The

Official®
DIRECTORY TO
U.S. FLEA
MARKETS

The
Official®
DIRECTORY TO
U.S. FLEA MARKETS

Edited by
Kitty Werner

FOURTH EDITION

House of Collectibles • New York

Important Notice: The publisher assumes no responsibility for any losses incurred as a result of consulting this directory, or for any objects or services bought, sold, or traded at any flea market listed in this publication. All information relating to specific flea markets has been obtained from the owner, manager, or promoter to the best of the publisher's knowledge and is accepted in good faith.

Copyright © 1994 by Random House, Inc.

This is a registered trademark of Random House, Inc.

All rights reserved under International and Pan-American Copyright Conventions.

Published by: House of Collectibles
                 201 East 50th Street
                 New York, New York 10022

Distributed by Ballantine Books, a division of Random House, Inc., New York, and simultaneously in Canada by Random House of Canada Limited, Toronto.

Manufactured in the United States of America

ISSN: 1073-208X

ISBN: 0-876-37925-0

Cover design by Kristine V. Mills
Cover photo by George Kerrigan

Fourth Edition: April 1994
10 9 8 7 6 5 4 3 2

Contents

INTRODUCTION

This year we have added over 300 markets including a few in Canada and Europe, some as new complete listings, some as a list at the end of the state's listings. Quite a few markets have closed, just as many have opened since the Third Edition. My children and I traveled around Europe for two summers and found that even in tiny villages in Provence, France, the Saturday market in my grandfather's hometown was similiar to the markets in tiny villages in northern Germany, near my husband's hometown. So much of the new merchandise is exactly the same as that sold here in the states. What makes a market different is the people, the atmosphere and the local produce and crafts. When you find a market that suits you—frequent it. Get to know its dealers and learn about the old treasures. Most of the dealers I have met love to talk about their wares and the history behind them.

In writing this book, I have spoken to hundreds of strangers in as many cities and towns around this country. I learned a great deal about flea markets in general, and collected some terrific stories. In this edition, these stories have been added to their respective market's listing. If you have a market story to share, send it along to me; my address is in the back of this book.

What I have gleaned from many conversations with these markets are these two basic facts:

1. The majority of people running flea markets are working for the fun of it, for the "family" a really good market becomes, and because they are, quite simply, dedicated to antiques, collectibles and the treasures that may show up.

2. Those markets opened up "just to make a buck" quickly fold. It takes a lot of work and dedication to make a market work and grow; and more important to the market's survival, a healthy, loyal following of customers and dealers.

In fact, some of these markets become so "family" to dealers and customers that weddings and other major events are planned around market days. In one case, an elderly gentleman who lived at "his other home" for twenty-some years of the market's existence, seated at a different dealer's booth each week, died just before the market re-opened in April. His funeral happened to fall on opening day. As a tribute, his funeral procession drove slowly through the market in a final salute.

1

Two dealers we heard about, again, both elderly, died at their booth spaces, one while laughing with his customers, the other, an 87-year-old who had vowed to die on "his space," did so after having driven completely around the market, pulling into his accustomed space, and getting out of his car.

Another market, newly opened, became "family" so fast, that when one dealer's husband required surgery, the other dealers kept her booth running for her so the family wouldn't go broke.

In a different vein, one market told me that one of their dealer spaces was lost/won (depending on your point of view) in a divorce settlement!

When it came to asking about the merchandise sold, I asked the same question: What sort of things does your market sell? The answer is invariably the same: "You name it, we've got it!" Perhaps we should rename this book.

Occasionally I encountered a nagging question, "Was this market really a flea market?" Some markets are, of course, flea markets by any definition of the phrase. One market I called had recently kicked out its three vendors "because they squabbled too much." Now the proud owner proclaims, he can sell anything! And does. Is this really a flea market now? Many calls between New York and Vermont answered this "moral dilemma" to our satisfaction, taken on a one-market-at-a-time basis. (Considering the market's peculiar circumstances, it was included.) Only one didn't really come near any remote definition of a flea market and it was not added. But still, what is the *real* definition of today's flea market? Do they sell only "old" items—a former qualification? Or is new merchandise fair game?

Recent changes in markets and what they sell stem from the simple fact that there are only a finite amount of antiques and collectibles available. Period. Chippendale only lived about 61 years and could only create a finite amount of furniture. The same goes for other "names" in the business. There were only so many baseball cards printed in any one year. That is what makes one card more valuable than another.

As more markets open for business, the fewer dealers there are to go around. If there are, in fact, more dealers (as more go into the business), there is still a "finite" amount of goods to spread even more thinly.

As a result many markets have opened their stalls to "new merchandise." Still, the die-hards hold out and you can still find markets that only deal in antiques and collectibles. They are mentioned in the description of each market. But remember, to keep the market doors open, many markets that may have been more selective are now forced to sell the products the dealers have to sell—namely new merchandise.

Many markets proudly boast about their size—"we are the largest in northeast Whatchamacallit!" Or we are the "largest Wednesday and Thursday market anywhere!" Sometimes you have to take such claims with a grain of sand. I had one man tell me he had the largest market in the business—"125,000 square feet!" I'm afraid I shattered his ego when I told him about a market that opened in an abandoned Ford factory (since gone out of business). Using only two of the six floors, they owned close to 750,000 square feet altogether. In fact, there are many markets in the 100,000 square foot category. And just as many smaller ones—they seem to have the richest stories to tell. Bigger isn't always better. It simply depends on what you are looking for: a good time, your "other" family, a specific object, just to waste a day, a carnival atmosphere, whatever.

Many of the markets listed have turned into semi-carnivals to attract buyers, or to provide a more interesting place to visit as a getaway with the family. One market owner bought the contents of a former amusement park and has all the gnomes and creatures scattered around his property, including a 30-foot totem pole and twin pink elephants. Colonial Valley in Pennsylvania had a 26-inch-tall steer named Clyde (who unfortunately died). Mt. Sterling, Kentucky, celebrates the Third Monday Court Days, started in 1870 when the circuit court judge would pass through the towns of Maysville, Flemingsburg, and then Mt. Sterling doing his business—including the sentencing of some offenders to hang! The entire town shuts down and celebrates for three days (with over 2,000 dealers). Maysville and Flemingsburg joined in the act around twenty years ago restarting their "Court Days." Their markets start Sunday after church and continue until the dancing ends on Monday night.

A neighbor of mine has found the greatest antique treasures in the local flea market, not noted for anything grand. She says you just have to look carefully and know what you are getting. Her house is furnished with numerous pieces of furniture, from chests and beds to baby high-chairs, mostly culled from this one market. She has collected complete sets of china and silverware in five different patterns for each of her five children—all from flea markets.

A caution about being sure of what you want and knowing its value. There are numerous stories sprinkled throughout this book of surprise finds—the dealer who sold a frame for $75 only to hear later that the savvy buyer sold the old master in it for $250,000. And so on. Look carefully. You never know.

FLEA MARKETS: THEN AND NOW

Look at the history and development of the phenomenon of flea markets as an alternative to *shopping*—that is, going to town and wandering from store to store. The term "flea market," a direct translation from the French phrase *marché aux puces*, has come to signify a specially designated occasion for the purpose of exchanging a wide variety of goods—anything from valuable antiques to backyard junk.

In France, where the term was coined, fleas were found to accompany old furniture and clothing drawn from attics or barns. Today, some flea markets in the United States maintain a curious tie to this tradition by demanding that all furniture be either fumigated or else banned from the sale area entirely.

The flea market in the United States, however, has taken on other European customs—customs found not only in France but throughout the Continent. One custom is Market Day, a regularly scheduled time when a portion of town, usually the main square, is closed off from traffic as farmers, itinerant tradesmen, butcher and bone-men, and other dealers sell their merchandise—anything from produce and clothing to fresh meats and kitchen appliances—to the people of the town and surrounding area. From early in the morning—6:00 AM, even earlier—to the middle of the afternoon, buyers and sellers get together in a particular place for the single purpose of striking bargains. In America, where so many ancestors came from rural Europe, small towns have since the first settlement conducted fairs, animal shows, and farmers' markets as means of distributing locally made products. For early farmers, tool makers, and other craftsmen, the local market could prove an effective gateway to the larger markets of other cities and large towns in the region, as buyers from nearby districts would frequently come looking for special deals. The flea market in the United States, then, is a bit of mongrel, with its Old World mixed parentage combined with that peculiarly American flair for the entrepreneurial. The giant flea markets like the Rose Bowl Flea Market in Pasadena, California, and the First Monday Trade Days in Canton, Texas, are cousins, and not very distant, to that of the antique shows and sales that keep popping up with increasing frequency throughout the country. The current popularity of flea markets large or small around urban centers as well as in the deep country, suggests that these events have become a welcome and permanent part of our day-to-day lives.

A flea market may range in size from just a few sellers standing on the side of a highway trying to clean out the unwanted contents of their homes to a complex, labyrinthine structure of dealers' booths sprawled out across acres of open space indoors or outdoors or both. In other words, a flea market is rather like beauty—it is all in the eye of the beholder.

Thinking another way, it is not so much a particular kind of event (whether it's a "swap meet" or an antique show and sale), but rather an alternative to shopping at the mall—a place where the individual buyer is on equal terms with the individual dealer, where no prices are fixed, and the fun comes in finding just what you want and buying or selling it for a price that feels right to *you*.

In this fourth edition, our directory has grown with over 300 new markets. We include just about any conceivable flea market from the one-man market to the gigantic San Jose market in California. One of my criteria was courtesy and friendliness. I didn't find every market that exists. I've been told that between Kansas and Texas, there must be 4,000 flea markets alone! But I did find some obscure markets that are fund-raisers for churches, schools, and firehouses. According to the people who run these markets, you wouldn't believe the treasures that can be found there. One Texas market is simply the local residents' once-a-year garage sale.

There are some newer markets that have opened and grown tremendously since the third edition was published and we've added them too.

I think you'll find this a wonderful mix. There are plenty of places that cater to families, providing rides, perhaps video arcades, games, petting zoos, and whatever they can think of that children might enjoy.

You could plan a vacation around many of the markets listed here. Don't be shy. The people I talked with represented a rich cross-section of America, doing this because they loved the people who came as dealers and those who came as visitors. They are having fun and they want to share it. It's up to you.

BUYING AT FLEA MARKETS
Coming Prepared

When shopping at flea markets—and this is as true for the fine antique shows as for the markets that feature new merchandise—be sure to distinguish between the valuable and not so valuable articles offered for sale. Keep in mind that flea markets trade in all kinds of things, not only antiques and fine collectibles, but also brand new objects and some odds and ends that have ended up, somehow, in the dealer's hands. Notes promoter R.G. Canning of his early days organizing California's world-famous Pasadena Rose Bowl Flea Market and Swap Meet: "It was amazing to me that people would come to buy all that junk."

Of course, there is nothing wrong with your paying money for someone else's junk; it just depends on how much you value it. The flea market (in the most general sense of the term) is really not unlike a communal yard sale. It often provides the opportunity to sell things to other people who might be able to find a use for them—though they might be hard pressed to say what that is exactly at the moment of purchase.

But whether it is a fine antique show or something as manic as the Rose Bowl Swap Meet, it is advisable to subject *all* merchandise to careful scrutiny, and not just the antiques and collectibles, either. When shopping for "brand-name" items, be especially careful to check for fakes—some imitations are so masterful that they can fool a seasoned shopper. While imitations of brand-names appear to match the originals in craftsmanship and quality of materials, there have been many disappointed shoppers who have watched their "once-in-a-lifetime" bargains disintegrate in a matter of weeks or even days under normal use. Most flea markets monitor and insist that their dealers represent their goods honestly and use fair business practices. Several listed herein make known their policy of having their dealers not only stand behind their merchandise, but also offer refunds if the merchandise fails to please. This serves the double purpose of protecting both the buyer and the reputation of the market. Be sure to report any unfair or dishonest practices to the owner or operator of the market where this occurs. It is always best to be an alert and educated shopper.

Knowing When to Haggle

At flea markets, as with just about any kind of trade, a deal is made when both the seller and the buyer think they are getting a bargain.

Put a value on an item as soon as you can and stick to it, as best you can. Changing your mind in the middle of a sale is a sign of weakness and uncertainty—one that a hardened seller will be quick to take advantage of. The more sure you are in your initial assessments, the easier and more pleasant your overall shopping will be. And when you encounter an object that is not marked with a price, don't suggest one, but rather prompt the seller to give you one. After all, it is the obligation of the seller to have a price to quote for any item he sells.

And don't forget that a main activity at the flea market isn't so much shopping as bargaining. In other words, don't automatically assume that the first price you hear is final, whether offered by voice or by a price tag. In fact, you have a right as a potential buyer to ask for a "last price" before you make up your mind on an item. (Remember, though, that you can only ask for a last price once.) You are not necessarily being rude by passing up an object after hearing the final offer, so long as you are polite in your refusal and thank the seller for his/her offer.

Don't ever let a seller use intimidation to force you to buy an object. You alone can know whether you want an object and, if so, how much it is worth to you.

Carry lots of cash, best of all in small denominations. As a general rule, always be working toward a deal in your negotiations with flea market salespeople. After all, their business is to sell, not to talk. Do not ask for a price on an item unless you are genuinely interested.

If you want to haggle, be careful how you do it. Part of the trick is in knowing real value, of course. Even if something is already priced low, a deft haggler takes the position that it can be driven down further. If he's going to make an offer he'll make a considerably lower one, representing maybe 50 percent of the asking price or even less, figuring that the end result is likely to be a compromise.

The wrong way to ask for a discount is by deriding the merchandise or the price, by suggesting that the dealer does not know his business, or by doing anything which could trigger a negative reaction. For example, never say "The shop down the street is selling one just like this for $20 less." Or, worse, "You don't really expect to get $75 for this, do you?"

Remember that the sellers have heard every possible pitch for discounts. They hear them every day, the same ones over and over. After just a short time in business they get thoroughly turned off by most types of discount-seeking approaches, and by most of the typical "I-want-a-discount" customers.

The majority of such customers act as if the dealer owes them a favor. You need to be a little original in trying to obtain a discount and, above all, courteous. Be inventive, use your imagination, and, most important, make a good impression. As they say in show biz, always leave'em laughing. You may want to return some day, and you will want to be welcome next time.

SELLING AT FLEA MARKETS

First of all, decide which markets you want to participate in. There may be several nearby. A beginner is apt to make his choice based on the wrong considerations, thinking in terms of which show offers the best rate on space, or how he can save $1.50 on gas by selling close to home. It's really useless to give much thought to these points. The important thing is at which flea market are you likely to do the most selling? Visit different markets as a browser; look at what is going on. How many dealers are present? Are nearly all the spaces taken, or are the grounds half empty? Unless the flea market is a new one, or in some cases the season is winding down, empty ground space indicates an unsuccessful market. What are the sellers offering? What percentage of the sellers are offering collectors' items? If you're interested in collectibles, for example, it is unwise to take a space at a show where collectibles are seldom sold.

After deciding on the flea market at which to sell, make arrangements for a space well in advance. Talk to the manager and find out about the rules and regulations. They are more or less the same from one show to another but there could be some differences. Every show has restrictions on what can and cannot be sold. With collectibles, you are not likely to run afoul of any taboos, except with firearms. Most flea markets do not permit the sale of firearms, antique or modern. Knives are almost always okay, except switchblades—some states have laws against them. Markets listed as "family" markets generally don't allow pornography either.

Mostly you'll want to find out what you will be getting for your rental money. Does the management provide a table? What is the exact size of the space you'll get? Will you be required to collect sales tax? Is this show held rain or shine? If the show is canceled because of bad weather, do you get a refund or a raincheck for the next show?

Put some thought into what you are going to take to the show. It's always better to have a variety of merchandise than to go heavy on just a few kinds of items. Large items such as furniture will cut down your exhibit space. If you are going to show small things of moderate or high value, such as jewelry or scarce coins, try to get a display box with a glass top and a lock. This will reduce the risk of theft. Clean up merchandise before packing it off to the show. This does not mean an indiscriminate scrubbing that could lessen the value and desirability of an antique, but dusting and (where appropriate) polishing. It does not enhance sales value when items have a just-out-of-the-dustbin appearance. Try to arrange everything in a way that will make browsing as easy as possible. If you are selling magazines, stand them upright in a carton so that customers can flip through them with a minimum of fuss. This will also help to keep the covers from tearing, which is sure to happen if they are just piled together in a heap. When selling magazines of high value, or old comic books, slip them into protective Mylar bags. Scarce coins should be displayed in 2" × 2" holders. Some items are, of course, more of a headache to display than others: with glassware and china you run the risk of breakage not only as a result of clumsy browsers but strong gusts of wind. If you are displaying a lot of breakables, you can take the precaution of making certain that your table is well anchored. One way of anchoring a table is by sinking the leg tips two or three inches into the ground, if this is feasible. Another is to place heavy stones or bricks on top for ballast. In any event, keep breakables toward the center of the table if you can, where they are not as likely to be swept away by an errant arm or sleeve.

Figure out how much you want to get for each item before the show whether or not you are going to use price tags. Don't wait until somebody asks the price before you start thinking about it. Most flea market exhibitors mark prices on their merchandise, and this is probably the best course to follow, simply because many browsers just won't bother to ask the price, even if they are mildly interested. Of course the marked price need not necessarily be the actual sum for which you would sell the item; you can leave yourself some leeway for bargaining, and it is usually a good idea to do this. But don't set your marked prices too much higher than what you would be willing to accept.

PERIODICALS OF INTEREST

Following is a selective list of periodicals with good coverage of flea markets. The approximate geographical scope of each publication is listed in parentheses after its name. The publications listed are all produced in tabloid newspaper format. This list, though far from complete, should help the reader find the most up-to-date listings for some of the many flea markets that, due to space limitations or our own oversight, have regrettably been omitted from this guide.

Antique Press, The (Florida). 12403 North Florida Avenue, Tampa, FL 33612. Published 18 times per year. Subscriptions are $12 per year.

Antique Review (Midwest). P.O. Box 538, Worthington, OH 43085. Tel: (614) 885-9757. Monthly. Subscriptions are $20 per year.

Antique Trader Weekly, The (Midwest). P.O. Box 1050, Dubuque, IA 52001. Tel: (319) 588-2073. Weekly. Subscriptions are $32 per year.

Antique Week (Two editions: Mid-Atlantic and Mid-Central). P.O. Box 90, Knightstown, IN 46148. Tel: (317) 345-5133. Weekly. Subscriptions are $21.95 per year Mid-Atlantic Edition, $25.95 per year for the Mid-Central Edition and $45.20 for both, includes Antique Shop Guide issue.

Antiques & Auction News, Joel Sater's (Pennsylvania/Northeastern U.S.). P.O. Box 500, Mount Joy, PA 17552. Tel: (717) 653-9797. Weekly. Subscriptions are $15 per year 3rd class, $35 for 6 months or $60 per year, first class mail.

Antiques & Collectibles (New York City/Long Island, NY). P.O. Box 33, Westbury, NY 11590. (516) 334-9650. Monthly. Subscriptions are $10 per year.

Antiques & The Arts Weekly (New England/Northeastern U.S.). c/o The Newtown Bee, Newtown, CT 06470. Tel: (203) 426-8036. Monthly. Subscriptions are $40 per year.

Buckeye Marketeer, The (Ohio). P.O. Box 954, Westerville, OH 43081 Tel: (614) 895-1663. Monthly. Subscriptions are $15 per year, or $24 for two years.

Collectors Journal (Midwest). P.O. Box 601, Vinton, IA 52349-0601. Tel: (319) 472-4763. Weekly (except last two weeks in December and first week in January). Subscriptions are $25 per year.

Collectors News (Midwest). P.O. Box 156, Grundy Center, IA 50638. Tel: 1-800-352-8039. Monthly. Subscriptions are regularly $36 per year, but will give readers of this guide one year at $24 per year.

Hudson Valley Antiquer, The, P.O. Box 561, Rhinebeck, NY 12572. Tel: (914) 876-8766. Distributed free at markets.

Maine Antiques Digest (New England). P.O. Box 645, Waldoboro, ME 04572. Tel: 1-800-752-8521. Monthly. Subscriptions are $29 per year.

Mid-Atlantic Antiques Magazine (Mid-Atlantic States). P.O. Box 908, Henderson, NC 27536. Tel: (919) 492-4001. Monthly. Subscriptions are $12 per year.

New England Antiques Journal (New England; formerly *New England Country Antiques*). 4 Church Street, Ware, MA 01082. Tel: (413) 967-3505. Monthly. Subscriptions are $19.95 per year.

New York Antique Almanac, The (New York State). P.O. Box 335, Lawrence, NY 11559. Tel: (516) 371-3300. Published 10 times per year, including two bi-monthly issues. Subscriptions are $10 per year.

New York-Pennsylvania Collector, The (Northern Atlantic States). P.O. Drawer C, Fishers, NY 14453. Tel: (716) 424-2880. Published 11 times per year. Subscriptions are $18 per year, $28 for two years, $39 for three years, $60 for five years.

MassBay Antiques, Box 192, Ipswich, MA 01938. Tel: (508)356-5141 x 5211. Monthly. Subscriptions are $15 a year, two years for $25.

Renninger's Antique Guide (Eastern U.S.). P.O. Box 495, Lafayette Hill, PA 19444. Tel: (215) 828-4614. Bi-weekly. Subscriptions are $15 year.

Today's Collector, 700 East State Street, Iola, WI 54990-0001. Tel: (715) 445-3775 ext. 257. Monthly. Subscriptions are $17.95 a year.

Treasure Chest, Venture Publishing, 253 West 72nd Street, #211A, New York, NY 10023. Tel: (212) 496-2234. Monthly. Subscriptions are $25 a year.

The Upper Canadian, P.O. Box 653, Smiths Falls, Ontario, Canada K7A 4T6. Tel: (613) 283-1168. Bi-monthly. Subscriptions are C$25 (US$26) for one year, C$44 (US$46) for two years.

HOW TO USE THIS BOOK

The flea markets listed in this book vary from those having fewer than 15 dealers to more than 2,000 dealers in some cases. The markets are listed alphabetically by state, and by town within each state. Each listing is broken down into the following subheadings:

DATES: Market days are listed here, including specific dates for 1994 where applicable. Rain dates are noted where applicable.

TIMES: Hours during which the flea markets are held are listed.

ADMISSION: If there is a cost to enter a market, the fee will be listed. Information about the availability and cost of parking is also presented.

LOCATION: A street address for the market is supplied where available; brief directions are provided for those traveling from out of town by car.

DESCRIPTION: This section discusses the size of the market, its age, the types of merchandise available, whether food is served on the premises, and any other interesting facts pertaining to its operation. All markets listed have toilet facilities on the premises or nearby, unless otherwise noted.

DEALER RATES: This section provides the most complete information available at press time regarding costs of selling space at the market, and whether advance reservations are required.

CONTACT: Complete mailing address and telephone number of the market operator are supplied wherever possible for dealer or shopper inquiries.

The Official Directory to U.S. Flea Markets has been designed to provide essential information about flea markets across the country selected for variety of merchandise, number of dealers attending, or other information of interest to the bargain hunter. The at-a-glance format previously outlined aids in making this guide the easiest as well as the most up-to-date reference available on the subject.

While the editors have made every effort to obtain the most exhaustive and accurate information available on a selection of flea markets from coast to coast in the continental United States, the reader is advised that in a work of this scope, inaccuracies may occur. House of Collectibles assumes no responsibility for any misprints or other errors found in this directory; all show dates, admission fees, dealer rates, etc. listed herein are subject to change at any time without notice. It is recommended that users of this directory call ahead or consult local sources whenever possible when planning a visit to a flea market.

FLEA MARKET
LISTINGS

ALABAMA

ATTALLA
Mountain Top Flea Market

DATES: Every Sunday, year round, rain or shine.
TIMES: 5:00 AM to dark.
ADMISSION: Free. Parking is free.
LOCATION: 11301 U.S. Highway 278 West. Six miles west of Attalla. Highway 278W at 101 mile marker.
DESCRIPTION: Located on a remote mountain top on 96 acres, this mostly outdoor flea market first started in 1971 and currently consists of approximately 1,000 dealers selling everything from antiques and collectibles to new merchandise (jewelry, clothing, shoes, tools, furniture), from handcrafted items from three states to fresh produce from local farmers. They describe themselves as "Alabama's longest market—with 2.6 miles of shopping." They average over 40,000 buyers every Sunday! Twelve snack bars are on the premises. Restrooms with handicap facilities are available.
DEALER RATES: $6 per 10' × 22' space outside per day, $6 for 10' × 10' booth inside (very limited inside space). Shed tops for rent at $4 per day. Call the toll-free number for the latest information. Overnight camping with showers and restrooms is available.
CONTACT: Janie Terrell, Mountain Top Flea Market, 11301 U.S. Highway 278 West, Attalla, AL 35952. Tel: 1-800-535-2286.

BESSEMER
Bessemer Flea Market

DATES: Every Friday, Saturday, and Sunday rain or shine.
TIMES: 8:00 AM–5:00 PM.
ADMISSION: Free. Parking is also free.
LOCATION: Highway 11 South off I-59. Take Exit 112 to Eighth Avenue North.
DESCRIPTION: This indoor/outdoor market accommodates approximately 500 dealers. As many as 15,000 people attend these shows. A variety of goods from antiques to new merchandise can be found. There is a snack bar serving fast food on the premises. A special treat is their homemade cotton candy. Restrooms are available.
DEALER RATES: $5 to $10 per day, depending on size. Weekend rates to $30 per space. Prepayment is required to reserve indoor space,

outside is always available. There are shower facilities for traveling dealers.

CONTACT: Bessemer Flea Market, 1013 8th Avenue N, Bessemer, AL 35020 Tel: (205) 425-8510.

BIRMINGHAM

The Birmington Fairgrounds Flea Market

DATES: First weekend of every month, year round, plus the second and third weekends in December.

TIMES: Friday, 3:00 PM–9:00 PM. Saturday and Sundays, 7:00 AM–6:00 PM.

ADMISSION: Free. Parking is free.

LOCATION: Alabama State Fairgrounds. Exit 120 off I-20/59, follow the signs to the Alabama State Fair Complex.

DESCRIPTION: Operating under its current management for six years, this market has 600 dealer spaces, mostly indoors. Billed as "Alabama's Largest Indoor Flea Market." Antiques; collectibles; furniture; oriental rugs; gold, silver, vintage and costume jewelry; gems; sterling silverware; glassware; vintage clothing; new clothing and accessories; purses, prints and framed art; giftware; ceramics; fishing gear; electronic equipment; golf clubs and accessories; automotive accessories; dolls; plants; tools; leather; toys; crafts; phones; makeup; bedding; coins; sport cards; comics; knives; books; CDs; cassettes; recrods; lamps; jewelry repair; crystal restoration; flowers; and "you name it!" There are concession stands and restrooms on the premises, all handicapped accessible.

DEALER RATES: $45–$60 per 10' × 10' indoor booth, per weekend; $25 for a "two-parking-space" size area outdoors. The fairgrounds provide camping facilities for a fee.

CONTACT: Cindy or Kenton, The Flea Market, P.O. Box 39063, Birmingham, AL 35208. Tel: 1-800-3-MARKET (1-800-362-7538).

Jefferson County Farmer's Market

DATES: Daily, rain or shine

TIMES: 8:00 AM–6:00 PM.

ADMISSION: Free. Parking is also free.

LOCATION: 342 Finley Avenue West.

DESCRIPTION: This market is held in a 100' × 200' building and on an acre lot outside. There is an average of 50 to 150 dealers selling a variety of collectible items. For your convenience, there are snacks and restrooms available on the premises.

DEALER RATES: $6 per space, inside; $4 per space, outside. Reservations are not required.

CONTACT: Jefferson County Farmer's Market, 342 Finley Avenue West, Birmingham, AL 35204. Tel: (205) 251-8737.

COLLINSVILLE
Collinsville Trade Day

DATES: Every Saturday, rain or shine.
TIMES: Sunup to sundown.
ADMISSION: Free.
LOCATION: Highway 11 South.
DESCRIPTION: Since 1955, this market averages about 1,000 vendors selling antiques, collectibles, books, jewelry, used and new clothing and tools, stamps, cookware, toys, fresh produce, and new merchandise. Up on Coon Dog Hill livestock is traded and sold. There are 15 concessions and snack bars to accommodate the hungry. Restrooms are available.
DEALER RATES: Call for more information. Reservations are not required.
CONTACT: Mrs. Harris, P.O. Box 256, Collinsville, AL 35961. Tel: (205) 524-2536.

Jim's Flea Market

DATES: Every Saturday. Also open Memorial Day, July 4, and Labor Day.
TIMES: 6:00 AM to sundown.
ADMISSION: Free. Parking is also free.
LOCATION: East on Highway 68 East off Highway 11.
DESCRIPTION: This show started in 1983. It is both an indoor and outdoor market consisting of approximately 100 dealers. Items sold include antiques, arts and crafts, new merchandise, and fresh produce. It is run by the original concept of a flea market—anything goes! There is also food available on the premises.
DEALER RATES: $2 for 10' × 20' space per day, includes parking space for vehicles; $8 per space, monthly. Reservations are not required.
CONTACT: Jim or Estellene Clayton, P.O. Box 334, Collinsville, AL 35961. Tel: (205) 524-2565.

CULLMAN
Cullman Flea Market

DATES: Every Saturday, Sunday, and major Monday holidays.

TIMES: 8:00 AM–5:00 PM.

ADMISSION: Free. Parking is also free.

LOCATION: 415 Lincoln Avenue Southwest. Next to I-65, on U.S. Route 278 at Exit 308.

DESCRIPTION: This market opened in May 1989 and added another addition in 1991. Located on 40 acres of land with 9 acres just for parking, this market has 300 dealer spaces indoors and more space outdoors. Their dealers sell a variety of antiques, collectibles, handmade and craft items, tools, hardware, jewelry, woodwork, handbags, glassware, baseball cards, coins, fresh produce, cheese and dairy products, and new merchandise. Three concession stands with seating areas provide food to hungry shoppers. Clean restrooms with handicapped facilities are on the premises.

Here, too, is Country Village, built of old barnboard, a collection of speciality shops selling mostly antiques. These shops are open from Thursday through Sunday, some from Tuesday through Sunday.

DEALER RATES: $20 per 9' × 10' booth for two days; $30 per 10' × 10' booth for two days. Reservations are required.

CONTACT: Frances Kilgo, Cullman Flea Market, P.O. Box 921, Cullman, AL 35056. Tel: (205) 739-0910.

DOTHAN
Sadie's Flea Market

DATES: Friday, Saturday, and Sunday, year round.

TIMES: 8:00 AM–5:00 PM.

ADMISSION: Free. Parking is free.

LOCATION: On Route 231 South, 5 miles south of Ross-Clark Circle in Dothan. From Route 109, turn left on 231; market is a few hundred yards down the road.

DESCRIPTION: Open since May 1989, this market has 250 booths with 60 permanent dealers, but many times is full to capacity. Dealers sell a large variety of everything including antiques, collectibles, crafts, produce, new and used merchandise—"real flea market stuff." A large Peanut Festival is held in the area in mid-to-late October. There are many antique car shows held in the area throughout the year. Two snack bars quell hunger, and there are two large restrooms; all handicapped accessible on the premises.

DEALER RATES: Indoors: $6 per day for a 10' × 10' booth; outside: $3 per day for a 4' × 8' table. Reservations are preferred.
CONTACT: Sadie, Sadie's Flea Market, Route 11 Box 165, Dothan, AL 36301. Tel: (205) 677-5138.

FALKVILLE
Lacon Trade-Day

DATES: Every weekend, year round, weather permitting.
TIMES: All day.
ADMISSION: Free. $.50 parking fee.
LOCATION: On Highway 31 South between Birmingham and Huntsville, off I-65. Two miles south of Falkville.
DESCRIPTION: This show opened in 1972. It is both an indoor and outdoor market that accommodates approximately 300 dealers. Items available include antiques, arts and crafts, and collectibles. There is also an assortment of new merchandise and fresh produce. Food is served on the premises.
DEALER RATES: $2 per 10' × 12' space. Reservations are suggested.
CONTACT: Charles Thornton, P.O. Box 1385, Hartselle, AL 35640. Tel: (205) 784-5091.

FLORENCE
Uncle Charlie's Flea Market

DATES: Every Saturday and Sunday.
TIMES: 8:00 AM–5:00 PM.
ADMISSION: Free. Ample free parking is available.
LOCATION: On Highway 72 West, 5 miles east of Florence, in the Killen area.
DESCRIPTION: This indoor market started in 1982 and accommodates approximately 400 dealers. They exhibit a wide variety of items including antiques, collectibles, arts and crafts, new merchandise, and fresh produce; there are also livestock exhibits. For your convenience, there are food and restrooms (with handicapped facilities) available on the premises.
DEALER RATES: $25 for 8' × 10' space per weekend. Reservations are required.
CONTACT: Mr. Tom Mabry, P.O. Box 190, Killen, AL 35645. Day of show call (205) 757-1771. Or call 1-800-542-2848.

GUNTERSVILLE

All American Tradè Day
Flea and Farmer's Market

DATES: Every Saturday and Sunday, rain or shine.

TIMES: 8:00 AM–5:00 PM.

ADMISSION: Free. Parking is available and free.

LOCATION: 11190 U.S. Highway 431. Along Highway 431 South, between Albertsville and Guntersville. Located just minutes from Boaz Outlets and Lake Guntersville.

DESCRIPTION: Established in 1989, this indoor/outdoor market on 30 prime acres has a daily attendance of 30,000 people. There are an average of 300 dealers indoors and 400 outdoors selling a variety of antiques and collectibles, "whatever you are looking for"—old, new or used. There is a large meat market, produce and grocery stores on the grounds. Fresh seafood and meats are cut while you wait. Over 45,000 square feet are under roof. This market has grown tremendously in the last few years. Sand Mountain Antique Mall is located next door and open Tuesday through Sunday. They have a concert hall seating 700 and hold special events: a tractor-truck pull, mud bogs, and bluegrass festivals. A restaurant, serving home-cooked meals, is on the premises. Clean restrooms are available.

DEALER RATES: $10 per 8' × 10' space under roof perimeter daily; $5 per day for a 10' × 12' booth outside under sheds. There is 24-hour security, electric at all booths, and vendors can park at their space. Reservations are not required.

CONTACT: Gladys and Jim Cornelius, All American Trade Day, 11190 U.S. Highway 431, Guntersville, AL 35976. Tel: (205) 891-2790.

HARPERSVILLE

Dixie Land Flea and Farmers Market

DATES: Friday, Saturday and Sunday, year round.

TIMES: 9:00 AM–5:00 PM.

ADMISSION: Free. Parking is also free.

LOCATION: I-280 East to Highway 25 South, exit at Harpersville about 4 miles south of Harpersville. On State Road 25 between Harpersville and Wilsonville.

DESCRIPTION: Opened in 1986 on 70 acres of land, this market has 400 booths inside a 70,000 square-foot building and acres of outside booths selling antiques, furniture, arts and crafts, jewelry, baseball cards, toys, evening gowns, fruits and vegetables, and plenty of new and used merchandise. Friday is Garage Sale Day with special rates for outside booths. Three hundred of the dealers are permanent and the market advertises heavily in newspapers, on radio and television and hosts "live remotes" for on-air promotions. They have "everything and anything" in this "country flea market" including a 2,000-square-foot grocery store. "Huge deer and wild turkeys" roam around this market "driving hunters crazy" during the appropriate seasons. This is a clean, well-run, friendly market. There is entertainment to keep the children busy. Plenty of food is available on the premises supplied by four restaurants, an ice cream parlor, and a barbeque pit. There are clean restrooms with handicapped facilities.

DEALER RATES: $12 per day for main aisle; perimeter at $10 space 10' × 10'. Monthly rates are $72 perimeter and $87 for main aisle. There are a few outside booths at $6 per day or $43 monthly. Electricity is $2 per day, extra tables are $1. Campers $5 per day. There is full-time security, showers for dealers, and special handicapped facilities. Each booth has its own entrance with parking behind it.

CONTACT: James Galantis, Dixie Land Flea Market, 3000 Highway 25 South, Harpersville, AL 35078. Tel: (205) 672-2022.

MADRID

J Hooter's Flea Market

DATES: Saturday and Sunday, year round.

TIMES: 9:00 AM–6:00 PM.

ADMISSION: Free. Parking is also free.

LOCATION: Highway 231—12 miles south of Dothan, 3 miles north of Alabama/Florida state line.

DESCRIPTION: Opened in November 1989, the owners have been expanding facilities. Alongside the 23,000 square foot building for the flea market they are constantly adding shops and attractions. "We are beginning to look like a western town." The 90 to 125 dealers sell antiques, collectibles, jewelry, tools, books, furniture, handmade and craft items, fresh produce, and new merchandise. There are campgrounds as well as family oriented attractions including shows featuring country and western, and gospel fare. The Hooterville General Store is open, as well as Jed's Salvage Food Store. The Gold Star Restaurant serves the hungry. Restrooms are available.

DEALER RATES: $6 per 8' × 10' booth per day. Reservations are strongly suggested. Outside booths with RV hookups and showers are available for traveling dealers.

CONTACT: Jim and Margaret Easterly, Route 1 Box 223E, Cottonwood, AL 36320. Tel: (205) 677-7234.

PHENIX CITY

Valley Flea and Farmers Market

DATES: Wednesday, Friday, Saturday, and Sunday.

TIMES: 8:00 AM–6:00 PM.

ADMISSION: Free. Parking is free.

LOCATION: 3864 U.S. Highway 80 West. Across from the Ladonia Elementary School. Or just ask anyone in Phenix City.

DESCRIPTION: This market, under new management as of summer of 1993, is now run like a carnival. Crazy Ray, the new owner, has 20 years of carnival experience in his background and runs this market with the notion that "party, party, fun, fun" is the way to go. As of September 1993, the market grew from 30 dealers to over 250 and is still growing. The dealers sell everything from appliances to antiques, collectibles, crafts, produce, livestock, and whatever else comes through (except illegal goods). There are carnival-style concessions throughout the market, as well as a printing shop and full-time airbrush artist. Wild "goings-on" include televised wrestling matches from the market, painted pellet fights, and once a Wild West shoot-out that scattered the shoppers, a "Little House on the Prairie" display of clothing from the show and the Little House that traveled with the clothing on tour. Carnival people come by and perform and a talk show is planned. Television advertising is a constant and Crazy Ray has made this market a household name already.

DEALER RATES: From $10 to $30 per weekend. Choices of location are outside tables, shed or the building itself. If you pay in advance, long-term, Crazy Ray will build you a shop. Camping is available for $25 a week for full hook-up or $2 a night for electric.

CONTACT: Crazy Ray, Valley Flea and Farmers Market, 3864 U.S. Highway 80 West, Phenix City, AL 36869. Tel: (205) 291-1496.

SCOTTSBORO

First Monday Flea Market

DATES: First Monday and preceding Sunday of each month.

TIMES: 8:00 AM until dark.

ADMISSION: Free. Parking is also free.
LOCATION: Courthouse Square in the center of downtown Scottsboro.
DESCRIPTION: This outdoor market accommodates 250 dealers in winter to 500 dealers in the summer. There are a variety of antiques, collectibles, and secondhand items available. For your convenience, food is served on the premises.
DEALER RATES: $25 per parking space. Availability of space is on a first come, first served basis.
CONTACT: Gayle Swafford, 916 South Broad Street, Scottsboro, AL 35768. Tel: (205) 574-3333.

SELMA
Selma Flea Market
DATES: Saturday, year round, rain or shine.
TIMES: 4:30 AM until whenever.
ADMISSION: Free. Parking is also free.
LOCATION: Selma by-pass at River Road.
DESCRIPTION: This market opened in 1986 in beautiful historic Selma. It attracts from 120 to 170 plus dealers in sheltered spaces selling antiques, collectibles, handmade crafts, fresh produce and meats, new merchandise, garage sale, and household items. There is food available on the premises.
DEALER RATES: $7 per 10' × 10' booth. Reservations are required.
CONTACT: Tyson Maluda, 606 River Road, Selma, AL 36703. Tel: (205) 875-0500.

SUMMERDALE
Highway 59 Flea Market
DATES: Every Friday, Saturday, and Sunday, year round.
TIMES: Sunup to sundown.
ADMISSION: Free. Parking is also free.
LOCATION: On Highway 59, between Foley and Robertdale, 13 miles north of Gulf Shores.
DESCRIPTION: This very busy market, "the best in this part of the country," has been in existence since the summer of 1985. The market accommodates approximately 300 to 400 dealers outdoors but under cover, and 35 individual shops. They do not specialize in one particular area; instead they sell a wide variety of goods. Included are antiques, fine art, repros, and fresh produce, to name a few. The mar-

ket is located on 33 acres which also includes a discount furniture store. There is a new restaurant and several snack shops, including an ice cream shop on the premises. There is a RV park with reasonable rates and full hook-ups here.

DEALER RATES: $8 for 10' × 20' space per day, per table. Reservations are not required.

CONTACT: Red Cotton, 1717 North T Street, Pensacola, FL 32505. Tel: (904) 433-4315 in FL. Day of show call Smitty on-site at (205) 989-6642.

THEODORE/MOBILE
Southern Alabama Flea Market

DATES: Daily.

TIMES: 9:00 AM–5:00 PM.

ADMISSION: Free. Parking is free.

LOCATION: 6280 Theodore Dawes Road. Take I-10 to Exit 13, go south 1 mile.

DESCRIPTION: Started in 1987 to give the retiring owner "something to do," this market hosts 35–50 dealers in buildings, under cover or outside under the trees. There are dealers specializing in dolls, cookie jars and the usual antiques and collectibles and used items. There "isn't much new" at this market. A snack bar, run by a "great cook," serves a varying menu of meals.

DEALER RATES: $3 per day for an 8' table, in the open or under a cover; $20 per week for a building. There is security on the premises. Dealer parking is available overnight.

CONTACT: Marie Massengill, 6511 Highmount Drive, Theodore, AL 36582. Tel: (205) 653-4736.

OTHER FLEA MARKETS

Albertville: U.S. Flea Market Mall, 5850 U.S. Highway 431, Suite 7, Albertville, AL 35950. Tel: (205) 891-3957. Open weekends.

Collinsville: Hawkins Collinsville Trade Days, Highway 11 South, Collinsville, AL 35961. Tel: (205) 524-2127. Open Saturdays.

Elmore: Bargain Place Flea Market, Highway 14, Elmore, AL 36025. Tel: (205) 567-7731. Open Friday through Sunday, 8:00 AM until whenever.

Mobile: Flea Market Mobile, 401 Schillinger Road North, Mobile, AL 36608. Tel: (205) 633-7533. Open weekends.

Montgomery: Grand Central Station, Inc., 425 Coliseum Boulevard, Montgomery, AL 36109. Tel: (205) 279-5794. Open daily.

Montgomery: International Flea Mall, 9310 Troy Highway, Montgomery, AL 36064. Tel: (205) 613-0438. Open daily except Monday.

Westover: 280 Flea Market, Highway 280 at Westover, Westover, AL 35078. Tel: (205) 678-6729. Open Friday through Sunday, 8:00 AM-6:00 PM.

Wetumpka: Santuck Flea Market, Route 2 Box 134 X, Wetumpka, AL 36092. Tel: (205) 567-7254. Open first Saturday of the month, March through December.

ARIZONA

APACHE JUNCTION
American Park N Swap

DATES: Wednesday, Friday, Saturday, and Sunday in winter. Friday and Saturday in summer. Rain or shine.

TIMES: Winter: Friday through Sunday 7:00 AM–4:00 PM, Wednesday 2:00 PM–8:00 PM; summer 4:00 PM–11:00 PM.

ADMISSION: $.50 per person walk-in or $1 per car.

LOCATION: 2551 West Apache Trail. U.S. 60 to Signal Butte exit, north on Signal Butte to Apache Trail, turn east on Apache Trail. Park N Swap is on the south side of the road.

DESCRIPTION: This market, started in 1965, houses up to 400 dealers daily in winter and 100 daily in summer selling everything from desert gold and crystals, hair cuts, Indian artifacts, golf clubs, redwood signs, silk plants, pet supplies, De Grazia, nuts, sandpaintings, kachinas, ironwood carvings, housewares, tools, books, produce, antiques, collectibles, crafts and handmade items, wind chimes, toys and bicycles, the list is endless! There is a huge barbecue pit in the center of the market and several smaller concessions are scattered conveniently around the selling floor. They are close to Superstition Mountain and recreational lakes.

DEALER RATES: $8 per 9' × 18' Friday through Sunday; $5 per 9' × 18' booth on Wednesdays. Reservations are suggested.

CONTACT: Mike Sleeseman, Manager, American Park N Swap, 2551 West Apache Trail, Apache Junction, AZ 85220. Tel: (602) 832-3270.

CASA GRANDE
Shoppers Barn and Swap Meet

DATES: Saturday and Sunday.

TIMES: 7:00 AM–4:00 PM.

LOCATION: Selma Road and Highway 84, between Tucson and Phoenix.

ADMISSION: Free. Parking is free.

DESCRIPTION: Open since 1983 under the same management, this outdoor market sells antiques, collectibles, new and used toys and merchandise, used auto parts, ceramics, and appliances. They are in town on a main road and next to many amenities.

DEALER RATES: $4 per day for center space, $6 per day for corner space, tables are $1 per day. First come, first served. There is security and the grounds are locked at night. Dealers can set up Friday night. **CONTACT:** Bud Grey, P.O. Box 10250, Casa Grande, AZ 85230. Tel: (602) 836-1934.

GLENDALE
Glendale Swap Meet

DATES: Saturday and Sunday.

TIMES: 5:30 AM–3:00 PM.

LOCATION: At 5630 55th Avenue between Bethany Road and Camelback Road, northwest of Phoenix.

ADMISSION: Free. Parking is free.

DESCRIPTION: This outdoor market of 250–300 dealers sells about half new and half used merchandise including Indian crafts, antiques, collectibles and garage sale treasures. There is a snack bar and some roaming food carts at the market.

DEALER RATES: $10 for a 36' × 10' space. Reservations are suggested.

CONTACT: Charles Barone, 5650 North 55th Avenue, Glendale, AZ 84301. Tel: (602) 931-0877.

PEORIA
Grand Avenue Swap Meet

DATES: Friday, Saturday, and Sunday.

TIMES: Friday 5:00 PM–10:00 PM; Saturday and Sunday 6:00 AM–4:00 PM.

ADMISSION: $.50. Parking is free.

LOCATION: Old Glendale Airport at 79th Avenue and Grand Avenue.

DESCRIPTION: Opened in 1989, this market has 75 (summer) to 350 (winter) dealers selling antiques, collectibles, crafts, produce, meats, cheeses and dairy, live plants and trees, new merchandise, and plenty of garage sale clean-outs. There is room for RVs with showers and a dump station available. Four snack bars take care of the famished. For entertainment, since it is an old airport, they've had ultralight airplane rides that lasted 15 minutes airborne; another time they threw out $100 worth of $1 bills; they hold auto auctions, play "Wheel of Fortune," or hold crazy scavenger hunts. Drop in and check it out!

DEALER RATES: $5 for a 10' × 20' space; $10 for a 30' × 20' space. Reservations are not required.
CONTACT: Bob Whittington, 7855 NW Grand Avenue, Peoria, AZ 85345. Tel: (602) 230-7927.

PHOENIX
American Park N Swap

DATES: Every Friday, Saturday, and Sunday, rain or shine.
TIMES: 4:00 PM–10:00 PM Wednesday; 6:00 AM–2:00 PM Friday; 6:00 AM–4:00 PM Saturday and Sunday.
ADMISSION: $.50 per person walk-in or $2 parking fee.
LOCATION: 3801 East Washington Street at 40th and Washington. From Loop 202 go south on 40th Street.
DESCRIPTION: This show first opened in 1961. It is both an indoor and an outdoor market that accommodates from 1,500 dealers in summer to 2,500 in winter. Billed as "the largest open air flea market in the southwest." Whatever you want, you will probably find at this market. There are dealers selling art, crystal, jewelry, musical instruments, toys, clothes, pictures, housewares, garage sale items, weight loss products, and tools. Even UPS has an outlet. There is also a printing service as well as a remodeling service in this enormous complex. Finally, when you grow hungry from shopping, there are many different types of foods available, from Mexican to Indian fry bread to American burgers and fries.
DEALER RATES: $12 per 9' × 21' booth per day, Saturday and Sunday. $5 per 9' × 21' booth per day, Wednesday and Friday. Reservations are not required.
CONTACT: Mr. Richard K. Hogue, P.O. Box 61953, Phoenix, AZ 85082. Tel: (602) 273-1259. Day of show contact: Monica Legliu or Susan Barrett.

Fairgrounds Antique Market

DATES: Third weekend of each month, except March, October, and December when it is held on the second weekend.
TIMES: Saturday 9:00 AM–5:00 PM; Sunday 10:00 AM–4:00 PM.
ADMISSION: Free. $3 parking fee per vehicle.
LOCATION: 1826 West McDowell Road, State Fairgrounds, at the intersection of Grand, 19th Avenue and McDowell.
DESCRIPTION: This show started in June, 1986. The indoor market currently draws over 150 dealers in summer and 300 in winter.

Dealers set up to sell a variety of antiques, collectibles, and handicrafts; expert crystal repair is also available. Food is served on the premises.

DEALER RATES: $40 for a 8' × 10½' space. $45 for a corner 8' × 10½' space. Reservations are advised.

CONTACT: Mr. Arthur J. Schwartz, Jack Black Enterprises, P.O. Box 61172, Phoenix, AZ 85082-1172. Tel: (602) 247-1004.

Paradise Valley Swap Meet

DATES: Saturday and Sunday.

TIMES: Summer: 5:30 AM–1:30 PM; winter: 5:30 AM–4:00 PM.

LOCATION: 2414 East Union Hills Drive. Go 1 mile north of Bell Road and Cave Creek Road. On the northeast corner of Cave Creek Road and Union Hills Road.

ADMISSION: Free. Parking is free.

DESCRIPTION: This market, in operation for over 14 years, has 125 spaces and hosts from 40 dealers in summer to capacity in winter. They sell everything from antiques and collectibles to soaps, tools, jewelry, boxed foods, produce, t-shirts, garage sale, new merchandise and the occasional reptile. The Chuck Wagon concession stand with outdoor tables and a hot dog cart provide food.

DEALER RATES: $10 per 10' × 10' or 10' × 29' space; corner space for $15; double space at $20 to $25 for 20' × 18' space; drop-off space at $10 for 10' × 10' or 10' × 15'. Reservations are a must in the winter, not required in the summer. Office is open Wednesday, Thursday, and Friday 10:00 AM–1:00 PM for reservations.

CONTACT: Jim Clark, Manager, Paradise Valley Swap Meet, 2414 East Union Hills Drive, Phoenix, AZ 85024. Tel: (602) 569-0052.

PRESCOTT

Peddler's Pass, Inc.

DATES: Friday, Saturday, and Sunday, year round.

TIMES: Sunup to sundown.

ADMISSION: Free. Parking is also free.

LOCATION: Six miles east of Prescott on Highway 69 in Prescott Valley.

DESCRIPTION: This growing market of 350 dealers in summer and 150 in winter started in 1987. The dealers feature a good mix of new and used merchandise and fresh produce with a strong market for antiques and collectibles. They are the "largest market in Northern Arizona," a clean, neat and well-organized "no hassle" market. In 1993 they added a 60' × 112' addition to house a 40-space farmer's market selling fresh produce and related items. Food is available on the premises.

DEALER RATES: $5 per 10' × 25'; $8 per 20' × 20'; $10 per 25' × 20' and $20 per 40' × 20' space. The largest space also comes with electric and water hook-ups. Reservations are suggested.

CONTACT: Robert H. Scott (Owner), 2201 Clubhouse Drive, Prescott, AZ 86301. Tel: (602) 775-4117 Wednesday through Sunday.

QUARTZSITE
The Main Event

DATES: The Big Show is held annually the second half of January. 1994 dates are January 15 until January 30. The area is open every day of the year.

TIMES: 8:00 AM–6:00 PM.

ADMISSION: Free. Parking is also free.

LOCATION: On I-10, Mile Post 17.

DESCRIPTION: This Annual Gemboree first began in 1982. It is held on 100 acres of land with over 1,000 dealers from all corners of the globe and is well known as one of the largest gem sales in the country, as well as one of the most exciting flea markets. Dealers set up to sell a virtually limitless range of antiques and collectibles including bottles, coins, hobby crafts, etc., along with lapidary equipment and thousands of specimens of gems and minerals from as far away as Brazil. The Main Event is a staging ground for the exchange of all sorts of out-of-the-ordinary objects. It is the brainchild of Howard and Marilyn Armstrong, who claim that "the world is missing out when they don't come to Quartzsite, Arizona... we have the largest collection of talent in the world." Food is served on the premises.

DEALER RATES: $300–$390 for 18' × 32' space. Reservations are advised.

CONTACT: The Main Event, P.O. Box 2801, Quartzsite, AZ 85346. Tel: (602) 927-5213.

TUCSON
MarketPlace USA

DATES: Friday, Saturday, and Sunday.

TIMES: Friday 12:00 NOON–9:00 PM; Saturday 10:00 AM–9:00 PM;

Sunday 10:00 AM–6:00 PM.

ADMISSION: Free. Parking is free.

LOCATION: 3750 East Irvington Road. Off I-10 at Palo Verde North exit, east on Irvington Road approximately 2 blocks.

DESCRIPTION: Opened in November 1990 with 500 dealer spaces this growing market currently has 300-400 dealers selling antiques, collectibles, crafts, produce, and new merchandise. Housed in a 150,000 square foot building they offer everything from plants, electronics, and tools to chiropractors. Billed as "the largest indoor marketplace for independent retailers in the Southwest" this market has 505 spaces plus a 26,000 square foot Exposition Center, five snack bars and one sports bar.

DEALER RATES: $200 for four weeks. Reservations are required.

CONTACT: Brian Weeks, General Manager, or Joanne Moebus, Assistant Manager, MarketPlace USA, 3750 East Irvington Road, Tucson, AZ 85714-1958. Tel: (602) 745-5000.

Tanque Verde Swap Meet

DATES: Wednesday, Friday, Saturday, and Sunday, year round, weather permitting.

TIMES: Wednesday and Friday 3:00 PM–11:00 PM; Saturday and Sunday two sessions: 7:00 AM–3:00 PM and 3:00 PM–11:00 PM.

ADMISSION: Free. Parking is free.

LOCATION: 4100 South Palo Verde. Just south of Ajo Way. Or take I-10 to Palo Verde North Exit 264B, go north 1 mile.

DESCRIPTION: This large outdoor family-owned market started in 1974 and is now considered a local tourist attraction as well as a city and county landmark. Its 800 dealers sell everything from antiques and collectibles to fresh produce; from unique Southwestern items to handcrafted treasures, to new and used merchandise. "Everything from toothpicks to houses, except processed food." There are 12 restaurants and snack bars. A well-equipped cafeteria, The Food Mercado, creates homemade Mexican dishes and assorted specials every weekend all at very reasonable prices. Live entertainment is scheduled periodically on a stage near the cafeteria.

DEALER RATES: $11 per 11' × 26' space; $12 per 11' × 35' space; $15 per corner space. Reservations are not required, unless for monthly reservations.

CONTACT: Tanque Verde Swap Meet, 602A South Pantano, Tucson, AZ 85710. Tel: (602) 294-4252.

Wilmot Bazaar and Swap Meet

DATES: Friday, Saturday, and Sunday.

TIMES: Friday 3:00 PM–11:00 PM; Saturday 7:00 AM–11:00 PM; Sunday 7:00 AM–10:00 PM.

LOCATION: Northwest corner of I-10 (Exit 296) and Wilmot, behind the Texaco Truck Stop.

ADMISSION: Free. Parking is free.

DESCRIPTION: This market averaging 120 dealers has been in operation since November 1991. Along with the usual antiques, collectibles, and new and used merchandise, they have one vendor specializing in "tons of old books," others bringing in the usual flea market fare, treasures, cars and RVs (yes, for sale), and garage sale items. They sell beer and wine, Mexican and the usual American fast food at their snack bars. A kiddie carnival will have spent the '93-'94 winter with them, and on weekends they have live music at their bandstand: Mexican and country western.

DEALER RATES: $22–$33 per weekend for a 12' × 26' booth; RV hook-ups with selling space $57 per week. Electric is available at all booths and water is available at some. Reservations are not required.

CONTACT: Jim Cummings or Jose, Wilmot Bazaar and Swap Meet, 6161 East Benson Highway, Tucson, AZ 85706. Tel: (602) 574-2772.

YUMA

Arizona Avenue Swap Meet

DATES: Daily, October through May.

TIMES: 8:00 AM–5:00 PM.

ADMISSION: Free. Parking is also free.

LOCATION: 1749 Arizona Avenue, 2 blocks south of 16th Street on Arizona Avenue.

DESCRIPTION: This outdoor show first began in 1976. Currently, approximately 50 to 100 dealers sell a wide range of goods, including antiques and collectibles, fine art, arts and crafts, books, tools, chalk, new merchandise, and fresh produce, to name a few. Food is served on the premises.

DEALER RATES: $5 per 18' × 20' space per day; $25 per 18' × 20' space per week. Tables available for $.50 per day.

CONTACT: Mr. Bob Butcher, 1749 Arizona Avenue, Yuma, AZ 85365. Tel: (602) 343-1837.

OTHER FLEA MARKETS

Chandler: Manufacturers and Merchants Flea Market, 670 North Arizona Avenue #1, Chandler, AZ 85224. Tel: (602) 963-8514. Open Friday through Sunday, 10:00 AM–6:00 PM.

Phoenix: Great Southwestern Swap Meet, 1820 South 35 Avenue, Phoenix, AZ 85009. Tel: (602) 352-1228. Open weekends, 6:00 AM–4:00 PM.

Phoenix: SwapMart, 5115 North 27 Avenue, Phoenix, AZ 85017. Tel: (602) 246-9600. Open Friday 12:00 NOON-8:00 PM, Saturday and Sunday 10:00 AM–6:00 PM.

Surprise: Surprise Swap Meet, 12912 Sante Fe Drive, Surprise, AZ 85374. Tel: (602) 972-7515. Open Thursday 3:00 PM–10:00 PM, Saturday and Sunday 5:30 AM–4:00 PM.

ARKANSAS

BATESVILLE
America's Flea Market

DATES: Every Friday, Saturday, and Sunday, year round, rain or shine.
TIMES: Friday 11:00 AM–6:00 PM, Saturday 8:30 AM–6:00 PM, and Sunday 11:00 AM–6:00 PM.
ADMISSION: Free. Free parking is provided.
LOCATION: 310 West Main Street, at the lower end of downtown Batesville. On the site of the historical Ringold home.
DESCRIPTION: This indoor/outdoor market first opened in 1950 and currently accommodates over 140 dealers. Everything from antiques and collectibles to new merchandise, and from fine art to fresh produce can be bought here. It is located on the historic home site of one of the founders of Batesville. Food is served on the premises.
DEALER RATES: Booth size is 10' × 10'; call for current rates. Advance reservations are required during winter months.
CONTACT: Ronald A. Newberry, 310 West Main Street, Batesville, AR 72501. Tel: (501) 793-7508.

FORT SMITH
Fort Smith Flea Market

DATES: Friday, Saturday, and Sunday.
TIMES: 9:00 AM–5:00 PM.
LOCATION: 3721 Towson Road. From the east: I-40, Route 540S to Phoenix exit, 2 to 3 miles down the road to Towson. From the west: take the first Fort Smith exit off I-40 and follow that road to Towson.
ADMISSION: Free. Parking is free.
DESCRIPTION: This long-time market averages from 60 to 70 dealers selling everything from antiques and collectibles to custom license plates, books, tools, t-shirts, baseball cards, and new and used merchandise. Food is available on the premises. Dave does extensive advertising on local cable and TV networks to promote this market.
DEALER RATES: $20 for a 10' × 8' space for the 3-day weekend and up depending on size. Reservations are strongly recommended.
CONTACT: Dave, Fort Smith Flea Market, 3721 Towson Avenue, Fort Smith, AR 72901. Tel: (501) 646-0410.

HOT SPRINGS
Hot Springs Flea Market

DATES: Thursday through Monday.

TIMES: 10:00 AM–6:00 PM.

LOCATION: 2156 Higdon Ferry Road. Just off Route 7 South, across from the Hot Springs Mall.

ADMISSION: Free. Parking is free.

DESCRIPTION: Opened in 1986 on 11 acres, and having become "a legend in our own mind," this market of approximately 50 dealers sells mostly antiques and collectibles. Everything from standard flea market fare to house plants is sold here, with a special area for "oldies and goodies" and an antique mall. This air-conditioned/heated market is a family operation with a skating rink included. "We grabbed the best cook in the county to run our snack bar," so the food should be special.

DEALER RATES: $150 for a 12' × 20' single space per month. Reservations are requested.

CONTACT: Rick Jackson, Manager, 2156 Higdon Ferry Road, Hot Springs, AR 71913. Tel: (501) 525-9927.

ROGERS
Rose Hall Mall Flea Market

DATES: Seven days a week.

TIMES: Monday through Saturday 9:00 AM–5:30 PM; Sunday 11:00 AM–5:30 PM.

ADMISSION: Free. Parking is also free.

LOCATION: 2875 West Walnut (Highway 71 North), exactly 1 mile east of new by-pass.

DESCRIPTION: With over 100 booths, this market is considered one of the friendliest markets around. Their dealers sell a good variety of antiques, collectibles, handmade crafts, and new merchandise at low prices. This market is located on scenic Highway 12. Rogers is the home of the nationally famous "War Eagle Days" Craft Fair.

DEALER RATES: Range from $30 to $200 per month. Reservations are required.

CONTACT: Wanda Doffin, Rose Hall Mall Flea Market, 2875 West Walnut, Rogers, AR 72756. Tel: (501) 631-8940.

SPRINGDALE
Discount Corner Flea Market Mall

DATES: Daily.

TIMES: 9:00 AM–6:00 PM.

ADMISSION: Free. Parking is also free.

LOCATION: 418 East Emma (downtown), approximately 3 blocks east of the railroad tracks.

DESCRIPTION: This indoor market started in 1987, and most of their 125 dealers have been with them since the beginning. These dealers sell antiques, collectibles, handmade and craft items, toys— both new and collectible, tools, and new merchandise. Other dealers from 19 states come shopping here. There are pleasant camper facilities nearby, as is the Shiloh Museum. A country music show is just down the street. Food is available on the premises.

DEALER RATES: No weekend space is currently available, however do call for information regarding monthly rates.

CONTACT: Harold or Frances Carpenter, Discount Corner Flea Market Mall, 418 East Emma, Springdale, AR 72764. Tel: (501) 756-0764.

Oak Grove Flea Market

DATES: Saturday and Sunday, year round.

TIMES: 8:00 AM–5:00 PM.

ADMISSION: Free. Parking is also free.

LOCATION: Corner of Oak Grove and Elm Springs Roads.

DESCRIPTION: Considered one of largest and oldest of northwest Arkansas's flea markets, having opened in 1977, this indoor/outdoor market hosts between 60 to 100 dealers depending on the season. They sell antiques, collectibles, furniture, fresh produce, crafts, and new merchandise. Food is available on the premises.

DEALER RATES: $4 per 12' × 14' space per day, outside; $50 per month inside. Reservations are required for inside space; outside is first come; first served.

CONTACT: Ramona or Bob Wallis, Route 5 Box 292, Fayetteville, AR 72701. Tel: (501) 756-0697 or (501) 521-5791.

SPRINGHILL
Springhill Flea Market

DATES: Daily.

TIMES: 8:00 AM–5:00 PM.

LOCATION: 660 Highway 65 North. Exactly 7 miles out of Conway going to Greenbrier, 5 miles from Pickle's Gap.

ADMISSION: Free. Parking is free.

DESCRIPTION: This market averages 32 vendors selling "antiques to junctiques," including a vendor specializing in *Star Wars* toys, baseball cards, and comics; one vendor with a collection of 30,000 books and "every variety of knife"; oil paintings; and opening in the spring of 1994, a new pet shop. Refreshments and restrooms are available on the premises.

DEALER RATES: $90 per month for a 16' × 20' inside booth; $35 per month for outside space; $3 per day for electric hook-up for dealers wishing to hang around awhile. Reservations are suggested, or at least a call, one week in advance for inside space; first come, first served for outside space.

CONTACT: Rita Camp, Manager, Springhill Flea Market, 660 Highway 65 North, Springhill, AR 72058. Tel: (205) 679-9106.

WEST MEMPHIS
West Memphis Flea Market

DATES: Wednesday through Sunday.

TIMES: 10:00 AM–6:00 PM.

LOCATION: 512 East Broadway. Easy access from either I-40 or I-55 from Exit 7 (both interstates), go to Broadway, right, 2 blocks to market on your left.

ADMISSION: Free. Parking is free.

DESCRIPTION: Located along the Mississippi River, this market of 45 permanent and up to a total of 75 dealers sells everything from antiques and collectibles to household goods, glassware, new and vintage clothing, jewelry, the latest fads, and new merchandise. Other dealers come here to shop because the deals and merchandise are so good. One snack bar feeds the famished. They are near a RV park, a dog track for the bold, and only seven miles from Memphis.

DEALER RATES: Daily, weekly, and monthly rates available. Reservations are strongly suggested, as sometimes they are quite full, but they will do their best to accommodate dealers even when full.

CONTACT: Juanita and Butch Mosier, 512 East Broadway, West Memphis, AR 72301. Tel: (501) 735-9332 or 735-1644.

OTHER FLEA MARKETS

Fort Smith: Zero Street Flea Market, 2425 South Zero Street, Fort Smith, AZ 72902. Tel: (501) 648-9909. Open Friday through Sunday.
Jubsonia: Thackerland Flea Market, Highway 367, Jubsonia, AR 72087. Tel: (501) 729-3063. Open weekends.

CALIFORNIA

ANTIOCH
Contra Costa County (Antioch) Flea Market
DATES: Friday through Sunday, year round.
TIMES: 5:00 AM-3:00 PM.
ADMISSION: $.50. Parking is free.
LOCATION: At 10th and L Streets.
DESCRIPTION: Open since 1981, this outdoor market has 300–500 dealers selling antiques, collectibles, crafts, produce, new merchandise, autos, tools, fishing equipment, and "everything under the sun." Five snacks bar deal with the hunger factor.
DEALER RATES: $10-$15 per 20' × 20' space. First come, first served.
CONTACT: Lou Briones, Contra Costa County Flea Market, 10th and L Streets, Antioch, CA 94509. Tel: (510) 778-6900.

BAKERSFIELD
Bakersfield Swap Meet
DATES: Saturday and Sunday.
TIMES: 5:00 AM-3:00 PM.
ADMISSION: $.75. Parking is free.
LOCATION: At the fairgrounds, at the intersection of Ming and Union, right on the corner.
DESCRIPTION: This outdoor market, open since 1984, attracts 500 to 700 dealers, year round, selling antiques, collectibles, crafts, produce, new merchandise, farm tools, cars, boats, motorhomes, used merchandise, and "everything under the sun." Ten snack bars feed the famished.
DEALER RATES: $10-$15 for a 20' × 20' space. Reservations are not required.
CONTACT: Ed Murphy, Bakersfield Swap Meet, Corner Ming and Union Streets, Bakersfield, CA 93307. Tel: (805) 397-1504.

Pacific Theater Swap-O-Rama
DATES: Every Saturday and Sunday, rain or shine.
TIMES: Saturday 6:00 AM-3:00 PM, Sunday 6:00 AM-4:00 PM.
ADMISSION: Saturdays free, $.75 Sundays, children under 12 free. Free parking is available.

LOCATION: 4501 Wible Road. Take Freeway 99, Exit White Lane and Wible Road exit, two blocks south.

DESCRIPTION: This market opened in 1971. It is an outdoor market that accommodates anywhere from 450 to 550 dealers. Antiques, fine art, arts and crafts, collectibles, fresh produce, and new merchandise are among the many items you will find. There is also an assortment of second-hand goods. For your convenience, there is a large variety of foods available on the premises, picnicking under the trees, carnival rides, carousel, ferris wheel, plenty to keep the kids happy, and live music.

DEALER RATES: Saturday $3 reserved space, $5 non-reserved; Sunday $15 reserved space, $20 for non-reserved. Reservations are suggested. The office is open Thursday for reservations from 9:00 AM–3:00 PM.

CONTACT: Pacific Theater Swap-O-Rama, 4501 Wible Road, Bakersfield, CA 93313. Tel: (805) 831-9342.

CAMPBELL
Second Saturday Flea Market

DATES: Second Saturday of every month, weather permitting.

TIMES: 7:00 AM to dusk.

ADMISSION: Free. Parking is also free.

LOCATION: South from Santa Cruz on Highway 17, turn west at Hamilton; then travel ½ mile to Winchester Boulevard; then turn left and go ½ block to Campbell Center Shopping Center.

DESCRIPTION: This show started in 1971. The outdoor market accommodates approximately 100 dealers. You can find almost anything here from antiques and collectibles to fine art and new merchandise—"whatever dealers bring that is legal to sell." Fresh produce is also available. Although it originally started as only a mini-market it has grown to a full-fledged flea market. Food is served on the premises.

DEALER RATES: $10 for 17' × 10' space. Reservations are not accepted. First come, first served.

CONTACT: Mr. Walt Landers, 1769 South Winchester Boulevard, Campbell, CA 95008. Tel: (408) 866-5131.

COLTON
Maclin's Colton Open Air Market and Auction

DATES: Every Thursday, Saturday and Sunday.

TIMES: 7:30 AM–3:00 PM. Antique auctions are held every Thursday at 10:00 AM.

ADMISSION: $.50, children 12 and under free. Free on Sundays. Parking is free.

LOCATION: 1902 West Valley Boulevard, Colton. From points west, take 10 Freeway east to Riverside Avenue, then north to Valley East. From points east, take Freeway 10 west to Pepper, then go north to Valley West.

DESCRIPTION: Maclin's has just celebrated its 50th anniversary. Over the years it has grown to accommodate 350 to 500 dealers and between 3,000 to 7,000 buyers daily. While the grounds are completely paved and the spaces are covered, it is considered an open-air outdoor market. Their furniture/antique/collectible auction, however, is held indoors. Their merchandise selection is huge and they claim it is unequaled for variety and quality. They sell antiques, fine art, collectibles, arts and crafts, gold jewelry, clothing, home furnishings, and shoes, just to name a few! There is also a wide range of foods available on the premises. The restaurants are run by the Marriott Corp.

DEALER RATES: $7–$40 depending on size and location. Reservations are suggested and are accepted on Wednesdays from 1:00 PM–4:00 PM by calling (909) 431-5353, but walk-ins are welcome and advised to be there before 7:30 AM to get a good spot.

CONTACT: Maclin Markets, Inc., 7407 Riverside Drive, Ontario, CA 91761. Tel: (909) 877-0790 or toll-free in California 1-800-222-7467 for information about Colton.

CRESCENT CITY
Redwood Flea Market

DATES: Irregular schedule but generally once a month; schedule cards printed in October for following year; contact market for exact dates. Open year round.

TIMES: 8:00 AM–4:00 PM.

ADMISSION: $.25 per person. Children under 12 free.

LOCATION: Del Nort County Fairgrounds on Main Street.

DESCRIPTION: Sister market to Eureka's Redwood Market and opened in October 1993, this market enjoys the same ambiance as Eureka: beautiful redwoods, the ocean, and lots of fishing. The climate is mild both summer and winter (cool to those from warm climates). Antiques, collectibles, craft items, and new and used mer-

chandise are displayed on 70 to 90 indoor tables during the summer; 80 to 140 during the winter months. Food is available at a snack bar.
DEALER RATES: $9 per 3' × 8' table. Advance reservations are suggested.
CONTACT: Amanda Plants, Redwood Flea Market, P.O. Box 2774, McKinleyville, CA 95521. Tel: (707) 839-3049 or leave message for Amanda.

CUPERTINO
De Anza College Flea Market
DATES: First Saturday of every month, rain or shine.
TIMES: 8:00 AM–4:00 PM.
ADMISSION: Free. Parking is $2 on campus.
LOCATION: Take Highway 280 north or south to Highway 85 west, then to De Anza College via Stevens Creek Boulevard.
DESCRIPTION: This outdoor market began in 1972 and is operated by the student government and the student activities committee, with proceeds benefiting the student body. There are approximately 850 booths selling antiques, fine art, arts and crafts, collectibles, and new merchandise. Food is served on the premises.
DEALER RATES: $15 for two parking spaces as selling area; $30 for four spaces as of 1991. Reservations must be made one month in advance.
CONTACT: De Anza Flea Market, 21250 Stevens Creek Boulevard, Cupertino, CA 95014. Tel: (408) 996-8946.

DALY CITY
Geneva Swap Meet
DATES: Saturday and Sunday.
TIMES: 7:00 AM–4:00 PM.
ADMISSION: $.75. Parking is free.
LOCATION: 607 Carter, at the Geneva Drive-In next door to the Cow Palace.
DESCRIPTION: This market hosts from 150 to 200 dealers selling about half new merchandise and half old or used. Food is served on the premises.
DEALER RATES: $10 for a 11'x 18' space on Saturdays; $15 Sundays. Reservations are suggested.
CONTACT: Laura Ross, Geneva Swap Meet, 607 Carter Street, Daly City, CA 94014. Tel: (415) 587-4606 or 587-0515.

ESCONDIDO
Escondido Swap Meet

DATES: Wednesday, Thursday, Saturday, and Sunday.

TIMES: Wednesday and Thursday 6:30 AM–4:00 PM; Saturday and Sunday 6:00 AM–4:00 PM.

ADMISSION: Wednesday and Saturday $.50, Thursday $.25, Sunday $.75.

LOCATION: 635 West Mission Avenue. Take 78 east to Centre City Parkway South, take next left at Mission Avenue, left at Quince Street. Market is on the right side.

DESCRIPTION: Since 1970, this indoor/outdoor market has drawn large crowds of sellers as well as buyers. There is a large variety of new and used merchandise, antiques, collectibles, and crafts to choose from. Eight concessions include Mexican, pizza, ice cream, fish and chips, barbeque, standard snack bar, and a bakery. A farmers market sells inexpensive fresh produce, cheeses, and dairy products and meats.

DEALER RATES: Per 18' × 20' booth: Wednesday $8, Thursday $6, Saturday $13, Sunday $16. Reservations are not required, first-come, first-served.

CONTACT: Lee Porter, Escondido Swap Meet, 635 West Mission Avenue, Escondido, CA 92025. Tel: (619) 745-3100.

EUREKA
Redwood Flea Market

DATES: Irregular schedule but generally twice a month; schedule cards printed in October for following year; contact market for exact dates. Open year round.

TIMES: 8:00 AM–4:00 PM.

ADMISSION: $.25 per person. Children 12 and under free.

LOCATION: 3750 Harris Street at Redwood Acres Fairgrounds.

DESCRIPTION: When visiting this indoor flea market, opened in 1969, visitors can enjoy the beautiful redwoods, the ocean, and lots of fishing. The climate is mild both summer and winter (cool to those from warm climates). Antiques, collectibles, craft items, and new and used merchandise are displayed on 70 to 150 indoor tables during the summer; 80 to 152 during the winter months. Food is available at a snack bar. See their sister market in Crescent City.

DEALER RATES: $9 per 3' × 8' table. Advance reservations are suggested.

CONTACT: Amanda Plants, Redwood Flea Market, P.O. Box 2774, McKinleyville, CA 95521. Tel: (707) 839-3049 or leave message for Amanda.

FOLSOM
Annual Peddlers Faire and Flea Market

DATES: Flea Market (spring) is the third Sunday in April and Peddler's Faire (fall) is third Sunday in September. Rain date is the following Sunday. Octoberfest is the second Saturday in October.

TIMES: 8:00 AM–5:00 PM.

ADMISSION: Free. Some parking is free, some paid.

LOCATION: On Sutter Street in historic Folsom. From Highway 50. Take Folsom Boulevard Exit, turn left, 2.9 miles to Sutter Street.

DESCRIPTION: Started in 1966, this outdoor market in the Sierra foothills now accommodates 300 dealers that sell antiques and collectibles. No new merchandise is allowed. More than 20,000 people attend this semi-annual fair. In the heart of "gold country" this fair is located in the middle of some fascinating history: the Folsom Powerhouse was the first commercial transporter of long-distance electricity, there are the logging and gold mining histories, chinese diggings, special exhibits of early Indian life at the History Museum on Sutter Street, and more. Food is plentiful.

DEALER RATES: $70 for 10' × 10' space. Reservations are required; setup starts at 2:00 AM and dealers should take note that crowds may start appearing as early as 3:00 AM.

CONTACT: Attn: Asta Peter, Sutter Street Merchants Association P.O. Box 515, Folsom, CA 95763. Tel: (916) 985-7452.

FRESNO
Cherry Auction

DATES: Open every Tuesday and Saturday.

TIMES: 6:30 AM–5:00 PM.

ADMISSION: $.50 for adults; children under 12 are free. Both free and pay parking are available.

LOCATION: 4640 South Cherry Avenue. Take Highway 99 north to Jensen Avenue exit; then go one block west to Cherry; then go two miles south to yard.

DESCRIPTION: This show began over 50 years ago. Booths are either outdoors or under a shed roof. The 700 plus dealers who attend this market sell "1,000 + 1 items," from antiques and collectibles to new merchandise and fresh produce—it can all be bought. This is one of the oldest outdoor markets in the area. There is also a unique "Auction Lane" where anything and everything is auctioned off. There is plenty of food available on the premises.

DEALER RATES: Reservations are taken only by the month. The cost for dealer space is $10 per 10' × 20' booth on Saturday; $8 per booth on Tuesday. Reservations are not required.

CONTACT: Richard Pilegard, Cherry Auction, 4640 South Cherry Avenue, Fresno, CA 93706. Tel: (209) 266-9856.

HOLLYWOOD
Hollywood Outdoor Flea Market

DATES: Fourth Sunday of every month.

TIMES: 8:00 AM–3:00 PM.

ADMISSION: $2, seniors $1, children under 12 free with an adult. Parking is where you can get it: lots or street.

LOCATION: 1540 Vine Street, in the heart of Hollywood, between Hollywood and Vine Streets.

DESCRIPTION: Open since 1992, this market has over 130 dealers, many permanent, selling strictly antiques and collectibles. There is a snack truck on site and a farmer's market across the street, as well as many restaurants in the surrounding blocks. Because of its location, you never know who you might run to (there have been sightings of the major star variety).

DEALER RATES: $30 per 3-car parking-lot space, $40 per 3-car parking-lot corner space. Reservations are required. They do keep a waiting list and sell the available spaces at 7:00 AM on a first come, first served basis.

CONTACT: Robert Cox, Hollywood Outdoor Flea Market, P.O. Box 1631, Hollywood, CA 90078. Tel: (213) 464-4276.

KING CITY
King City Rotary Flea Market

DATES: First Sunday in April, rain or shine.

TIMES: 7:00 AM–4:00 PM.

ADMISSION: $2 for adults. $1 for children age 12 and under. Parking is free.

LOCATION: Salinas Valley Fairgrounds. Take Highway 101 to Canal Street, then follow signs to Fairgrounds.

DESCRIPTION: This show began in 1969 and is both an indoor and outdoor market that accommodates approximately 150 dealers selling antiques as well as new merchandise, crafts, collectibles, and fresh produce. There is also a variety of foods available, including American, Mexican, and Oriental.

DEALER RATES: $15 for 10' × 15' space. $10 for each additional space. Reservations are required.

CONTACT: Paul T. Becket, King City Rotary, P.O. Box 611, King City, CA 93930. Tel: (408) 385-0414. Day of show call Paul Beckett on fairgrounds at (408) 385-3243.

LAKE PERRIS
Maclin's Open-Air Market at Lake Perris

DATES: Every Saturday and Sunday.

TIMES: 7:30 AM–3:00 PM.

ADMISSION: Free. Parking is also free.

LOCATION: Lake Perris Fairgrounds at 18700 Lake Perris Drive.

DESCRIPTION: This outdoor market first began in San Jacinto in 1936 and moved here in June 1993. There are antiques, arts and crafts, and collectibles, as well as new merchandise, fishing and hunting equipment, pets and supplies, and grocery items. Between 200 and 300 dealers are there to help you find what you want "without emptying your wallet." When you're ready for a break, relax in one of their restaurants or beer gardens and enjoy some live entertainment.

DEALER RATES: $12 to $25 depending on space and reservation status: prepaid $12–$20; unreserved $15–$25. Reservations are suggested and can be made in person Fridays at the market between 1:00 PM–4:00 PM.

CONTACT: Maclin's, 7407 Riverside Drive, Ontario, CA 91761. Tel: (909) 654-2546. Or Toll-free in California 1-800-222-7467.

LANCASTER
Lancaster Chamber of Commerce
Semi-Annual Flea Market

DATES: Third weekend in May; first weekend in October, rain or shine.

TIMES: 7:00 AM–5:00 PM.

ADMISSION: $2 per person. Parking fee is $2.

LOCATION: Antelope Valley Fairgrounds. 155 East Avenue I. Take the 14 Freeway (Antelope Valley Freeway) to Avenue I exit and head east exactly 2 miles to the fairgrounds at the corner of Avenue I and Division Street.

DESCRIPTION: This indoor/outdoor market has been operating since 1967 as *the* fundraiser for local chamber of commerce. Approximately 1,800 dealers from five states are attracted to this well-organized market selling antiques, arts and crafts, collectibles, fine art, fine jewelry, food, new merchandise, and whatever is legal. It is getting more upscale as the years pass. About ¼ of all the vendors sell food, from Mexican, Thai, Oriental, Italian, barbeques, whatever your palate fancies. Restrooms are available.

When this market first opened, vendors would wait impatiently until the gates were thrown open, then race for whatever spot they could get. Now it is a finely-tuned event run by 300 volunteers.

DEALER RATES: $35–$105 for 8' × 10' space inside; $35–$60 per 10' × 10' booth outside, depending on the location. Reservations are required on a first come, first served basis. Dealers must be set up and ready by 3:00 AM.

CONTACT: Lancaster Chamber of Commerce, 44335 Lowtree Avenue, Lancaster, CA 93534. Tel: (805) 948-4518.

LODI

Lodi Street Faire

DATES: First Sunday in May and October. Rain or shine.

TIMES: 8:00 AM–4:00 PM.

ADMISSION: Free. Parking is free.

LOCATION: Downtown Lodi on School Street, between Lodi Avenue and Lockeford Street.

DESCRIPTION: This annual fundraiser attracts 400 dealers selling antiques, collectibles, arts and crafts, and new merchandise. Food vendors sell a variety of treats in the Food Alley and beer gardens. One parking lot is devoted to tables and chairs for those eating or resting. Over 20,000 attend this fair. There are volunteers roaming the fair in golf carts waiting to be flagged down by weary or overloaded shoppers looking for a lift. Entertainment is provided.

DEALER RATES: $30 for 13' × 13' space, $95 for 13' × 13' corner space. Reservations are required.

CONTACT: Lodi District Chamber of Commerce, 1330 South Ham Lane, P.O. Box 386, Lodi, CA 95242. Tel: (209) 367-7840. Day of show contact workers in on-site information booth.

LONG BEACH
Outdoor Antique and Collectible Market

DATES: Third Sunday of every month, rain or shine. Extra holiday show first Sunday in November.

TIMES: 8:00 AM–3:00 PM.

ADMISSION: $3.50 for adults. No fee for children under 12. Free parking.

LOCATION: Veterans Stadium at Lakewood Boulevard and Conant Street. Take Lakewood Boulevard North exit from Freeway 405, turn right onto Lakewood Boulevard, go north approximately 2 miles, turn right on Conant Street.

DESCRIPTION: This outdoor market opened in 1982 and is the largest regularly scheduled antique and collectible show in the west. It draws over 800 dealers.

DEALER RATES: Booths measure 19' × 16' and range in cost from $40 to $50 to $60 and $80 for corners. Advance reservations are required.

CONTACT: Americana Enterprises Inc., P.O. Box 69219, Los Angeles, CA 90069. Tel: (213) 655-5703.

LOS ANGELES
Alameda Swapmeet

DATES: Wednesday through Monday.

TIMES: Weekdays: 10:00 AM–7:00 PM; weekends: 8:00 AM–7:00 PM.

ADMISSION: Free. Parking is free. Make it snappy on weekends, as you only have 3 hours of free parking.

LOCATION: 4501 Alameda Street. 1½ blocks from the Vernon stop on the Blue Line metro. Off I-10 take the Alameda Exit, go south; from I-110 take Vernon Exit, east to Alameda.

DESCRIPTION: Opened in 1987, this indoor market of 200 dealers sells only new merchandise including electronics and clothes. Twice a month they hold a big party with live entertainment, clowns, and other activities for families.

DEALER RATES: Call for information, as they are full of permanent dealers now.

CONTACT: Alameda Swapmeet, 4501 South Alameda Street, Los Angeles, CA 90058. Tel: (213) 233-2764.

MARIN CITY
Marin City Flea Market
DATES: Saturday and Sunday, weather permitting.
TIMES: Saturday 6:00 AM–4:00 PM; Sunday 5:00 AM–4:00 PM.
ADMISSION: Free. Parking is $2 per car.
LOCATION: Off Highway 101, Marin City Exit.
DESCRIPTION: Opened in 1978, this market of 500 dealers is held outdoors. Besides the standard flea market fare, the dealers sell antiques, collectibles, and everything else. One dealer said "this place is better than Reno" and another dealer keeps bringing in "basement loot" that turns out to be treasures! Food is available on the premises.
DEALER RATES: Per vehicle; $20 per car; $30 per van or truck; large vehicles over 18 feet $35; buses $40; food vendors are also $40. If reserved, it's $5 more. Reservations are required on Sunday; not Saturday.
CONTACT: Marin City Flea Market, 740 Drake Avenue, Marin City, CA 94965. Tel: (415) 332-1441.

MORGAN HILL
Morgan Hill Flea Market
DATES: Every Saturday and Sunday, year round.
TIMES: 7:30 AM–6:00 PM.
ADMISSION: Free. Parking is also free.
LOCATION: 140 East Main Street in Morgan Hill, 25 miles south of San Jose.
DESCRIPTION: This show first began in 1964. The market is held outdoors and consists of over 200 dealers selling under shade trees. Shoppers may find antiques and collectibles, as well as new and used merchandise and fresh produce. Food is served on the premises.
DEALER RATES: $12 for 3' × 10' table on Saturdays and $15 on Sundays. Reservations are not required.
CONTACT: Mr. James Ahlin, 140 East Main Street, Morgan Hill, CA 95037. Tel: (408) 779-3809.

NILES
Niles Antique Faire
DATES: Last Sunday in August.
TIMES: 4:00 AM–4:00 PM.
ADMISSION: Free. Parking is $3 and is run as a Boy Scout fund raiser. Some free parking is available early.

LOCATION: In the Niles Business District. Take Highway 680 to Mission Boulevard north to Niles Boulevard; or take Highway 880 to Alvarado Boulevard and Niles Boulevard east.

DESCRIPTION: This one-day event has been a successful fundraiser for many local non-profit organizations since 1925. Most of Niles Boulevard and side streets are closed as over 500 dealers turn Niles into antique heaven. Buyers may start arriving as early 3:00 AM and continue to shop throughout the day. Antiques, arts and crafts, and a variety of collectibles can be found. Niles itself is an historic landmark, home of the former Essanay Studios (of Charlie Chaplin, Ben Turpin fame), Vallejo's Mill (the first flouring mill), and its Railroad Depot Museum with a large railroad layout. Non-profit organizations run the many food concessions as their fundraiser.

DEALER RATES: $110 for 10' × 12' space with early reservations, $135 for later reservations. Reservations are suggested. First come, first served. There are advance shopping hours for dealers from 4:00 AM–7:00 PM.

CONTACT: Flea Market Committee, Niles Merchant Association, P.O. BOX 2672, Niles District, Fremont, CA 94536. Tel: (415) 792-8023.

OAKHURST
Mountain Peddler's Show

DATES: The Sunday of Memorial Day weekend; the Sunday of Labor Day weekend; rain or shine.

TIMES: 8:00 AM–4:00 PM.

ADMISSION: Free admission.

LOCATION: State Highway 41 and County Road 426. Oakhurst is located in the Sierra Nevada foothills on California State Highway 41, 36 miles north of Fresno, and 16 miles south of Yosemite National Park.

DESCRIPTION: Initiated as a revenue source for the chamber of commerce, the first flea market was held in 1979. There were 186 booths and a crowd of 10,000. Today, there are over 400 booths of antiques, collector's items, arts and crafts, and food displays—everything from a pancake breakfast to Indian tacas, barbecue hamburgers, hot dogs, and French dip sandwiches are freshly prepared for the visitors. Arts and hand-crafts are well represented with paintings in all media, wall hangings, baskets, dried flowers, etc. Live entertainment, free to the public, is provided.

DEALER RATES: $100 per booth of various depths with 20' frontage. Saturday setup 3:00 PM. Sundowner sale Saturday 5:00 PM.
CONTACT: Harry Fries, Eastern Madera County Chamber of Commerce, P.O. Box 369, Oakhurst, CA 93644. Tel: (209) 683-3560.

OAKLAND
Coliseum Swap Meet

DATES: Wednesday through Sunday.
TIMES: 6:30 AM–4:00 PM.
ADMISSION: Wednesday $.25, Thursday $.50, Friday $.75, Saturday and Sunday $1. Parking is free.
LOCATION: 5401 Coliseum Way. At I-880 and Coliseum Way, ½ mile south of the Oakland Coliseum.
DESCRIPTION: Next door to the Oakland "A's," this market averages 400 dealers selling "everything" including antiques, collectibles, fruits, vegetables, meats, used and new merchandise, and craft items during the holidays. Plenty of south-of-the-border fruits are sold here. Food is served on the premises.
DEALER RATES: $10 per 10' × 15' space Wednesday through Friday, $15 per space on weekends. They only handle monthly or yearly reservations. You must come in person Thursday through Sunday to make your reservations.
CONTACT: Bob Darrow, Coliseum Swap Meet, 5401 Coliseum Way, Oakland, CA 94601. Tel: (510) 534-0325 or 533-1601.

OCEANSIDE
Oceanside Drive-In Swap Meet

DATES: Every Friday, Saturday, and Sunday, and holiday Mondays. Rain or shine.
TIMES: Saturday and Sunday 6:00 AM–4:00 PM; Friday and Holidays 6:00 AM–3:00 PM.
ADMISSION: Mondays and Saturdays $.50 fee; Fridays $.35, Sundays $.75. Parking is free.
LOCATION: 3480 Mission Avenue, 2 miles East of Interstate Freeway 5.
DESCRIPTION: This show started in 1971. There are now more than 1,000 dealers featured in this outdoor market. All types of new, used, and collectible merchandise are sold on approximately 40 acres of land, which includes places to purchase food.

DEALER RATES: Saturday $13; Sunday $16; Friday $6.50; Monday $8 for 18' × 24' space. Reservations are not required.
CONTACT: Joe C. Crowder, 635 West Mission Avenue, Escondido, CA 92025. Tel: (619) 745-3100. Day of show call Ernie Murray at (619) 757-5286, Saturday and Sunday.

ONTARIO
Maclin's Chino Open Air Market

DATES: Every Tuesday, Saturday, and Sunday.
TIMES: 7:30 AM–3:00 PM.
ADMISSION: $.50, children under 12 free. Free on Saturdays. Parking is free.
LOCATION: 7407 Riverside Drive. From points west, take Freeway 60 east to Euclid south, then east on Riverside Drive. From points east, take Freeway 60 west to Grove south, then west on Riverside Drive.
DESCRIPTION: This unique place to sell and shop has been serving the public since 1936. It is a cross between a swap meet, a mall, and a country fair, with not just dealers but exotic foods and children's attractions. There is a genuine livestock auction on Tuesdays and a restaurant with a 40-foot beer and wine bar with a widescreen T.V. Between 350 to 500 dealers sell everything from antiques and collectibles to clothing and gold jewelry. There are even children's pony rides. There is also a bakery and fish market on the premises. The restaurants are run by the Marriott Corp.
DEALER RATES: Rates are from $15 to $40. Reservations are suggested and are accepted on Fridays from 1:00 PM–4:00 PM by calling (909) 431-5353. Walk-ins are welcome, just be there before 7:30 AM.
CONTACT: Maclin's, 7407 Riverside Drive, Ontario, CA 91761. Tel: (909) 984-5131. Or Toll-free in California 1-800-222-7467.

ORANGE
Troubleshooters Antiques Only Round-Up

DATES: The first Sunday in June and October, rain or shine.
TIMES: 9:00 AM–3:00 PM.
ADMISSION: $4. Parking is free.
LOCATION: "The City" Shopping Center.
DESCRIPTION: This outdoor show, started in 1962, is sponsored by the Register Charities (*Orange County Register* newspaper) with all profits going to charity. The 800 dealers sell antiques, collectibles.

It is the largest antique related event in Orange County. Food is available on the premises.
DEALER RATES: $40 for 9' × 20' booth. Reservations are suggested.
CONTACT: R.G. Canning, P.O. Box 400, Maywood, CA 90270-0400.
Tel: (213) 587-5100.

PALMDALE
Antelope Valley Swap Meet at Four Points
DATES: Saturday and Sunday, year round.
TIMES: Saturday 7:00 AM–4:00 PM; Sunday 6:00 AM–4:00 PM.
ADMISSION: Saturday $.50; Sunday $1; parking is free.
LOCATION: 5550 Pearblossom Highway. Intersection of Highway 138 and Pearblossom Highway. Five miles east of Palmdale.
DESCRIPTION: "Everything under the sun!" describes this swap meet opened in 1977. About 300 dealers sell antiques, collectibles, crafts, garage sale goods, old and new merchandise, tools, fresh produce, and "soup to nuts." Great food is easily found including homemade tamales and corn dogs, authentic Mexican food, and biscuits and gravy to mention a mouth-watering few. This market, with its country/western atmosphere, live entertainment, and pony rides for the kids, seems to offer more than something for everyone.
DEALER RATES: Saturday: $7 per 20' × 20' booth; Sunday $12 per booth. Storage sheds are available. Reservations are not required; first come, first served.
CONTACT: Joyce Bruce, Antelope Valley Swap Meet, P.O. Box 901807, Palmdale, CA 93590. Tel: (805) 273-0456. Day of show call (805) 944-9116.

PASADENA
Rose Bowl Flea Market and Swap Meet
DATES: Second Sunday of each month, rain or shine.
TIMES: 9:00 AM–3:00 PM.
ADMISSION: $5 per person. Free parking.
LOCATION: Pasadena Rose Bowl, at the corner of Rosemont Avenue and Aroyo Boulevard. Well marked.
DESCRIPTION: This monthly market ranks among the largest and best known in the country. It has operated outdoors on the grounds of the Rose Bowl Stadium since 1968 and currently hosts over 1,500 sellers and approximately 20,000 shoppers at each sale. Virtually anything under the sun can be found here, from antiques and collectibles

to new merchandise and arts and crafts. Buyers often include Hollywood celebrities. Vendors may not sell food, animals, drug-related items, or ammunition.

DEALER RATES: $40 and up per 10' × 20' space per day depending upon location. Advance reservations suggested.

CONTACT: R.G. Canning Enterprises, P.O. Box 400, Dept. 44, Maywood, CA 90270. Tel: (213) 588-4411. Mondays and Wednesdays 10:00 AM–5:00 PM call main office at (213) 587-5100, ext 44.

PORTERVILLE
Porterville College Swap Meet

DATES: Every Saturday, weather permitting.

TIMES: 5:00 AM until dark.

ADMISSION: Free. Parking is also free.

LOCATION: From Bakersfield. Go north on Highway 99 to Highway 65. Then 50 miles to Highway 190, then east 2 miles to college. From Fresno, go south on Highway 99 to Highway 190, then go east 17 miles to college.

DESCRIPTION: Started in 1981, this market has an average of 350 dealers attending. There is always plenty of elegant junk available along with an ample supply of antiques, arts and crafts, collectibles, jewelry, and music tapes, along with new merchandise and fresh produce. This market is run for the benefit of the student scholarship fund and is a student body function. There is always plenty of food available on the premises.

DEALER RATES: $10 for 24' × 36' space (electricity costs an additional $1). Reservations are advised.

CONTACT: Bill Goucher, Porterville College Swap Meet, 900 South Main Street, Porterville, CA 93257. Tel: (209) 781-3130 (college) or Mr. Goucher at (209) 784-9161.

REDDING
Epperson Brothers Auction and Flea Market

DATES: Saturday and Sunday, year round, rain or shine.

TIMES: Sunup to sundown. Also, auctions are held at 6:30 AM every Wednesday and at 1:00 PM every Sunday.

ADMISSION: $.50 per carload Sundays; Saturdays admission is free.

LOCATION: 5091 Fig Tree Lane, 1 mile south of Redding International Airport, off Airport Road.

DESCRIPTION: The market first opened in 1962 and now consists of 75 to 100 dealers selling their goods both indoors and outdoors. Antiques, collectibles, arts and crafts, and new and used furniture can be purchased. There is also food available on the premises.

DEALER RATES: $5 for 4' × 8' table (plus space for vehicle) on Saturday. $8 per space on Sunday.

CONTACT: Mr. Jack L. Epperson, 5091 Fig Tree Lane, Redding, CA 96002. Tel: (916) 365-7242.

ROSEVILLE

Denio's Roseville Farmer's Market and Auction, Inc.

DATES: Every Monday, Tuesday, Wednesday, Saturday, and Sunday, rain or shine.

TIMES: 7:00 AM–5:00 PM.

ADMISSION: Free Admission. $2 parking fee.

LOCATION: 1551 Vineyard Road. Take I–80 to Roseville/Riverside Avenue off-ramp, turn left on Cirby, right on Foothill to Vineyard, right on Vineyard Road.

DESCRIPTION: Denio's is a family owned and operated business in the same location since 1947, serving northern California, southern Oregon, and western Nevada. Denio's is known as northern California's oldest and largest outdoor shopping attraction. It averages 1,500 to 2,000 dealers selling everything imaginable—antiques, collectibles, handmade/craft items, fresh produce, and new merchandise. Delicious corn dogs and other international foods are available on the premises.

DEALER RATES: Start at $15 per 18' × 20' space. Reservations are not required.

CONTACT: Ken Denio, 1551 Vineyard Road, Roseville, CA 95678. Tel: (916) 782-2704 seven days a week from 8:00 AM–5:00 PM.

SACRAMENTO

Auction City and Flea Market

DATES: Every Saturday and Sunday, rain or shine.

TIMES: 7:00 AM–5:00 PM.

ADMISSION: Free. Parking is free.

LOCATION: 8521 Folsom Boulevard. Use Highway 50 going to Lake Tahoe, take Watt Avenue south to Folsom Boulevard, turn right, go .8 miles to market on right.

DESCRIPTION: This show first opened in 1966. It accommodates over 350 dealers in both an indoor and outdoor market. You can find everything from antiques to new merchandise, from collectibles to fresh produce. This is said to be the longest-operating flea market within the city limits of Sacramento. There is also food available on the premises.

DEALER RATES: $20 for one 4' × 8' table. $10 for each additional table. Reservations are accepted Wednesday through Friday 9:00 AM–5:00 PM.

CONTACT: Emil Magovac, Owner, Auction City and Flea Market, 8521 Folsom Boulevard, Sacramento, CA 95826. Tel: (916) 383-0880. Day of show call Harold Hennessey, Manager, at the above number.

Forty-Niner (49er) Drive-In Swap Meet

DATES: Thursday through Sunday.

TIMES: 7:00 AM–4:00 PM.

ADMISSION: Free. Parking is free.

LOCATION: At the 49er Drive-In Theater. I-80 at Raley Boulevard Exit, 2 miles west of McClellan Air Force Base.

DESCRIPTION: Now open about 8 years, this growing outdoor market draws from 152 to 200 dealers selling mostly garage- and attic-found treasures including old clothes, furniture and "a little bit of everything." Because so much of the stuff coming in is from "Auntie's attic" there are a lot of "great finds" waiting to be discovered. A hot dog cart serves the starved.

DEALER RATES: Thursday $4; other days $8 per 15' × 15' space. However, if you come for Thursday, it's $4 for Thursday, then $4 for each consecutive day after, that weekend. Reservations are required for monthly rental; otherwise, first come, first served.

CONTACT: Rosemary Hallett, 49er Swap Meet, 4450 Marysville Boulevard, Sacramento, CA 95838. Tel: (916) 920-3530.

SAN BERNADINO

San Bernadino Swap Meet/Outdoor Market

DATES: Every Sunday, rain or shine.

TIMES: 6:00 AM–3:00 PM.

ADMISSION: $1, children under 12 are free. Free and paid parking is available.

LOCATION: National Orange Showgrounds.

DESCRIPTION: There are almost 800 dealers attending this outdoor show. An enormous selection of merchandise can be found. Antiques, collectibles, crafts, and new merchandise are just some of the items you may find. Many sellers are "the average guy cleaning out his garage." For your convenience, food is also available on the premises.

DEALER RATES: $8 to $40 depending on location of space. Reservations are suggested.

CONTACT: R. G. Canning, P. O. Box 400, Maywood, CA 90270-0400. Tel: (714) 795-0984.

SAN FRANCISCO
America's Largest Antique & Collectible Sale

DATES: 1994 DATES: Feb 12 & 13; May 21 & 22; Aug 27 & 28.

TIMES: Saturday 8:00 AM–7:00 PM; Sunday 9:00 AM–5:00 PM.

ADMISSION: $5. Parking is $3.

LOCATION: Cow Palace exit off Highway 101, San Francisco.

DESCRIPTION: This indoor market opened in 1988 and attracts over 350 dealers selling antiques and collectibles. Food is available on the premises.

DEALER RATES: $100 per 10' × 10' booth.

CONTACT: Chuck Palmer, Palmer/Wirfs & Associates, 4001 NE Halsey, Portland, OR 97232. Tel: (503) 282-0877. Fax: (503) 282-2953.

SAN JOSE
The Flea Market Inc.

DATES: Wednesday through Sunday, year around.

TIMES: Dawn to dusk.

ADMISSION: Free. Parking is $3 Saturday and Sunday; free Wednesday through Friday.

LOCATION: 12000 Berryessa Road between Highways 680 and 101.

DESCRIPTION: This market is billed as the "Original Flea Market" started in 1960 and is the world's largest covering 120 acres with 3,000 dealers selling everything! From antiques and collectibles to garage sales. They have a ¼ mile long produce row, 35 restaurants, clean, attended restrooms and an average of 110,000 visitors each weekend.

DEALER RATES: Wednesday $15; Thursday and Friday $10 per space per day; Saturday and Sunday $25 per space per day. No reservations are necessary, but suggested if you have a preference for a space.

CONTACT: Pat Detar, Reservation Manager, The Flea Market, Inc., 12000 Berryessa Road, San Jose, CA 95133. Tel: (408) 453-1110.

Capitol Swap Meet

DATES: Thursday, Saturday, and Sunday.
TIMES: Thursday 7:00 AM–5:00 PM, Saturday and Sunday 6:00 AM–5:30 PM.
LOCATION: Capitol Expressway at Highway 82, Monterey Road.
ADMISSION: $1. Children under 12 free. Parking is free.
DESCRIPTION: This outdoor market, in business since 1982, hosts from 800 to 1,000 dealers depending on the season. They sell mostly antiques, collectibles, and garage sale specials. Very little new merchandise is sold here. They describe themselves as an "old-fashioned" flea market in the best sense of the word. Covering 35 acres in a drive-in theater, they park from 4,000 to 12,000 cars a day! "We are crammed!" says their manager, Glen Norris. He advises you to "Come *early* for the bargains." They cater to families. There are restaurants and snack bars on site with a wide range of food available.
DEALER RATES: $12 on Thursday, $15 on Saturday, $20 on Sunday for a 16' × 24' space. Although spaces may vary, they all accommodate a car or truck and ample selling space. Reservations are required.
CONTACT: Glen Norris, Capitol Swap Meet, 3630 Hillcap Avenue, San Jose, CA 95136. Tel: (408) 225-5800.

· SAN JUAN BAUTISTA
San Juan Bautista Annual Flea Market

DATES: First Sunday in August, rain or shine.
TIMES: 8:00 AM–5:00 PM.
ADMISSION: Free. Some parking lots nearby are free, some aren't.
LOCATION: In downtown San Juan Bautista, 30 miles south of San Jose on Highway 101.
DESCRIPTION: This show first began in 1963, and nowadays over 500 vendors from nine states and 165 California cities come to participate in this event, all conducting their business outdoors on the main streets of the town. Antiques and collectibles, fineart, and craft items can be purchased. This market is claimed to be the oldest and largest one-day street show in California and has been named one of the top four flea markets in California by *Good Housekeeping* magazine. There are ten restaurants and plenty of street vendors providing food.

DEALER RATES: $150 for 10' × 14' space. Reservations are required. Dealers start arriving as early as 4:00 AM.

CONTACT: Chamber of Commerce, P.O. 1037, San Juan Bautista, CA 95045. Day of show call Rosanna Lepiane at (408) 623-2454.

SAN LUIS OBISPO

Sunset Drive-In Theatre Swap Meet

DATES: Every Sunday, rain or shine.

TIMES: 6:00 AM–1:00 PM.

ADMISSION: $1 per carload.

LOCATION: One-half mile south of San Luis Obispo, off Elks Lane.

DESCRIPTION: This outdoor show began in 1978. Dealers set up to sell a variety of antiques, arts and crafts, collectibles, and fresh produce as well as plain old "odds and ends." This market attracts approximately 200 dealers per show. "This show just keeps getting better." Food is served on the premises.

DEALER RATES: $7 for a 12' space. Reservations are not required.

CONTACT: Mr. Larry Rodkey, 255 Elks Lane, San Luis Obispo, CA 93401. Tel: (805) 544-4592 after 6 PM. Day of show call same number.

SANTA FE SPRINGS

Santa Fe Springs Swap Meet

DATES: Every Wednesday, Thursday, Saturday, and Sunday. Thursday and Friday nights May through October, rain or shine.

TIMES: Days: 5:30 AM–3:30 PM. Night hours: 5:00 PM–10:00 PM.

ADMISSION: $.50 on Wednesday; $.25 on Thursday; $.75 on Saturday and Sunday; nights $.50. Parking is free.

LOCATION: 13963 Alondra Boulevard. Valley View exit off I-5.

DESCRIPTION: This market first began in 1960 and is said to be the first swap meet in Southern California. Held at a drive-in theater, this market averages 700 dealers on weekends and 500-plus during the week selling arts and crafts, fine art, new merchandise, and fresh produce. There are kiddie rides and a video arcade to keep children busy. Food is served on the premises.

DEALER RATES: $10 for approximately 15' × 20' space on Wednesday; $4 per space on Thursday; $15–$35 per space on Saturday and Sunday; $15–$20 Friday nights; depending on location. Reservations are required, although non-reserved space is available at a higher rate.

Monthly rates are available. Advance shopping hours for dealers begins at 5:30 AM.
CONTACT: Gary Rollins, Santa Fe Springs Swap Meet, 13963 Alondra Boulevard, Santa Fe Springs, CA 90670. Tel: (213) 921-4359.

SANTEE
Santee Swap Meet

DATES: Saturday and Sunday, rain or shine.
TIMES: 6:30 AM–2:00 PM.
ADMISSION: $.50. Parking is free.
LOCATION: 10990 Woodside Avenue North. Take 67 north to Riverford Road exit. Turn left at exit, then left at Riverford Road, left at Woodside Avenue North. Market is on the right side at the drive-in theater.
DESCRIPTION: Open since 1984, this outdoor market draws large crowds of buyers as well as sellers. Many a garage is cleaned out here as well as vendors selling new merchandise, antiques, collectibles, crafts, and produce. A snack bar serves a wide variety of sandwiches, snacks, and breakfasts.
DEALER RATES: Saturday $6 per 20' × 20' booth, Sunday $8 per 20' × 20' booth. Reservations are not required, it's a first-come, first-served market.
CONTACT: Joe Crowder, 635 West Mission Avenue, Escondido, CA 92025. Tel: (619) 745-3100. Day of show contact Greg Crowder at (619) 449-7927.

SAUGUS
Saugus Swap Meet

DATES: Every Sunday, rain or shine.
TIMES: 6:00 AM–3:00 PM.
ADMISSION: $1 for adults, children under 12 are admitted free. Parking is free.
LOCATION: 22500 Soledad Canyon Road. From Los Angeles, take I-5 to Valencia Boulevard exit, turn right on Valencia Boulevard, then go 3¼ miles. Market is on the right.
DESCRIPTION: This show originally began in 1965. There are now approximately 900 dealers conducting their business outdoors and selling everything from antiques and collectibles to new merchandise and fresh produce. The market is held on the grounds of movie star Hoot Gibsons former ranch. They also have stock car racing every

Saturday night, March through mid-October. There is food available on the premises.

DEALER RATES: $20 for 20' × 16' space. Reservations are not required. Park on a space.

CONTACT: Mr. Ray Wilkings, Manager, Saugus Swap Meet, Box 901, Santa Clarita, CA 91380-9001. For information contact the office Sunday through Friday 8:00 AM–3:00 PM.

SEBASTOPOL
Midgley's Country Flea Market

DATES: Every Saturday and Sunday year round. Closed only when there is a "downpour."

TIMES: 6:30 AM–4:30 PM.

ADMISSION: Free. Parking is free.

LOCATION: Off Highway 101 to Gravenstein Highway or Highway 116. Market is about 5 miles at 2200 Gravenstein Highway South.

DESCRIPTION: This outdoor market has been open since 1972. There are approximately 600 dealers during the summer and anywhere from 300 to 400 dealers selling their goods during the winter months. There is a large variety of antiques, collectibles, handmade craft items, new merchandise and even fresh produce available Basically anything new or used is sold. Included are clothes, books, pictures, jewelry, tires, and furniture, just to name a few. For your convenience there are two snack bars on the premises.

DEALER RATES: $15 per 4' × 8' space for a table and car. $18 per 4' × 8' covered space. Reservations are not required.

CONTACT: Rosalie Midgley, 2200 Gravenstein Highway, South, Sebastopol, CA 94572. Tel: (707) 823-7874.

STOCKTON
San Joaquin County Fairgrounds Flea Market

DATES: Friday, Saturday, and Sunday.

TIMES: 5:00 AM–3:00 PM.

ADMISSION: $.50. Parking is free.

LOCATION: Corner of Airport Way and Charter Way.

DESCRIPTION: Open since 1984, this indoor/outdoor market draws from 400 dealers in summer to 600 in winter selling antiques, collectibles, crafts, produce, autos, boats, motorhomes, new merchandise, and "everything under the sun." Plenty of snack bars provide the goodies to fill the famished.

DEALER RATES: $17 for a 20' × 20' space. First come, first served.
CONTACT: Nacho Garcia, San Joaquin County Fairgrounds Flea Market, Corner of Airport Way and Charter Way, Stockton, CA 95205. Tel: (209) 476-8609.

TORRANCE
Alpine Village Swap Meet

DATES: Tuesday through Sunday, year round.
TIMES: 8:00 AM–3:00 PM.
ADMISSION: $.50. Parking is free.
LOCATION: 833 West Torrance Boulevard. At the corner of Torrance Boulevard and Vermont Avenue. Off Harbor Freeway Route 110 at the base of the Torrance Boulevard off-ramp.
DESCRIPTION: For about 11 years, this indoor/outdoor market of over 100 dealers has been selling antiques, collectibles, crafts, new merchandise, jewelry, t-shirts, and garage sale goodies. There are two restaurants, the Alpine Inn and Alpine Cafe, as well as several snack bars and clean restrooms.
DEALER RATES: $9 per day, weekdays; $27 per day, weekends. Reservations are requested.
CONTACT: Inge or Gerald, Alpine Village Swap Meet, 833 West Torrance Boulevard, Torrance, CA 90502. Tel: (213) 770-1961.

VACAVILLE
Vacaville Chamber of Commerce
Bizarre Bazaar

DATES: Two Saturday shows, one in October and one in April. Call for 1994 dates and information.
TIMES: 9:00 AM–5:00 PM.
ADMISSION: Free. Parking is wherever in town.
LOCATION: In the center of Vacaville. I-80 between San Francisco and Sacramento.
DESCRIPTION: This show first began in the 1960s. In 1993, it moved to the center of town and is aimed a bit more at arts and crafts. In the past it has been an outdoor market with 200 dealers selling their antiques, arts and crafts, collectibles, plants, clothing, brass, jewelry, and new merchandise. The chamber of commerce handles all food concessions that are on premises.

DEALER RATES: $11 for 10' × 10' space; $22 for 10' × 20' space; $44 for 20' × 20' space. Reservations are required, first come, first served.

CONTACT: Vacaville Chamber of Commerce, 400 East Monte Vista Avenue, Vacaville, CA 95688. Tel: (707) 448-6424.

VALLEJO
Napa-Vallejo Flea Market & Auction

DATES: Every Sunday, rain or shine.

TIMES: 6:00 AM–5:00 PM.

ADMISSION: Free. $1 parking fee.

LOCATION: On Highway 29, half way between Napa and Vallejo.

DESCRIPTION: This show began in 1947. It is both an indoor and outdoor market situated on 25 acres of land. The market accommodates approximately 600 dealers who sell antiques and collectibles, arts and crafts, jewelry, books, sporting goods, and tools, to name a few. There are four snack bar facilities on the premises which have been family owned and operated for 40 years.

DEALER RATES: $15 for 3' × 8' table, vehicle space is included. No reservations are accepted.

CONTACT: Nelson or Tom Harding, 303 Kelly Road, Vallejo, CA 94590. Tel: (707) 226-8862.

VENTURA
Ventura Flea Market

DATES: Held six times per year. Call for dates.

TIMES: 9:00 AM–3:00 PM.

ADMISSION: $3, children under 12 are free. Parking is free.

LOCATION: Ventura County Fairgrounds.

DESCRIPTION: There are over 600 dealers attending this outdoor show. Everything from antiques to collectibles to crafts and new merchandise to garage specials can be found here. It is one of California's most popular markets with 10,000 to 15,000 buyers. For your convenience, there is also food available on the premises.

DEALER RATES: $20, $30, or $40 per 10' × 20' space. Reservations are suggested.

CONTACT: R. G. Canning, P.O. Box 400, Maywood, CA 90270-0400. Tel: (213) 588-2727.

VISALIA
Visalia Sales Yard, Inc.
DATES: Thursday through Sunday, year round.
TIMES: 6:00 AM–3:00 PM.
ADMISSION: Free. Parking is also free.
LOCATION: 29660 R.D. 152, 1½ miles east of Visalia.
DESCRIPTION: This show began in 1948 and is currently an all-outdoor market that accommodates approximately 300 dealers. Among the items to be found here are antiques and collectibles, new merchandise, and fresh produce. Food is available on the premises.
DEALER RATES: $5 per 10' × 10' space.
CONTACT: Mr. Paul Furnas, 29660 Road 152, Visalia, CA 93291. Tel: (209) 734-9092.

WOODLAND HILLS
Pierce College Swap Meet
DATES: Saturday and Sunday.
TIMES: 5:00 AM–4:00 PM.
ADMISSION: $.50. Parking is free.
LOCATION: At the corner of Mason and Victory.
DESCRIPTION: Open since 1988, this outdoor market's 600 dealers sell antiques, collectibles, produce, crafts, new merchandise, and "everything under the sun." There are five snack bars on the premises.
DEALER RATES: $14 per 20' × 20' space. Reservations are suggested.
CONTACT: Ed Saleedo, Pierce College Swap Meet, 6201 Winnetka Avenue, Woodland Hills, CA 91303. Tel: (818) 773-3661.

OTHER FLEA MARKETS
Anaheim: Anaheim Swap Meet, 1520 North Lemon—Off 91 Freeway, Anaheim, CA 92801. Tel: (714) 525-3606. Open weekends, year round, 6:00 AM–3:00 PM.
Anderson: Jolly Giant Flea Market, 6719 East Side Road, Anderson, CA 96007. Tel: (916) 365-6458. Open weekends, 7:30 AM–4:00 PM.
Bakersfield: DeAnza Mercado Swap Meet, 1110 Quantico, Bakersfield, CA 93306. Tel: (805) 322-1476. Open weekends, 6:00–4:00 PM.
Calexico: Calexico Price Center, 121 Hacienda Drive, Calexico, CA 92231. Tel: (619) 357-8668. Open Tuesday through Sunday, 8:00 AM–9:00 PM; Wednesday, 6:00 AM–9:00 PM. Food court on premises.

Ceres: Ceres Drive-In Flea Market, Highway 99 and East Whitmore Avenue, Ceres, CA 95307. Tel: (209) 537-3323. Open weekends, year round, 7:00 AM–5:00 PM.

City of Industry: Vineland Swap Meet, 443 North Vineland Avenue, City of Industry, CA 91744. Tel: (818) 369-7224. Open daily 6:00 AM–3:00 PM except Christmas Day.

Concord: Solano Swap Meet, 1611 Solano Way, Concord, CA 94520. Tel: (510) 687-6445. Open weekends, year round, 6:00 AM–4:00 PM.

Fontana: Belair Swap Meet, 15895 Valley Blvd, Fontana, CA 92335. Tel: (714) 822-2617. Open Wednesday, Friday through Sunday, year round from 6:00 AM–3:00 PM.

Fresno: Sunnyside Swap Meet, 5550 East Olive Street, Fresno, CA 93727. Tel: (209) 255-7469. Open weekends, 6:00 AM–3:00 PM.

Galt: City of Galt Flea Market, 380 Civic Drive, P.O. Box 97, Galt, Sacramento County, CA 95632. Open Wednesdays 5:30 AM–5:30 PM.

Gardena: Vermont Swap, 17737 South Vermont Avenue, Gardena, CA 90247. Tel: (310) 324-0923. Open weekends 6:00 AM–3:00 PM.

Goleta: Santa Barbara Swap Meet, 907 South Kellogg, Goleta, CA 93117. Tel: (805) 964-9050. Open Sundays 7:00 AM–3:00 PM.

Indio: Sunair Swap Meet of Indio, 84-245 Indio Springs Drive, Indio, CA 92201. Tel: (619) 342-1113. Open Tuesdays 4:00 PM–11:00 PM; Sundays 7:00 AM–4:00 PM, September through May.

Madera: Madera 2 Swap Meet, 201 Lincoln, Madera, CA 93637. Tel: (209) 661-SWAP. Open Sundays 6:00 AM–3:00 PM, year round.

Marin City: Marin City Flea Market, 630 Drake Avenue, Marin City, CA 94965. Tel: (415) 332-1441. Open Saturdays 5:00 AM–6:30 PM; Sundays 4:00 AM–6:30 PM.

Marysville: Marysville Flea Market, 1468 Simpson Lane, Marysville, CA 95901. Tel: (916) 743-8713. Open weekends 6:00 AM–2:00 PM.

Nipomo: Nipomo Buyers Mart, 263 North Frontage Road, US Highway 101, Nipomo, CA 93444. Tel: (805) 929-7000. Open Friday–Sunday, 6:00 AM–6:00 PM, year round.

Norwalk: Norwalk Indoor Swap Meet, 11600 Alondra Boulevard, Norwalk, CA 90650. Tel: (213) 402-1007. Open Wednesday through Monday, 10:00 AM–7:00 PM.

Orange: Orange Swap Meet, 291 North State College Boulevard, Orange, CA 92668. Tel: (714) 634-4259. Open weekends, 6:00 AM–3:00 PM, year round.

Oroville: Chappell's Flea Market, 1141 Oro Dam Boulevard West, Oroville, CA 95965. Tel: (916) 533-1324. Open Friday through Sunday, year round, 6:30 AM–4:00 PM.

Panorama City: Valley Indoor Swap Meet, 14650 Parthenia Street, Panorama City, CA 91402. Tel: (818) 892-0183. Open Friday through Sunday 10:00 AM–6:00 PM.

Pasadena: Pasadena City College Flea Market, Pasadena City College, 1570 East Colorado at Hill-Pasadena. Free parking and admission. First Sunday of the month, 8:00 AM–3:00 PM.

Pico Rivera: Fiesta Swap Meet, 8462 East Whittier Boulevard, Pico Rivera, CA 90660. Tel: (213) 949-5918. Open weekends 6:00 AM–3:00 PM.

Pomona: Valley Indoor Swap Meet, Indian Hill Mall, 1600 East Holt Boulevard, Pomona, CA 91767. Tel: (714) 620-4792. Open Friday through Sunday 10:00 AM–6:00 PM.

Ridgecrest: Tro-Am Swap Meet, Desert Empire Fairgrounds, Ridgecrest, CA 93555. Tel: (619) 872-2318. Open first and third weekends of every month, Saturdays 8:00 AM–4:00 PM; Sundays 8:00 AM–3:00 PM.

San Diego: Kobey's Swap Meet at the Sports Arena, 3500 Sports Arena Boulevard, San Diego, CA 92110. Tel: (619) 226-0650. Open Thursday through Sunday, 7:00 AM–3:00 PM.

Santa Fe Springs: Santa Fe Springs Swap Meet, 13963 Alondra Boulevard, Santa Fe Springs, CA 90670. Tel: (213) 921-9996 or (714) 523-3014. Open Wednesday, Thursday, Saturday, and Sunday 6:00 AM–3:00 PM.

Santa Maria: Santa Maria Highway Drive-In, 3085 Santa Maria Way, Santa Maria, CA 93455. Tel: (805) 937-9715. Open Sundays, 6:00 AM–1:00 PM.

Sepulveda: Van Nuys Indoor Swap Meet, 8345 Havenhurst Place, Sepulveda, CA 91343. Tel: (818) 891-0983. Open weekends 10:00 AM–6:00 PM.

Simi Valley: Simi Valley Swap Meet, 361 Tierra Rejada Road, Simi Valley, CA 93065. Tel: (805) 526-6048. Open Sundays, year round, 7:00 AM–4:00 PM; Saturdays, October through December, 7:00 AM–4:00 PM.

Spring Valley: Spring Valley Swap Meet, 6377 Quarry Road, Spring Valley, CA 91977. Tel: (619) 463-1194. Open weekends.

Stanton: Indoor Swap Meet of Stanton, 10401 Beach Boulevard, Stanton, CA 90680. Tel: (714) 527-1234 or 527-1112. Open weekdays 10:00 AM–7:00 PM; weekends 10:00 AM–6:00 PM.

Torrance: Roadium Open Air Market, 2500 Redondo Beach Boulevard, Torrance, CA 90504. Tel: (213) 321-3709 or 321-3920. Open daily 7:00 AM–4:00 PM.

Tulare: Tulare Fairgrounds Swap Meet, 215 Alpine Street, Tulare, CA 93274. Tel: (209) 686-8566. Open Wednesday, Friday, and Saturday 5:30 AM–4:00 PM.

Tulare: Open Country Flea Market, 23090 Road 152, Tulare, CA 93274. Tel: (209) 686-9588. Open Sundays 6:00 AM–3:00 PM.

Venice: Fox Indoor Swapmeet, 620 Lincoln Boulevard, Venice, CA 90291. Tel: (213) 392-3477. Open Friday and Saturday 10:00 AM–8:00 PM; Sunday through Thursday 10:00 AM–7:00 PM.

Ventura: 101 Swap Meet, 4826 East Telephone Road, Ventura, CA 93003. Tel: (805) 644-5043. Open weekends 6:00 AM–2:00 PM.

Vernalis: Orchard Flea Market, 2553 East Highway 132, Vernalis, CA 95385. Tel: (209) 836-3148. Open Friday, Saturday, and Sunday 6:00–4:00 PM.

Yucca Valley: Sky Drive-In Swap Meet, 7028 Theater Road, Yucca Valley, CA 92284. Tel: (619) 365-9934. Open Saturday and Sunday, year round, 5:30 AM–2:00 PM.

Whittier: Sundown Swap Meet, 12322 East Washington Boulevard, Whittier, CA 90606. Tel: (213) 696-7560. Open Thursday through Sunday 6:00 AM–2:00 PM.

Woodland Hills: Valley Indoor Swap Meet, 6701 Variel Avenue, Woodland Hills, CA 91303. Tel: (818) 340-9120. Open Friday through Sunday 10:00 AM–6:00 PM.

COLORADO

DENVER
Mile High Flea Market, Inc.

DATES: Every Wednesday, Saturday, and Sunday year round.
TIMES: 6:00 AM–5:00 PM.
ADMISSION: $2 per person weekends, $1 per person Wednesdays, under 12 free. Parking is free.
LOCATION: I-76 and 88th Avenue.
DESCRIPTION: This indoor/outdoor flea market started in 1977 and is currently America's third largest flea market and Denver's largest attraction bringing over 1.6 million bargain hunters to 22 paved acres of brand name, close-out, garage sale, and seasonal merchandise. It features from 1,800 dealers in summer to 1,500 in winter selling antiques, fine art, collectibles, new merchandise, sports shoes, socks and underwear, clothing, silk plants, crystals, sunglasses, tires, auto parts, tools, luggage, furniture, bicycles, fishing tackle, cowboy boots, baby clothes to army surplus, antique train bells, hog greasers, steam ship whistles, one left mannequin leg, bowling balls, jackalopes, and seasonal merchandise, including bedding plants, Christmas trees, pumpkins, and fresh produce. About 800 of the dealers are cleaning out their garages, over 700 vendors are regulars. This is billed as a family event with plenty of parking for motorhomes and tour buses. A restaurant, seven food stands, two beer tents, corn and potato roasters, outdoor grills and four food carts provide ample food. You can also rent shopping carts, wheelchairs, wagons, and tables.
DEALER RATES: $17 per 12' × 25' space per day for Saturday and Sundays; $10 per day on Wednesday. Reservations are required and payable in advance (credit cards accepted).
CONTACT: Peter Balderston, Operations Manager, 7007 East 88th Avenue, Henderson, CO 80640. Tel: (303) 289-4656.

DENVER (NORTHGLENN)
Collector's Corner

DATES: Daily.
TIMES: 10:00 AM–6:00 PM.
ADMISSION: Free. Parking is free.
LOCATION: 10615 Melody Drive. From Denver take I-25 North, go west on 104th 2 blocks, then 2 blocks north.

DESCRIPTION: This market, started in 1989, is housed in a relatively new, large building across from the Northglenn Shopping Mall. It has 130 dealers selling antiques, collectibles, primitives, furniture, and new merchandise. Restaurants and shops surround this market.

DEALER RATES: $120 per 8' × 10' space per month. Reservations are not necessary.

CONTACT: Jean or Pat Corwin, Collector's Corner, 10615 Melody Drive, Northglenn, CO 80234. Tel: (303) 450-2875.

FORT COLLINS
Foothills and Fort Collins Indoor Flea Markets

DATES: Daily.

TIMES: 10:00 AM–6:00 PM.

ADMISSION: Free. Free parking is available.

LOCATION: Just off I-25, between Fort Collins and Loveland on Highway 287. These two markets are one block apart at 6200 and 6300 South College.

DESCRIPTION: Both these shows opened in 1982. They accommodate approximately 100 dealers each. These indoor markets contain over 500,000 different items. Sold here are antiques, arts and crafts and collectibles. There is also a selection of new merchandise. There is no food available on the premises.

DEALER RATES: $135 plus a 5% fee per 100 square foot space, per month. Reservations are required; monthly rates only are available.

CONTACT: Mr. John Sollo, 6300 South College, Fort Collins, CO 80525-4044. Tel: (303) 223-9069.

LAFAYETTE
Lafayette Flea Market

DATES: Daily, year round.

TIMES: 10:00 AM–6:00 PM.

ADMISSION: Free. Parking is free.

LOCATION: 130 East Spaulding, just behind the Conoco gas station on the corner of Highway 287 and Spaulding Street.

DESCRIPTION: This brand new market started on April 1, 1990 with 20,000 square feet in a climate-controlled, heated and cooled former bowling alley. Antique stores are two blocks away. There are 125 dealer spaces, with 90 dealers specializing in glassware, hobbies, stamps, coins, antique furniture, collectibles, sports cards, secondhand items, jewelry, and consignments.

DEALER RATES: $1.35 per square foot per month, or $135 per month for a 20' × 10' booth. Reservations are required.
CONTACT: Bill Hopkins, Lafayette Flea Market, 130 East Spaulding, Lafayette, CO 80026. Tel: (303) 665-0433.

LONGMONT
Front Range Flea Market

DATES: Daily.
TIMES: 10:00 AM–6:00 PM.
ADMISSION: Free. Parking is also free.
LOCATION: 1420 Florida Avenue. West off U.S. 287 on Colorado Route 119.
DESCRIPTION: This growing market opened in 1989 and currently has 50 dealers with room for more. Housed in a 17,000 square foot building, these dealers sell new merchandise, collectibles, antiques, jewelry, furniture, sports cards, tack, and "a lot of everything." A second store has opened across the street. No food is available.
DEALER RATES: $1.45 per square foot plus 10%. Reservations are required as there is a waiting list.
CONTACT: Richard Schweger, Front Range Flea Market, 1420 Florida Avenue, Longmont, CO 80501. Tel: (303) 776-6605.

PUEBLO
Sunset Flea Market

DATES: Saturday and Sunday, rain or shine.
TIMES: 7:00 AM–5:00 PM.
ADMISSION: Free. Parking is also free.
LOCATION: Colorado State Fairgrounds. Follow the signs.
DESCRIPTION: Since 1981 this indoor/outdoor market has been hosting between 100 and 175 dealers selling antiques, collectibles, or "whatever you want"—everything and anything. There is unlimited space available to grow. Food is available on the premises.
DEALER RATES: $10 general space, $12 reserved space. Reservations are not required; first come, first served.
CONTACT: Sunset Flea Market, Sunset Enterprises, 1400 Santa Fe Drive, Pueblo, CO 81006. Tel: (719) 584-2000 or 1-800-647-8368.

OTHER FLEA MARKETS

Colorado Springs: The Flea Market, 5225 East Platte, Colorado Springs, CO 80933. Tel: (719) 380-8599. Open weekends 7:00 AM–4:00 PM.

CONNECTICUT

CANTON
The Cob-Web

DATES: Every Sunday, May through September.
TIMES: 9:00 AM–whenever.
ADMISSION: Free. Parking is also free.
LOCATION: At the junction of Routes 44 and 202 near Route 179, about 20 miles west of Hartford. (On Dyer Cemetery Road.)
DESCRIPTION: This show first opened in 1968 and currently draws approximately 50 dealers outdoors. Shoppers may purchase just about anything: antiques, arts and crafts, plants, jewelry, tools, coins, collectibles, furniture, and new merchandise. The fare changes weekly. There is always a friendly atmosphere here. There are restaurants, stores, motels and campgrounds nearby. Food is available on the premises from a Food Wagon serving "great big hamburgers!"
DEALER RATES: $17 for an approximately 20' × 20' space. Reservations are advised. Space is available.
CONTACT: Dolly or Dawn, P.O. Box 354, Canton, CT 06019. Tel: (203) 693-2658.

COVENTRY
Coventry Indoor Outdoor Flea Market

DATES: Every Sunday, year round except Christmas Sundays.
TIMES: 9:00 AM–4:00 PM.
ADMISSION: Free. Parking is free.
LOCATION: 44 Lake Street. Junction of Routes 31 and 275.
DESCRIPTION: Open since October 1990, and now under new management, this indoor/outdoor market of approximately 80 dealers sells baseball cards, coins, comics, custom-made furniture, jewelry, tag sale items, antique paper, fabrics and linens, depression glass, antiques and collectibles. In 1993, they opened the Coventry General Store selling Coventry-made products: vinegars, dried flowers, furniture, and Westerwald pottery from Pennsylvania with the Coventry pattern. There is a "great clean snack bar with more than hot dogs," as well as handicapped-accessible clean restrooms.
DEALER RATES: $12 to $25 depending on size and location. Reservations are requested.
CONTACT: Joseph and Rose Fowler, Coventry Flea Market, 110

Wall Street, Coventry, CT 06238. Tel: (203) 742-9362. Day of market call: (203) 742-1993.

DANBURY

The Country Peddler Show

DATES: Friday, July 8 through Sunday, July 10.

TIMES: Friday 4:00 PM–9:00 PM, Saturday 9:00 AM–5:00 PM, Sunday 11:00 AM–4:00 PM.

ADMISSION: Adults $5, children 2–12 $2.

LOCATION: O'Neill Center at Western Connecticut State University, 181 White Street.

DESCRIPTION: This new show is one of a series of highly successful folk art shows held around the East Coast. They feature only top-quality folk artists from across the nation selling only handmade decorating and quality items such as herb arrangements, country furniture, salt-glazed pottery, and more.

DEALER RATES: $375 for a 10' × 10' space and up. Reservations are mandatory as this is a juried show.

CONTACT: American Memories., Inc. P.O. Box 249, Decatur, MI 49045. Tel: (616) 423-8367 or fax: (616) 423-2421.

EAST HARTFORD

Connecticut Comic Book Flea Market

DATES: Sundays, bi-monthly, year-round. Monthly during the summer months.

TIMES: 11:00 AM–5:00 PM.

ADMISSION: $.99 fee. Parking is free.

LOCATION: Elks Hall at 148 Roberts Street. Take Exit 58 off I-84, follow the signs.

DESCRIPTION: This show started in 1974 and has approximately 30 dealers. It is an indoor market selling collectibles, antiques, and new merchandise, as well as pulp magazines, science fiction collectibles, gum cards, and movie items, but they specialize in comic books for collectors. They also run a convention twice a year with guest artists and writers. Food is available on the premises.

DEALER RATES: $35 for an 8' table. Advance reservations are required.

CONTACT: Mr. Harold E. Kinney, c/o The Bookies Bookstore, 206 Burnside Avenue, East Hartford, CT 06108. Tel: (203) 289-1208 in afternoons.

FARMINGTON
Farmington Antiques Weekend

DATES: Second weekend in June and Labor Day weekend. 1994: June 11–12, September 3–4; 1995: June 10–11, September 2–3; 1996: June 8–9, August 31–September 1; 1997: June 14–15, August 30–31.

TIMES: 10:00 AM–5:00 PM. Early admission 7:00 AM.

ADMISSION: $5 for adults. Parking is free. Early admission fee $20.

LOCATION: At the Farmington Polo Grounds, 10 miles west of Hartford and 3 miles from Exit 39 off I-84.

DESCRIPTION: This national antiques event opened in 1980 and is held both outdoors and under tents. There are around 600 dealers at each show selling antiques, fine art, and collectibles, but this market specializes in antiques from rural America. This claims to be the number one large antiques and better collectibles event in the United States, and it draws approximately 30,000 people per show. All merchandise is guaranteed to be as represented: no new merchandise, no reproductions. Good home-cooked food is available on the premises.

DEALER RATES: $250 on the lawns, $350 under the tents. Reservations are required well in advance. Write for map and motel list.

CONTACT: Abby or Bob McInnes, Revival Promotions, Inc., P.O. Box 388, Grafton, MA 01519. Tel: (508) 839-9735. Week of show call (203) 677-7862.

JEWETT CITY
College Mart Flea Market

DATES: Every Sunday.

TIMES: 9:00 AM–4:00 PM.

ADMISSION: Free. Parking is free.

LOCATION: Wedgewood Drive. Exits 84 and 85 off I-395.

DESCRIPTION: Started in 1982 in the old Slater Textile Mill, this market now hosts 140 vendors indoors and outdoors selling antiques, glassware, clothing, collectibles, toys, crafts, furniture, all types of old and new jewelry, gold, silver, and new merchandise. Food is available on the premises.

DEALER RATES: $12.50 for a half space to $25 for a full space. Reservations are strongly recommended.

CONTACT: Bob Leone, College Mart Flea Market, Wedgewood Drive, Jewett City, CT 06351. Tel: (203) 376-3935 or 642-6248.

MANSFIELD
Eastern Connecticut Flea Market

DATES: Sundays, first Sunday in April through Thanksgiving, weather permitting.

TIMES: 8:00 AM–3:00 PM.

ADMISSION: Free. Parking is $1 from 8:00 AM–9:00 AM; $.50 after that.

LOCATION: Mansfield Drive-In Theatre at 228 Stafford Road. At the junction of Routes 31 and 32.

DESCRIPTION: Operating since 1975, and one of the first markets in Connecticut, this outdoor market's 200-plus dealers sell antiques, clothes, collectibles, new and used books, tools, toys and more. Breakfast and lunch are served at the market, or bring your own. This market is held at a thriving three-screen drive-in theater and its concession is open during the market.

DEALER RATES: $20 for a 14' × 14' space weekly; or $17.50 per week on a monthly basis. Rental tables are $2.50 per week, if you need one. Reservations are taken on a monthly basis only; not necessary for weekends only.

CONTACT: Michael Jungden, 228 Stafford Road, Mansfield, CT 06250. Tel: (203) 456-2578.

NAUGATUCK
Peddlers Market

DATES: Every Sunday from the beginning of first Sunday in April to the end of November, rain or shine.

TIMES: Dawn to dusk.

ADMISSION: Free. Parking is also free.

LOCATION: On Route 63 (New Haven Road) between Waterbury and New Haven.

DESCRIPTION: This market began operation in 1969 but was taken over by the present owners in 1980. There are anywhere from 75 to 150 dealers at this outdoor market. This is a family oriented market. You can find most anything here from antiques and collectibles to new merchandise and fresh produce, including fishing equipment, furniture, and household items. It is located in a beautiful setting not far from the highway. For your convenience, this clean market maintains a lunch wagon and toilet facilities on the premises.

DEALER RATES: $25 for 20' front per day. Reservations are not required.

CONTACT: Mr. Thomas Murray, Gunntown Road, Naugatuck, CT 06770. Tel: (203) 729-6339; or Mr. Gerald Garceau, 3 Hazel Avenue, Naugatuck, CT 06770. Tel: (203) 729-7762.

NEW MILFORD
Elephant's Trunk Flea Market

DATES: Sundays only, April through Sunday before Christmas, except Easter Sunday.
TIMES: 7:00 AM–4:00 PM.
ADMISSION: Free. Parking is free and plentiful. No pets allowed!
LOCATION: Route 7. Exit 7 from I-84, 7 miles north of Danbury.
DESCRIPTION: This market started in 1977. The 300-plus dealers break down their sales as approximately 30 percent antiques and collectibles; 30 percent general line merchandise; 20 percent new items: tools, jewelry, etc.; and 20 percent anything and everything else. There are dealers who have been with this market since the beginning and buyers who return the same time every weekend and have, over the years, become friends. There are 55 acres with room for 500 dealer spaces. Food is available on the premises.
DEALER RATES: $25 per 25' × 20' space. All dealers are urged to have a Connecticut tax number. Reservations are not required.
CONTACT: Greg Baecker. Tel: (203) 355-1448.

NIANTIC
Between the Bridges
Antique and Collectibles Flea Market

DATES: Thursday through Tuesday, year round.
TIMES: 10:00 AM–5:00 PM.
ADMISSION: Free. Parking is free.
LOCATION: 65 and 57 Pennsylvania Avenue. Take Exit 74 off I-95, turn right, 3 miles.
DESCRIPTION: Opened in May 1991, this new market has 60 dealers and a waiting list, selling just antiques, collectibles, and used furniture. No new merchandise or crafts. There is a restaurant next to the market for the hungry.
DEALER RATES: $25 for 65 square feet of space; 10% service charge. You don't have to be there to sell. There is a waiting list, so call first.
CONTACT: John and Diane Deer, 65 Pennsylvania Avenue, Niantic, CT 06357. Tel: (203) 691-0170.

OLD MYSTIC
Old Mystic Antique Flea Market

DATES: Every Sunday, weather permitting.

TIMES: 8:00 AM–5:00 PM.

ADMISSION: Free. Parking is free.

LOCATION: Route 27 in Old Mystic. Across from the southern entrance to I-95.

DESCRIPTION: This market, in business since 1974, has from 20 dealers in winter to 40 in summer. While the market deals mostly in antiques, there is some new merchandise sold as well, including toys. One dealer specializes in antique Matchbox cars. Mystic Seaport is less than one mile away. Snacks are available on the premises.

DEALER RATES: $25 per Sunday for 14' × 22' space. Reservations are strongly recommended.

CONTACT: Sonny Hendel, 6 Hendel Drive, Old Mystic, CT 06372. Tel: (203) 536-2223.

TORRINGTON
Wright's Barn and Flea Market

DATES: Saturday and Sunday, year round, rain or shine.

TIMES: 10:00 AM–4:30 PM.

ADMISSION: Free. Parking is also free.

LOCATION: Wright Road off Route 4, between Torrington and Goshen. Follow the large signs on Route 4.

DESCRIPTION: This indoor market opened in 1981 in a huge 10,000 square foot barn with 40 dealers selling mostly antiques and some collectibles. Most of their dealers are permanent (12 dealers having been there over eight years) and come from over 20 miles away. There is one snack bar.

DEALER RATES: $20 for 10' × 14' booth, Saturday and Sunday. Reservations are required. Ask about the special monthly treats for dealers.

CONTACT: Millie Wright, Wright's Barn, Wright Road, Torrington, CT 06790. Tel: (203) 482-0095.

WALLINGFORD
Redwood Country Flea Market

DATES: Every Saturday and Sunday, and some holidays, year round, weather permitting (even in snow!).

TIMES: 8:00 AM–4:00 PM.

ADMISSION: Free. Parking is also free.

LOCATION: At 170 Hartford Turnpike in Wallingford. Take Exit 13 off I-91, or take Exit 64 off Wilbur Cross Parkway.

DESCRIPTION: This show began in 1973. There are approximately 75 to 90 dealers at this outdoor market selling almost anything from antiques and collectibles to new merchandise and fresh produce. The Dubar's have a restaurant on the premises that is well known to the rich and famous whose pictures cover the walls. Walter Dubar, the original founder of this market, has retired, leaving his son and grandsons to run this unique place. However, if you can find Walter, he has some wonderful stories to tell!

DEALER RATES: For space measuring 20' × 10', the fee is $18 for holidays, $23 for Saturday, $17 for Sunday, and $40 for Saturday and Sunday.

CONTACT: Ken Dubar, Steven and Mark Hugo, Redwood Country Flea Market, 170 Hartford Turnpike, Wallingford, CT 06492. Tel: (203)269-3500 between 1:00 PM–7:00 PM weekdays or all day Saturday and Sunday.

Wallingford YMCA Antiques and Collectibles Show

DATES: Annually in February, usually President's Weekend Sunday.

TIMES: 9:00 AM–4:00 PM.

ADMISSION: $2.75 per person, or $2.50 with discount coupon. Parking is free.

LOCATION: 81 South Elm Street. Take Exit 13 off I-91 North; or take Exit 14 South off I-91.

DESCRIPTION: This show started in 1978. The market is held indoors and accommodates approximately 35 dealers who sell a variety of unusual and unique antique and collectible items. Snack food is served on the premises.

DEALER RATES: $65 for 10' × 10' space. A booth with electricity is $70. Reservations are required.

CONTACT: Wallingford Family YMCA, 81 South Elm Street, Wallingford, CT 06492. Tel: (203) 269-4497.

WOODBURY

Woodbury Antiques and Flea Market

DATES: Every Saturday, weather permitting.

TIMES: 7:00 AM–4:00 PM.

ADMISSION: Free. Parking is free.

LOCATION: Junction of Routes 6 and 64. Off I-84, take Exit 15, go 3½ miles on Route 6E to market.

DESCRIPTION: For over 26 years this outdoor market has been considered one of the best antiques markets in Connecticut. Located in a beautiful country setting, their 90 to 180 dealers sell primarily antiques, collectibles, furniture, memorabilia, coins, antique tools, jewelry, books, military items, art, and books. Newer merchandise includes tools, jewelry, clothes, household goods, produce, and plants. It is described as the "#1 Saturday market in Connecticut" with "great browsing and buying in Woodbury, the Antique Capital of Connecticut." This market has a strong following because of the quality of the goods sold. Food is available on the premises.

DEALER RATES: $25 for a 20' × 20' space. Reservations are not required.

CONTACT: Don and Diane Heavens, P.O. Box 184, Woodbury, CT 06798. Tel: (203) 263-2841.

OTHER FLEA MARKETS

New Haven: Boulevard Flea Market, 520 Ella T Grasso Boulevard, New Haven, CT 06519. Tel: (203) 772-1447. Open weekends, year round, 8:00 AM–4:00 PM.

DELAWARE

LAUREL

Bargain Bill, The Shore's Largest Flea Market, Inc.

DATES: Every Friday, Saturday, and Sunday, rain or shine.

TIMES: 6:00 AM–5:00 PM.

ADMISSION: Free. Free parking is provided.

LOCATION: At the intersection of U.S. 13 Dual and Route 9 East, 14 miles north of Salisbury. From Washington, D.C., take Route 50 West to Route 404 East, then Route 13 South.

DESCRIPTION: This indoor/outdoor show began in 1978 and is located just 30 minutes from the Atlantic Ocean and listed as a Delaware tourist attraction. People come from all over the United States to buy from the 200 (in winter) to 500 (in summer) dealers who sell everything from antiques to new merchandise, from collectibles to fresh produce—all tax free! Other items to be found are: a large selection of depression glass, electronics, books, airbrush artist, baked goods, records, jewelry, vacuums, new and used clothing and tools, wicker, doors, portable buildings, and groceries among others. They built a unique covered market with skylights to illuminate the merchandise, where vendors can park next to their treasures. When this market first opened, vendors laid their merchandise on the ground. Now they have a 400' air-conditioned/heated indoor market with over 800 tables. Talk about having everything, in December 1992 they even had a wedding here, complete with wedding gown, tuxedo, minister, cake, and music. An extension of this market, Sir William's Antiques, opened in November 1990 and operates six days a week (closed Tuesday). Food is served on the premises. Overnight camping with electric hook-ups and air-conditioned/heated restrooms with showers are available.

DEALER RATES: $18.75 per 8' × 10' indoor space. $10 per 16' frontage outdoor space, includes two 3' × 8' tables. Reservations are not required.

CONTACT: Bill and Leslie Brown, R.D. 4, Box 547, Laurel, DE 19956. Tel: (302) 875-9958 or 875-2478.

Route 13 Outlet Market

DATES: Friday, Saturday, and Sunday, year round.

TIMES: 9:00 AM–7:00 PM.

ADMISSION: Free. Parking is also free.

LOCATION: Route 13 at State Road 462.

DESCRIPTION: Started in 1985, they now have over 100 vendors selling "duck decoys to watches to pianos" in this 84,000 square foot building. There are some antiques and collectibles, loads of tools, seafood, produce, clothing, and jewelry. Twelve restaurants feed the famished including one Amish restaurant. Ninety percent of the merchandise is new and 80 percent of the vendors have been with this market from the beginning. If an item fails to satisfy, it is quite common to be able to return it to the original vendor.

DEALER RATES: $48 per 12' × 7' space per weekend and up. Reservations are not required.

CONTACT: Lisa Fanugao, Route 13 Outlet Market, P.O. Box 32, Laurel, DE 19956. Tel: (302) 875-4800.

NEW CASTLE
New Castle Farmers Market

DATES: Friday, Saturday, and Sunday, year round.

TIMES: Friday and Saturday 10:00 AM–10:00 PM; Sunday 10:00 AM–6:00 PM.

ADMISSION: Free. Parking is also free.

LOCATION: Route 13 and Hares Corner.

DESCRIPTION: Started in 1954, this indoor/outdoor market is really two markets in one. The outside is the flea market restricted to used items only, antiques, and collectibles; the inside market is the farmer's market with over 60 merchants. This is said to be one of the premier markets on the East Coast with genuine Pennsylvania Dutch merchants selling outstanding quality beef, pork, poultry, cheeses, and homemade baked goods. The produce stands are works of art. Food is available on the premises.

DEALER RATES: Friday $12 per day; Saturday and Sunday $15 per day. First come, first served.

CONTACT: Steven Stein, New Castle Farmers Market, Route 13 and Hares Corner, New Castle, DE 19720. Tel: (302) 328-4102.

FLORIDA

APOPKA
Three Star Flea Market

DATES: Every Saturday and Sunday, rain or shine.
TIMES: Dawn to dusk.
ADMISSION: Free. Free parking is available.
LOCATION: 2930 South Orange Blossom Trail. Highway 441.
DESCRIPTION: This market began in 1966. About 60 dealers sell their antiques, collectibles, handicrafts, garage sale items, and produce from covered stalls outdoors. They are only 18 miles from Disney World. There is a food wagon on the premises.
DEALER RATES: $10.80 per space and parking per day. They provide tables and clothes racks. Reservations are required.
CONTACT: Mary C. Markeson, Owner, c/o Three Star Flea Market, 2390 South Orange Blossom Trail, Apopka, FL 32703. Tel: (407) 293-2722.

AUBURNDALE
International Market World

DATES: Every Friday, Saturday, and Sunday, rain or shine.
TIMES: 8:00 AM–5:00 PM.
ADMISSION: Free. Free parking is available.
LOCATION: 1052 Highway 92 West. Between Orlando and Tampa, just outside the city limits of Lakeland.
DESCRIPTION: This market opened in 1981 and currently attracts anywhere from 750 (summer) to 1,000 plus (winter) dealers. A new building was added in 1991 adding another 200 stalls. As one of Florida's largest markets, Market World attracts customers from throughout Central Florida as it is only a short 45 minute drive from either Tampa or Orlando down I-4. There is an endless variety of merchandise from antiques and collectibles to new merchandise and fresh produce. A gem mine where you can pan for precious gems is one of several attractions including a fishing pond and an auto repair center. There is a delightful country atmosphere and an eager-to-please management. There are numerous concessions serving a variety of foods on the premises.
DEALER RATES: $35 per 8' × 10' space weekly; $140 monthly. Reservations are not required. Dealers may start setting up shop at 7:00 AM.

CONTACT: International Market World, Box 1052 Highway 92 West, Auburndale, FL 33823. Tel: (813) 665-0062.

BROOKSVILLE
Airport Mart

DATES: Every Saturday and Sunday, rain or shine.
TIMES: 8:00 AM–3:00 PM.
ADMISSION: Free. Parking is also free.
LOCATION: 17375 Spring Hill Drive. Six miles south of Brooksville, just off U.S. 41.
DESCRIPTION: This show started in 1978. The market accommodates approximately 300 dealers and is held both indoors and outdoors. There are no specialties but rather a large assortment of goods is offered including antiques, fine art, arts and crafts, collectibles, new merchandise, fresh produce, used household items, and tools. Seventy percent used and 30 percent new. Both inside and outside concessions serve food on the premises.
DEALER RATES: $70 for 8' × 12' space indoors, per month; $8.50 for three table set-up under covered space outdoors, per day. Reservations are required during the winter only.
CONTACT: Scott Barker, Manager, Airport Mart, 17375 Spring Hill Drive, Brooksville, FL 34609. Tel: (904) 796-0268.

CHIEFLAND
McCormack Flea Market, Inc.

DATES: Friday through Sunday, year round, rain or shine.
TIMES: 7:00 AM–4:00 PM.
ADMISSION: Free admission and free parking.
LOCATION: U.S. Highway 19 and 98, Alt 27, North. Market located across from ABC Pizza and Best Western Motel.
DESCRIPTION: Since 1983, this indoor flea market has expanded four times on its 23 acres and is in the Suwannee River area, in the center of town, near motels. There are a total of 310 selling spaces, all under one roof, with concrete floors and screens. Water and electricity are available to each booth, as well as RV electricity. There is an RV park close by for the customers. Dealers can park their RV next to their booth or in the park. Currently the market attracts approximately 55 dealers in the summer and 100 in the winter selling antiques, collectibles, handmade crafts, vegetables, meats, cheeses, dairy products, plants, flowers, nuts, birds, and new merchandise among

other treats. In addition, there is a small grocery store, bake shop, tools, tape store, leather craft shop, pump sales, RV parts, laundry, cabinet shop, and carpet and vinyl store. Three restaurants feed the hungry.

DEALER RATES: $6 per 10' × 10' booth on Friday and Sunday; $7 on Saturday; $17.50 for three days. Reservations are suggested.

CONTACT: Jack McCormack, P.O. Box 1970, Chiefland, FL 32626. Tel: (904) 493-1493.

DAYTONA
Daytona Flea Market

DATES: Friday, Saturday, and Sunday, year round.

TIMES: 8:00 AM–5:00 PM.

ADMISSION: Free. Parking is free.

LOCATION: 1425 Tomoka Farms Road, Southwest corner of I-95 and U.S. 92 intersection.

DESCRIPTION: This indoor/outdoor market opened in 1981 just five miles from the "World's Most Famous Beach" attracting 2.2 million visitors in 1990. Over 1,000 dealers on 40 acres sell antiques, collectibles, craft items, used and new merchandise, produce, meats, cheeses, and just about everything imaginable. One section of the market is fully air-conditioned. Twelve concession provide ample food for the hungry.

DEALER RATES: $12 for a booth with 10' frontage. Ninety percent of this market is under roof. Reservations are suggested, in some cases required.

CONTACT: John Schnebly, Manager or Sylvia Graves, Rental Agent, P.O. Drawer 2140, Daytona Beach, FL 32115. Tel: (904) 252-1999.

DELRAY BEACH
Delray Swap Shop

DATES: Always Friday through Sunday. Seasonally during peak seasons also open Wednesdays and Thursdays.

TIMES: Wednesday and Thursday, 8:00 AM–2:00 PM, Friday 8:00 AM–2:00 PM; Saturday and Sunday 8:00 AM–3:00 PM. Longer hours during peak seasons.

ADMISSION: Free. Parking is free on Thursday and Friday, $2 Saturday and Sunday.

LOCATION: 2001 North Federal Highway. Take I-95 to Atlantic Boulevard in Delray Beach to North Federal Highway, north 3 miles.

DESCRIPTION: This market has been open since 1976 with 430 dealer spaces, mostly outdoors. Items for sale are mostly new merchandise including: health and beauty aids, clothing, jewelry, hats, pictures and frames, household goods, and vegetables in season. In November 1993 they opened a special antique section of this market. Several snack bars serve the hungry.

DEALER RATES: Wednesday $1; Thursday free; Friday $5; Saturday and Sunday from $50 to $100 for 11' x 15' spaces. For the antique mall: $25 Saturday and Sundays. Reservations are required. There is a wait-list for no-shows, at $25 for space at the last minute with no guarantees.

CONTACT: Loretta Shaw, Manager, Delray Swap Shop, 2001 North Federal Highway, Delray, FL 33444. Tel: (407) 276-4012.

FORT LAUDERDALE

Oakland Park Boulevard Flea Market

DATES: Every Wednesday through Sunday, rain or shine.

TIMES: 10:00 AM until closing. Wednesdays 10:00 AM–6:00 PM.

ADMISSION: Free. Parking is available and is also free.

LOCATION: 1½ miles west of I-95, and ½ mile east of State Route 7, at 3161 West Oakland Park Boulevard.

DESCRIPTION: This is the oldest indoor flea market in the Fort Lauderdale area. It accommodates approximately 120 dealers, with room for more. There are antiques, collectibles, gold jewelry, and new merchandise to be found. For your convenience, there is also food available on the premises.

DEALER RATES: $400 and up per space per month. Reservations are required. Currently there is a waiting list.

CONTACT: Leonard Bennis, Manager, Oakland Park Boulevard Flea Market, 3161 West Oakland Park Boulevard, Fort Lauderdale, FL 33311. Tel: (305) 731-1150.

Swap Shop of Ft. Lauderdale

DATES: Everyday including holidays, year round, rain or shine.

TIMES: 7:00 AM–5:00 PM.

ADMISSION: Free. Free parking is available. Preferred parking Saturday and Sunday is $1.50.

LOCATION: 3291 West Sunrise Boulevard, between I-95 and the Turnpike.

DESCRIPTION: This well-known show began in 1967. About 2,000 dealers sell both indoors and out on 70 acres of grounds. All sorts of things can be found here—antiques, crafts and collectibles, new and used items, produce, watches, electronics, clothing, plants—you name it! They say they are "the largest flea market in the Eastern United States." Free circus shows are presented daily, and they feature 17 international restaurants.

DEALER RATES: Call for current rates. Reservations are advised during the winter season.

CONTACT: Reservation Office, c/o Swap Shop, 3501 West Sunrise Boulevard, Fort Lauderdale, FL 33311. Tel: (305) 791-SWAP (7927) or 1-800-345-7927.

FORT MYERS

Fleamasters Fleamarket

DATES: Friday, Saturday and Sunday, year around.

TIMES: 8:00 AM–4:00 PM.

LOCATION: 4135 Dr. Martin Luther King, Jr. Boulevard.

ADMISSION: Free. Parking is free.

DESCRIPTION: Opened in 1985, this completely undercover outdoor market, billed "as the largest market in southwest Florida," hosts an average of 1,200 dealers year round. It is still growing—they added another 200 stalls in 1993. Their dealers sell everything "from fruit to nuts," including antiques, collectibles, clothing, wheelchair rentals and psychic readings. The food courts provide an ample feast from pizza to ice cream, Mexican, Greek, Oriental, and good-old-USA fast food. In fact, this market is so popular, it has become a tourist attraction in its own right.

DEALER RATES: $48–$61, plus tax and license, per 10' × 12' booth for a 3-day weekend, depending on location. Reservations are not required, first come, first served. Although dealers can continue to hold the same spot week after week.

CONTACT: Donna Matthews, Fleamaster Flea Market, 4135 Dr. Martin Luther King, Jr. Blvd, Ft. Myers, FL 33916. Tel: (813) 334-7001.

FRONTENAC

Frontenac Flea Market

DATES: Friday, Saturday, and Sunday.

TIMES: 6:30 AM–5:00 PM.

LOCATION: 5605 North U.S. Highway 1, midway between Cocoa and Titusville, right on U.S. 1.

ADMISSION: Free. Parking is free.

DESCRIPTION: In operation over 17 years, this market has an average of 300 dealers selling antiques, collectibles, new and used merchandise, silk flowers, and a farmers market selling fresh fruits and vegetables. One of the several food concessions sells a "famous quarter-pound hot dog." This market is close to the Kennedy Space Center and beaches.

DEALER RATES: $14.84 per day for a 10' × 8' space indoors; $10.60 for a 10' × 20' space outdoors. First come, first served.

CONTACT: Mike Christian, Frontenac Flea Market, P.O. Box 10, Sharpes, FL 32959. Tel: (407) 631-0241.

GAINESVILLE
Smiley's Antique Mall

DATES: Daily.

TIMES: 10:00 AM–6:00 PM.

ADMISSION: Free. Parking is free.

LOCATION: Off I-75 Exit 73, the Michanopy Exit, 7 miles south of Gainesville.

DESCRIPTION: Brand new! Opened in April 1994, this market deals only with antiques and collectibles. It has 175 dealers indoors. There is a restaurant next door and clean modern restrooms on site. This mall is an extension of the three Smiley's flea markets in Macon, Georgia; Fletcher, North Carolina; and Waldo, Florida. There is RV parking available.

DEALER RATES: Vary according to size and location of space. Reservations are required.

CONTACT: Barbara or Christie, Smiley's Antique Mall, P.O. Box 129, Gainesville, FL 32603-0129. Tel: (904) 335-2821 or 466-0707.

KEY LARGO
Key Largo Warehouse Market

DATES: Saturday and Sunday.

TIMES: 8:00 AM–5:00 PM.

ADMISSION: Free. Free parking is available.

LOCATION: on U.S. Route 1, at Mile Marker 103.5.

DESCRIPTION: This small, selective, but excellent market has 60 dealers selling "everything you could want," with an emphasis on antiques and collectibles. Charlie's vegetables are said to be "the best on the Keys." A sampling of some of their dealers' specialties are baskets, bathing suits, marine and fishing gear, orchids and exotic plants, ceramic goods, and bikes. A snack bar serves American and Thai dishes to the hungry. This is the only market open all year long on the Keys. They place a high value on "treating our people right."

DEALER RATES: $262.15 for a front row 10' × 40' space if you are lucky enough to get one; $174.50 for a second row 10' × 30' space; and $101 for a 10' × 10' space. Reservations are most necessary.

CONTACT: Elsie Click, 103530 Overseas Highway, Key Largo, FL 33037. Tel: (305) 451-0677.

LAKE CITY
Lake City Flea Market

DATES: Every Saturday and Sunday, rain or shine. Closed from mid-October to mid-November for Columbia County Fair.

TIMES: 8:00 AM–5:00 PM.

ADMISSION: Free. Free parking is available.

LOCATION: Columbia County Fairgrounds, one mile east of I-75 on U.S. 90 at State Road 247 (Branford Highway).

DESCRIPTION: This indoor/outdoor market opened in 1980 and now accommodates approximately 100 to 150 dealers selling everything from antiques and collectibles to new merchandise and fresh produce. There is a weekly auction every Saturday. There are 1,500 motel rooms available at reasonable rates located within ½ mile of the flea market. Food is served on the premises.

DEALER RATES: $7 per 10' × 10' space indoors, per day; $4 and up per day outdoors. Reservations for space indoors are required, it gets full.

CONTACT: Lake City Flea Market, Ralph Tiner, Route 5 Box 1025, Lake City, FL 32056. Tel: (904)752-1999.

LAKELAND
Lakeland Farmer's Market

DATES: Every Thursday through Sunday, rain or shine.

TIMES: 6:00 AM–5:00 PM.

ADMISSION: Free. Free parking is available.

LOCATION: 2701 Swindell Road. Take I-4 to West Memorial Boulevard exit, then go 1 mile. At the intersection of Swindell Road and West Memorial Boulevard at Kathleen High School.

DESCRIPTION: This market started out as a "Curb Market" in the 1930s and moved to its present location in 1971 where local farmers and craftsmen could sell their goods; some of these original sellers still work here. The market now accommodates from 225 to 350 dealers that sell collectibles, arts and crafts, new merchandise, used items, clothing, tools, household necessities, used farm and work related items, fresh produce, and meats. Thursday and Friday's market is mainly produce and plants. This is a rustic, down-to-earth flea market with a museum, free of charge, on the premises. There are five restaurants and snack bars to choose from.

DEALER RATES: $10 per 10' × 10' space under cover on Saturday and Sunday. Rates in the open field are $6 per 25' × 15' space on Saturday and Sunday; $4 per space uncovered on Friday; Thursday is free. $76 per month. Reservations are advised.

CONTACT: Bill Hudson, 2701 Swindell Road, Lakeland, FL 33805. Tel: (813) 682-4809 or 665-3723.

MAITLAND
Ole Red Barn Flea Market

DATES: Saturday and Sunday, with a few dealers opening as early as Wednesday.

TIMES: 9:00 AM–5:00 PM.

ADMISSION: Free. Parking is available at no extra charge.

LOCATION: East on Maitland Interchange I-4, then .2 of a mile north on Highway 17-92, at 8750 South Highway 17-92.

DESCRIPTION: This old-fashioned flea market began in 1968 but has been under new management since March 1984. This indoor/outdoor market has 30 permanent dealers with space for more. A variety of antiques, furniture, advertising articles, primitives, glassware, china and pottery, collectibles, and general used merchandise can be found. Included in the items you may find are furniture, jewelry, and household goods. Beverages are available, but there is no food sold on the premises.

DEALER RATES: $5 per day per table. There is also booth space available, size and price vary. Reservations are not required and are given on a first come, first served basis.

CONTACT: Betty L. Smith, 2001 El Campo Avenue, Deltona, FL 32725. Tel: (904) 789-3945.

MARGATE
Margate Swap Shop

DATES: Saturday, Sunday, and Tuesday.

TIMES: 5:00 AM–2:00 PM.
ADMISSION: Free. Parking is $1.
LOCATION: 1000 North State Road 7 (U.S. 441). West of Pompano Beach; west of Florida Turnpike and I-95 (Atlantic Boulevard to Route 441 then north several blocks).
DESCRIPTION: This indoor/outdoor market opened in 1976 with 300 to 550 dealers selling collectibles, new and used merchandise, and fresh produce. This family-type flea market has one of the largest produce sections around. The Lake Shore Motel is on the property as well. Two snack bars are on site.
DEALER RATES: $8 per 10' × 20' space. Reservations are suggested.
CONTACT: Sheree, Margate Swap Shop, 1000 North State Road 7, Margate, FL 33063. Tel: (305) 971-7927.

MIAMI BEACH
"World's Largest" Indoor Flea Market

DATES: For 1994: March 8–13; June 7–12; December 13–18. 1995: March 7–12, June 27–July 2, November 14–19.
TIMES: Tuesday, Wednesday, and Thursday 12:00 PM–10:00 PM; Friday and Saturday 12:00 PM–11:00 PM; Sunday 12:00 PM–8:00 PM.
ADMISSION: $3.50 for adults, $1 for children (6–12 years); or $5 for a six-day unlimited pass. Parking costs $.50 per hour for city meters or $2 for use of the parking lot, but as we go to press these parking fees were being renegotiated. Valet parking is also available.
LOCATION: At the Miami Beach Convention Center, 1901 Convention Center Drive. Take I-95 to 195, then east to Alton Road; follow signs to Convention Center.
DESCRIPTION: Started in 1979 and in March, celebrating their 50th phenomenally successful edition of this event. 1994 saw record-breaking attendance and booth rentals. This is a show that has something for everyone. Exhibitors include nationally prominent firms, hundreds of local companies, individual dealers, artists and craftsmen from throughout the United States and overseas. Used merchandise is not permitted, but there is a large selection of antiques, collectibles, and fine art. There are many special attractions such as guest lecturers and well-known celebrities. There is also the Elvis Presley Museum and Buffalo Bill's Wild West Show replica, just to name a few. There are continuous broadcasts from the show's "celebrity corner" where a prize machine promotion is a favorite treat for visitors.

DEALER RATES: $550 to $650 per 10' × 10' space depending on location, $775 for 10' × 18' space. Reservations are required as most shows are sold out before the show date.

CONTACT: I.B.S. Shows, Inc., 190 Northeast 199 Street (Ives Dairy Road) Suite 203, North Miami Beach, FL 33179-2918. Call Mr. Louis Shelley, Show Director, at (305) 651-9530, Monday–Friday 9:00 AM–5:00 PM. For special show date information, call (305) 673-8071.

South Florida Kids' Show

DATES: January 21–22, 1995.

TIMES: 10:00 AM–8:00 PM.

ADMISSION: $3.50 for adults, $1 children 6–12, under 6 free. Parking is available at cost from valet parking or city meters.

LOCATION: Miami Beach Convention Center, 1901 Convention Center Drive. Take I-95 to 195, then east to Alton Road; follow signs to Convention Center.

DESCRIPTION: A huge new market centered around families with young children, this market will fill its 600 vendor spaces. If it has to do with families, from safety seats to education, from swimming (lessons and/or clothing) to music, nutrition and cooking lessons to summer camp, toys, and computers, this market will have it all! A "vast array of services and products for parents and their kids" is premise of the show. There will be special attractions and entertainment for families. This is one of a series of markets offered by I.B.S. Shows and they suggest that you call them for more information about other venues.

DEALER RATES: $550 for a 10' × 10' space, $650 for a 10' × 10' corner space, $775 for a 10' × 18' perimeter space. Reservations are mandatory. These shows are well known, well attended and quickly sold-out.

CONTACT: Lou Shelley, I.B.S. Shows, Inc., 190 Northeast 199 Street (Ives Dairy Road) Suite 203, North Miami Beach, FL 33179-2918. Call Mr. Louis Shelley, Show Director, at (305) 651-9530, Monday-Friday 9:00 AM–5:00 PM. For special show date information, call (305) 673-8071.

NORTH FORT MYERS

North Side Drive-In Swap Shop

DATES: Summer, end of April to end of October: Wednesday, Saturday, and Sunday. Winter: Wednesday through Sunday, weather permitting.

TIMES: 5:30 AM–3:00 PM.

ADMISSION: Free. Free parking is available.

LOCATION: On Route 41 north, in the old business district.

DESCRIPTION: This show, also known as the "Thunderbird," began around 1982. It is an outdoor market that accommodates approximately 200 dealers selling antiques, arts and crafts, collectibles, fresh produce, and both new and used merchandise. Food is served on the premises.

DEALER RATES: Wednesday $6, Thursday $1, Friday free; Saturday and Sunday $5. Reservations are not required.

CONTACT: North Side Drive-In and Flea Market, P.O. Box 1629, Ft. Myers, FL 33902. Call Claire Rose at (813) 995-2254.

NORTH FORT PIERCE
Biz-E-Flea Market

DATES: Saturday and Sunday, year round.

TIMES: 7:00 AM until whenever!

ADMISSION: Free. Parking is also free.

LOCATION: 3252 North U.S. 1, 1 mile north of St. Lucie Boulevard (Airport Road) and 5 miles south of Vero Beach.

DESCRIPTION: This covered outdoor market first opened in 1980. There are anywhere from 50 dealers during the summer to 100 dealers during the winter selling antiques, collectibles, crafts, tools, electronic equipment, carpeting, and new and good used merchandise. Fresh vegetables are also sold. This is a family-style market boasting sidewalks for easy walking. Food is available on the premises.

DEALER RATES: Fees vary per 10' × 10' covered booth. Reservations are suggested. They teach new sellers how to succeed.

CONTACT: Irma Partridge, 1000 Southwest 27th Avenue #61, Vero Beach, FL 32968. Tel: (407) 569-0147.

NORTH MIAMI
Seventh Avenue Flea Market and
North Miami Flea Market

DATES: Every Wednesday through Sunday; open daily Thanksgiving through Christmas, rain or shine.

TIMES: Wednesday and Sunday 10:00 AM–7:00 PM; Thursday through Saturday; 10:00 AM–9:00 PM.

ADMISSION: Free. Free parking is available.

LOCATION: 14135 NW Seventh Avenue, one block west of I-95 off north 135th Street. (The Blue Building.)

DESCRIPTION: This is South Florida's original indoor flea market, and it all began in 1967. More than 200 dealers assemble to sell a variety of goods including antiques as well as new merchandise, fine art, and fresh produce. There is also clothing for the entire family, housewares, electronics, toys—the list goes on. Actually, due to the many fine jewelry dealers in the markets, it is practically a jewelry exchange and flea market all in one! This famous Miami landmark, also referred to as "the Blue Building," is conveniently located to South Florida's major artery, I-95. The indoor market is clean and air-conditioned and features deluxe snack bars, a new ice cream shop and the Busy Bee Restaurant.

DEALER RATES: $400 and up (plus tax), for 10' × 15' space, monthly with annual lease required. Includes telephone service, advertising, security service, electric, and maintenance.

CONTACT: Marion Brown, Market Managers, 14135 NW SEventh Avenue, North Miami, FL 33168. Tel: (305) 685-7721.

OCALA

Ocala Drive-In Flea Market

DATES: Saturday and Sunday, year round, rain or shine.

TIMES: 7:00 AM–4:00 PM.

ADMISSION: Free admission and free parking.

LOCATION: 4850 South Pine Avenue (South 441-301-27).

DESCRIPTION: Started in 1979, the Ocala Flea Market is located at the only drive-in theater in the county, which is open on Friday, Saturday, and Sunday. Approximately 300 dealers occupy selling space in the summer and 450 in the winter, offering antiques, collectibles, handmade crafts, vegetables, tools, clothes, plants, birds, and new merchandise. There is a pawn shop on the premises. Food is available.

DEALER RATES: $8 per day for a 10' × 10' booth under roof; $6 per day for a 10' × 10' booth outside. Reservations are suggested.

CONTACT: Sheri Williams, 4850 South Pine Avenue, Ocala, FL 34480. Tel: (904) 629-1325.

OLDSMAR
Oldsmar Flea Market

DATES: Saturday and Sunday, year round.

TIMES: 9:00 AM–5:00 PM.

ADMISSION: Free admission and free parking available.

LOCATION: 180 Racetrack Road, at the corner of Hillsboro Avenue and Racetrack Road.

DESCRIPTION: This market began in 1980. About 1,100 dealers sell to the public. Ninety-five percent of them are indoors and offer antiques, collectibles, handmade and craft items, produce, meats, and cheeses. New merchandise is also sold. In addition, there are two bakeries, two nurseries, and even beauticians on the premises. Ten snack bars provide plenty of food and refreshment.

DEALER RATES: Prices vary from $11 to $235 per month, depending on size and location, rented on a first come, first served basis.

CONTACT: Oldsmar Flea Market, P.O. Box 439, Oldsmar, FL 34657. Tel: (813) 855-5306 or (813) 855-2587.

ORLANDO
Country Peddler Show

DATES: Annually. Usually the same weekend each year. For 1994: September 16, 17, and 18.

TIMES: Friday 4:00 PM–9:00 PM; Saturday 9:00 AM–5:00 PM; Sunday 11:00 AM–4:00 PM.

ADMISSION: Adults $5; children 2-12 years $2.

LOCATION: Central Florida Fairgrounds, 4603 West Colonial Drive, Route 50.

DESCRIPTION: This is the fourth year of this market, one of a series of highly successful shows specializing in folk art, collectibles, and crafts with 75 exhibitors displaying their wares. Their specialty is the folk artisans that create the collectibles of the future. Food is available on the premises. This show is one of a series held all over the East Coast from Michigan to Florida.

DEALER RATES: $375 per 10' × 10' booth; $562.50 per 10' × 15' booth; $750 per 10' × 20' booth. Reservations are required as this is a juried show.

CONTACT: American Memories, Inc., P.O. Box 249, Decatur, MI 49045-0249. Tel: (616) 423-8367, fax: (616) 423-2421.

PENSACOLA
T & W Flea Market

DATES: Saturday and Sunday, rain or shine.
TIMES: Dawn to dusk.
ADMISSION: Free. Free parking is available.
LOCATION: 1717 North "T" Street, on the west side of Pensacola.
DESCRIPTION: This indoor/outdoor market started in 1979. There are 400 dealers per weekend selling a variety of objects including antiques, fine art, arts and crafts, new merchandise, fresh produce, etc. it's all here. They have made many improvements here including concrete aisles. Four snack bars provide food for the hungry.
DEALER RATES: From $10 for 10' × 20' space; $12 for 12' × 20' space. Reservations are required for the more desirable spaces.
CONTACT: Red Cotton, 1717 North T Street, Pensacola, FL 32505. Tel: (904) 433-4315 or 433-7030.

PLANT CITY
Country Village Flea Market

DATES: Every Wednesday, Saturday, and Sunday, rain or shine.
TIMES: 7:00 AM–2:00 PM.
ADMISSION: Free. Free parking is available.
LOCATION: On corner of State Road 39 and Sam Allen Road, one mile north of I-4. (Tampa area.)
DESCRIPTION: This market began in 1979 and currently ranks among the largest Wednesday markets. It accommodates dealers both indoors and outdoors, selling plenty of used goods. Also available are antiques, collectibles, and fresh produce. Food is served on the premises. Their Wednesday market is so popular that they have turned away dealers for lack of room! There is a wholesale produce market seven days a week from 6:00 AM to whenever.
DEALER RATES: $5–7 for 10' × 24' indoor space. $5 for 24' outdoor space. No reservations are required and there are no advance shopping hours for dealers.
CONTACT: Ferris Waller, 3301 North Highway 39, Plant City, FL 33566. Day of show call Sylvia the manager at (813) 752-4670.

RIVIERA BEACH
Riviera Swap Shop

DATES: Wednesday, Friday, Saturday, and Sunday.
TIMES: 6:00 AM–2:00 PM.

ADMISSION: Saturday and Sunday $.50 per car.
LOCATION: 1301 Old Dixie Highway. Between I-95 and U.S. 1.
DESCRIPTION: This outdoor market started in 1965 and attracts 400 dealers selling mostly used and new merchandise and fresh produce. "All kinds of goodies," according to the manager. There is a nice snack bar on premises.
DEALER RATES: Wednesday free, Friday $4; Saturday and Sunday $7. Reservations are not required.
CONTACT: Rubin Rodriguez, Riviera Swap Shop, 1301 Old Dixie Highway, Riviera Beach, FL 33404. Tel: (407) 844-5836.

ST. AUGUSTINE
St. Johns Flea Market

DATES: Saturday and Sunday.
TIMES: 9:00 AM–5:00 PM.
ADMISSION: Free. Parking is also free.
LOCATION: I-95 and State Road 207, Exit 94.
DESCRIPTION: This market opened in 1985 and has 500 spaces indoors and out with dealers selling "everything;" antiques, collectibles, new and used merchandise, produce, plants, and more. It is all under roof. Located in historic St. Augustine, the country's oldest city and a major tourist attraction. Food is available on the premises as are clean restrooms and RV facilities.
DEALER RATES: $11 per day. Reservations are suggested.
CONTACT: St. Johns Flea Market, P.O. Box 1284, St. Augustine, FL 32085. Tel: (904) 824-4210.

SANFORD
Flea World

DATES: Every Friday, Saturday, and Sunday, rain or shine.
TIMES: 8:00 AM–5:00 PM.
ADMISSION: Free. Free parking is available for 4,000 cars.
LOCATION: On Highway 17-92, Sanford. From I-4, take Exit 50 east to Highway 17-92, turn right one mile.
DESCRIPTION: This show started on May 20, 1982, with just a 12-acre tract. It has now grown to accommodate 1,600 dealers on 104 acres of land. There is an "all-under-one-roof" air-conditioned building and three mini-malls as well as booths outside. Shoppers really can "get it all" here from antiques and collectibles to the unusual: a lawyer, an optometrist, a barber and beauty shop, and an exotic pet

shop. Other attractions include a children's petting zoo featuring numerous animals. Fifteen fun food stops quell hunger and a Family Fun Park is located next door.

DEALER RATES: $10–16 per space and up. Reservations are required.

CONTACT: Mary Disque, Rental Manager, Flea World, Highway 17-92, Sanford, FL 32773. Tel: (407) 647-3976 or (407) 330-3976.

STUART
B & A Flea Market

DATES: Every Saturday and Sunday, rain or shine.

TIMES: 8:00 AM–3:00 PM.

ADMISSION: Free. Free parking is available. Other parking for $1.

LOCATION: 2201 S.E. Indian Street. East of U.S. 1, across from Martin Square Mall.

DESCRIPTION: This market first opened in 1975. It accommodates approximately 400 to 500 dealers both indoors and outdoors who assemble to sell just about everything including antiques, collectibles, fine art, arts and crafts, new merchandise, fresh produce, and everything else imaginable. Food is served on the premises.

DEALER RATES: $12–$20 per space. Reservations are not accepted; set up is first come, first served.

CONTACT: Tara Linn, B & A Flea Market, 2201 S.E. Indian Street, Stuart, FL 34997. Tel: (407) 288-4915.

TAMPA
Big Top Flea Market

DATES: Every Saturday and Sunday, year round, rain or shine.

TIMES: 8:00 AM–5:00 PM.

ADMISSION: Free. Parking is $1 per vehicle.

LOCATION: Take I-75 south to Fowler Avenue (S.R. 582), Exit 54, heading east. Market is 500 yards east of I-75.

DESCRIPTION: The Big Top Flea Market, opened in October 1990, was built in a unique hub and spoke design so that every booth is well traveled and easily accessible. The market is named after the 27,000 square foot center core that resembles a huge circus tent. It houses 620 booths with 160,000 square feet of both covered and enclosed spaces. Eventually the Market will have over 1,100 spaces. While there is a wide variety of merchandise from produce to fine jewelry, the center core features antiques, collectibles and crafts. This market

is keeping the true spirit of a flea market: value, bargains and fun.
DEALER RATES: Summer: $67 to $147; Winter: $74 to $173 depending on location. Rates are based on a 4-week month. Daily and weekend rates are available.
CONTACT: Mark Hintz, Vice President or Janet Adie, Reservation Manager, P.O. Box 18444, Tampa, FL 33679-8444. Tel: (813) 986-4004.

Sunshine State Marketplace
DATES: Saturday and Sunday, year round, rain or shine.
TIMES: 9:00 AM–4:00 PM.
ADMISSION: Free. Parking is free.
LOCATION: 8120 Anderson Road, 1 block from the new Veterans Expressway, Waters Exit.
DESCRIPTION: In the tradition of the original idea behind a "flea market" this indoor/outdoor market, now over 27 years old, sits on 13 acres of prime location. It is described by its owners as an "old-fashioned flea market with a new-fashioned look." Dealers sell more used than new merchandise including antiques, collectibles, and garage sale treasures. A food concession and beer vendor are on the premises.
DEALER RATES: $88 per month; $5 per day. Reservations are not accepted. First come, first served.
CONTACT: John Gardner or Joanne, Sunshine State Marketplace, 8120 Anderson Road, Tampa, FL 33634. Tel: (813) 884-7810.

WALDO
Smiley's Pocket Change Flea Market
DATES: Saturday and Sunday.
TIMES: 8:00 AM–5:00 PM.
ADMISSION: Free. Parking is free.
LOCATION: One mile north of Waldo on west side of U.S. 301.
DESCRIPTION: Started in 1982, this indoor/outdoor market of 100 dealers sells mostly antiques and collectibles. There is some new merchandise, but basically, it's all old treasures and goodies. One snack bar and clean restrooms are on site. An RV park is next door.
DEALER RATES: $5 for a 10' × 10' outside space, $10 for inside space. Reservations are recommended.
CONTACT: Sylvia Hall, Smiley's Pocket Change Flea Market, P.O. Box 194, Waldo, FL 32694-0194. Tel: (904) 468-1785 or 375-6600.

Waldo Farmer's and Flea Market

DATES: Every Saturday and Sunday, rain or shine.

TIMES: 7:30 AM–5:00 PM.

ADMISSION: Free. Free parking available.

LOCATION: Located on Highway 301 North, north of Waldo.

DESCRIPTION: This Farmer's and Flea Market attracts an average of 650 dealers in the summer and 800 dealers during the winter who sell antiques, collectibles, handmade craft items, vegetables meats, and new merchandise. The market has been running since 1973. There is a new antique mall here, open every day. The majority of spaces are under cover sheds, however outside space and lock-up stalls are also available. Dealers may stay overnight and no county or city licenses are required. There are two snack bars on the premises and camping nearby. The office is open everyday except Wednesday. "Look for the Big Horse."

DEALER RATES: $6 and up per 10' × 10' space. Reservations are suggested. You can go to the market to make the reservation, or call and give them a credit card number, otherwise first come, first served. $1.06 extra for electric.

CONTACT: Waldo Farmer's and Flea Market, Rt 1 Box 85, Waldo, FL 32694. Tel: (904) 468-2255.

WEBSTER

Sumter County Farmer's Market, Inc.

DATES: Every Monday year round. Rain or shine.

TIMES: 8:00 AM–3:00 PM.

ADMISSION: Free. Free parking is provided on market grounds.

LOCATION: On Highway 471 in Webster. Accessible from Highway 50, Highway 301, or Highway 98.

DESCRIPTION: This market opened in 1937 and currently attracts between 1,200 (winter) and 2,000 (summer) dealers who sell a range of antiques, collectibles, craft items, new merchandise, and fresh produce, including citrus and flower plants. This market is well known for its selection of antique items and locally grown vegetables. Snack food is available on the premises.

DEALER RATES: $7 per 10' × 10' booth, covered with 2 tables; $6 per 12' × 12' booth, open without tables. All reservations are first come, first served. All dealers must have city and county licenses, available at office every Monday between 6:00 AM and 9:00 PM, for $7 per day or $35 for the year.

CONTACT: Margie Hayes, Office Manager, P.O. Box 62, Webster, FL 33597. Tel: (904) 793-3551.

OTHER FLEA MARKETS

Belleview: Flea City USA, US 441, Belleview, FL 32620. Tel: (904) 245-FLEA. Open Friday through Sunday 7:00 AM–9:00 PM.

Belleview: The Market of Marion, 12888 SE U.S. Highway 441, Belleview, FL 32620. Tel: (904) 245-6766. Open summers: weekends; winters: Friday through Sunday.

Big Pine: Big Pine Flea Market, Mile Marker 30.5, U.S. Highway 1, Big Pine, FL 33043. Tel: (305) 872-4221. Open weekends October through May.

Bradenton: Red Barn Flea Market Plaza, 301 and 41 at 17th Avenue, Bradenton, FL 34208. Tel: (813) 747-3794. Open Wednesday through Sunday.

Crystal River: Stokes Flea Market, Highway 44 East, Crystal River, FL 32629. Tel: (904) 746-7200. Open Wednesday and weekends.

DeFuniak Springs: DeFuniak Flea Market, Highway 90 East, Route 1 Box 527, DeFuniak Springs, FL 32433. Tel: (904) 892-3668. Open Friday through Sunday 8:00 AM–4:00 PM.

De Land: Volusia County Farmer's Market, 3090 East New York Avenue at the County Fairgrounds, De Land, FL 32724. Tel: (904) 734-1614. Open Wednesdays.

Delray Beach: Delray Indoor Flea Market, 5283 West Atlantic Avenue, Delray Beach, FL 33484. Tel: (407) 499-9935. Open Thursday through Sunday 9:00 AM–5:00 PM.

Ellisville: GrandPa's Farmers & Flea Market, Exit 80 from I-75 and U.S. Route 41, Ellisville, FL 32055. Tel: (904) 758-5564. Open weekends 6:00 AM–6:00 PM.

Fort Lauderdale: The Value Mart, 7350 West Commercial Boulevard, For Lauderdale, FL 33325. Tel: (305) 370-8205.

Fort Myers: Ortiz Avenue Flea Market, 1501 Ortiz Avenue, Fort Myers, FL 33905. Tel: (813) 694-5019. Open Friday through Sunday.

Hallandale: Hollywood Dog Track Flea Market, U.S. 1 at Pembroke Road, Hallandale, FL 33022. Tel: (305) 454-8666. Open weekends 8:00 AM–3:00 PM.

Homosassa: Howard's Flea Market, 6373 South Suncoast Boulevard, Homosassa, FL 32646. Tel: (904) 628-3437. Open weekends 6:30 AM–4:00 PM.

Homosassa Springs: Homosassa Springs Flea Market, Highway 19S, Homosassa Springs, FL 32647. Tel: (904) 628-4656. Open weekends 6:30 AM–4:00 PM.

Jacksonville: Bargain House of Fleas, 6016 Blanding Boulevard, Jacksonville, FL 32244. Tel: (904) 772-8008. Open weekends.

Jacksonville: Beach Boulevard Flea and Farmers Market, 11041 Beach Boulevard, Jacksonville, FL 32216. Tel: (904) 645-5961. Open Friday 1:00 PM–9:00 PM; weekends 8:00 AM–5:00 PM.

Jacksonville: The Market Place, Inc., 6839 Ramona Boulevard, Jacksonville, FL 32205. Tel: (904) 786-1153. Open weekends.

Jacksonville: Pecan Park Road Flea Market, Pecan Park Road at I-95, Jacksonville, FL 32218. Tel: (904) 751-6770. Open weekends 8:00 AM–5:00 PM.

Jacksonville: Playtime Drive-In Theatre Flea Market, 6300 Blanding Boulevard, Jacksonville, FL 32210. Tel: (904) 771-9939. Open Wednesday through Sunday 7:00 AM–4:00 PM.

Kissimmee: Osceola Flea and Farmer's Market, 2801 East Irlo Bronson Highway, Kissimmee, FL 34744. Tel: (407) 846-2811. Open Friday through Sunday 8:00 AM–5:00 PM.

Lakeland: King Flea Inc., 333 North Lake Parker Avenue, Lakeland, FL 33801. Tel: (813) 688-9964. Open Friday through Sunday 8:30am–5:00 PM.

Lauderlakes: The Bazaar, 3200 West Oakland Park, Lauderlakes, FL 33311. Tel: (305) 739-2805. Open Wednesday, Thursday, and Sunday.

Melbourne: Flea Mall, 915 South Babcock Street, Melbourne, FL 32901. Tel: (407) 951-2240. Open daily.

Melbourne: Super Flea and Farmers Market, 4835 West Eau Gallie Boulevard, Melbourne, FL 32934. Tel: (407) 242-9124. Open Friday through Sunday 9:00 AM–4:00 PM.

Miami: 183 Street Flea Market, 18200 NW 27th Avenue, Miami, FL 33056. Tel: (305) 624-1756. Open Wednesday through Sunday.

Miami: #1 Market, 11000 NW 7th Avenue, Miami, FL 33168. Tel: (305) 751-8664. Open Wednesday through Sunday.

Miami: Flagler Flea Market, Flagler Greyhound Track, NW 7th Street and 37th Avenue, Miami, FL 33126. Tel: (305) 649-3022. Open weekends 9:00 AM–5:00 PM.

Miami: Flea Market USA, 3015 NW 79th Street, Miami, FL 33147. Tel: (305) 836-3677. Open Wednesday through Sunday.

Miami: Opa Locka/Hialeah Flea Market, 12705 NW 42nd Avenue, Miami, FL 33054. Tel: (305) 688-0500. Open Friday through Sunday 5:00 AM–7:00 PM.

Mount Dora: Florida Twin Markets, U.S. Highway 441, Mt Dora, FL 32757. Tel: (904) 383-8393. Open weekends 8:00 AM–5:00 PM.

Naples: Naples Drive-In Theatre Flea Market, Highway 84 East, Naples, FL 33939. Tel: (813) 774-2900. Open weekends.

New Port Richey: Indoor Fleas, 3621 U.S. 19 South (Moog Road), New Port Richey, FL 34652. Tel: (813) 842-3665. Open Friday through Sunday 9:30 AM–5:30 PM.

North Miami: North Miami Flea Market, 14135 NW 7th Avenue, North Miami, FL 33168. tel: (305) 685-7721. Open Wednesday through Sunday 10:00 AM–7:00 PM.

Odessa: Gunn Highway Flea Market, 2317 Gunn Highway, Odessa, FL 33556. Tel: (813) 920-3181. Open weekends 8:00 AM–4:00 PM.

Okeechobee: The Market Place Flea Market, 3600 Highway 441 South, Okeechobee, FL 34974. Tel: (813) 467-6803. Open weekends 7:00 AM–4:00 PM.

Okeechobee: Whispering Pines Flea Market, 250 NW 34th Street, Okeechobee, FL 34972. Tel: (813) 763-7702. Open Thursday through Monday.

Orlando: Central Florida Fairgrounds, 1552 Daly Street, Orlando, FL 32808. Tel: (407) 295-9448. Open weekends.

Orlando: Colonial Flea Market, 11500 East Colonial Drive, Orlando, FL 32817. Tel: (407) 380-8888. Open Friday through Sunday.

Orlando: Great American Bazaar, 7551 Canada Avenue, Orlando, FL 32819. Tel: (407) 363-0505. Open daily 10:00 AM–10:00 PM.

Orlando: Our Place, 3569 Old Wintergarden, Orlando, FL 32805. Tel: (407) 345-5475.

Ormond Beach: Nova Swap Shop, 700 South Nova Road, Ormond Beach, FL 32174. Tel: (904) 672-3014. Open Wednesday through Sunday 6:00 AM–2:00 PM.

Palmetto: Country Fair Flea Market, Junction of Routes 301 and 41, Palmetto, FL 34220. Tel: (813) 722-5633. Open weekends.

Panama City: Springfield Flea Market, 3425 East Business I.S. 98, Panama City, FL 32401. Tel: (904) 769-4999. Open Wednesday through Sunday.

Pinnelas Park: Wagon Wheel Flea Market, 7801 82nd Avenue North, Pinnelas Park, FL 33565. Tel: (813) 544-5319. Open weekends.

Plant City: The Value Mart, 1864 Jim Redman Parkway, Plant City, FL 33566. Tel: (813) 754-8222.

Pomona Park: Frank's Flea Market, 1814 Highway 17, Pomona Park, FL 32181. Tel: (904) 649-0608. Open Friday through Sunday 7:00 AM–5:00 PM.

Pompano Beach: Festival Flea Market, 2900 West Sample Road, Pompano Beach, FL 33073. Tel: (305) 979-4555. Open Thursday through Sunday 9:30 AM–5:00 PM.

Port Charlotte: Poor Jed's Flea Market, 4628 Tamiami Trail, Port Charlotte, FL 33980. Tel: (813) 629-1223. Open Friday through Sunday 8:30 AM–4:00 PM.

Port Richey: USA Fleamarket, 11721 U.S. 19, Port Richey, FL 34668. Tel: (813) 862-5724. Open Friday through Sunday.

Tallahassee: Flea Market Tallahassee, 200 Capital Circle SW, Tallahassee, FL 32310. Tel: (904) 877-3811. Open weekends 9:00 AM–5:00 PM.

Tampa: American Legion Market Place, 929 East 139th Avenue, Tampa, FL 33612. Tel: (813) 971-3699. Open weekends.

Tampa: Great American Flea Market, 5050 East 10th Avenue Columbus Plaza, Tampa FL 33619. Tel: (813) 247-3532. Open Friday through Sunday 9:00 AM–6:00 PM.

Waldo: Trading Post, Route 1 Box 244, Waldo, FL 32694. Tel: (904) 468-2622. Open Friday through Sunday.

Winter Garden: The Value Mart, 401 West Highway, Winter Garden, FL 34787. Tel: (407) 654-0909.

GEORGIA

ACWORTH

Lake Acworth Antique and Flea Market

DATES: Every Saturday and Sunday, rain or shine.

TIMES: 7:00 AM–5:00 PM.

ADMISSION: Free. Parking is $1 per car.

LOCATION: 4375 Cobb Parkway, N.W., approximately 35 miles north of Atlanta and 5 miles west of I-75, off Highway 92 exit. Follow Highway 92 to Cobb, turn right, go approximately 1 mile. Market is on the left.

DESCRIPTION: Started in 1978, this flea market was formerly known as Delight's. It is held indoors, in the open air, and under cover. There are 400 dealers exhibiting antiques, arts and crafts, fresh produce, collectibles, and new merchandise—something for everyone. Located near Allatoona Lake on Lake Acworth, the average daily attendance ranges between 5,000 and 6,000 people. Food is available.

DEALER RATES: $5, $7, and $10 depending upon size of space. Reservations are recommended.

CONTACT: James Little, 4375 Cobb Parkway North, Acworth, GA 30101. Tel: (404) 974-5896 (Friday and Saturday only). Day of show call James Little at (404) 974-5896.

ALBANY

Kitty's Flea Market

DATES: Friday, Saturday, and Sunday, year round.

TIMES: 7:00 AM–6:00 PM.

ADMISSION: Free. Parking is also free.

LOCATION: 3331 Sylvester Road. On U.S. 82, 3 miles north of Albany.

DESCRIPTION: This market opened in 1985 in the middle of a pecan orchard and accommodates 320 regular dealers under roof and another 350 in the open or under shade, and they are adding new tables all the time. "Anything you can think of" is sold here, including produce, furniture, clothes, and jewelry. It is described by one regular as real "country, very laid back" and agreeable. This market is doing a booming business. If you love pecans, you can even pick your own!

DEALER RATES: $5 per table under the shed. Reservations are required under the shed only. Outside: no reservation required.

CONTACT: Jim Andrews, Kitty's Flea Market, 3331 Sylvester Road, Albany, GA 31705. Tel: (912) 432-0007.

ATLANTA
Country Peddler Show

DATES: February 4–6.

TIMES: Friday 4:00 PM–9:00 PM; Saturday 9:00 AM–5:00 PM; Sunday 11:00 AM–4:00 PM.

ADMISSION: Adults $5, children 2–12 $2 each day.

LOCATION: Cobb Galleria Centre, 300 Galleria Parkway, Suite 200.

DESCRIPTION: One of a series of highly successful folk art shows around the East Coast featuring decorating and quality handmade items such as herb arrangements, country furniture, salt-glazed pottery, and more.

DEALER RATES: $375 for a 10' × 10' space, $562.50 for a 10' × 15' space, and $750 for a 10' × 20' space. Reservations are required as this is a juried show.

CONTACT: American Memories, Inc. P.O. Box 249, Decatur, MI 49045. Tel: (616) 423-8367 or fax: (616) 423-2421.

Lakewood Antiques Market

DATES: Second weekend of every month, Friday through Sunday, year round. Extravaganzas held in April and November for four days.

TIMES: Friday 9:00 AM–8:00 PM; Saturday 9:00 AM–6:00 PM; Sunday 10:00 AM–5:00 PM.

ADMISSION: $3.00. Parking is free.

LOCATION: 2000 Lakewood Way. Take I-75-85 South, Exit 88 East and follow the signs.

DESCRIPTION: Since 1969, this market has been hosting from 800 to 1,200 dealers selling at least 75 percent antiques and collectibles. Their historic buildings are situated on 117 acres of land with a fully equipped bar and restaurant, and dealer camping stops on-site. They have added new air-conditioned and heated buildings.

DEALER RATES: $75 per 8' × 10' booth inside space; $65 per 11' × 15' outside space. After advance reservations are filled, then it is first come, first served.

CONTACT: Ed Spivia, P.O. Box 6826, Atlanta, GA 30315. Tel: (404) 622-4488. Day of show contact Diane Kent at above number.

Scott Antique Market

DATES: 1994: April 8–10, May 13–15, June 10–12, July 8–10, August 12–14, September 9–11, October 7–9, November 11–13, December 9–11.

TIMES: Friday and Saturday 9:00 AM–6:00 PM, Sunday 10:00 AM–5:00 PM.

ADMISSION: $3. Parking is free.

LOCATION: Atlanta Expo Center, 3650 Jonesboro Road.

DESCRIPTION: Since 1986 this indoor/outdoor market has 1,600 dealers selling the finest in antique and collectibles only. Four snack bars and one restaurant supply the energy to keep you browsing.

DEALER RATES: Indoors: $75 for a 8' × 10' space; outdoors: $55 for a 10' × 15' open space or 10' × 10' covered space. Reservations are required.

CONTACT: Scott Antique Market, P.O. Box 60, Bremen, OH 43107. Tel: (614) 569-4112 or fax: (614) 569-7595.

CALHOUN

New Town Flea Market

DATES: Saturday and Sunday, year round, rain or shine.

TIMES: Sunup until sundown.

ADMISSION: Free. Parking is also free.

LOCATION: One mile out on New Town Road next to I-75 on the west side.

DESCRIPTION: This outdoor market began in 1979 and accommodates 50 to 60 dealers. There are mostly secondhand and household items, with some antiques, collectibles, and new merchandise available. This market prides itself on its reputation as a good, clean, small market. Food is served on the premises.

DEALER RATES: $5 per 12' × 12' covered shed with table; $2 per table outside. Monthly rental is available for inside booths. Reservations are suggested.

CONTACT: Earl Abernathy, 257 Iracille Lane N.E., Calhoun, GA 30701. Tel: (706) 625-1157. Day of show call: (706) 625-9088.

CHAMBLEE

Atlanta Antique Center and Flea Market

DATES: Every Friday, Saturday, and Sunday, rain or shine.

TIMES: 11:00 AM–7:00 PM.

ADMISSION: Free. Free parking is available.
LOCATION: 5360 Peachtree Industrial Boulevard, 1½ miles inside I-285, off Exit 23.
DESCRIPTION: This indoor show began in 1974 and is said to feature the largest selection of antiques under one roof in the Southeast. Over 150 independent merchants offer collectibles, art, gold, silver, crystal, plants, baskets, pottery, brass, books, vintage clothing, etc. This permanent flea market is housed in 80,000 square feet of climate-controlled selling space. It offers the same sense of excitement, and more importantly, the chance for bargain hunting, that exists in the bazaars in Damascus, Syria, Cairo, the Casbah, and, most famous of all, the Paris Flea Market. There is a restaurant on the premises.
DEALER RATES: No weekend rentals.
CONTACT: W.S. Malone, 5360 Peachtree Industrial Boulevard, Chamblee, GA 30341. Tel: (404) 458-0456.

DECATUR
Kudzu Antique Flea Market
DATES: Friday, Saturday, and Sunday.
TIMES: Friday and Saturday 10:30 AM–5:30 PM; Sunday 12:30 PM–5:30 PM.
ADMISSION: Free. Parking is also free.
LOCATION: 2874 East Ponce de Leon. Off I-285, Exit 31.
DESCRIPTION: This dealer's paradise opened in October 1980. Their 27 dealers, in a 27,000 square foot barnlike building, sell mostly American antiques, collectibles, and furniture. There is very little new merchandise sold here and what comes in is exceptionally good. No food is available on the premises.
DEALER RATES: Rarely any vacancies; call for information.
CONTACT: Emily Campbell, 178 Lamont Drive, Decatur, GA 30030. Tel: (404) 373-6498 or 378-3909.

EAST POINT
Greenbriar Flea Market
DATES: Wednesday through Sunday, year round.
TIMES: Wednesday through Saturday noon–9:00 PM; Sunday noon–6:00 PM.
ADMISSION: Free. Parking is also free.
LOCATION: 2925 Headland Drive. Across from the Greenbriar Mall.
DESCRIPTION: Opened in 1983, this market hosts 136 dealers sell-

ing all new merchandise including jewelry, clothes, hats, fragrance, shoes, photos, and endless amounts of more at very reasonable prices. They remodeled the entire market in 1993 adding 10,000 square feet, a few retail stores, and a little restaurant to handle your hunger.

DEALER RATES: $225 and up per month. Reservations are suggested, especially around the holidays.

CONTACT: Marvin Davis, Greenbriar Flea Market, 2925 Headland Drive, East Point, GA 30344. Tel: (404) 349-3994.

GAINESVILLE
Mule Camp Trade Days Gainesville Flea Market

DATES: First weekend of each month and preceding Friday, rain or shine.

TIMES: Friday and Saturday 9:00 AM–6:00 PM; Sunday noon–6:00 PM.

ADMISSION: Free. Free parking is available.

LOCATION: Gainesville Fairgrounds, Highway 13 South, between Atlanta and Helen, 50 miles north of Atlanta, Exit 4 off I-985.

DESCRIPTION: Known for its friendliness and courtesy, many of the 75 dealers have been with this flea market since it opened in 1978. Antiques, arts and crafts, collectibles, and new merchandise are exhibited both indoors and out. The concession is excellent, serving home-cooked food that includes home-baked cakes and cookies.

DEALER RATES: A three-day weekend fee of $30 for space measuring 10' × 10', which includes two tables. Reservations are preferred.

CONTACT: Johnny and Barbara Benefield, P.O. Box 224, Oakwood, GA 30566. Tel: (404) 536-8068. Day of show call Barbara Benefield at (404) 534-9157.

MACON
Smiley's Flea Market

DATES: Saturday and Sunday.

TIMES: 7:00 AM–5:00 PM.

ADMISSION: Free. Parking is free.

LOCATION: On U.S. 129/GA 247, 4 miles south of Macon.

DESCRIPTION: Opened in 1985, this indoor/outdoor market's 500 dealers sell mostly antiques and collectibles, although "anything goes." There is a huge antique mall on the premises. There are snack bars to satisfy the "munchies," and clean handicapped-accessible restrooms.

RV parking is available.

DEALER RATES: $5 for 10' × 10' outside space, $15 for inside space. Reservations are recommended.

CONTACT: Cletus Smith, 6717 Hawkinsville Road, Macon, GA 31206. Tel: (912) 788-3700.

OTHER FLEA MARKETS

Acworth: Great American Bargain Market, 3355 Cobb Parkway, Acworth, GA 30101. Tel: (404) 974-9660.

Atlanta: Flea Market USA, 1919 Stewart Avenue, Atlanta, GA 30315. Tel: (404) 763-3078. Open Thursday through Sunday 10:00 AM–7:00 PM, Friday and Saturday until 9:00 PM.

Cumming: Dixie 400 Flea Market, Highway 400, Cumming, GA 30130. Tel: (404) 889-5895. Open weekends 9:00 AM–6:00 PM.

Decatur: Flea Mart-Candler, 1954 Candler Road, Decatur, GA 30032. Tel: (404) 289-0804. Open Friday noon–9:00 PM, Saturday 10:00 AM–9:00 PM, Sunday noon–6:00 PM.

Grantville: Grantville "Good Times" Flea Market, 5320 Highway 29 North, Grantville, GA 30220. Tel: (404) 583-3442. Open weekends 8:00 AM–6:00 PM.

Helen: Alpine Valley Complex, Route 1, Helen, GA 30545. Tel: (404) 878-2803. Open daily.

Lake Park: Bargainville Flea-Esta Flea Market, Frontage Road (at I-75, Exit 2), Lake Park, GA 31636. Tel: (912) 559-0141. Open weekends 9:00 AM–5:00 PM.

Savannah: Kellers Flea Market, 5901 Ogeechee Road, Savannah, GA 31419. Tel: (912) 927-4848. Open Friday through Sunday 8:00 AM–5:00 PM.

Waycross: Chrystal's Flea Market, 1631 Genoa Street, Waycross, GA 31501. Tel: (912) 283-9808. Open Saturday 8:00 AM–5:00 PM, Sunday 1:00 PM–5:00 PM.

Whittier: Uncle Bill's Cherokee Flea Market, Highway 441 North, Whittier, NC 28789. Tel: (704) 586-9613. Open daily 8:00 AM–6:00 PM, April through November.

Wilmington: Trade Winds Swaperama, 5919 Market Street, Wilmington, NC 28405. Tel: (919) 395-6880. Open Friday through Sunday 9:00 AM–5:00 PM.

HAWAII

AIEA
Kam Super Swap Meet

DATES: Wednesday, Saturday, and Sunday and most holidays, weather permitting.
TIMES: 5:30 AM–3:00 PM.
ADMISSION: Free. Parking is free.
LOCATION: 98-850 Moanalua Road, across from the Pearlridge Shopping Center.
DESCRIPTION: This outdoor meet started in 1966. There are 600 dealers in Polynesian and Hawaiian handicrafts and collectibles, new items, slightly used items, fresh produce, milk caps, ethnic delicacies, and much more. You will also find a varied assortment of clothes and Polynesian-made arts and crafts. Food is available on the premises.
DEALER RATES: *Unreserved Sellers:* $7 per stall Saturday and Sunday, $6 Wednesday and weekday holidays.
Reserved Sellers: Monthly reservations are $15 per stall per day of the week, for an entire month (i.e., a month of Sundays, a month of Wednesdays). Holidays are free to reserved sellers. There is also a daily charge for reserved sellers: $5 per Saturday and Sunday, $4 per Wednesday and weekday holiday.
Marketplace Sellers: $60 per stall per day per month (i.e., a month of Sundays, etc.) for Saturdays and Sundays; $50 per stall per day per month for Wednesdays.
CONTACT: Kam Super Swap Meet, 98-850 Moanalua Road, Aiea, HI 96701. Tel: (808) 483-5933 for recorded message and instructions, or (808) 847-9248 between 8:00 AM–4:00 PM.

HONOLULU
Aloha Flea Market

DATES: Wednesday, Saturday, Sunday, and some holidays. The week before Christmas open every day.
TIMES: 6:00 AM–3:00 PM.
ADMISSION: $.35 per person. Children 12 and under are free. Parking is free.
LOCATION: Aloha Stadium. Right across the street from the Arizona Memorial in Pearl Harbor. Fifteen minutes from Waikiki.
DESCRIPTION: This market opened in 1979 and averages 1,200

vendors selling shirts, antiques, collectibles, diving gear, tools, sporting goods, shoes, and new and used merchandise. During the holiday season, the dealer ranks swell to monumental proportions. Rows of shade trees line the market, so it stays cool. Of course, it offers the ideal weather. No flammables are allowed. Food and restrooms are on the premises. This is the largest market in the state of Hawaii and "on a per capita basis, the largest in the U.S."

DEALER RATES: Wednesday $10–$40.75 per space; Saturday $10.75–$42.75; Sunday $12.75–$42.75 per stall. One of the four stall sizes is 18' × 20'. Reservations are not required.

CONTACT: Aloha Flea Market, 99-500 Salt Lake Boulevard, Honolulu, HI 96818. Tel: (808) 486-1529.

HONOMU
Akaka Falls Flea Market

DATES: Daily.

TIMES: 9:00 AM–5:00 PM.

LOCATION: Akaka Falls Road, two minutes from the Akaka Falls.

ADMISSION: Free. Parking is free.

DESCRIPTION: While this market isn't truly a flea market with vendors, it seems to cover everything flea markets generally do, selling local crafts and goods, musical instruments, coral, clothes, imports, jewelry, flowers, plants, and other specialties.

DEALER RATES: N/A.

CONTACT: Dennis Seville, P.O. Box 11, Honomu, HI 96728. Tel: (808) 963-6171.

IDAHO

KETCHUM-SUN VALLEY
Antique Peddler's Fair Antique Show

DATES: July 4th weekend and Labor Day weekend, each year; rain or shine.

TIMES: 9:00 AM–7:00 PM.

ADMISSION: Free. Free parking is available.

LOCATION: In Warm Springs Village, Ketchum-Sun Valley.

DESCRIPTION: This show first opened in 1970 in the heart of Wood River Valley, Ketchum, and Sun Valley. It is Idaho's largest antique market and accommodates anywhere from 85 to 100 dealers, coming from Maine to California, bringing a nice variety of antiques and fine art. There is always a large selection of furniture, china, jewelry, silver, and vintage clothes, to name a few. Because of its extraordinary natural beauty, this area has become a summer playground offering guided pack and river trips, hiking, swimming, fantastic fishing, and ice shows featuring the champions. These shows attract many famous people including some Hollywood stars who have homes in the area. Food is served on the premises.

DEALER RATES: $135 per 10' × 12' space for all three days. Reservations are required. Bring your own canopy and booth set-up.

CONTACT: Jan or Jeffrey Perkins, 2902 Breneman Street, Boise, ID 83703. Tel: (208) 345-0755 or 368-9759.

ILLINOIS

ALSIP

Tri-State Swap O Rama

DATES: Every Saturday and Sunday, rain or shine.

TIMES: 7:00 AM–4:00 PM.

ADMISSION: $.75 per person. Free parking available for 1,500 cars.

LOCATION: 4350 West 129th Street. Take I-294 to Cicero Avenue (Route 50) south to 131st, east to Door or Pulaski Road to 129th west.

DESCRIPTION: The Tri-State Swap O Rama is held both indoors and outdoors. Started in 1979, there are now 500 to 750 dealers selling antiques, fresh produce, meats, collectibles, and new merchandise. Food is served on the premises.

DEALER RATES: $18 for space measuring 8' × 12' indoors or $14 per 12' × 24' outdoor booth. Advance reservations are suggested.

CONTACT: Jim Pierski, Swap O Rama, 4600 West Lake Street, Melrose Park, IL 60160. Tel: (708) 344-7300.

AMBOY

Amboy Happening Flea Market

DATES: Third Sunday of each month except December and January, rain or shine.

TIMES: 8:00 AM–4:00 PM.

ADMISSION: $1 per person. Free parking with lots of available space.

LOCATION: 4-H Fairgrounds, 1 mile east of Route 52 and 30 on U.S. 30.

DESCRIPTION: Started in 1965, this market is held both indoors and outdoors. It consists of 72 dealers indoors selling antiques, arts and crafts, collectibles, new merchandise, coins, jewelry, and furniture. Others exhibit outdoors. A full kitchen serves good food on the premises. They feature a special guest collector at each market, lecturing in their specialty. However, the guest's goods are not for sale. There are special events scheduled throughout the year. Watch for announcements. Some past events included a John Deere antique tractors show, English horse jumping, and more.

DEALER RATES: $35 for three tables inside; $15 outside. Set up on Saturday and there is security. Reservations are required inside only; first come, first served outside. Free coffee is available to all dealers.

CONTACT: Bill Edwards, Bil-Mar Promotions, P.O. Box 99, Amboy, IL 61310. Tel: (815) 626-7601. Day of show call (815) 857-3488.

CHICAGO
Ashland Avenue Swap-O-Rama

DATES: Thursday, Saturday and Sunday.

TIMES: Thursday 2:00 PM–9:00 PM; Saturday and Sunday 7:00 AM–4:00 PM.

ADMISSION: $.50 per person; free parking.

LOCATION: 4100 South Ashland Avenue. One mile west of I-94, near White Sox Park.

DESCRIPTION: Started in 1990, there are now 500 to 600 indoor and outdoor dealers exhibiting fresh produce and new merchandise. Three restaurants serve the hungry.

DEALER RATES: $17 per 12' × 8' inside space; $6 per 24' × 12' outside space. Reservations are suggested.

CONTACT: Jim Pierski, Swap O Rama, 4600 West Lake Street, Melrose Park, IL 60160. Tel: (708) 344-7300.

CHICAGO HEIGHTS
Country Peddler Show

DATES: November 11–13, 1994.

TIMES: Friday 4:00 PM–9:00 PM; Saturday 9:00 AM–5:00 PM; Sunday 11:00 AM–4:00 PM.

ADMISSION: Adults $5; children 2–12 years $2. Parking is free.

LOCATION: Chicagoland Convention Center. 90 North Street, Park Forest.

DESCRIPTION: This show specializes in collectibles and craft items, with top exhibitors displaying the finest in folk art in the United States. Food is available on the premises. There is a sister market in Lincoln at the end of April. This show is one of a series run throughout the East Coast from Michigan to Florida.

DEALER RATES: $375 per 10' × 10' booth; $562.50 per 10' × 15' booth; $750 per 10' × 20' booth. Reservations are required.

CONTACT: American Memories, P.O. box 249, Decatur, MI 49045-0249. Tel: (616) 423-8367 or fax: (616) 423-2421.

CICERO
Cicero Swap O Rama

DATES: Saturday and Sunday, year round.

TIMES: 7:00 AM–4:00 PM.

ADMISSION: $.50. Parking is free.

LOCATION: 1333 South Cicero Avenue. Just south of I-290 on Cicero Avenue (Route 50).

DESCRIPTION: This market started in 1980 with between 150 to 300 dealers selling antiques, collectibles, handmade crafts, fresh produce, and new merchandise. A full service restaurant is on the premises.

DEALER RATES: $15 per 8' × 12' booth indoors: $8 per 12' × 24' booth outdoors. Reservations are suggested.

CONTACT: Jim Pierski, Swap O Rama, 4600 West Lake Street, Melrose Park, IL 60160. Tel: (708) 344-7300.

LINCOLN
Country Peddler Show

DATES: April 29–30, May 1, 1994. Check for the same weekend in following years.

TIMES: Friday 4:00 PM–9:00 PM; Saturday 9:00 AM–5:00 PM; Sunday 11:00 AM–4:00 PM.

ADMISSION: Adults $5; children 2–12 years $2. Parking is free.

LOCATION: Logan County Fairgrounds. Take I-55 City Loop at Woodlawn, Exit 126, follow fairground signs.

DESCRIPTION: Started in 1982, this show specializes in collectibles, and craft items, with 100 top exhibitors displaying the finest in folk art in the United States. Food is available on the premises.

DEALER RATES: $375 per 10' × 10' booth; $562.50 per 10' × 15' booth; $750 per 10' × 20' booth. Reservations are required.

CONTACT: American Memories, P.O. box 249, Decatur, MI 49045-0249. Tel: (616) 423-8367 or fax: (616) 423-2421.

MELROSE PARK
Melrose Park Swap-O-Rama

DATES: Every Friday, Saturday, and Sunday.

TIMES: 7:00 AM–4:00 PM Saturday and Sunday; Friday 10:00 AM–5:00 PM.

ADMISSION: $.50 per person. Free parking is available for 600 cars.

LOCATION: 4600 West Lake Street, at corner of Lake Street (Route 20) and Mannheim Road (Route 45).

DESCRIPTION: Started in 1975, 350 dealers both indoors and outdoors offer antiques, fine art, arts and crafts, fresh produce, collectibles, and new merchandise. Food is served on the premises.

DEALER RATES: $18 per 12' × 8' space inside, and $10 per 12' × 24' space outside. Reservations are suggested.
CONTACT: Jim Pierski, Swap O Rama, 4600 West Lake Street, Melrose Park, IL 60160. Tel: (708) 344-7300.

PECATONICA
The "Pec-Thing"

DATES: May 14 & 15 (third Sunday weekend); September 17 & 18.
TIMES: 8:00 AM–5:00 PM.
ADMISSION: $2 per person. Plenty of free parking is available.
LOCATION: Winnebago County Fairgrounds in Pecatonica, 7th and 4th Street entrances.
DESCRIPTION: Started in 1980, this market operates both indoors and out. Over 400 dealers sell antiques, collectibles, handmade crafts, and new and used items. All food must pass Fair Board approval. Several local homes are listed in the National Registry. Breakfast and lunch are served on the premises by one restaurant and six snack bars.
DEALER RATES: $25 per 10' × 25' space outdoors per weekend; $35 per 16' × 12' open outdoor shed; $50 per 16' × 12' indoor space per weekend. Tables are extra. Reservations are required. Friday setup 2:00 PM–9:00 PM, gates open at 6:00 AM for set up Saturday and Sunday. Also they have some space on a first come, first served basis.
CONTACT: Manager, P.O. Box 38, Pecatonica, IL 61063. Tel: (815) 239-1188. Day of show call (815) 239-1641.

PEOTONE
Antique Show

DATES: Fourth Sunday of each month except August and December. Also May 29 and October 30, 1994. Rain or shine.
TIMES: 7:00 AM–4:00 PM.
ADMISSION: $2 per person. Free parking is available.
LOCATION: Will County Fairgrounds. South of Chicago between Chicago and Kankakee, one mile east of I-57.
DESCRIPTION: Started in 1967, this show is held inside an air-conditioned building. Sixty-five dealers display a variety of antiques and collectibles. The market boasts lots of good glassware and primitives, and excellent meals. If it's possible, they manage to have a two-day show on the fourth weekend in December. When weather permits, there are outside dealers as well.

DEALER RATES: $60 for four-table booth approximately 15' × 10', $70 for a 5-table booth. Large space outside: $25. Reservations are not required.

CONTACT: Robert W. Mitchell, Jr., 223 E. Main Street, Amboy, IL 61310. Tel: (815) 857-2253 days; (815) 857-3328 evenings. Day of show call Will County Fairgrounds at (312) 258-3266.

ROCKFORD
Greater Rockford Antique and Flea Market
DATES: Every Saturday and Sunday, rain or shine.
TIMES: 9:00 AM–5:00 PM.
ADMISSION: Free admission and parking.
LOCATION: Alpine/Sandy Hollow Road at 3913 Sandy Hollow Road. Take Highway 20 to Alpine exit, go north to Sandy Hollow, then west 1½ blocks.
DESCRIPTION: Started in 1976 at Alpine Village. At the current location, this market has room for 200 dealers outside and 60 indoors, offering antiques, fresh produce, collectibles (books, records, coins, baseball cards, etc.), and new merchandise. Food is served on the premises.
DEALER RATES: $22 per weekend for space measuring 10' × 12' inside (dealers must furnish own tables). Reservations are required in advance for indoor space only. $10 set-up fee outdoors.
CONTACT: Carol A. Fritsch, 6350 Canyon Wood Drive, Rockford, IL 61109. Tel: (815) 397-6683.

SANDWICH
Sandwich Antiques Market
DATES: Fourth Sundays in May, July, August, September, and October. But call just to make sure.
TIMES: 8:00 AM–4:00 PM.
ADMISSION: $3 per person. Parking is free.
LOCATION: The Fairgrounds, State Route 34. From I-88, Sugar Grove Exit to Route 30 to Hinckley. Follow signs on west side of Hinckley.
DESCRIPTION: Started in 1988, this 160-acre shaded outdoor market attracts 550 dealers selling only top-quality antiques and collectibles. It is the only market in Illinois where dealers must give a 10-day money back guarantee that the merchandise is as represented.

There is a furniture delivery service available. Food is available on the premises.

DEALER RATES: $80 per 25' × 25' outside booth: $85 per 10'x 10' inside booth. Reservations are required.

CONTACT: Robert C. Lawler, Show Manager, Sandwich Antiques Market, 1510 North Hoyne, Chicago IL 60622-1804. Tel: (312) 227-4464. Day of show call: (815) 786-3337.

SAUGET
Archview Flea Market

DATES: Saturday and Sunday, year round, floods permitting.

TIMES: 8:00 AM–5:00 PM.

ADMISSION: Free. Parking is free.

LOCATION: Route 3, from I-255 take Exit 13 (Cahokia) to U.S. 157 to Route 3, go north for about 3 miles.

DESCRIPTION: Opened in November 1992, a survivor of the 1993 Mississippi floods, this market has from 60 to 150 dealers selling mostly new merchandise. A sampling of the fare: Ozark Village wooden furniture, scissors, figurines, jewelry, sweatshirts, paper products, tools, wood, games, electronics (from TVs to computers to microwave ovens), some garage sale items, and collectibles. A "mini" restaurant serves homemade hot lunches on weekends (real good deal) and regular fare the rest of the time. Two sets of clean restrooms are available.

DEALER RATES: $15 for 100 square feet inside, $8 for outside. Reservations are requested, as many of their vendors are permanent.

CONTACT: Ron or Sandy Newsome, 1401 Mississippi Avenue, Bay 5, Sauget, IL 62202. Tel: (618) 271-1021.

ST. CHARLES
Kane County Flea Market

DATES: First Sunday of every month and preceding Saturday, rain or shine.

TIMES: Saturday 1:00 PM–5:00 PM; Sunday 7:00 AM–4:00 PM.

ADMISSION: $3. Free parking is available.

LOCATION: Kane County Fairgrounds (Randall Road); west side of St. Charles between Route 64 and Route 38.

DESCRIPTION: Having started with a humble 35 dealers in 1967, there are currently as many as 1,400 dealers (average 1,200 in summer, 800 in winter) selling antiques, fine art, collectibles, coins, fancy "junque" and the occasional new merchandise. Dealers, shoppers and collectors have come from as far away as Korea and all over the United States to shop here. "If you can't find it at Kane County, it was probably never made." There are four indoor buildings for winter months, and nine indoor buildings and seven sheds for summer months. This market has been listed in *Good Housekeeping* as one of the top 25 markets in the United States. So popular is this market, it prompted a local minister to ask: "Would Jesus skip church to shop at the Kane County Flea Market?" Plenty of good food—served by two restaurants and several snack bars, including country-style breakfast—is served on the premises.

DEALER RATES: $110 per 14' × 14' space indoors; $100 per weekend for a 10' × 20' space outdoors. Advance reservations are required for space under cover only; outside space is first come, first served. Setup Saturday at 9:00 AM. There is a parking lot in back for dealers.

CONTACT: Helen Robinson, Kane County Flea Market, Inc., P.O. Box 549, St. Charles, IL 60174. Tel: (708) 377-2252.

STERLING

Antique Show

DATES: March 12–13, July 9–10, and October 8–9.

TIMES: Saturday 10:00 AM–9:00 PM; Sunday 10:00 AM–5:00 PM.

ADMISSION: Free. Parking is also free.

LOCATION: Inside Northland Mall on Highway 2 East end of Sterling.

DESCRIPTION: This market started in 1973 with 50 to 55 dealers selling primarily antiques and collectibles and some flea market goods. This is a well-established show that attracts quite a crowd. Food is available on the premises.

DEALER RATES: $60 for two days and three-table booth (tables, furnished) and plug in for lights in all booths. Reservations are required, paid in advance. $85 for five-table booth.

CONTACT: Lois and Bob Mitchell, 223 East Main Street, Amboy, IL 61310. Tel: (815) 857-2253. After 5:00 PM call (815) 625-6909.

SYCAMORE

Antique, Craft, and Flea Market

DATES: The last full weekend in October.

TIMES: 9:00 AM–5:00 PM.

ADMISSION: $1.50 for adults; $1 senior citizens and students K-12, $.50; under 5 free. Free parking is available.

LOCATION: At the Sycamore High School. Take Route 23 south through downtown Sycamore to the south edge of town. Turn onto Spartan Trail at stop light on Route 23.

DESCRIPTION: This flea market, started in 1973 and currently consisting of 155 dealer booths, is operated by the Sycamore Music Boosters. It is run in conjunction with Sycamore's Annual Pumpkin Festival, which includes a variety of activities on that weekend, such as carved and decorated pumpkins on the Court House lawn (approximately 1,000), 10K race on Sunday, food booths, art fair, a haunted house, and a giant parade Sunday afternoon. Proceeds from all activities associated with the weekend are used to support music programs and activities in the community school district. It is estimated that approximately 100,000 people will visit the community over Pumpkin Festival weekend. This is a juried show, which in the past has had wool products, stained glass, handmade dolls, hand-carved wood products and other non-commercial goods produced by artists. Food is available on the grounds. The Huskie Bus Line will provide transportation between the school and the downtown area for $.50 per person. A "stroller park" is available, with attendants, as strollers are not allowed in the market. Sycamore is only 65 miles northwest of Chicago on Route 64.

DEALER RATES: $60 for 10' × 12' booth, reservations required.

CONTACT: Sycamore Music Boosters, P.O. Box 432, Sycamore, IL 60178. (Show chairmen change yearly.) Day of show call Beverly Smith at (815) 895-6750.

TOWANDA

Towanda Antique Flea Market

DATES: Every July 4th.

TIMES: 9:00 AM–5:00 PM, rain or shine.

ADMISSION: Free. Free parking is available.

LOCATION: Northwest of Bloomington, Illinois, on I-55, Exit 171.

DESCRIPTION: Started in 1968, the show has grown larger every year and currently features 200 dealers outdoors selling antiques, arts and crafts, collectibles, and new merchandise. This market has become known as a buyer's market because of the fair prices. Food is available on the premises.

DEALER RATES: $25 per 12' × 12' space. Reservations are required.
CONTACT: Lyle and Mary Merritt, P.O. Box 97, Towanda, IL 61776.
Tel: the Merritts at (309) 728-2810 or Linda Potts at (309) 728-2384.

WOODSTOCK

Woodstock Antiques and Collectibles Market

DATES: 1994 dates: Third Saturday monthly, April through September.
TIMES: 8:00 AM–4:00 PM.
ADMISSION: $2, kids under 12 free. Parking is free.
LOCATION: McHenry County Fairgrounds. From Chicago: take Route 90 north (to Rockford) Exit 47 north to Woodstock. From Milwaukee: Route 43 West to Route 120 South, through Lake Geneva, 15 minutes south of Lake Geneva (Route 120 becomes 47 over the Illinois border).
DESCRIPTION: Over 200 sellers have been vending primarily antiques, collectibles, old toys, bric-a-brac, and furniture at this market held both indoors and out. It is run more like a flea market than an antique show. Since 1989, several thousand buyers per week have been "picking up antiques and collectibles at flea market prices."
DEALER RATES: Outside $25 for 20' × 15' space; pavilions $35 for 20' × 10' space; inside $45 for 20' × 10' space. First come/first served, reservations are not required.
CONTACT: Zurko's Midwest Promotions, 211 West Green Bay Street, Shawano, WI 54166. Call Eileen Potasnik or Bob Zurko at (715) 526-9769 or 1-800-842-5174.

OTHER FLEA MARKETS

Chicago: Double Indoor Flea Market, 2750 West Columbus Avenue, Chicago, IL 60652. Tel: (312) 925-9602. Open weekends 6:00 AM–5:00 PM.

Chicago: Loew's Double Outdoor Flea Market, 2800 West Columbus Avenue, Chicago, IL 60652. Tel: (312) 925-9602. Open weekends 6:00 AM–4:00 PM.

Chicago: The Buyer's Flea Market, 4545 West Division Street, Chicago, IL 60651. Tel: (312) 227-1889. Open weekends 8:00 AM–5:00 PM.

Cicero: Casablanca Flea Market, 3200 South Cicero Avenue, Cicero, IL 60650. Tel: (708) 652-0867. Open weekends 8:00 AM–5:00 PM.

Danville: North Vermillion Flea Market, 120 East Wilson Street, Danville, IL 61832. Tel: (217) 431-4982. Open Friday 4:00 PM–9:00 PM, Saturday 8:00 AM–6:00 PM, Sunday 8:00 AM–5:00 PM.

Melrose Park: A.M. Bargain Bazaar Flea Market, 1945 Cornell, Melrose Park, IL 60160. Tel: (708) 450-0277. Open weekends 9:00 AM–5:00 PM.

South Chicago Heights: Show and Sell, Inc., Halsteds and Souk Trail Road, South Chicago Heights, IL 60661. Tel: (708) 574-3737. Open Friday and Saturday 12:00 PM on, Sunday 8:00 AM–4:00 PM.

Tinley Park: I-80 Collectable & Flea Market, 191 and Oak Park Avenue, Tinley Park, IL 60477. Tel: (708) 532-8238. Open weekends 6:00 AM–2:00 PM.

Waukegan: Waukegan Swap'N'Swap Flea Market, Belvidere Mall, Route 120 East & Lewis Avenue, Waukegan, IL 60085. Tel: (708) 263-0160. Open Friday through Sunday 9:00 AM–6:00 PM.

Wheeling: Loews Twin Drive-In Flea Market, 1010 South Milwaukee Avenue, Wheeling, IL 60090. Tel: (708) 537-8223. Open weekends 6:00 AM–4:00 PM from March through November.

INDIANA

BROOKVILLE
White Farmers Market

DATES: Every Wednesday, rain or shine. Saturday and Sunday during the summer.

TIMES: Wednesday: 5:00 AM–1:30 PM. Saturday: 9:00 AM–1:00 PM, Sunday: 9:30 AM–2:00 PM.

ADMISSION: Free. Free parking is available.

LOCATION: White's Farm on Holland Road, three miles southeast of town on Highway 52. Thirty miles northwest of Cincinnati, Ohio.

DESCRIPTION: A combination flea market and livestock auction, this market was originally started by the present owner's grandfather in 1940. Currently there are between 350 and 400 dealers in summer and between 50 and 75 dealers in the winter selling antiques, arts and crafts, fresh produce and fruits, collectibles, and new merchandise on a 160-acre farm. Amish baked goods are offered as well as farm fresh eggs and small animals such as ducks, rabbits, and chickens. Next door to the farm one can see and visit the oldest church in Indiana on its original foundation. The market is located in the scenic Whitewater Valley. Indoor setups are located in the farm's original granary and tobacco barns. The buildings have been refurbished in the original antique atmosphere. They added more storage buildings for inside setups. Special events are held throughout the year. Be advised that Wednesday is still considered the *big* day.

DEALER RATES: $8 per 20' × 22' space outdoors. Reservations are not necessary for outside space, but are required for inside space. Inside spaces from $10 to $18, depending on size and location.

CONTACT: Dave or Paula White, 6119 Little Cedar Road, Brookville, IN 47012. Tel: (317) 647-3574 (business) or 647-5360 if desperate.

CANAAN
Canaan Fall Festival

DATES: Second weekend in September, rain or shine.

TIMES: Friday and Saturday 9:00 AM–10:00 PM; Sunday 9:00 AM–6:00 PM.

ADMISSION: Free. Free parking is available.

LOCATION: On the Canaan Village Square.

DESCRIPTION: Publicized as an old-fashioned event, this outdoor festival draws a very large crowd to this small village. Approximately

160 dealers sell a range of items from antiques and collectibles to craft items, fresh produce, and some new merchandise. Highlights include the longest-running annual Pony Express in the United States, plus many games, contests, and stage entertainment. On Saturday, the old-fashioned parade starts at 10:30 AM and features floats, bands, horses, a Postal Representative swearing in the Pony Express rider, and other events. The Fire Department's food concession does something special with its fish dish, it's a perennial favorite. The Kremer House Museum with three generations of furnishings was donated to the town in 1980 and is open to the public during this festival.

DEALER RATES: $25 per 20' × 20' space outside for the entire weekend plus $5 for electric. Or $10 per day.

CONTACT: Gale H. Ferris, President, Canaan Restoration Council, Inc., 9713 North State Road 62, Canaan, IN 47224. Tel: (812) 839-4770.

Wandering Pets

Years ago, a buffalo got loose from Rising Sun, a town in Ohio County, and wandered across two more counties, and through the Canaan Fall Festival. He didn't seem to be a problem, just visiting, but he really had people wondering. By the time the wanderer got to the Proving Grounds, he was deemed a hazard to population and killed. But the people of Canaan haven't forgotten their buffalo visitor.

CEDAR LAKE
Barn and Field Flea Market

DATES: Every Saturday and Sunday, rain or shine.

TIMES: Dawn to dusk.

ADMISSION: Free admission and free parking for 400 cars on the premises.

LOCATION: 150th and Parrish Avenue, 1 mile east of Route 41. Take I-65 to Lowell exit, then take west Route 2 to Parrish Avenue, then north on Parrish to 150th (approximately 7 miles).

DESCRIPTION: Started in 1978, there are now between 150 and 200 dealers at this indoor/outdoor market. The barn is open year round, the field as soon as or as late as weather permits. The atmosphere is country; the barn is 100 years old and houses antiques and collectibles from furniture and dolls (some of which are home-made antique dolls) to bottles, guns, jewelry, and bric-brac. Food is served on the premises, including home-baked goodies.

DEALER RATES: $2 per 18' space on Saturday; $3 on Sunday. Advance reservations are required only if electricity is needed. Dealer overnighters are welcome from Thursday noon until Monday noon.

CONTACT: C. and D. Corey (they live on the premises), P.O. Box 411, Cedar Lake, IN 46303-0411. Tel: (219) 696-7368.

CENTERVILLE

Big Bear Flea Market

DATES: Saturday and Sunday, April through October.

TIMES: 7:00 AM–5:00 PM.

ADMISSION: Free. Parking is free.

LOCATION: On I-70 at Centerville, Exit 145 at the south-east corner, 4 miles west of Richmond, Indiana.

DESCRIPTION: Opened in July, 1993, this market has hundreds of spaces with 80 under canopies. Their dealers sell everthing from antiques and collectibles to crafts, new merchandise, secondhand merchandise and produce. Delicious barbecue ribs, chicken, and other delectables are cooked onsite as well as lunch and short orders. There is a complete campground with RV hook-ups.

DEALER RATES: $8 a day or $15 for 2 days. Reservations are not required.

CONTACT: Ed or Shelby Newman, 2131 North Centerville Road, Centerville, IN 47330. Tel: (317) 855-3912.

FRANKLIN

Franklin Antique Flea Market

DATES: Third Saturday and Sunday, September through April, rain or shine.

TIMES: 9:00 AM–5:00 PM.

ADMISSION: Free admission and free parking.

LOCATION: At the Franklin County Fairgrounds on Fairgrounds Street. Take I-65 south from Indianapolis to Route 44 to Franklin. Junction 31 at Fairgrounds.

DESCRIPTION: This indoor show began operation in 1966 and is southern Indiana's largest. Although a small market with 40-45 dealers, they carry a variety of antiques and collectibles, as well as new merchandise. This is a very friendly market with good dealers. Concessions and a full kitchen provide food on the premises.

DEALER RATES: $28 for a 12' × 14' area and two tables, for both days. Reservations are required inside; not required outside.
CONTACT: Elmer Judkins, 122 Woodland Drive, New Whiteland, IN 46184. Tel: (317) 535-5084. Day of show call (317) 736-9800.

FRIENDSHIP
Friendship Flea Market

DATES: Two nine-day shows. 1994: June 10–18; September 12–20. Call for 1995 dates.
TIMES: All day and night, really, rain or shine.
ADMISSION: Free admission. Parking is available at $2 per vehicle.
LOCATION: On State Highway 62, 6 miles west of Dillsboro, Indiana.
DESCRIPTION: Started in 1968, this indoor/outdoor market consists of approximately 500 dealers selling antiques, arts and crafts, fresh produce, collectibles (such as guns, knives, and beads), and new merchandise. It is located on the grounds adjoining the National Muzzle Loading Rifle Association. Up to 100,000 people attend this event. Food is served on the premises. In 1984, this market was listed by *Good Housekeeping* magazine as one of the 25 best flea markets in the United States. It is the largest of the four markets within ½ mile of each other. Every night of the market, a campfire is crackling with country music entertainment. They really mean it is open day and night!
DEALER RATES: $110 for nine days per 10' × 10' space indoors or a 20' × 20' space outdoors. Advance reservations are required.
CONTACT: Tom Kerr or Jan Hopkins, 654 Wayskin Drive, Covington, KY 41015. Tel: (606) 356-7114. Days of the show call the flea market at (812) 667-5645.

FT. WAYNE
Fort Wayne Flea Market

DATES: Friday, Saturday and Sunday, year round, rain or shine.
TIMES: Friday 12:00 PM–6:00 PM; Saturday and Sunday 9:00 AM–6:00 PM.
ADMISSION: $.50. Free parking is available.
LOCATION: Highways 27 and 33 and South Hanna Street.
DESCRIPTION: Opened on August 1, 1990, this already successful market has 153 dealers in an air-conditioned and heated building sell-

ing typical flea market fare including: T-shirts, tools, coins, and quite a bit of new merchandise. There are some antiques and collectibles now, but they are planning to use a 33,000 square foot building next door for an antique mall. For your convenience, a food concession is on the premises.

DEALER RATES: $36 for 15' × 10' per weekend. Reservations are required as there is a waiting list.

CONTACT: Dean Morris, Fort Wayne Flea Market, 6901 South Hanna Street, Ft. Wayne, IN 46816. Tel: (219) 447-0081 Friday through Monday.

Indiana Flea Market at Ft. Wayne

DATES: 1994 dates: January 14–16, February 25–27, April 22–24, July 29–31, September 23–25, and November 11–13.

TIMES: Friday 3:00 PM–9:00 PM; Saturday 10:00 AM–7:00 PM; Sunday 11:00–5:00 PM.

ADMISSION: $1. Parking is free.

LOCATION: Allen County War Memorial Coliseum. Corner of Coliseum and Parnell Avenues.

DESCRIPTION: This new market started in 1991 with 400 dealers selling antiques, collectibles, and the usual flea market hode-podge. Already it is quite successful. Food is available on the premises.

DEALER RATES: $65 per 14' × 8' space; $98 per 21' × 8' space; $130 per 28' × 8' space. Reservations are required.

CONTACT: Stewart Promotions, 2950 Breckinridge Lane, Suite 4A, Louisville, KY 40220. Tel: (502) 456-2244 except Tuesday.

INDIANAPOLIS

Liberty Bell Flea Market

DATES: Friday through Sunday, year round.

TIMES: Friday 12:00 PM–8:00 PM; Saturday 10:00 AM–7:00 PM; Sunday 10:00 AM–6:00 PM.

ADMISSION: Free. Free parking is available.

LOCATION: 8949 East Washington Street (U.S. 40).

DESCRIPTION: This indoor/outdoor show has been operating for 16 years. Over 88 dealers spread over 200 spaces (they like this market!) sell everything and anything from antiques, collectibles, and new merchandise to produce, meats, cheese, and handmade items. There are food concessions on the grounds.

DEALER RATES: $45 per 12' × 14' booth per weekend. No advance reservations required.
CONTACT: Mr. Noble Hall, Liberty Bell Flea Market, 8949 East Washington Street, Indianapolis, IN 46219. Tel: (317) 898-3180.

Indiana Flea Market

DATES: 1994: January 21–23, February 11–13, March 18–20, April 8–10, May 20–22, June 24–26, July 15–17, September 3–5 (special), 23–25, October 14–16, November 25–27, and December 9–11. Three-day show monthly except for August during State Fair. Usually the second weekend each month, depending on availability of the fairgrounds.
TIMES: Friday noon to 8:00 AM; Saturday 10:00 AM–8:00 PM; Sunday 11:00 AM–5:00 PM.
ADMISSION: Free. Parking is also free.
LOCATION: Indianapolis State Fairgrounds.
DESCRIPTION: This indoor market opened in 1976 and hosts between 400 to 1,000 dealers depending on the season. There are special Antique and Country Craft shows scattered throughout their schedule in addition to the flea markets. Some of these scheduled events fill three buildings! The dealers sell mostly antiques, collectibles, and flea market treasures. Food is available on the premises.
DEALER RATES: $75 ($80 Labor Day) per 14' × 8' space; $113 ($120 Labor Day) per 21' × 8' space; $150 ($160 Labor Day) per 28' × 8' space depending on the building the show is housed in. Reservations are required, and there is a waiting list.
CONTACT: Stewart Promotions, 2950 Breckinridge Lane, Suite 4A, Louisville, KY 40220. Tel: (502) 456-2244 (except Tuesday).

LAWRENCEBURG

Tri-State Antique Market

DATES: Always the first Sunday of the month, from May through October.
TIMES: 7:00 AM–3:00 PM.
ADMISSION: $1 per adult. Free parking is available.
LOCATION: On Route 50, one mile west from Exit 16, off I-275.
DESCRIPTION: Started in 1986, this indoor/outdoor market now draws between 175 and 200 dealers from three surrounding states. The promoter of this show has said that this is where many shop owners come to stock their shelves and floor space, buying both fur-

niture and small items. "Lots of good treasures." Only antiques and old collectibles are sold. Food is served on the premises.

DEALER RATES: $20 per 20' × 20' outside space paid in advance or $25 at site; $20 per 10' × 15' space indoors. Advance reservations are not required for outside space, required for inside space; early birds are admitted for advance shopping.

CONTACT: Bruce Metzger, P.O. Box 238, Miamitown, OH 45041. Tel: (513) 353-2688. Day of show call Bruce Metzger at the number listed above.

Classic Market Tales

In 1989, in Lawrenceburg, there was a "dust devil" during the show. Hypnotized, the vendors and buyers watched this little mini-tornado form at the end of the fairgrounds. Slowly, it moved down the midway street of the market flipping tables, toppling cupboards, lifting cast iron ware and dropping it through glass showcases, scattering the "smalls" and lightweight merchandise. After traveling about 100 feet, the twister stood still, lifted off the ground and retreated back to the rear of the grounds, leaving choking dust in the air and wreckage marking its route.

Says Bruce Metzger, the promoter of this show: "No one was injured in this occurrence, although some merchandise sustained damage and some was just plain lost. It's a hell of a thing to be remembered for, but people still like to talk about the dust devil at Lawrenceburg."

METAMORA
Canal Days Flea Market

DATES: The first weekend in October, rain or shine.

TIMES: All day Saturday and Sunday.

ADMISSION: Free. Parking is available at $3 to $5 per vehicle.

LOCATION: From Indianapolis, take U.S. 52 east. From Cincinnati, go west on I-74 to Exit 169, then west on U.S. 52, and then go 8 miles west of Brookville.

DESCRIPTION: An estimated 125,000 people attend this October weekend, initiated in 1968. Currently between 700 and 1,000 dealers set up to sell antiques, fine art, arts and crafts, collectibles, and new merchandise. Metamora is a lovely old town with a canal and canal boat pulled by horses, and there is an old Grist Mill which still operates. There are over 150 shops open year round, and a passenger train runs on the weekends.

DEALER RATES: From $100 per 20' × 20' space. Reservations are required.

CONTACT: Al Rogers, P.O. Box 76, Metamora, IN 47030. Tel: (317) 647-2194.

MICHIGAN CITY
Lilac Park Country Fair, Craft and Flea Market

DATES: Friday, Saturday and Sunday, May through October.

TIMES: 10:00 AM–6:00 PM.

ADMISSION: Free. Parking is also free.

LOCATION: On County Road 1000 North, 1 mile west of State Route 39, 3 miles east of U.S. Route 12 on County Road 1000 North.

DESCRIPTION: Started in 1990, this market has 100 spaces and more available, with dealers selling wind chimes, wood crafts, toys, used merchandise, tapes, pottery, used clothes, crafts, and more. A snack bar serves food on the premises.

DEALER RATES: Free. First come, first served.

CONTACT: Don or Leona Turner, 2612 West 1000 North, Michigan City, IN 46360. Tel: (219) 874-6048.

MUNCIE
Greenwalt's Flea Market

DATES: January 8–9, February 12–13, March 5–6, April 9–10, May 7–8, September 10–11, October 8–9, November 5–6, and December 3–4.

TIMES: 9:00 AM–5:00 PM on Saturday; 9:00 AM–4:00 PM on Sunday.

ADMISSION: Free admission and free parking.

LOCATION: At Delaware Fairgrounds-Memorial Building. Take I-69 to Muncie/Frankton Exit 332. Go approximately 7 miles (becomes McGalliard Avenue) to Wheeling Avenue, then turn south and go 7 blocks to the Fairgrounds.

DESCRIPTION: This indoor market, which opened in 1976, houses approximately 65-70 dealers selling antiques, collectibles, handmade/craft items, toys, jewelry, baseball cards, and new merchandise. Food is available on the premises.

DEALER RATES: $35 a weekend for a 10' × 10' booth. Advance reservations are required.

CONTACT: Mary Greenwalt, 604 North Kettner Drive, Muncie, IN 47304. Tel: (317) 289-0194.

ROCKVILLE

RocKERRville Flea Market Extravaganza

DATES: October 14–23, 1994.
TIMES: 9:00 AM–6:00 PM.
LOCATION: Just 3 miles north of Rockville on U.S. 41.
ADMISSION: Free. Parking is free.
DESCRIPTION: Held at the same time as the Covered Bridge Festival in historic Parke County, this outdoor market hosts approximately 200 dealers selling antiques, crafts, collectibles, and new merchandise. Just for the record, there are 33 covered bridges in the area. There is food available.
DEALER RATES: $150 for the 10-day festival for a 20' × 20' space.
CONTACT: Tom Kerr or Jan Hopkins, RocKERRville, 654 Wayskin Drive, Covington, KY 41015. Tel: (606) 356-7114. For reservations call: (317) 498-8988.

SHIPSHEWANA

Shipshewana Auction and Flea Market

DATES: Every Tuesday and Wednesday, May through October; Wednesdays only, November through April, rain or shine.
TIMES: Tuesday 7:00 AM–6:00 PM, Wednesday 7:00 AM–4:00 PM, May through October; Wednesdays 8:30 AM–whenever the auction ends, November through April.
ADMISSION: Free. $2 per car parking.
LOCATION: On State Route 5 on the southern edge of Shipshewana, 160 miles north of Indianapolis, 50 miles east of South Bend and 100 miles south of Grand Rapids.
DESCRIPTION: This show first opened in 1922 and moved to its present location in 1947. It is held both indoors and outdoors and accommodates approximately 800 dealers (fewer in winter) and has room for more. Just about anything you might want can be found at this market, from antiques and collectibles to fine art, arts and crafts, new merchandise, and fresh produce. There is also a Miscellaneous and Antique Auction every Wednesday at 8:00 AM, and a livestock auction at 11:00 AM. The widely known Horse Sale is held on Fridays at 9:30 AM and always draws a full house of spectators. One full ser-

vice, and three fast food restaurants, one snack bar and four drink stands take care of any possible hungers.

DEALER RATES: Approximately $18–$28 per 20' × 25' space outdoors, for two days; $25–$45 per 8½' × 10' spaceindoors, for two days. Reservations are required.

CONTACT: Kevin Lambright, P.O. Box 185, Shipshewana, IN 46565. Tel: (219) 768-4129.

SOUTH BEND
Thieves' Market Mall

DATES: Every Saturday and Sunday, rain or shine.
TIMES: 10:00 AM–6:00 PM.
ADMISSION: Free. Free parking is available.
LOCATION: 2309 East Edison Road at Ironwood.
DESCRIPTION: This indoor/outdoor market has been operating for 24 years. It is a true mall, with 30 permanent vendors selling their antiques and collectibles from individual shops. They now have a train shop, baseball cards and hobby shop. With room for more dealers outside, sellers offer everything from jewelry to antiques to new merchandise. Food is available at three nearby restaurants.
DEALER RATES: $5 per 12' × 30' space outside per day. $80 per month for a 8' × 12' inside space, more if a larger space is available. Inside space is rented by the month. No lease is required.
CONTACT: David Ciesiolka, P.O. Box 6114, South Bend, IN 46615. Tel: (219) 233-9820.

TERRE HAUTE
Terre Haute Flea Market

DATES: April 16–17, June 11–12, and August 6–7
TIMES: Saturday 8:00 AM–6:00 PM, Sunday 9:00 AM–5:00 PM.
ADMISSION: Free. Parking is free.
LOCATION: Vigo County Fairgrounds.
DESCRIPTION: This market, one of several run by Stewart Promotions in Indiana and Kentucky has over 200 dealers inside selling about 60 percent antiques and collectibles and 40 percent crafts and new items. Generally, the collectible dealers set-up under the sheds.
DEALER RATES: $15 daily outside; indoor $55 for a 14' × 8' space; sheds $45 for a 12' × 12' space.
CONTACT: Stewart Promotions, 2950 Breckenridge Lane, Suite 4A, Louisville, KY 40220. Tel: (502) 456-2244 except Tuesdays.

Vigo County Historical Society Flea Market

DATES: 1994 dates: June 4 and September 25. Usually the first Saturday in June and and fourth Sunday in September. Rain or shine.
TIMES: 9:00 AM–4:00 PM.
ADMISSION: Free. Free parking is available.
LOCATION: Spring show: Historical Building, 1411 South Sixth Street. Turn east off U.S. 41 onto College and go 2 blocks down. Fall show: Paul Dresser Memorial Birthplace, Fairbanks Park. Call for directions.
DESCRIPTION: This is an outdoor market which opened in 1976 and now accommodates approximately 20 to 25 dealers. All participants are cautioned that items sold must be primarily antiques, collectibles, or related to the traditional craft markets. The market also has a nice variety of ornamental plants and herbs. It is interesting to note that dealers consist of professionals in the antiques and collectibles field, some who are breaking up family estates, as well as those who are just cleaning out their attics. This market is a fund-raising activity for the Historical Society. The Saturday June market coincides with the local Historic District of Farrington Grove's annual "neighborhood party—street faire" used as a fund-raiser for the Historical Society. Food booths are everywhere, activities for children, yard sales and loads of events. Restroom facilities are available.
DEALER RATES: $15 per space. Reservations are preferred. Booth space fees go the Society and are tax-deductible.
CONTACT: Marylee Hagan, Vigo Historical Society, 1411 South Sixth Street, Terre Haute, IN 47802. Tel: (812) 235-9717.

OTHER FLEA MARKETS

Fort Wayne: Speedway Mall, 217 Marciel Drive, Fort Wayne, IN 46825. Tel: (219) 484-1239. Open Friday 9:00 AM–9:00 PM, weekends 9:00 AM–5:00 PM.

Indianapolis: West Washington Flea Market, 6445 West Washington Street, Indianapolis, IN 46241. Tel: (317) 244-0941. Open Friday 1:00 PM–9:00 PM, Saturday 11:00 AM–7:00 PM, Sunday 11:00 AM–6:00 PM.
Lake Station: Central Avenue Flea Market, 2750 Central Avenue, Lake Station, IN 46405. Tel: (219) 962-5524. Open weekends 9:00 AM–4:00 PM.
Muncie: Main Street Flea Market, 1710 East Main Street, Muncie, IN 47303. Tel: (317) 289-5394. Open weekends 9:00 AM–5:00 PM.

IOWA

AMANA COLONIES
Collector's Paradise Flea Market

DATES: Fourth weekend in June.

TIMES: Saturday 7:00 AM–5:00 PM, Sunday 7:00 AM–4:00 PM.

LOCATION: Amana Colonies Outdoor Convention Facility. At Exit 225 off I-80, 12 miles north. Across from the Visitors Center.

ADMISSION: $1, 12 and under free with an adult. Parking is free. Early bird admission $2 on Friday.

DESCRIPTION: Opened in 1992, this indoor/outdoor market hosts 200 dealers selling antiques, collectibles, old tools, primitives, coins, furniture, glassware, jewelry, stamps, postcards, baseball cards, and new merchandise. If this market is as successful as their What Cheer markets, buyers and sellers are in for a treat. Food is available at the market. Amana Colonies is a top tourist attraction in Iowa. See their companion market at What Cheer three times a year.

DEALER RATES: $30 for 20' × 40' booth. Dealer set-up starts Friday at 7:00 AM. No reservations taken; first come, first served.

CONTACT: Larry D. Nicholson, P.O. Box 413, What Cheer, IA 50268. Tel: (515) 634-2109.

DUBUQUE
Dubuque Flea Market

DATES: February 20, April 24, October 9.

TIMES: 8:00 AM–4:00 PM.

ADMISSION: $1 for 12 and over, 11 and under free. Parking is free.

LOCATION: Five miles west of town on Highway 20, at Dubuque County Fairgrounds.

DESCRIPTION: This indoor/outdoor market began in 1970. Approximately 100 to 160 dealers sell a variety of antiques, collectibles, art objects, and crafts. Among the local attractions are a dog track and river boats. For your convenience, there is food available on the premises.

DEALER RATES: $11 per 8' space inside including a table; wall space is $12; $10 per 20' × 20' space outside with no table. Reservations are required for inside space. Outside is first come, first served.

CONTACT: Norma and Francis Koppen, 1887 Carter Road, Dubuque, IA 52001. Tel: (319) 583-7940.

LAKE OKOBOJI AT MILFORD
Treasure Village Flea Market and Antiques Shows

DATES: Memorial Day weekend (Saturday through Monday); July 4th weekend; Labor Day weekend (Saturday through Monday); and first weekend in August (Saturday and Sunday). Call for specific dates as July 4th falls on different days each year.

TIMES: 8:00 AM–6:00 PM.

ADMISSION: Free. Parking is also free.

LOCATION: Treasure Village, 2033 Highway 86, 3 miles northwest of Milford.

DESCRIPTION: Held outdoors under the trees, this market generally limits its dealers to about 70. They show a variety of toys, coins, collectibles, primitives, antiques, sports cards, crafts, tools, and novelties, among other treasures. To amuse the children there is a children's theater, and for everyone there is miniature golf. Hand-dipped ice cream, sandwiches, and the usual concession fare are available. This is a real family affair and social gathering for the local residents. Lake Okoboji is one of only three "blue-water lakes" in the world; the others are Lake Geneva in Switzerland and Lake Louise in Canada. It is also the number one tourist attraction in Iowa.

DEALER RATES: $55 for a 20' × 20' space Memorial Day, Labor Day and July 4th; August first weekend $40. Reservations are required. Prepaid reservations are allowed a discount.

CONTACT: Garth Neisess, Manager, 2033 Highway 86, Milford, IA 51351. Tel: (712) 337-3730.

OTTUMWA
Collector's Fair

DATES: Saturday and Sunday.

TIMES: 9:00 AM–4:00 PM.

ADMISSION: $.50. Parking is free.

LOCATION: Ottumwa Coliseum basement, between Highways 34 and 63.

DESCRIPTION: This indoor market began in 1970. It attracts approximately 40 dealers selling antiques and collectibles. Food is served on the premises.

DEALER RATES: $12.50 per 2½' × 8' table. Reservations are required.

CONTACT: Dwight Jones, RR#2 Box 228, Ottumwa, IA 52501. Tel: (515) 684-6719.

SPIRIT LAKE

Annual Antique Show and Flea Market at Vick's Corner

DATES: Memorial Day, July 4th, and Labor Day weekends.

TIMES: 8:00 AM–6:00 PM.

ADMISSION: Free. Parking is also free.

LOCATION: Junction of Highways 9 and 86 at Vick's Corner.

DESCRIPTION: This market started the Spirit Lake market corner in 1966. Sixty-nine dealers from 10 different states sell antiques, collectibles, and primitives. Absolutely no junk is allowed. People plan their vacations around these market days as the dealers who come here are famous throughout the country for the quality of their goods. This is a ten-acre grove area, all grassed, and kept up like a golf course. Vick's Corner is a general store established in 1930 and a well-known landmark in the area. Food concessions and restrooms are onsite.

DEALER RATES: $75 per booth for one show. Reservations are highly recommended.

CONTACT: L.W. Vick, Vick's Corner, Junction of Highways 9 and 86, Box 9131, Spirit Lake, IA 51360 Tel: (712) 336-1912 or 336-1496.

Wa-Hoo Market

DATES: Weekends of Memorial Day, July 4th, and Labor Day.

TIMES: 9:00 AM–dark.

ADMISSION: Free. Parking is also free.

LOCATION: On the southwest corner of the junction of Routes 9 and 86. About 10 miles south of I-90, Exit 64 (Highway 86) to junction of 86 and 9. In the northwest corner of the state. About 90 miles southeast of Sioux Falls.

DESCRIPTION: This market started in 1979 with overflow from the other two markets at Spirit Lake in 1979. There are from 45 to 55 dealers and the number is growing rapidly. They added more space in 1993 and can accommodate up to 150 dealers. Selling antiques, collectibles, and "good rummage sale stuff to classic antiques," the market also sells some newer items, but the latter aren't encouraged. Crafts are not encouraged here simply because they don't sell very well. People from all over the country plan their vacations to come to the three markets here in Spirit Lake. From 3,000 to 7,000 visitors come through here per weekend and most of them are buyers. Suppers and breakfasts are available plus regular concession food. Meals are reasonably priced.

DEALER RATES: $45 plus electric for a 20' deep by 50' frontage space. If you need more than 50', add $1 per foot. Reservations are not required, but suggested if traveling quite a distance to get there. The managers are also dealers and hold regular meetings after supper on the second evening of each market to exchange ideas.

CONTACT: Doc Howard, Box 385, Howard, SD 57349. Tel: (605) 772-5376. Best time to call is evenings (between 9:00 PM and 2:00 AM, really!). A few days before and during the show, you can call (712) 336-1453.

WHAT CHEER

Collectors Paradise Flea Market

DATES: Weekends of the first Sundays in May, August, and October.

TIMES: Saturday 7:00 AM–5:00 PM, Sunday 7:00 AM–4:00 PM.

ADMISSION: $1 per person, 12 and under free with adult. Free parking is available.

LOCATION: At the Keokuk County Fairgrounds in What Cheer. Take Exit 201 off I-80 and drive south 20 miles on Highway 21.

DESCRIPTION: According to local shoppers, Larry Nicholson's Collectors Paradise is well named. Having started this indoor/outdoor market in 1977, Mr. Nicholson has raised dealer attendance up to around 400, with some dealers showing up for setup as early as the Wednesday before the show. Dealers come from all of the Midwest states. This market is one of the major antique and collectible markets in the Midwest. Shoppers, who can number as many as 7,000, are invited on the Saturday preceding the main sale day, for the same $1 fee, to get an early chance to browse through the innumerable bargains. Antiques and collectibles of every shape and size are to be found here including glassware, toys, tools, coins, jewelry, stamps, baseball cards, postcards, primitives, furniture, and more. Among the foods served is funnel cake, a favorite among local flea marketeers. Lunch is available.

DEALER RATES: $30 for outside space for the weekend. Reservations are required.

CONTACT: Larry D. Nicholson, P.O. Box 413, What Cheer, IA 50268. Tel: (515) 634-2109.

KANSAS

HUTCHINSON
Mid-America Flea Markets

DATES: First Sunday of each month, October through June.

TIMES: 9:00 AM–4:00 PM.

ADMISSION: $.50 per person. Free parking is available.

LOCATION: At the Kansas State Fairgrounds, well marked in Hutchinson.

DESCRIPTION: This indoor market first opened its doors in 1964. Currently there are approximately 200 dealers that specialize in a variety of types of antiques and collectibles, exhibiting miscellaneous items at a wide range of prices. There is food available on the premises.

DEALER RATES: $15 per 10' × 12' space. Reservations are required.

CONTACT: Av Hardesty, Mid-America Flea Markets, P.O. Box 1585, Hutchinson, KS 67504. Tel: (316) 663-5626.

OPOLIS
Opolis Flea Market

DATES: Most Saturdays, every Sunday, and by chance, year round, rain or shine.

TIMES: Daylight hours.

ADMISSION: Free, with free parking.

LOCATION: On the Kansas-Missouri State Line; junction of U.S. 171 and 57.

DESCRIPTION: Since 1978 this relatively small flea market sells mainly antiques and collectibles, including miscellaneous Volkswagen autos and parts. They have four permanent dealers, including one who has "the most gorgeous things." It is held both indoors and outdoors in this historic town—one of the oldest in Kansas. Snacks and refreshments are available on the premises. I've heard from the grapevine that this is definitely a market to visit. Especially for dealers.

DEALER RATES: Call for availability, as there wasn't any space available as we went to press. But you never know.

CONTACT: Norma Kukovich, Box 42, Opolis, KS 66760. Tel: (316) 231-2543.

PITTSBURGH
The Warehouse

DATES: Daily.

TIMES: 10:00 AM–6:00 PM, except Sundays 1:00 PM–6:00 PM. They have been known to stay open until 9:30 PM because the customers are having too much fun to leave. Try the door, if it's open, enter. Otherwise, try again.

ADMISSION: Free. Parking is free.

LOCATION: 612 South Broadway.

DESCRIPTION: Opened in 1993, this market has 50 dealers (and growing) year round, selling antiques, collectibles, toys, primitives, tools, beer signs, and whatever. If a customer wants something, they will look for it. After the infamous '93 floods, the dealers went looking to fill in the household goods blanks with affordable merchandise to help their customers. Located in a 10,000 square-foot building they can just keep going and going. And the building is located in the center of a city block with glass windows facing the street and surrounded by huge parking lots used for market space.

DEALER RATES: Outdoors–free; indoors from $20 to $50 per space. Reservations are required.

CONTACT: Jody Monsour, The Warehouse, 612 South Broadway, Pittsburg, KS 66762. Tel: (316) 231-6429.

WICHITA
Village Flea Market

DATES: Every Friday, Saturday, and Sunday, rain or shine.

TIMES: 9:00 AM–6:00 PM.

ADMISSION: Free. Parking is also free.

LOCATION: At 2301 South Meridian.

DESCRIPTION: This indoor/outdoor market first opened in 1974. Their 125 to 150 dealers sell everything from antiques and collectibles to handmade craft items, vegetables, meats, and cheeses. An interesting variety of garage items are also available. For your comfort the building is heated as well as air-conditioned. It is also equipped with a modern security system. Food is available on the premises.

DEALER RATES: $27 per 10' × 10' booth. Space is rented on a first come, first served basis.

CONTACT: Dale Cooper, 2301 South Meridian, Wichita, KS 67213. Tel: (316) 942-8263.

Mid-America Flea Markets

DATES: Irregular dates. Either 3rd or 4th Sunday, September through June.

TIMES: 9:00 AM–4:00 PM.

ADMISSION: $.50 per person. Free parking is available.

LOCATION: At the Kansas Coliseum, at the intersection of 85th Street and I-135.

DESCRIPTION: This market opened in 1977. It accommodates approximately 650 dealers and is among the largest indoor market in the Midwest. Approximately 5,000 people attend each Sunday to view a large selection of antiques and collectibles; there is always a wide variety to choose from, at a wide range of prices. For your convenience, food is served on the premises.

DEALER RATES: $15 per 8' × 10' space. Reservations are required.

CONTACT: Av Hardesty, Mid-America Flea Markets, P.O. Box 1585, Hutchinson, KS 67504. Tel: (316) 663-5626.

OTHER FLEA MARKETS

Kansas City: Boulevard Swap & Shop, 1051 Merriam Lane, Kansas City, KS 66103. Tel: (913) 262-2414. Open weekends 7:00 AM–2:00 PM.

KENTUCKY

FLEMINGSBURG

Flemingsburg Monday Court Days

DATES: Second Monday and preceding weekend of October, rain or shine.

TIMES: Saturday, sunup to whenever; Sunday 12:00 NOON until Monday 10:00 PM.

ADMISSION: Free. Parking is also free.

LOCATION: The entire town of Flemingsburg! In the center of town, on Main Street.

DESCRIPTION: Started in 1969 to continue the tradition of the circuit judge plying this trade (trials and hangings), this town turns into a huge market centered in downtown Flemingsburg. From 450 to 600 outside vendors sell everything and anything you can imagine—old, new, and otherwise. They do try to have a booth or two of unusual things like games and rides for kids, clogging, and live entertainment. For 1994, they are arranging a traveling carnival to coincide with Court Days. This shebang ends with a good old-fashioned square-dance on Monday night. See also Maysville and Mt. Sterling for the first and third Monday Court Days markets and you too can follow the judge's historical circuit.

DEALER RATES: Setup anytime after 6:00 PM Saturday. $40 per space for the two days; $20 per day. Reservations are strongly recommended.

CONTACT: June Mason, Route 3 Box 159A, Flemingsburg, KY 41041. Tel: (606) 849-4942.

FORT MITCHELL

Country Peddler Show

DATES: Annually. Third weekend in August. 1994: August 19–21.

TIMES: Friday, 4:00 PM–9:00 PM; Saturday 9:00 AM–5:00 PM; Sunday 11:00 AM–4:00 PM.

ADMISSION: $5 for adults, $2 for children 12 and under. There is ample free parking.

LOCATION: Drawbridge Estates and Convention Center. Take I-75 at Buttermilk Pike exit, 5 miles south of Cincinnati.

DESCRIPTION: This indoor market, started in 1986, features 100 dealers. They gather annually to sell a variety of collectibles, arts and crafts, fine art, and new merchandise. What makes this event special are the folk artisans featuring one-of-a-kind heirlooms of the future. For your convenience there is food available on the premises. This show is one of a series of Country Peddler Shows held throughout the East Coast from Florida to Michigan and Wisconsin. All products at these shows are American made.

DEALER RATES: $375 per 10' × 10' booth; $562.50 per 10' × 15' booth; $750 per 10' × 20' booth. Reservations are required.

CONTACT: American Memories, Inc., P.O. Box 249, Decatur, MI 49045-0249. Tel: (616) 423-8367 or fax: (616) 423-2421.

GEORGETOWN
Country World Flea Market

DATES: Friday through Sunday, April through November.

TIMES: Friday 7:00 PM–Sunday afternoon, sometime.

ADMISSION: Free. Parking is free.

LOCATION: On U.S. Route 460 off I-75, Georgetown interchange at Exit 125.

DESCRIPTION: Founded in 1967, and temporarily closed for two and a half years, this market is back! With up to 250 dealers selling antiques, collectibles, crafts, farm goods, and "everything in the world." (Even coffins occasionally.) There are food concessions on-site.

DEALER RATES: $8 on Saturday, $10 on Sunday for 14' × 30' space per day. First come, first served. No reservations needed or taken.

CONTACT: Glenn Juett, 111 Montgomery Avenue, Georgetown, KY 40324. Tel: (502) 863-0474 (business) or 863-0289 (home).

GREENVILLE
Luke's Town and Country Flea Market

DATES: Monday and Tuesday, year round, weather permitting.

TIMES: 8:00 AM–dark Monday; 6:00 AM–2:00 PM Tuesday.

ADMISSION: Free, with free parking.

LOCATION: Highway 62 West 1 mile from Greenville city limits.

DESCRIPTION: This outdoor market has been operating since May, 1979. On Monday about 25 to 50 dealers show. Tuesdays are busier, with between 200 and 400 dealers selling antiques, collectibles, crafts, new merchandise, and produce, as well as poultry and livestock. The surrounding area is rustically scenic, with Lake Malone and many other state parks nearby. There is a real family atmosphere here and a large antique display and collection to view (but not for sale) and three antique shops nearby. Food is available on the grounds.

DEALER RATES: $3 and up per 8' × 10' space per day Tuesdays; $2 on Mondays. Reservations are appreciated but not necessary.

CONTACT: Wayne and Judy Rice, Managers, Luke's Town and Country Flea Market, Route #1, Highway 62 West, Greenville, KY 42345. Tel: (502) 338-4920.

HENDERSON
Ellis Park Flea Market

DATES: May 13–15, June 17–19, September 9–11, October 7–9, 1994.

TIMES: Friday 1:00 PM–6:00 PM, Saturday 10:00 AM–6:00 PM, Sunday 10:00 AM–5:00 PM.

ADMISSION: Free. Parking is free.

LOCATION: Ellis Park Race Track.

DESCRIPTION: This market is one of a series of highly successful markets held throughout Indiana and Kentucky. With almost as many outside booths as there are inside booths (300 total), it sells mostly newer merchandise and crafts—a good mix of merchandise. This can be a very adventurous market to visit. Because it is actually on the *north* side of the Ohio River and *still* in Kentucky (a most unusual occurrence to be blamed on the shifting river), this market tends to experience strange weather patterns—a mini-tornado, 85° one day, snow the next—particularly during the May and October shows. Just come prepared.

DEALER RATES: $65 for 14' × 8' space, $98 for 21' × 8' space, $130 for 28' × 8' space.

CONTACT: Stewart Promotions, 2950 Breckinridge Lane, Suite 4A, Louisville, KY 40220. Tel: (502) 456-2244 or fax: (502) 456-2298.

LEITCHFIELD
Bratcher's Flea Market

DATES: Wednesday and Saturday, year round, weather permitting.

TIMES: Dawn–2:00 PM.

ADMISSION: Free admission and parking, including overnight before show days.

LOCATION: On Highway 62, 1 mile east of Leitchfield.

DESCRIPTION: This market opened over 30 years ago and is run by the daughter of the founder. Approximately 100 dealers sell their antiques and collectibles outdoors. Handicrafts, new merchandise, and produce in season are also for sale. This is a well-managed, well-run market. There is a food concession at the market.

DEALER RATES: $6 per 8' × 10' space per day. Reservations for the month are suggested.

CONTACT: Mrs. Gladys Bratcher, Owner, Bratcher's Flea Market, P.O. Box 396, Leitchfield, KY 42754-0396. Tel: (502) 259-3571.

LEXINGTON
Antique and Flea Market

DATES: January 7–9, March 25–27, June 3–5, July 22–24, August 26–28, October 21–23, November 18–20, December 2–4, 1994.

TIMES: Friday and Saturday 11:00 AM–8:00 PM; Sunday 11:00 AM–5:00 PM.

ADMISSION: Free. Parking is also free.

LOCATION: Lexington Center. Downtown Main and Patterson.

DESCRIPTION: Started in 1980 this market has about 250 dealers selling antiques, collectibles and flea market fare and everything else but food or weapons. This is considered a fine antique market. Food is available on the premises.

DEALER RATES: $70 per 14' × 8' space; $105 per 21' × 8' space; $140 per 24' × 8' space. Reservations are not required.

CONTACT: Stewart Promotions, 2950 Breckinridge Lane, Suite 4A, Louisville, KY 40220. Tel: (502) 456-2244 except Tuesday.

LOUISVILLE
Country Peddler Show

DATES: Annually. Usually the second weekend in March. 1994: March 11–13.

TIMES: Friday 4:00 PM–9:00 PM; Saturday 9:00 AM–5:00 PM; Sunday 11:00 AM–4:00 PM.

ADMISSION: Adults $5; children 2–12 years $2 each day.

LOCATION: Commonwealth Conference Center at 221 Fourth Avenue.

DESCRIPTION: This indoor market, started in 1983, features 70 exhibitors. They gather annually to sell a variety of collectibles, arts and crafts, fine art, and new merchandise. Exhibiting here are folk artisans featuring one-of-a-kind heirlooms of the future. For your convenience there is food available on the premises. This show is one of a series of Country Peddler Shows held throughout the East Coast. All items shown here are completely American made.

DEALER RATES: $375 per 10' × 10' booth; $562.50 per 10' × 15' booth; $750 per 10' × 20' booth. Reservations are required.
CONTACT: American Memories, Inc., P.O. Box 249, Decatur, MI 49045-0249. Tel: (616) 423-8367 or fax: (616) 423-2421.

Derby Park Trader's Circle

DATES: Friday, Saturday, and Sunday, year round, rain or shine.
TIMES: 8:00 AM–6:00 PM.
ADMISSION: Free. Free parking for public.
LOCATION: I-264 to Taylor Boulevard North exit. Turn right on Taylor and go 4 stoplights. Turn left on Arcade. At light make a left onto 7th Street Road and the market is on the right at 2900 7th Street Road.
DESCRIPTION: Located .7 of a mile from Churchill Downs, this indoor/outdoor market has been operating since 1985. It attracts an average of 90 dealers in the summer and 200 in the winter selling antiques, collectibles, handmade crafts, vegetables, furniture, clothing, knives, guns, toys, carpet, baseball cards, and new merchandise. They have 75,000 square feet under roof and are adding another 50,000! There was an "Outrageous Giveaway Promotion" going on until February 1994, giving away a 1969 Rolls Royce or a trip to Las Vegas, an in-ground pool, Pepsi for a year, and more. Wonder what they'll do next time? Three snack bars provide food on the premises.
DEALER RATES: $21 per 6' × 20' indoor booth for the weekend; $31 per weekend for 18' × 10' booth; $6–$8 per outdoor booth per day.
CONTACT: Terry Martian, Derby Park Traders Circle, 2900 7th Street Road, Louisville, KY 40216. Tel: (502) 636-3532.

Kentucky Flea Market

DATES: 1994: February 4–6, March 11–13, April 1–3, 29–30, May 1, 27–30, July 1–4, September 2–5, 30, October 1–2, December 29–31, January 1, 1995. Rain or shine.
TIMES: Friday 12:00 noon–8:00 PM; Saturday 10:00 AM–8:00 PM; Sunday 11:00 AM–5:00 PM.
ADMISSION: Free. $2 for parking in 15,000 spaces.
LOCATION: Kentucky Fair and Exposition Center. Junction of I-264 and 65. Follow the signs.
DESCRIPTION: Started in 1972, and housed in a 250,000 square foot climate-controlled building, this market consists of 1,000 to 2,000

dealers selling antiques, fine arts, arts and crafts, collectibles, and new merchandise. It is promoted as one of the largest indoor flea markets in the United States, in one of this country's finest facilities. On regular show days the market draws between 30,000 and 50,000 shoppers; on holidays, the crowds can swell to 100,000 or more. Food is served on the premises.

DEALER RATES: $70 ($95 holidays) per 14' × 8' space per show; $105 ($143 holidays) per 21' × 8' space; $140 ($190 holidays) per 28' × 8' space. Larger spaces are available. Higher holiday rates. Reservations are required well in advance.

CONTACT: Stewart Promotions, 2950 Breckinridge Lane, Suite 4A, Louisville, KY 40220. Tel: (502) 456-2244 (except Tuesday).

MAYSVILLE

Maysville Monday Court Days

DATES: First Monday in October plus preceding Sunday, rain or shine.
TIMES: Sunday 12:00 noon through Monday exhaustion.
ADMISSION: Free. Parking is also free.
LOCATION: The streets of Market Street and another parking lot nearby and McDonald Parkway.
DESCRIPTION: Started in the horse and buggy days of 1870 when the circuit judge would ride from town to town in Kentucky, then try and hang offenders, this series of Court Days (including Flemingsburg and Mt. Sterling) blossomed from the trading that naturally happened when people where brought together from outlying districts for a common gathering once a year. "If you can't find it on one of those trading days, then it doesn't exist, from jewelry to bent hinges (and bent nails!), even dogs!" Apples, crafts, wooden tool handles, at one time, to goldfish, sorghum molasses, collectibles, new merchandise, parts of kitchen sinks, furniture, and anything. Food is available on the premises and run by local charity and fraternal groups. Country ham and cheese sandwiches are one of the specialties sold. "The best beef and country ham you ever put in your mouth." An auctioneer comes in selling tools, ropes, and lamps among other treasures. Find Colonel Bower and ask him to tell you some of his market stories (and say "Hi" from Kitty); they *are* funny!

DEALER RATES: $2 a running foot (8' table is $16). First come, first served.

CONTACT: Col. George Bowers, 876 Fleming Road, Maysville, KY 41056. Tel: (606) 564-6026.

Entrepreneur in the Making:

A small boy carrying a bucket of bent nails was stopped by a dealer. He asked the boy how much he wanted for the bucket of nails? The child answered "Thirty-five cents."

"I'll give you twenty-five."

"No, thirty-five." After a bit of this haggling, the child got his thirty-five cents and watched the man go off with the bucket. But then the man put the bucket down on a nearby table and walked off into the crowd. The boy snatched his bucket from the table and went the opposite direction and sold the bucket of nails again.

MT. STERLING
October Court Days

DATES: The weekend of and including the third Monday in October, annually.

TIMES: 6:00 AM Saturday through 12:00 midnight Monday, non-stop.

ADMISSION: Free admission; parking from $5 to $10 per day or wherever you can find it.

LOCATION: The entire town of Mt. Sterling! Take Exit 110 off I-64, 35 miles east of Lexington; or take Exit 113 off I-64, 100 miles west of Ashland, Kentucky. Hint: Take U.S. 60 into town.

DESCRIPTION: Mt. Sterling has always been a big trading center. Around 1870, it was traditional for the local county judge to hang convicted offenders on the third Monday in October, which naturally started people trading over the entire weekend. People came from miles away to buy and sell cows, horses, dogs, produce, tools, and other farm goods. This market attracts 2,000 dealers and up to 100,000 shoppers (although another flea marketeer in the know says closer to 200,000 shoppers). Even now, during Court Days, people bring objects of all shapes and sizes for sale or trade—guns, axe handles, hammer handles, and antiques of all kinds that defy cataloging. Among the various foods for sale are corn meal and real Kentucky Sorghum Molasses, which is still made right in this mountain area. See also Flemingsburg and Maysville Court Days and follow the judge's circuit.

DEALER RATES: Average rate is $125 plus $20 for city license per 20' × 20' space for three days. Reservations are required in advance.

Don't even consider selling anything that isn't legal—after all, this is a hangout of the "judge."

CONTACT: Chamber of Commerce, 51 North Maysville Street, Mt. Sterling, KY 40353. Tel: (606) 498-5343.

RICHWOOD
Richwood Flea Market

DATES: Tuesday, Saturday, and Sunday, year round.

TIMES: Saturday and Sunday 9:00 AM–5:00 PM; Tuesday outdoors daybreak to 1:00 PM.

ADMISSION: Free. $1 per car.

LOCATION: 10915 U.S. 25, Richwood exit. I-75 to Exit 175, north on U.S. 25. Fifteen minutes south of Cincinnati.

DESCRIPTION: Opened in 1980, this market has about 300 indoor and 100 outdoor sellers. The indoor sellers are housed in a former tobacco warehouse over three acres *big*. There are many antiques, collectibles, craft items, sporting goods, tools, guns and knives, shoes, general merchandise, as well as farm goods, jewelry, and new merchandise to be found. Food is available on the premises.

DEALER RATES: $60 per 15' × 16' space per weekend. Reservations are suggested.

CONTACT: Mike Stallings, P.O. Box 153, Florence, KY 41022-0153. Tel: (606) 371-5800.

OTHER FLEA MARKET

Elizabethtown: Bowling Lanes Flea Market, 4547 North Dixie, Elizabethtown, KY 42701. Tel: (502) 737-5755. Open weekends 8:00 AM–5:00 PM.

London: Flea World Flea Market, 192 by-pass at Highway 22, London, KY 40741. Tel: (606) 864-3532. Open weekends 9:00 AM–5:00 PM.

New London: New London Flea Market, Tobacco Road, New London, KY 40741. Tel: (606) 878-9000. Open Friday through Sunday 7:00 AM on.

Russell Springs: Russell Springs Flea Market, Highway 80, Russell Springs, KY 42642. Open Friday through Sunday 7:00 AM–4:00 PM, February through November.

Simpsonville: Shelby County Flea Market, I-64, Exit 28, Simpsonville, KY 40067. Tel: (502) 722-8883. Open weekends 9:00 AM–5:00 PM.

LOUISIANA

ARCADIA
Bonnie & Clyde Trade Days, Inc.

DATES: The weekend before the third Monday of each month, Friday through Sunday.

TIMES: Dawn to dark.

ADMISSION: Free. Parking is $3.

LOCATION: Take Exit 69 off I-20 in Arcadia and go south 3½ miles to market.

DESCRIPTION: Since its opening in September 1990, this show has grown from the original 635 dealers to over 1,100 dealer spaces. The grounds feature three stocked lakes for free fishing, a restaurant, amphitheater, and stage, 100 RV hook-ups and facilities. There are dozens of concessions and dealers selling just about anything and everything. They have added both a washateria and free shower facilities.

DEALER RATES: $30 per 12' × 20' booth. Reservations are suggested.

CONTACT: Lamar E. Ozley, Jr., Bonnie & Clyde Trade Days, Inc., P.O. Box 243, Arcadia, LA 71001. Tel: (318) 263-2437.

BATON ROUGE
Deep South Flea Market

DATES: Every Friday, Saturday, and Sunday, rain or shine.

TIMES: 10:00 AM–6:00 PM.

ADMISSION: Free. Parking is also free.

LOCATION: 5350 Florida Boulevard.

DESCRIPTION: This indoor market began in 1974. Approximately 275 dealers sell everything from antiques and collectibles to a variety of crafts, art work, secondhand merchandise, and produce. For your convenience, food is available on the premises.

DEALER RATES: $70 per 8' × 10' space, per weekend. Reservations are not required.

CONTACT: Bill Vallery, 5350 Florida Boulevard, Baton Rouge, LA 70806. Tel: (504) 923-0142 or 923-0333.

CROWLEY
Crowley Flea Market
DATES: First full weekend of every month.
TIMES: 8:00 AM-5:00 PM.
ADMISSION: Small fee. Parking is free with hook-up available.
LOCATION: 407 South Avenue H.
DESCRIPTION: This indoor market has around 50 dealers selling a variety of antiques, collectibles, crafts, glassware, clothing, jewelry, and dolls. There is a concession stand on site.
DEALER RATES: $35 for a 12' × 15' space per weekend. Reservations are suggested.
CONTACT: Larry and Maureen Dubois, Crowley Flea Market, 407 South Avenue H, Crowley, LA 70526. Tel: (318) 783-3944 or 783-5326.

GREENWOOD/SHREVEPORT
Greenwood Flea Market
DATES: Saturday and Sunday, year round.
TIMES: 10:00 AM–6:00 PM.
ADMISSION: Free. Parking is free Saturday. Sunday $.25 per car.
LOCATION: 9249 Jefferson-Paige Road. I-20, Exit 5.
DESCRIPTION: This unusual market started in 1982, with 150 dealer spaces inside, 25 railroad boxcars and numerous outside setups. Their dealers sell antiques, collectibles, primitives, baseball cards, glassware, furniture, jewelry, and everything old and new. One of the owners saw the railroad boxcars sitting around a Texas siding and decided they would be fun and brought them over to Louisiana. Restrooms and food are available on the premises.
DEALER RATES: $30 per weekend; $110 per month. $110 per railroad car plus electric. $7.50 per day outside. Reservations are required.
CONTACT: Lou Forrest, Greenwood Flea Market, 9249 Jefferson-Paige Road, Greenwood, LA 71033. Tel: (318) 938-7201.

LACOMBE
190 Trading Post Flea Market
DATES: Every Saturday and Sunday, rain or shine.
TIMES: From 9:00 AM until dark.
ADMISSION: Free. Free parking is available.

LOCATION: On Highway 190, 4 miles east of Lacombe and 6 miles west of Slidell, Louisiana.

DESCRIPTION: Started in 1958, this indoor/outdoor market is said to be the oldest in Louisiana, having been in continuous operation since that time. There are 20 dealers selling antiques, fine art, arts and crafts, fresh produce, collectibles, new merchandise, appliances, and furniture, as well as unusual items such as farm equipment, American made tools, etc. One can find anything and everything here, even hard-to-find items. Food is available nearby.

DEALER RATES: From $5 to $40 depending upon size of space.

CONTACT: Mary and Harold Fayard, 470 Pine Street, Slidell, LA 70460. Tel: (504) 882-6442. Day of the market call Sharon Fayard at (504) 641-3476.

LAFAYETTE
Common Market

DATES: Daily.

TIMES: 10:00 AM–6:00 PM.

ADMISSION: Free. Parking is also free.

LOCATION: 3607A Ambassador-Caffrey Street.

DESCRIPTION: Open since 1986, this market with 15 dealers, sells a variety of merchandise including gold and silver jewelry, watches, shoes and handmade leather goods including purses and boots, and some antiques.

DEALER RATES: $125 per 6' × 6' space a month. Reservations are required.

CONTACT: Robert, Common Market, 3607A Ambassador-Caffrey Street, Lafayette, LA 70508. Tel: (318) 981-4428.

NEW ORLEANS
French Market Community Flea Market

DATES: Daily.

TIMES: 9:00 AM–5:00 PM.

ADMISSION: Free. Parking is free.

LOCATION: 1235 North Peters Street. Located on the riverfront behind the old U.S. Mint (yes, coins were minted here) between the Mint and Cafe duMont. It is quite the tourist attraction.

DESCRIPTION: This has got to be the great-grandaddy of all U.S. flea markets, started in 1791! Located in a historic part of New Orleans, this market (and the adjoining markets that sort of just run together) has around 300 dealers selling just about everything: African clothes and artifacts, antiques, collectibles, quilts, Guatemalan clothes, tie-dye clothing, t-shirts, stain-glass, purses, dolls, toys, ceramics, glasses, masks, furniture, stones and rocks, jewelry, plenty of produce, seafood, and whatever. Many of the dealers are permanent fixtures, some are seasonal.

DEALER RATES: Weekdays: $7 to $17 a space; weekends: $12 to $33 a space, depending on what is available. Spaces are given out by tenure on a weekly basis. All vendors must have city and state licenses and current photo ID and social security number.

CONTACT: French Market Corp., 108 North Peters Street, New Orleans, LA 70116. Tel: (504) 522-2621 (office) or 596-3420 for the market.

PONCHATOULA

Ponchatoula Antiques, Inc.

DATES: Friday, Saturday and Sunday following the second Monday of each month.

TIMES: 10:00 AM–6:00 PM.

ADMISSION: Free. Parking is free.

LOCATION: 400 West Pine Street, Highway 22.

DESCRIPTION: In 1989 Ponchatoula began developing into "antique city" by utilizing old buildings deserted in the downtown area. There are 30 to 40 businesses within 3 miles and about 100 dealers set up permanently. This market has 25 covered spaces and 30 open selling spaces for dealers. There is a Strawberry Festival in April, an Antique Festival in June and an Oktoberfest each October. There is lodging nearby.

DEALER RATES: $25 per 10' × 27' covered space per weekend; $12.50 for a 10' × 12' open space per weekend.

CONTACT: Jake Walden, 601 East Robert Street, Hammond, LA 70401. Tel: (504) 345-2381. Day of Show call: (504) 386-7809.

OTHER FLEA MARKETS

Baton Rouge: Merchants Landing, 9800 Florida Boulevard, Baton Rouge, LA 70815. Tel: (504) 925-1664. Open weekends 10:00 AM–7:00 PM.

MAINE

FREEPORT
Red Wheel Flea Market

DATES: Saturdays, Sundays, and holidays; from April through October; rain or shine.

TIMES: 9:00 AM–5:00 PM.

ADMISSION: Free. Free parking is available.

LOCATION: U.S. Route 1 in Freeport on the south side.

DESCRIPTION: This show is in its 25rd year, with 120 dealers selling both indoors and out. About 80 percent of the show is antiques, but collectibles, handicrafts, new merchandise, and produce in season are also available. Right in town is the Freeport Mall with over 90 new outlet stores (L.L. Bean included). Food is available from a snack bar serving all home-cooked food.

DEALER RATES: Outside: $7 per 8' × 10' table with parking frontage and table; $10 on Sunday. Inside: $10 on Saturday, $12 on Sunday. Reservations are suggested.

CONTACT: Ed Collett, 275 U.S. Route 1 South, Freeport, ME 04032. Tel: (207) 865-6492.

OXFORD
Undercover Antiques & Flea Market

DATES: Thursday through Sunday, year round.

TIMES: Thursday and Friday 7:00 AM–4:00 PM; Saturday and Sunday 7:00 AM–5:00 PM.

ADMISSION: Free. Parking is also free.

LOCATION: Route 26. One-half mile north of Oxford Plains Speedway on left. Only 30 minutes from I-95 Gray exit and 45 minutes from Conway.

DESCRIPTION: Under new ownership since June 1991, this market originally opened in 1984. There are 65 dealers inside year round and 20 to 30, and growing, outside in summer under awnings selling antiques, collectibles, appliances, baseball cards, coins, books—you name it. There isn't much new merchandise as it is discouraged. There is a snack bar on premises serving snacks, full breakfasts, and lunches.

DEALER RATES: $5 a day for outside three-table setup. Inside: $108 to $120 a month for a 8' × 10' booth, tables $60 a month if the market does the selling.

CONTACT: Dale Farrar or Paul Chretien, Undercover Flea Market, Route 1 Box 1550, Oxford, ME 04270. Tel: (207) 539-4149 or (207) 897-4018.

PORTLAND
Portland Expo Flea Market

DATES: Every Sunday October through March, rain or shine.
TIMES: 9:00 AM–4:00 PM.
ADMISSION: Free. Free parking is also available.
LOCATION: Portland Exposition Building, 239 Park Avenue. From Maine Turnpike Exit 6A or Exit 7, follow I-295 to Exit 5A Congress Street (Maine Route 22). At the first set of lights, take a left onto St. John Street, then at the next set of lights take a right onto Park Avenue. Expo is on the left.
DESCRIPTION: Started in 1981, this is Maine's largest indoor flea market located in the historic Portland Exposition Building, one of the oldest arenas in continuous operation in the United States. It is heated, clean, and friendly. There are an average of 150 dealers selling antiques, fine art, arts and crafts, collectibles, new merchandise, and "junque." Full service concessions provide home-style food on the premises.
DEALER RATES: $20 for regular space and table; $26 for bleacher space (includes table); $32 for corner space (includes 2 tables in "L" formation). Reservations are advised.
CONTACT: Arthur Stephenson or Norma Littlefield, Portland Exposition Building, 239 Park Avenue, Portland, ME 04102. Tel: (207) 874-8200.

TRENTON
Bargain Barn Flea Market

DATES: Saturday, Sunday and holidays, Memorial Day through September, weather permitting.
TIMES: 7:00 AM–5:00 PM.
ADMISSION: Free. Parking is free if you can find a place. Hint: Look behind the building, there is plenty of room there.
LOCATION: Route 3, between Elsworth and Bar Harbor, ¼ mile from the bridge entering Acadia National Park and Mt. Desert Island.
DESCRIPTION: Over 12 years old, this market has between 40 and 50 dealers with room for more. Everything from collectibles to junk, new merchandise, expensive collectibles, good old "stuff," to good

new stuff, "quite a mixture" including some crafts. Food is available on the premises.

DEALER RATES: $10 per space, seasonal rates available. Reservations are suggested.

CONTACT: George Wallace, Bargain Barn Flea Market, RD 1 Box 176, Trenton, ME 04605. Tel: (207) 677-5022.

WOOLWICH

Montsweag Flea Market

DATES: Saturday and Sunday, May through October. Also, Wednesday and Friday, June through August.

TIMES: 6:30 AM–5:30 PM.

ADMISSION: Free. Free parking is available.

LOCATION: On Route 1 in Woolwich, 5 miles north of Bath.

DESCRIPTION: The promoter tells us that this market, started in 1977, is rated number one in Maine and number three in New England. It is pictured in the book, *Coastal Maine, A State of Maine*. There are about 100 dealers selling antiques, arts and crafts, fresh produce, collectibles, new merchandise, tools, plants and seedlings, early primitives, and fine jewelry. This market mainly deals with antiques and collectibles. The market is held outdoors and there is food served on the premises.

DEALER RATES: $5 and $9 for 3' × 8' tables, depending on market day. Advance reservations are required.

CONTACT: Norma Thompson Scopino, P.O. Box 252, Woolwich, ME 04579. Tel: (207) 443-2809.

MARYLAND

BALTIMORE

North Point Drive-In Outdoor/Indoor Flea Market

DATES: Every Saturday and Sunday, rain or shine.

TIMES: 7:00 AM–3:00 PM.

ADMISSION: $.25 per person. Parking for 800 cars is free.

LOCATION: 4001 North Point Boulevard. Take the Beltway 695, off at Exit 41, bear right, then take a left at the first light.

DESCRIPTION: Started in 1971, this indoor/outdoor market runs year round in a 24,000 square foot building next to a drive-in theater. It is claimed to be the oldest and one of the largest flea markets in the area. On Saturdays, 100 dealers (200 on Sunday) sell antiques, arts and crafts, fresh produce, collectibles, new merchandise, used items, junk, plants, furniture, etc. Food is available.

DEALER RATES: $5 on Saturday, $10 on Sundays. Please call for information.

CONTACT: Frank Durkee, North Point Drive-In Flea Market, 7721 Old Battlegrove Road, Baltimore, MD 21222. Day of market call (410) 477-1337.

Patapsco Flea Market

DATES: Saturday and Sunday, rain or shine.

TIMES: 7:00 AM–4:00 PM.

ADMISSION: $.25. Parking is free.

LOCATION: Corner of West Patapsco Avenue and Annapolis Road.

DESCRIPTION: Started in 1982 in a former "strip mall," this market has 300 to 500 dealers indoors and outdoors selling "everything"— antiques, new and used merchandise, collectibles, and more. There are weekly bingo games, a warehouse across the street for dealers, a restaurant, bakery, deli, ice cream parlor, carry-out lunch counters, barbecue pit, hot dog stand, and more for the hungry.

DEALER RATES: From $15 a table space and up. Reservations are not required.

CONTACT: Patapsco Flea Market, 1402 Patapsco Avenue, Baltimore, MD 21230. Tel: (410) 354-3040.

BETHESDA

Farmer's Flea Market

DATES: Every Sunday, April through November.

TIMES: 9:00 AM–5:00 PM.
ADMISSION: Free. Free parking is available.
LOCATION: Two miles south of Route 495 at 7155 Wisconsin Avenue in Bethesda (Northwest Washington, D.C. area).
DESCRIPTION: Started in 1974, 50 to 60 outside dealers now sell antiques, collectibles, and furniture. Great sales are available at the Montgomery County Farm Women's Market. Food is served on the premises.
DEALER RATES: $15 per 10' × 20' space. Reservations are not required.
CONTACT: James R. Bonfils, P.O. Box 39034, Washington, D.C. 20016. No phone available.

COLUMBIA
The Columbia Market

DATES: Every Sunday mid-April to mid-October, rain or shine.
TIMES: 10:00 AM–4:00 PM.
ADMISSION: Free. Parking is available and is also free.
LOCATION: Between Baltimore and Washington, D.C. Off I-95 to Route 175, at the mall.
DESCRIPTION: This market first opened in 1972. It is held outdoors, but protected from weather, and accommodates up to 300 dealers—200 undercover and 100 in the open. There is a huge variety of antiques, collectibles, and crafts for sale under a double-deck parking lot. Food is available at the mall.
DEALER RATES: $55 per 16' × 16' space undercover, $45 per space unprotected, pre-paid. Call for more rates. Reservations are suggested.
CONTACT: Bellman Promotions, Inc., 11959 Philadelphia Road, Bradshaw, MD 21021. Tel: (410) 329-2188 or (410) 679-2288.

EDGEWOOD
Bonnie Brae Flea Market

DATES: Every Saturday and Sunday, weather permitting.
TIMES: 7:00 AM–until whenever.
ADMISSION: Free. Free parking is available.
LOCATION: 1301 Pulaski Highway in Edgewood, Harford County, Company grounds. Take Route 40 (Pulaski Highway), 20 miles N.E. of Baltimore, between Joppa and Aberdeen; near Exit 152 off I-95.
DESCRIPTION: Opened in 1974, this indoor/outdoor flea market was at one time one of the largest truck stops on the East Coast. When

I-95 was built the traffic left. Now it's coming back. There are now approximately 50 dealers (meaning they are mostly full in summers), selling antiques, fine art, arts and crafts, depression glass (many patterns), some Flo-blue and Carnival, oyster cans, dolls, Roseville and other pottery, some furniture, marbles, clocks, record players, china dishes, collectibles, new merchandise, baseball cards, and much more. The market specializes in depression and Carnival glass. Snacks are available.

DEALER RATES: $15 per 12' × 10' space per day. No advance reservations required.

CONTACT: Juanita Merritt, 1003 Magnolia Road, Joppa, MD 21085. Tel: (410) 679-2210 or (410) 679-6895.

ELDERSBURG

Flea Market, Craft Show and Pancake Breakfast

DATES: Annually on the last Saturday of April. For 1994: April 30. Rain date May 1.

TIMES: 8:00 AM–4:00 PM.

ADMISSION: Free and parking is free.

LOCATION: In Carroll County, 2 miles south of Eldersburg at the Freedom District Fire Company Carnival Grounds. Only 20 minutes NW of Baltimore and about 8 miles north of I-70.

DESCRIPTION: Limited to 150 quality dealers, this market is the fundraiser for the Freedom District Lions Club and benefits the Maryland Eye Bank. among the treasures sold are: antiques, collectibles, baseball cards, homemade dolls, tools, and spring flowers. There is a variety of food to please everyone.

DEALER RATES: $15 for a 24' × 24' space. Reservations are required.

CONTACT: Denton or Janet Boyd, 229 East Nicodemus Road, Westminster, MD 21157. Tel: (410) 857-5362.

FREDERICK

Canon Hills Flea Market

DATES: Open 7 days a week.

TIMES: 9:00 AM–5:00 PM.

ADMISSION: Free. Free parking is available.

LOCATION: 111 South Carroll Street in Frederick.

DESCRIPTION: This 11-year-old indoor show has 35 permanent dealers. Everything from antiques and collectibles to craft items and new merchandise can be found here. Business here increases yearly.

The building itself is of interest, built in 1780 by the Hessians. For your convenience, food is available on the premises.

DEALER RATES: Available upon request.

CONTACT: John Hornick, Canon Hills Flea Market, 111 South Carroll Street, Frederick, MD 21701. Tel: (301) 695-9304.

Country Peddler Show

DATES: Annually. Usually first weekend in August. 1994: August 5–7.

TIMES: Friday 4:00 AM–9:00 PM, Saturday 9:00 AM–5:00 PM, Sunday 11:00 AM–4:00 PM.

ADMISSION: $5 for adults, $2 for children 12 and under. Parking is $1.

LOCATION: At Great Frederick County Fairgrounds; Franklin Street to fairgrounds.

DESCRIPTION: This indoor show has been exciting dealers and bargain hunters since 1983. The 120 exhibitors show a variety of collectibles, as well as arts and crafts, fine art, baskets, tin, herb arrangements, pottery, furniture, homespun and new merchandise. Their specialty is their folk artisans who sell the treasures of the future. For your convenience, there is food available on the premises.

DEALER RATES: $375 per 10' × 10' booth; $562.50 per 10' × 15' booth; $750 per 10' × 20' booth. Reservations are required.

CONTACT: American Memories, Inc., P.O. Box 249, Decatur, MI 49045-0249. Tel: (616) 423-8367 or fax: (616) 423-2421.

Odds and Ends

DATES: Every Friday, Saturday, and Sunday, year round.

TIMES: 9:00 AM–5:00 PM.

ADMISSION: Free. Free parking is available.

LOCATION: At the intersection of Carroll and South Streets.

DESCRIPTION: Started 24 years ago, this indoor market has about 20 permanent dealers selling antiques, collectibles, postcards, books, and curios. Food is served in several nearby restaurants.

DEALER RATES: Start at $85 per 8' × 10' booth or tables per month. Reservations are required.

CONTACT: Dennis Dugan, Odds and Ends Shop, Carroll and South Street, Frederick, MD 21700. Tel: (301) 662-5388.

INDIAN HEAD
Village Green Flea Market

DATES: Saturdays, April through October, weather permitting.

TIMES: 8:00 AM–2:00 PM.

ADMISSION: Free. Parking is also free.

LOCATION: On the Village Green. From out of town take I-210 South to the very end, right behind the post office.

DESCRIPTION: Started in 1987 by the Town of Indian Head as a way for local residents to have a flea market and a place to have yard sales, this market usually has about 20 to 25 dealers and residents selling flea market goods, yard sale items, some new merchandise, woodwork, local fresh foods (jelly and bread), and whatever comes in. A hot dog stand is on the premises.

DEALER RATES: $5 per space. Reservations are not required.

CONTACT: Indian Head Town Hall, 1107 Strauss Avenue, Indian Head, MD 20640. Tel: (301) 743-5511.

NORTH EAST
North East Auction Galleries and Flea Market

DATES: Every day, rain or shine.

TIMES: 8:00 AM–dusk.

ADMISSION: Free. Ample free parking is provided.

LOCATION: Off I-95, on the corner of Route 40 and Mechanics Valley Road.

DESCRIPTION: This market has been in operation since 1973, and currently attracts between 50 dealers in winter and 150 in summer who sell a variety of goods including antiques, collectibles, craft items, new merchandise, auto parts, furniture, household goods, appliances, baseball cards, Oriental rugs, and fresh produce. The market is located at the head of the picturesque Chesapeake Bay, in a high traffic area near state parks, marinas, campgrounds, yacht clubs, and other local attractions. In addition, a consignment auction is held every Tuesday evening and an automobile auction held every Thursday evening. Food is available on the premises.

DEALER RATES: $15 per 8' × 10' booth. Reservations are suggested.

CONTACT: Mr. R. C. Burkheimer, North East Auction Galleries, P.O. Box 551, North East, MD 21901. Tel: (800) 233-4169. In Maryland, call (410) 287-5588. Fax number is (410) 287-2029.

OCEAN CITY

Antiques and Crafts Flea Market

DATES: Starts with Saturday and Sunday in May, then Friday, Saturday, and Sunday through first weekend in October.

TIMES: 9:00 AM–5:00 PM.

ADMISSION: Free. Parking is also free.

LOCATION: Parking lot of the Ocean City Convention Center.

DESCRIPTION: Started in 1970 and operated by the town of Ocean City, this market has 35 vendors, under shelter, selling antiques, collectibles, small furniture, baseball cards, coins, glassware, assorted old treasures, used or old merchandise only. No new merchandise or food is allowed. There are two baseball card shows scheduled by the Center not connected with this flea market and also separate antique shows held in the same building but scheduled by others. This is the beach—there is plenty of food around on the boardwalk, from local restaurants to concessions.

DEALER RATES: $30 per day per 20' × 26' space; or $25 per day if staying for two days; $20 for each of three days. A $6 daily sales license is required and issued on-site. Reservations are suggested.

CONTACT: C. Preston Phillips, Ocean City Convention Center, 4001 Coastal Highway, Ocean City, MD 21842. Tel: (301) 289-8313.

RISING SUN

Hunter's Sale Barn, Inc.

DATES: Every Monday, rain or shine.

TIMES: 3:00 PM–9:00 PM, auction at 6:00 PM.

ADMISSION: Free. Free parking is available.

LOCATION: Take Exit 93 off I-95, then go north 2½ miles to a dead end, turn right on Route 276; market is 2½ miles down, on the right.

DESCRIPTION: Originally this business was a livestock market. The flea and farmers market started in 1975, and the livestock sales stopped in 1985. This indoor/outdoor market has 120 dealers selling antiques, arts and crafts, fresh produce, collectibles, and new merchandise. This is a family oriented market kept clean and very pleasant. In addition, an auction is also conducted at the market at 6:00 PM, selling eggs, produce, and general merchandise. Monday night is Sale Barn Auction Night for the county. There is a full restaurant on the premises. This is a well-attended market drawing 300 plus people to the auction alone.

DEALER RATES: $20 per 4' × 8' space, $40 for a 16' × 16' space. First come, first served.

CONTACT: Norman E. Hunter and Carol A. or Ronda L. Hunter, P.O. Box 427, Rising Sun, MD 21911. Tel: (410) 658-6400 or fax: (410) 658-3864.

OTHER FLEA MARKETS:

Jessup: Flea Market World, Route 1 and 175, Columbia Eastgate Shopping Center, Jessup, MD 20794. Tel: (410) 796-1025. Open weekends 8:00 AM–4:30 PM.

Millersville: Big Indoor Outdoor Flea Market, 8370 Jumpers Hole Road, Millersville, MD 21108. Tel: (410) 647-3545. Open weekends 7:00 AM–4:00 PM.

MASSACHUSETTS

ANDOVER
Country Peddler Show

DATES: October 28–30, 1994.

TIMES: Friday 4:00 PM–9:00 PM; Saturday 9:00 AM–5:00 PM; Sunday 11:00 AM–4:00 PM.

ADMISSION: Adults $5; children 2–12 years $2. Parking is $1.

LOCATION: Ramada Hotel, Rolling Green at 311 Lowell Street.

DESCRIPTION: This indoor market features 90 folk artisans selling a variety of collectibles, arts and crafts, and fine art—the one-of-a-kind heirlooms of the future. For your convenience food is available on the premises. This show is one of a series of Country Peddler Shows held throughout the East Coast. For more information regarding these shows, call or check the other state's listings.

DEALER RATES: $375 per 10' × 10' booth; $562.50 per 10' × 15' booth; $750 per 10' × 20' booth. Reservations are required.

CONTACT: American Memories, P.O. Box 249, Decatur, MI 49045-0249. Tel: (616) 423-8367 or fax: (616) 423-2421.

AUBURN
Auburn Antique and Flea Market, Inc.

DATES: Every Sunday indoors and outdoors, year round, rain or shine. April through November, Saturdays outdoors, weather permitting.

TIMES: 9:00 AM–4:00 PM.

ADMISSION: $.50 for adults, children free during winter. Free during summer months.

LOCATION: 773 Southbridge Street Route 12. From Massachusetts Turnpike take Exit 10, follow Route 12 south for ½ mile. From I-290 take Exit 8, follow Route 12 south for ½ mile. From I-395 take Exit 7, follow Route 12 south ½ mile.

DESCRIPTION: This indoor/outdoor market has been open since 1975. It accommodates approximately 100 dealers indoors, and 75 dealers outdoors. Many items such as antiques, arts and crafts, collectibles, new merchandise, and even fresh produce can be found. Many dealers also sell a variety of stamps, coins, and baseball cards. Food is served on the premises.

DEALER RATES: $30 per 9' × 9' space indoors; $15 per space outdoors on Sundays; $10 on Saturdays. Reservations are required for indoor space during the winter season only. Dealers may arrive at 7:00 AM to shop early.

CONTACT: Auburn Antique and Flea Market, Inc., 773 Southbridge Street, P.O. Box 33, Auburn, MA 01501. Tel: (508) 832-2763.

AVON
Rainbow Flea Market, Inc.

DATES: Saturday and Sunday, rain or shine.

TIMES: 9:00 AM–5:00 PM.

ADMISSION: $.50. Parking is free.

LOCATION: 44 Bodwell Street.

DESCRIPTION: Started in a new building in 1989, this market has150 vendors selling antiques, collectibles, new merchandise, china, computers, craft supplies, a "Pretty Punch" craft corner, Indian objects, coins, stamps, western jewelry, "cigar store" candies and smokes, custom-designed shirts, more jewelry, everything! The owners encourage dealers with good, low prices and wonderful deals abound. There is one vendor creating custom-made jewelry to order on premises. A full snack bar serves breakfast and lunch.

DEALER RATES: $30 and up for a booth per weekend. Outside space in summer is $10. Reservations are not required.

CONTACT: Joe Kelly or Gary Montgomery, Rainbow Flea Market, 44 Bodwell Street, Avon, MA 02322. Tel: (508) 583-3781.

BRIMFIELD
Crystal Brook Antique Show

DATES: 1994: May 10–15, July 5–10, and September 5–11. Usually the same weekends every year.

TIMES: 6:00 AM–5:00 PM.

LOCATION: On Route 20. Take the Palmer exit off the Massachusetts Turnpike, to Route 20, then 10 miles west of Sturbridge. Or Sturbridge exit on Massachusetts Turnpike.

DESCRIPTION: This show began about 35 years ago. It is an outdoor market that accommodates approximately 35 dealers. This is considered a relatively small market, but there are many quality antiques and collectibles sold.

DEALER RATES: Call for current rates.

CONTACT: Maureen Ethier, Route 20, Brimfield, MA 01010. Tel: (413) 245-7647.

J & J Promotions Antiques and
Collectibles Shows

DATES: 1994: May 13–14, July 8–9; September 9–10. Rain or shine.
TIMES: Friday 6:00 AM–5:00 PM; Saturday 8:00 AM–5:00 PM.
ADMISSION: $4 per person. $4 parking fee.
LOCATION: From Boston: take Massachusetts Turnpike west to Exit 9 at Sturbridge; follow Route 20 west to Brimfield for approximately 7 miles to Auction Acres. From New York City: take I-95 North to I-91 North. Go through Hartford to I-84 east to Sturbridge and Route 20 west for about 6 miles. Or, I-95 North to I-91 through Hartford to Springfield to I-291 East to I-90 (Massachusetts Turnpike) East to Exit 8 at Palmer, go beyond exit booth and turn right at stop light, then left to Route 20 East for approximately 6 miles.
DESCRIPTION: This outdoor show first opened in 1959. Auction Acres is the home of Gordon Reid's original Antique Market. Now owned by his two daughters, this prestigious property covers 40 acres at the center of Brimfield. Today, antiques and collectibles enthusiasts from all over the world continue to visit this famous market. Dealers and exhibitors alike have year after year relied on the experience and quality in the organization and presentation of these shows of antiques and collectibles. Food is served on the premises.
DEALER RATES: Space size and prices vary. Please call for more information.
CONTACT: Jill Reid Lukesh and Judith Reid Mathieu, J & J Promotions, Auction Acres, P.O. Box 385, Brimfield, MA 01010-0385. Tel: (413) 245-3436 or (508) 597-8155.

New England Motel Antiques Market, Inc.

DATES: 1994: May 12–16, July 7–11, September 8–12.
TIMES: Wednesday opening days 6:00 AM–dusk; other days, 8:00 AM to dusk.
ADMISSION: $3. Parking is $4.
LOCATION: Route 20, Palmer Road in the center of the Mart.
DESCRIPTION: This show started in 1986 and is said to be the first show to open in Brimfield (at 6:00 AM). The finest and freshest merchandise is found here. About 300 reputable dealers sell quality antiques and collectibles in the center of the Northeast's greatest outdoor show. Food is available on the premises.
DEALER RATES: $170 for a 20' × 24' booth. Reservations are required.

CONTACT: Marie Doldoorian, P.O. Box 186, Sturbridge, MA 01566. Tel: (508) 347-2179. Day of show call: (413) 245-3348.

Shelton Antique Shows

DATES: 1994: May 10–15, July 5–10, September 6–11.
TIMES: Daybreak on.
LOCATION: Route 20, Brimfield. Between Exit 9 Sturbridge or Exit 10 Palmer off Massachusetts Turnpike. Exit Sturbridge Route 86 from Connecticut.
ADMISSION: Free. Parking is $4 a day, overnight parking is $10.
DESCRIPTION: This market started in 1975 and is located on a 1 mile strip of the largest outdoor antique event in the United States. Approximately 150 dealers sell antiques and collectibles. There are dealer showers, food service, and table rentals available.
DEALER RATES: $190–$250 per 20' × 20' booth. Reservations are required. One-day rates offered after opening day.
CONTACT: Lois J. Shelton, Palmer Road, P.O. Box 124, Brimfield, MA 01010-0124. Tel: (413) 245-3591.

GRAFTON

Grafton Flea Market, Inc.

DATES: Every Sunday, rain or shine.
TIMES: 6:00 AM–5:00 PM.
ADMISSION: $.50 for an adult, children free. Free parking is available.
LOCATION: On Route 140 near the Grafton-Upton town line. Take the Massachusetts Turnpike to Route 495 South, then take Upton Exit 21B to Route 140.
DESCRIPTION: This show first opened in 1970. There are approximately 200 to 250 dealers attending this market, which is held both indoors and outdoors. A variety of items such as antiques, collectibles, arts and crafts, new merchandise, and fresh produce can be found. There is also a selection of baseball cards, stamps, and coins. There is catered food available on the premises.
DEALER RATES: $20 per space, outdoors. $25 per space, indoors. Reservations are required for indoor space only.
CONTACT: Mr. Harry Peters, P.O. Box 206, Grafton, MA 01519. Tel: (508) 839-2217.

HADLEY
Olde Hadley Flea Market

DATES: Every Sunday from the third Sunday in April through the first Sunday in November, weather permitting.

TIMES: 7:00 AM–5:00 PM.

ADMISSION: Free. Free parking is available.

LOCATION: On Route 47 South, Lawrence Plain Road. Take Exit 19 off Route 91 North. Or, take Exit 20 off Route 91 South. Follow Route 9 East to center of Hadley, then 2 miles south on Route 47.

DESCRIPTION: This show opened in 1980. There are 200 plus dealers selling their goods at this outdoor market. There is everything from antiques and collectibles, from new merchandise to fresh produce sold here including maple sugar, honey, and plants. Excellent catered food is available on the premises. This flea market has a beautiful country setting at the foot of the Mount Holyoke Range. Special features of this flea market include antique auto viewing and the Silver Eagle Hot Air Balloon lift-off. There is also the Old Hadley Museum, Skinner State Park, Mitch's Marina, Young Meadow Farms, as well as shopping malls and many fine restaurants nearby.

DEALER RATES: $15 per 25' × 25' space. Reservations are not required. First come, first served. There are advance shopping hours for dealers starting at 6:00 AM.

CONTACT: Raymond and Marion Szala, 45 Lawrence Plain Road, Hadley, MA 01035. Tel: (413) 586-0352.

HUBBARDSTON
Rietta Ranch Flea Market

DATES: Sundays, April through November, rain or shine.

TIMES: 6:00 AM–dusk.

ADMISSION: Free admission and free parking.

LOCATION: On Route 68.

DESCRIPTION: Opened in 1967, this market attracts 600 dealers offering antiques, collectibles, handmade/craft items, vegetables, and new merchandise. They offer a full concession with three kitchens and indoor and outdoor dining. There is a country fair atmosphere with cotton candy, ice cream and fried dough. Plenty of restrooms and 20 acres of parking make this an easy place to spend the day. They are in the process of restoring a complete antique train with a 1915 steam engine for display.

DEALER RATES: Dealers are charged $10 for outside space about the size of a large car including one table. $15 for two tables on the inside. First come, first served or reserve for the season only.
CONTACT: Ronnie and Joyce Levesque, P.O. Box 35, Hubbardston, MA 01452-0035. Tel: (508) 632-0559.

HYANNIS

Hyannis Indoor Flea Market and Antique

DATES: Daily.
TIMES: Winter months: 9:00 AM–5:00 PM; May through September 9:00 AM–10:30 PM.
ADMISSION: Free. Parking is also free.
LOCATION: 500 Main Street. Downtown Hyannis.
DESCRIPTION: Opened in October 1989, this mall/flea market includes vendors and shops. There is an antique co-op, furniture consignments, merchandise mart, collectibles, new merchandise, and "Something for everyone!"
DEALER RATES: Rates vary. Reservations are required.
CONTACT: Jeff Rose, Hyannis Indoor Flea Market and Antique, 500 Main Street, Hyannis, MA 02639. Tel: (508) 790-3412.

KINGSTON

Kingston 106 Antiques and Collectibles

DATES: Every Sunday, year round.
TIMES: 9:00 AM–4:00 PM.
ADMISSION: $.50 per person. Free parking is available.
LOCATION: On Route 106, at 20 Wapping Road, 30 miles from Boston and 5 miles from Plymouth. Market is off Southeast Express.
DESCRIPTION: This show opened in 1980. There are approximately 50 dealers that attend this indoor market. There is a large selection of antiques, collectibles, and bureaus. Smaller items include depression glass, jewelry, dolls, and postcards. There is also a fine selection of military items. Homemade food is available on the premises.
DEALER RATES: $25 per week or $125 per 10' × 15' space, per month. Reservations are required.
CONTACT: Barbara Stevens, Church Street, Duxbury, MA 02332. Tel: (617) 934-6711. Day of show call (617) 585-2885.

LAWRENCE
Pacific Mills Indoor Flea Market

DATES: Saturday and Sunday, year round, rain or shine.
TIMES: 9:00 AM–5:00 PM.
ADMISSION: Sunday $.50; Saturday free. Parking is also free.
LOCATION: 300 Canal Street.
DESCRIPTION: Opened in the fall of 1989, this former old brick, woolen textile mill houses 270 dealers selling antiques, collectibles, old and new merchandise inside on about two acres of floor space. "Even Elvis showed up." (Just ask about this one.) This market is very family oriented with "Family Fun Flea Market" as their theme. Food is available on the premises.
DEALER RATES: $25–$55 depending on size; off-season adjustments.
CONTACT: Vince Michaels, Pacific Mills Indoor Flea Market, 300 Canal Street, Lawrence, MA 01840. Tel: (508) 683-7107.

RAYNHAM
Raynham Flea Mart

DATES: Every Sunday, rain or shine.
TIMES: 8:00 AM–6:00 PM.
ADMISSION: $.75. Free parking is available.
LOCATION: At junction of Route 24 and Route 44.
DESCRIPTION: This show began in 1974. There are 350 dealers indoors in a 50,000 square foot one-story building and over 200 dealers outdoors. This market screens its dealers to ensure variety and quality of items. These include antiques, arts and crafts, collectibles, jewelry, new merchandise, fresh produce, and everything. There are four new buildings on eight acres of land. There are six snack bars, a full restaurant, and parking for 1,000 cars.
DEALER RATES: $20 per space outdoors, $25 per 9' × 9' space indoors. Reservations are recommended.
CONTACT: J. Mann, Raynham Flea Market, Judson and South Street, Raynham, MA 02767. Tel: (508) 823-8923.

SHREWSBURY
Shop 'Til You Drop Gigantic Flea Market
and Farmer's Market

DATES: Saturday and Sunday, March through November, weather permitting.

TIMES: 7:00 AM–5:00 PM.

ADMISSION: Yes. Parking is free.

LOCATION: Edgemere Drive-In Theatre. Route 20, 4 miles west of Route 9 on Route 20, or 4 miles east of Route 146 on Route 20, or ½ mile west of Route 140 on Route 20. Exit 11 off the Massachusetts Turnpike. Follow the signs.

DESCRIPTION: This fairly new market attracts large crowds for its dealers. They sell everything. There is also a tailgate auction on Saturdays at 11:00 AM. Some of the items sold (either way) are: antiques, collectibles, furniture, art, household items, tools, box lots of "stuff," whatever. There is a separate antique and collectible section.

DEALER RATES: Yard/garage sale area: $10; large field space: $15; large tent space: $20; tables $3 and $4.

CONTACT: Jeff Saletin, Shop Til You Drop, Edgemere Drive-In, Route 20, Shrewsbury, MA 01545. Tel: (508) 831-3696.

STURBRIDGE
Country Peddler Show

DATES: Annually. 1994: July 22–24. Usually the same weekend each year.

TIMES: Friday 4:00 AM–9:00 PM, Saturday 10:00 AM–6:00 PM, Sunday 11:00 AM–5:00 PM.

ADMISSION: $5 for adults, $2 for children 12 and under. There is plenty of free parking.

LOCATION: Sturbridge Host Hotel and Convention Center. Take Route 20, 1 mile west of I-86 and Massachusetts Turnpike, to Exit 9. Show is opposite Old Sturbridge Village.

DESCRIPTION: This indoor show has been held on these grounds since 1985. There are 100 exhibitors showing variety of collectibles as well as arts and crafts, fine art, and new merchandise available. Their specialty is the folk artisans that hold the collectibles of the future. For your convenience there is food served on the premises.

DEALER RATES: $375 per 10' × 10' booth; $562.50 per 10' x15' booth; $750 per 10' × 20' booth. Reservations are required.

CONTACT: American Memories, Inc., P.O. Box 249, Decatur, MI 49045-0249. Tel: (616) 423-8367 or fax: (616) 423-2421.

WELLFLEET
Wellfleet Drive-In Flea Market

DATES: Every Saturday and Sunday, and holiday Mondays, April through October. Also open every Wednesday and Thursday during July and August. Rain or shine.

TIMES: 8:00 AM–4:00 PM.

ADMISSION: $1 per carload. $2 per carload during Sundays in high season.

LOCATION: On Route 6 towards Provincetown, on Wellfleet-Eastham line. Once you are on Cape Cod, just follow the road to Provincetown.

DESCRIPTION: This show started about 22 years ago in the Cape Cod National Seashore at Wellfleet. They have 26 acres of family entertainment. Depending upon the season, there can be anywhere from 50 to 250 dealers at this outdoor market. They specialize in antiques, collectibles, local shellfish, furniture, and new merchandise. There are also arts and crafts vendors, tarot readers, artists, and anything else that is legal is here! For your convenience, food is available on the premises. The owners of this market pride themselves on running a very clean market with a very fine reputation.

DEALER RATES: Saturday and Thursday $15 per 18' × 22' space; Wednesday and Sunday $20 for a 18' × 22' space. Reservations are not required.

CONTACT: Eleanor Hazen, Wellfleet Drive-In Flea Market, Box 811 Wellfleet, MA 02667-0811. Tel: (508) 349-2520.

WILLIAMSBURG

Flea Market at Colonial Shops

DATES: Saturday and Sunday, year round.

TIMES: Saturday 10:00 AM–5:00 PM, Sunday 12:00 NOON–5:00 PM.

ADMISSION: Free. Parking is free.

LOCATION: At the Colonial Shops at 50 Main Street.

DESCRIPTION: Opened in 1992, this admittedly small market of five dealers sells basically antiques and collectibles. There is a dealer in old coins who is quite knowledgeable in her field and other dealers with glassware and silver.

DEALER RATES: $20 a weekend for about 8' × 10' space. Reservations are required.

CONTACT: Greg Conz or Louise Henry (manager), 50 Main Street, Williamsburg, MA 01039.

OTHER FLEA MARKETS

Ashland: Ashland Craft and Flea Market, 250 Elliot Street, Ashland,

MA 01721. Tel: (508) 881-4918. Open Sunday 7:00 AM–4:30 PM, September through December and March through June.

Brockton: Cary Hill Flea Market, 220 East Ashland Street, Brockton, MA 02402. Tel: (617) 783-3040. Open weekends 9:00 AM–5:00 PM.

Dennisport: Dennisport Flea and Antique Market, Route 28, Dennisport, MA 02639. Tel: (508) 394-6752. Open Thursday through Sunday 10:00 AM–6:00 PM.

Dudley: Dudley Flea Market, Dudley Plaza, Airport Road, Dudley, MA 01571. Tel: (508) 949-3552. Open weekends 9:00 AM–5:00 PM.

East Douglas: Douglas Flea Market Antiques and Collectibles, NE Main Street, East Douglas, MA 01516. Tel: (508) 278-6027. Open Saturday 9:00 AM–1:00 PM, Sunday 9:00 AM–4:00 PM.

Fall River: Old Ironworks Marketplace, 18 Pocasset Street, Fall River, MA 02721. Tel: (508) 678-7133. Open weekends 9:00 AM–5:00 PM.

Lynn: Massachusetts Merchandise Mart, 810 Lynnway, Lynn, MA 01901. Tel: (617) 598-5450. Open Wednesday through Sunday 10:00 AM–6:00 PM, Thursday and Friday until 9:00 PM.

Malden: Malden Flea Market, Route 60 and Ferry Street, Malden, MA 02148. Tel: (617) 321-9374 or (617) 324-9113. Open weekends 9:00 AM–5:00 PM.

Mashpee: Dick and Ellie's Flea Market, Route 28, Mashpee, MA 02649. Tel: (508) 477-3550. Open Tuesday, Friday through Sunday 6:00 AM–dusk, April through November 15.

New Bedford: Country Fair Antiques and Flea Market, 127 West Rodney French Boulevard, New Bedford, MA 02740. Tel: (508) 999-4414. Open Sunday 9:00 AM–4:00 PM.

New Bedford: The Whaling City Flea Market, 1145 Kempton Street, New Bedford, MA 02740. Tel: (508) 999-6225. Open Sunday 9:00 AM–5:00 PM.

North Plymouth: Plymouth Flea Market, Cordage Park Marketplace, Route 3A, North Plymouth, MA 02360. Tel: (508) 747-5252. Open weekends and holiday Mondays 9:00 AM–5:00 PM.

North Quincy: Naponset Flea Market, 2 Hancock Street, North Quincy, MA 02171. Tel: (617) 472-3558. Open weekends 9:00 AM–5:00 PM.

Somerset: Sunday Marketplace, Route 138, County Street, Somerset, MA 02726. Tel: (508) 677-2244. Open Sunday 9:00 AM–5:00 PM.

Swansea: Patriot Flea Market, 1049 GAR Highway, Route 6, Swansea, MA 02777. Tel: (508) 679-9466. Open weekends and holiday Mondays 9:00 AM–5:00 PM.

Taunton: Taunton Expo Center Antiques Show and Flea Market, Route 44, Taunton, MA 02780. Tel: (508) 880-3800. Open Sunday and holiday Mondays and the four Saturdays before Christmas.

Worcester: Worcester Flea Market, 72 Pullman Street, Worcester, MA 01606. Tel: (508) 852-6622. Open weekends 7:30 AM–4:30 PM.

MICHIGAN

ANN ARBOR
Country Peddler Show

DATES: Annually. 1994 dates: August 26–28. Usually the same weekend each year.

TIMES: Friday 4:00 PM–9:00 PM; Saturday 9:00 AM–5:00 PM; Sunday 11:00 AM–4:00 PM.

ADMISSION: Adults $5; children 2–12 years $2. Parking is $1.

LOCATION: Washtenaw Fairgrounds. Take Exit 175 off I-94, go south to Ann Arbor-Saline Road. Go left to Fairgrounds 1/8 mile on the left.

DESCRIPTION: This indoor market, started in 1988, features 100 folk artisans selling a variety of collectibles, arts and crafts, and fine art; the one-of-a-kind heirlooms of the future. For your convenience there is food available on the premises. This show is one of a series of Country Peddler Shows held throughout the East Coast. For more information regarding these shows, call or check the other state's listings.

DEALER RATES: $375 per 10' × 10' booth; $562.50 per 10' × 15' booth; $750 per 10' × 20' booth. Reservations are required.

CONTACT: American Memories, P.O. Box 249, Decatur, MI 49045-0249. Tel: (616) 423-8367 or fax: (616) 423-2421.

CENTREVILLE
Caravan Antiques Market

DATES: First Sunday in May, second Sunday in June, July, August, and October.

TIMES: 7:00 AM–4:00 PM.

ADMISSION: $3. Free parking is available.

LOCATION: St. Joseph's County Fairgrounds on M-86. In the heart of Michigan's Amish area, halfway between Chicago and Detroit.

DESCRIPTION: This show opened in 1973. It is both an indoor and outdoor market that accommodates approximately 650 dealers. This show is limited to antiques, fine art, and selected collectibles. There is also plenty of food available on the premises. This show provides a chance to "slip back in time and visit a part of small-town America." One can stroll around the 174 acres on the fairgrounds and recheck the merchandise, or walk to the fence near the viewing stand and watch a driver take a practice run around the track. This show is well thought out and well-planned. Although this is a rather large market, Robert Lawlor, the show manager, has done his very best to maintain a cozy, family-like environment.

DEALER RATES: $75 per 25' × 25' space. Reservations are required.

CONTACT: Robert L. Lawler, Show Manager, 1510 North Hoyne, Chicago, IL 60622-1804. Tel: (312) 227-4464.

FLAT ROCK

Flat Rock Historical Society Antique and Flea Market

DATES: First Sundays in May and October, rain or shine.

TIMES: 8:00 AM–5:00 PM.

ADMISSION: Free. Parking is free.

LOCATION: At the Flat Rock Speedway, 1 mile north of Flat Rock on Telegraph Road.

DESCRIPTION: This outdoor market opened in 1973 and accommodates about 350 dealers. There are a variety of antiques, arts and crafts, and collectibles. The money from this show is used to support the Flat Rock Historical Society Museum. Food is served on the premises.

DEALER RATES: $25 for a 20' × 20' space. Reservations are not required.

CONTACT: Flat Rock Historical Society, P.O. Box 336, Flat Rock, MI 48134. Tel: (313) 782-5220.

KALAMAZOO

Country Peddler Show

DATES: Annually in February. 1994: February 18–20. Usually the same weekend each year.

TIMES: Friday 4:00 PM–9:00 PM; Saturday 9:00 AM–5:00 PM; Sunday 11:00 AM–4:00 PM.

ADMISSION: Adults $5; children 2–12 years $2.

LOCATION: Kalamazoo County Fairgrounds, Hazel Grey Building at 2900 Lake Street. Exit 80, north off I-94 to Business Loop. Exit to Lake Street, right, follow fairground signs.

DESCRIPTION: This indoor market, started in 1988, features 80 folk artisans selling a variety of American-made collectibles, arts and crafts, and fine art. All these products are one-of-a-kind heirlooms of the future. For your convenience there is food available on the premises. This show is one of a series of Country Peddler Shows held throughout the East Coast. See next listing.

DEALER RATES: $375 per 10' × 10' booth; $562.50 per 10' × 15' booth; $750 per 10' × 20' booth. Reservations are required.
CONTACT: American Memories, P.O. Box 249, Decatur, MI 49045-0249. Tel: (616) 423-8367 or fax: (616) 423-2421.

LAWTON
Country Peddler Show

DATES: November 18–20, 1994.
TIMES: Friday 4:00 PM–9:00 PM; Saturday 9:00 AM–5:00 PM; Sunday 11:00 AM–4:00 PM.
ADMISSION: Adults $5; children 2–12 years $2.
LOCATION: Lawton Community Center, 646 North Nursery.
DESCRIPTION: This indoor market features folk artisans selling a variety of American-made collectibles, arts and crafts, and fine art. All these products are one-of-a-kind heirlooms of the future. For your convenience there is food available on the premises. This show is one of a series of Country Peddler Shows held throughout Michigan and the East Coast. For more information regarding these shows, call or check the other state's listings.
DEALER RATES: $375 per 10' × 10' booth; $562.50 per 10' × 15' booth; $750 per 10' × 20' booth. Reservations are required.
CONTACT: American Memories, P.O. Box 249, Decatur, MI 49045-0249. Tel: (616) 423-8367 or fax: (616) 423-2421.

MASON
Country Peddler Show

DATES: Annually. For 1994: September 16–18. Usually the same weekend each year.
TIMES: Friday 4:00 PM–9:00 PM; Saturday 9:00 AM–5:00 PM; Sunday 11:00 AM–4:00 PM.
ADMISSION: $5 for adults; children 2–12 $2. Parking is $1.
LOCATION: Ingham County Fairgrounds, Arena Building. Exit Kipp Road off Route 127, follow fairgrounds signs (south of Lansing).
DESCRIPTION: Started in 1981, this indoor market features 90 folk artisans gathering annually to sell a variety of collectibles, arts and crafts, and fine art—the one-of-a-kind heirlooms of the future. For your convenience there is food available on the premises. This show is one of a series of Country Peddler Shows held throughout the East Coast. For more information regarding these shows, call or check the other state's listings. Also see the previous two listings for Michigan.

DEALER RATES: $375 per 10' × 10' booth; $562.50 per 10' × 15' booth; $750 per 10' × 20' booth. Reservations are required.

CONTACT: American Memories, Inc., P.O. Box 249, Decatur, MI 49045-0249. Tel: (616) 423-8367 or fax: (616) 423-2421.

MONTAGUE

Hump-T-Dump

DATES: Monday, Wednesday, Thursday, Friday, and Saturday; May through August, weather permitting.

TIMES: 10:30 AM–6:30 PM.

ADMISSION: Free admission and free parking.

LOCATION: 9510 Oceana Drive (Old U.S. 31). Three miles north of Montague, Michigan or 2½ miles south of Rothbury, Michigan on old U.S. 31.

DESCRIPTION: This one-man flea market opened in 1978, specializing in general, used merchandise, some antiques, and collectibles. They have a unique Peddler's Cart to mark their entrance and a large Humpty-Dumpty by the building. Candy and soda are available.

DEALER RATES: Not applicable.

CONTACT: Sharon Briggs, Route #2 Box 131, Montague, MI 49437. Tel: (616) 894-8753.

MT. CLEMENS

Gibraltar Trade Center North

DATES: Friday through Sunday, year round.

TIMES: Friday 12:00 PM–9:00 PM, Saturday 9:00 AM–9:00 PM, Sunday 9:00 AM–6:00 PM.

ADMISSION: $1.50 a carload.

LOCATION: I-94 to Exit 237 North River Road, go 1 mile down on right-hand side.

DESCRIPTION: Opened in 1990, this market has 1,200 dealer spaces and 50,000 square feet of selling space indoors. Dealers sell through special shows: Sports Cards, Gun and Knife, Antiques, Home Improvement, Boat and Fishing, Arts and Crafts, etc. Watch for the ads with the listing as to what show is on for the weekend. There is plenty of food available in snack bars and restaurants, and clean handicapped-accessible restrooms.

DEALER RATES: $65–85 for a 12' × 6' space, $75–100 for 12' × 8' space, $150 for 12' × 10', and $250 for 12' × 16. Outdoors at $10 a day for a 10' × 8' booth under canopy April through October only.

CONTACT: Gibraltar Trade Center North, Inc., 237 North River Road, Mt. Clemens, MI 48043. Tel: (313) 465-6440 or fax: (313) 465-0458.

MUSKEGON
Golden Token Flea Market

DATES: Saturdays.
TIMES: 6:00 AM–2:00 PM.
ADMISSION: Free. Parking is also free.
LOCATION: 1300 East Laketon Avenue. One block west of U.S. 31 on Laketon Avenue.
DESCRIPTION: Started in 1985, this growing market of about 75 dealers fills two rooms selling whatever—from antiques and collectibles to whatever comes in. In summer the market is held outside. Food, from hot dogs to shrimp dinners, is available on the premises.
DEALER RATES: $5–6 per table. Reservations are not required. Yearly rates are available. There is plenty of room!
CONTACT: Golden Token, 1300 East Laketon Avenue, Muskegon, MI 49442. Tel: (616) 773-1137 or 722-4646.

PAW PAW
Reits Flea Market

DATES: Saturdays, Sundays, and summer holidays, rain or shine.
TIMES: All day.
ADMISSION: Free. Free parking is available.
LOCATION: Five miles west of Paw Paw on Red Arrow Highway.
DESCRIPTION: This indoor/outdoor market opened in 1965 and currently accommodates approximately 550 dealers. There are many garage sale items along with antiques, toys, tools, household items, jewelry, collectibles, art, and much more. This is a clean and well-managed family market with events all summer long including a wine fest and S & L train rides nearby. Food is available on the premises.
DEALER RATES: $8 per 22' × 20' space per day, outdoors. $9 per space indoors. Reservations are not required.
CONTACT: Bob Hixenbaugh and Deno Broadwater, 45146 Red Arrow Highway, Paw Paw, MI 49079. Tel: (616) 657-3428 or (219) 259-8292.

RAVENNA
Ravenna Monday Market

DATES: Mondays, April through November, weather permitting.

TIMES: 7:00 AM until everyone goes.

ADMISSION: Free. Parking is also free.

LOCATION: Two miles north of the Ravenna Livestock Sales Grounds. Take I-96 from Grand Rapids west to Muskegon to Coopersville Exit, north about 13 miles.

DESCRIPTION: Having been forced out of their original location (in place for over 45 years), they have moved to this new 100-acre location just two miles down the road. The owner/managers ran the previous market until forced out and decided, after many calls and much soul-searching, to start again and duplicate the old market—atmosphere and all. The original market started as a junk yard next to a downtown livestock lot around 1948. It was known locally as the "junk lot" until it outgrew its location and the owners built a proper building and sales lot and moved over one block. Over the years the "junk lot" evolved into a flea market. There are plenty of reasonably priced goods, just-discovered attic treasures, and easy-to-get-along-with people. It has been estimated that 3,000 people come through here on any given Monday. The mostly repeat dealers sell from 150–200 stalls. A miscellaneous auction starts at 8:00 AM until whenever, depending on goodies sold. The items sold at the auction usually comprise loads of "stuff" dealers just don't want to set up for.

DEALER RATES: $5 per space. Reservations are not required. There is a 20% commission to the market on auction sales.

CONTACT: Collette and James Lund, 1685 19-Mile Road, Cedar Springs, MI 49319. Tel: (616) 696-1247.

ROMULUS
Green Lawn Grove Flea Market

DATES: Saturday, Sunday, and holiday Fridays and Mondays.

TIMES: 7:00 AM–4:00 PM.

ADMISSION: Free. Parking is also free.

LOCATION: 16447 Middlebelt Road, between Pennsylvania and Eureka Streets, 5 miles south of the airport.

DESCRIPTION: Since 1973 this market has 220 dealers in summer and 80 in winter, selling everything "from soup to nuts" including novelties, some antiques and collectibles, baseball cards, crafts, produce, and new merchandise. Two kitchens and two restrooms are available on the premises.

DEALER RATES: Reserved space is $12, unreserved is $14 for a 4' × 10' space. Reservations are required.

CONTACT: William Pai, Green Lawn Grove Flea Market, 16447 Middlebelt Road, Romulus, MI 48174. Tel: (313) 941-6930.

WARREN
Country Fair Flea Market

DATES: Every Friday, Saturday, and Sunday, year round.
TIMES: Friday 4:00 PM–9:00 PM, Saturday and Sunday 10:00 AM–6:00 PM.
ADMISSION: Free. Parking is also free.
LOCATION: 20900 Dequindre Boulevard, 2 blocks north of Eight Mile Road.
DESCRIPTION: This indoor show began in 1978 and currently has about 300 dealers exhibiting antiques, collectibles, produce, meats and cheeses, handcrafted wares, new merchandise, 14-carat gold and silver jewelry, and brass items. Food is served on the premises.
DEALER RATES: $40 per 5' × 10' space per weekend. Reservations are suggested.
CONTACT: Katie Holland, Owner, or Joe Sherman, Country Fair Flea Market, 20900 Dequindre, Warren, MI 48091. Tel: (313) 757-3740 or 757-3741.

WATERFORD
Dixieland Antique Flea Market

DATES: Inside: Friday, Saturday, and Sunday, year round. Outside: Memorial Day to Labor Day.
TIMES: Friday 4:00 PM–9:00 PM, Saturday and Sunday 10:00 AM–6:00 PM.
ADMISSION: Free. Parking is also free.
LOCATION: On corner of Dixie Highway and Telegraph Road.
DESCRIPTION: It is nice to discover a market that hangs on to local color. Garland Brown, the "Mayor" of Dixieland, is one of the fixtures of Dixieland. Since 1975 and under its present ownership since 1986 this market has over 200 dealers selling antiques, collectibles, new and used merchandise, and a food court. "Every day is a treasure hunt." This market has been described as a giant garage sale. In summer, when the outside is open, then it becomes a *humongou*s garage sale. If you are interested, they have a real mummy coffin for sale.
DEALER RATES: Inside: $45 and up. Outside: $18 for one day, $28 for the weekend. Reservations are accepted upon availability.

CONTACT: Jill Gurwin, Dixieland Flea Market, 2045 Dixie Highway, Waterford, MI 48328. Tel: (810) 338-3220.

WYOMING
Beltline Flea Market

DATES: Saturday and Sunday, mid-April through October, weather permitting.

TIMES: 5:00 AM–1:00 PM.

ADMISSION: $.50 per person. Free parking is available.

LOCATION: At 1400 28th Street SW, 3 miles west of State Route 131.

DESCRIPTION: This outdoor market, comprising 300 dealers, is 15 years old. A wide variety of antiques and collectibles is sold. New merchandise and some produce are also available. For your convenience, food is served on the premises.

DEALER RATES: $8 per 8' × 20' stall. First come, first served rentals. Seasonal rentals are available.

CONTACT: Beltline Flea Market, 1400 28th Street SW, Wyoming, MI 49509. Tel: (616) 532-6302.

OTHER FLEA MARKETS

Lake City: Lake City Flea Market, 518 Union Street, Lake City, MI 49651. Tel: (616) 839-3206. Open daily 9:00 AM–5:00 PM, May through October.

Lexington: Lexington Harbor Bazaar, 5590 Main Street, Lexington, MI 48450. Tel: (313) 359-5333. Open weekends 10:00 AM–6:00 PM.

Muskegon: Muskegon Farmers Flea Market, 700 Yuba Street, Muskegon, MI 49442. Tel: (616) 728-6433. Open Wednesday 6:00 AM–6:00 PM, May through October.

Muskegon: Select Auditorium Flea Market, 1445 East Laketon, Muskegon, MI 49442. Tel: (616) 726-5707. Open Saturday 6:00 AM–6:00 PM.

Ypsilanti: The Huron Trade Center, 210 East Michigan Avenue, Ypsilanti, MI 48198. Tel: (313) 480-1539. Open Friday 4:00 PM–9:00 PM, weekends 10:00 PM–6:00 PM.

MINNESOTA

BLAINE
Blaine Flea Market

DATES: Daily.

TIMES: Monday through Friday 10:00 AM–8:00 PM; Saturday and Sunday 10:00 AM–6:00 PM.

ADMISSION: Free. Parking is also free.

LOCATION: In Blaine, off Highway 65 or Central.

DESCRIPTION: With 35,000 square feet of indoor space, this unusual flea market has dealer spaces ranging in size from 10' × 10' to 5,000 square feet. Dealers sell "odds and ends," furniture, food, used office furniture, computers, gifts, silk, appliances, and there's even a thrift store.

DEALER RATES: $175 per month for 10' × 10'. Reservations are required. Thirty day rental.

CONTACT: Floyd, Blaine Flea Market, 10980 Central Avenue NE, Blaine, MN 55434. Tel: (612) 757-9906.

DULUTH
23rd Annual Studebaker Drivers Club
Swap Meet Flea Market and Classic Car Show

DATES: Annually, the second Sunday in August, rain or shine.

TIMES: 8:00 AM–5:00 PM.

ADMISSION: $2 donation per person. Free parking is available.

LOCATION: Duluth Technical College Campus, 2101 Trinity Road, near Miller Hill Mall.

DESCRIPTION: This show opened in 1972. It is both an indoor and outdoor market that accommodates anywhere from 200 to 250 dealers. You can buy anything from antiques and collectibles to junk, coins, gifts, crafts, glass, hobbies, new merchandise, and fresh produce at this market. Many old and restored antique cars are on display for the Car Show. There are also old car parts for all makes and models on sale. Food is served on the premises.

DEALER RATES: $10 per 10' × 20' space outdoors; $10 per 10' × 10' space indoors. Reservations are recommended. There are advance shopping hours for dealers on the Saturday before the show.

CONTACT: Shirley D. Van Dell, 102 North Boundary Avenue, Duluth, MN 55810. Tel: (218) 624-5932.

MONTICELLO
Orchard Fun Market

DATES: Every Saturday and Sunday, rain or shine.

TIMES: 9:00 AM–5:00 PM.

ADMISSION: Free. Acres of free parking are provided.

LOCATION: On Orchard Road. Take Route 75 three miles west from the stoplight in downtown Monticello, then turn at Orchard Road and go approximately ¼ mile.

DESCRIPTION: This indoor/outdoor market began around 1972 and currently attracts between 250 and 500 dealers per market day, depending on the season; the facilities include 250 tables inside and 400 outside. The fare at this market includes antiques, collectibles, and used household items, as well as new merchandise and fresh produce. Other attractions include live entertainment on two stages, bumper boat rides, and "slick-rack racers" for the kids. Chicken dinners, bratwurst, hot dogs, funnel cakes, corn dogs, and more are served on the premises.

DEALER RATES: $10–$11 per 8' × 10' table per day. Reservations are not accepted.

CONTACT: Orchard Fun Market, 1479 127th Street NW, Monticello, MN 55362. (612) 295-2121.

ORONOCO
Downtown Oronoco Gold Rush, Inc.

DATES: Third Saturday and Sunday in August, rain or shine.

TIMES: Sunup to sundown.

ADMISSION: Free. Parking is also free. The town provides free outlying parking with bus transportation into town. Hint: Don't try to park in town.

LOCATION: The entire downtown Oronoco!

DESCRIPTION: Started in 1972, the entire town participates in this weekend-long flea market. The main street is closed off to traffic and over 1,000 dealers set up selling antiques, collectibles, flea market goodies, crafts, and unfound and re-found treasures. As one organizer says "if they don't have it here in those two days, you can't find it!" Some residents sell right out of their garages. Over 30,000 people come through here each day. The money raised is used to help the City of Oronoco finance their First Response system, the fire department, planting new trees, fixing the community center, fireworks for July 4th, and whatever else is needed. Ample food is available.

DEALER RATES: $50 per 15' × 15' space for the weekend. Reservations are required. Many spaces are reserved well in advance.
CONTACT: Sara Krause, Oronoco Gold Rush, P.O. Box 266, Oronoco, MN 55960.

WABASHA
Wabasha Indoor/Outdoor Flea Market
DATES: Saturday and Sunday, year round.
TIMES: 9:00 AM–5:00 PM.
ADMISSION: Free. Parking is also free.
LOCATION: Highway 61 and Industrial Court.
DESCRIPTION: Since 1988, this market of 120 tables, has been selling new and used merchandise, carpet, furniture, antiques, and collectibles. Coinciding with the arrival of the Mississippi Queen Riverboat, usually in September, the town celebrates Riverboat Days with a parade as well as a huge celebration. Food is available on the premises.
DEALER RATES: $8 per table. Reservations are required.
CONTACT: Doc Carlson, Wabasha Indoor/Outdoor Flea Market, P.O. Box 230, Wabasha, MN 55981. Tel: (612) 565-4767.

OTHER FLEA MARKETS
Detroit Lakes: Shady Hollow Flea Market, 5 miles south of Detroit Lakes on Highway 59. Contact Ardis R. Hanson, Route 5 Box 227, Dtroit Lakes, MN 56501. Tel: (218) 847-9488. Or Monte D. Jones, Route 3 Box 86D, Detroit Lakes, MN 56501. Tel: (218) 847-5706. Open Sundays, Memorial Day through Labor Day, and July 4th, We-Fest Saturday and the weekend of Labor Day. Averages 100 vendors.

MISSISSIPPI

AMORY

Bigbee Waterway Trade Days

DATES: The weekend after the first Monday of the month.
TIMES: Daylight hours, whatever they are.
ADMISSION: Free. Parking is free.
LOCATION: Three miles north of Amory on Highway 371. Only ½ mile from the Ten Tom Waterway.
DESCRIPTION: Opened in July 1991, this market attracts about 100 dealers selling the usual flea market fare: antiques, collectibles, crafts, new merchandise, coins, stamps, cards, and whatever. There are two concession stands on the grounds selling ice cream, plate lunches, snacks, nachos, funnel cakes, etc. Restrooms and showers are available. There's fishing on the waterway nearby, just in case you need something extra to do.
DEALER RATES: $15 for a 20' × 20' space. Reservations are recommended. They have sheds and full hook-ups.
CONTACT: Teresa Roby, Bigbee Waterway Trade Days, 30211 Highway 371, Amory, MS 38821. Tel: (601) 256-1226.

It is said that a picture and frame were sold for $5 at an auction near here. The new owner took the picture and frame to another auction and sold it for $115 and thought he did real well! The savvy New York buyer took it back to New York and reportedly sold it for over $50,000. So there.

JACKSON

Fairgrounds Antique Flea Market

DATES: Saturday and Sunday, year round.
TIMES: Saturday 8:00 AM–5:00 PM; Sunday 10:00 AM–5:00 PM.
ADMISSION: $.75 per person. Free parking.
LOCATION: Take High Street exit off I-55 to 801 Mississippi Street at the State Fairgrounds. In the big "steel building."
DESCRIPTION: This indoor flea market is in its seventh year and has over 200 dealers in antiques, collectibles, handicrafts, produce, and new merchandise. There are also some primitives and books. This

is a very well-rounded flea market. A complete concession provides food on the premises. Camper hook-ups are available.

DEALER RATES: $30 for a wall booth, $40 for an aisle booth, $4 each for tables. Reservations are required one week in advance.

CONTACT: Frank Barnett, Fairgrounds Antique Flea Market, P.O. Box 23579, Jackson, MS 39225. Tel: (601) 353-5327.

PASCAGOULA
Super Flea Market

DATES: Daily except Wednesdays, year round.

TIMES: 9:00 AM–6:00 PM.

ADMISSION: Free. Parking is also free.

LOCATION: 4502 Chico Road. Corner of Highway 90 and Chico Road.

DESCRIPTION: Started on March 16, 1990 and taken over by a local ministry, this indoor/outdoor market now uses this business to help the local homeless and other community services. Some of the homeless men work at the market assisting visitors and dealers, cleaning up, and working their way back into society. Their 100 dealers sell arts and crafts, antiques, coins, stamps, woodwork, yard sales, tools, clothing, and more. There are 100 booths inside an air-conditioned building with security. More booths are outside. A produce market runs daily as do lawn booths. This is a clean family environment. Food is available on the premises. There is also entertainment for your enjoyment.

DEALER RATES: Daily rates: $10 per 8' × 10' space; $12.50 for wall space; outside $5 per 20' × 20' space. Offer daily, weekly and monthly rates. Reservations are suggested.

CONTACT: Reverend Bill Day, Super Flea Market, 4502 Chico Road, Pascagoula, MS 39567. Tel: (601) 769-8714 or 826-5651.

RIPLEY
First Monday Flea Market

DATES: First Monday and preceding Saturday and Sunday of each month.

TIMES: Dawn to dusk.

ADMISSION: Free. $1.50 parking fee.

LOCATION: On Highway 15, 85 miles from Memphis and 45 miles from Tupelo.

DESCRIPTION: This outdoor market has operated under present management since the mid-1970s, although local sources claim to be able to trace it back to first Mondays as early as 1893, ranking it among the nation's most venerable. Presently accommodating an average of 700 dealers, there is everything from antiques, collectibles, fresh produce, and new merchandise to a variety of crafts and reproduction oak furniture available. Food is served on the premises.

DEALER RATES: $22.50 for a 18' × 18' booth. Reservations are suggested.

CONTACT: Ripley First Monday Trade Days, 10590 Highway 15 South, Ripley, MS 38663. Tel: (601) 837-4051.

OTHER FLEA MARKETS

Amory: 41 Flea Market, U.S. 278 and U.S. 45, Amory, MS 38821. Tel: (601) 224-6237. Open third weekends, Friday through Sunday during daylight.

Columbus: Traders Village Flea Market, 2608 Highway 82 East, Columbus, MS 39701. Tel: (601) 328-6750. Open Friday 10:00 AM–6:00 PM, Saturday 9:00 AM–6:00 PM, Sunday 12:00 noon–6:00 PM.

Corinth: Corinth Flea Market, 1224 Highway 72 East, Corinth, MS 38824. Tel: (601) 287-9110 or 287-1387. Open Wednesday through Saturday 10:00 AM–7:00 PM, Sunday 1:00 PM–6:00 PM.

Pascagoula: Jackson County Flea Market, 2519 Telephone Road, Pascagoula, MS 39567. Tel: (601) 762-9994. Open daily, 7:30 AM–5:00 PM.

MISSOURI

JOPLIN
Joplin Flea Market

DATES: Every Saturday and Sunday, year round. Rain or shine.
TIMES: 8:00 AM–5:00 PM.
ADMISSION: Free admission and free parking.
LOCATION: 1200 block of Virginia Avenue; 1 block east of 12th and Main Streets.
DESCRIPTION: This indoor/outdoor show is in its 12th year. It comprises 150 dealers selling all kinds of curios and antiques. There are crafts, collectibles, new and used merchandise, produce, meats and cheeses, primitives, stamps and coins, tools, jewelry, clothing, postcards, and the list goes on. An entire city block of flea market space has grown behind this market until the cold sends the dealers home for warmth. For your convenience, food is available on the premises.
DEALER RATES: $5 per 10' × 18' space per day outside; $10 per 9' × 20' space each day. Free storage for the following week is provided with advance payment. Reservations are suggested.
CONTACT: Laverne Miller, c/o Joplin Flea Market, 2572 Markwardt Avenue, Joplin, MO 64801. Tel: (417) 623-3743 or 623-6328.

KANSAS CITY
Jeff William's Everything Show and Flea Market

DATES: One or two Sundays each month. (Dates vary; please write for latest schedule.)
TIMES: 8:00 AM–4:00 PM.
ADMISSION: $1. Free parking is available.
LOCATION: Governor's Building (Kemper Arena Complex), 1800 Genessee. Go west on 12th Street and follow signs to Kemper Arena.
DESCRIPTION: Opened in 1973, this indoor market accommodates over 500 dealers. Along with a large variety of antiques, collectibles, arts and crafts, and new merchandise, they sell lots of nostalgia and memorabilia. Because this monthly flea market has recently moved to a larger facility, it no longer takes two years to rent a space! This show is definitely worth calling for more information about dates. Food is served on the premises.
DEALER RATES: $35 per 10' × 10' space, $70 for a 10' × 20' space. Reservations are required.

CONTACT: Jeff Williams Productions, P.O. Box 543, Blue Springs, MO 64013. Tel: (816) 228-5811.

LEBANON
Country Corner Flea Market

DATES: Daily.

TIMES: Monday through Saturday 9:00 AM–6:00 PM; Sunday 12:00 PM–6:00 PM.

ADMISSION: Free. Free parking is available.

LOCATION: 585 North Jefferson Street.

DESCRIPTION: This indoor market started in 1974. Over 40 dealers are on hand selling antiques, collectibles, handicrafts, gift items, primitives, and new merchandise.

DEALER RATES: $5 to $10 per 8' × 10' booth per day. Reservations are suggested.

CONTACT: Marilyn Allen, c/o Country Corner Flea Market, 585 Jefferson Street, Lebanon, MO 65536. Tel: (417) 588-1430.

PEVELY
The Big Pevely Flea Market

DATES: Every Saturday and Sunday, year round, rain or shine.

TIMES: 7:00 AM–5:00 PM.

ADMISSION: Free admission and free parking.

LOCATION: Take I-55 south from St. Louis to Pevely/Hillsborough Highway Z Exit to Highway 61/67, then go ¼ mile to market on the right hand side.

DESCRIPTION: This indoor/outdoor market opened in 1969 in an old drive-in theater. Over the years they have added two buildings housing about 200 dealers each. Altogether, their 500 to 600 dealers sell antiques, collectibles, crafts, furniture, cards, clothing, garage sale goodies, vegetables, and new merchandise. A snack bar serves the hungry. There is a special place outdoors for the "garage sale" vendors.

DEALER RATES: Outside: $8 a day. Inside: $12 a single space, $30 for a corner double space. If you rent by the month, you get one day free. Reservations are required indoors. Outdoor space is allocated on a first come, first served basis.

CONTACT: Charlie Thomas, Ken Smith or Lee Douglas, The Big Pevely Flea Market, P.O. Box 300, Pevely, MO 63070-0300. Tel: (314) 479-3215 or 479-5400.

SIKESTON
Tradewinds Flea Market

DATES: Every Thursday through Sunday, rain or shine.
TIMES: All day.
ADMISSION: Free. Free parking is available.
LOCATION: 875 West Malone. Sikeston is 150 miles south of St. Louis, 150 miles north of North Memphis.
DESCRIPTION: This indoor/outdoor market opened in 1974 and now accommodates approximately 300 dealers. There is everything here from antiques and collectibles to arts and crafts to new merchandise. Tools, toys, fresh produce, as well as chickens, turkeys, guinea pigs, and rabbits are available. The Tradewinds Restaurant is in the middle of the market and open daily. This market has been growing steadily since it began, as more and more dealers are coming from all over the United States to sell their goods.
DEALER RATES: $7 per 14' × 14' space per day. Reservations are required during the summer months.
CONTACT: Tradewinds Flea Market, 165 Lee Street, Sikeston, MO 63801. Call the Tradewinds Restaurant at (314) 471-3965.

SPRINGFIELD
Swap Shop, Flea Market and Swap Meet

DATES: Wednesday through Sunday.
TIMES: 10:30 AM–5:00 PM.
ADMISSION: Free. Parking is also free.
LOCATION: 1024 NW By-pass.
DESCRIPTION: Opened in 1989, and expanded at this new location in 1992, this market hosts 60 to 100 dealers on 20 acres selling tools of all sorts, toy collections, used and new merchandise, antiques and collectibles, and whatever else there is. There are several bargain tables—the ½ mile long "everything for a quarter" and the "everything for a buck." The same management runs another market in another part of town (next entry).
DEALER RATES: $5 per space. Reservations are not required.
CONTACT: Butch Koonce or Bob, Swap Shop, 1024 NW By-Pass, Springfield, MO 65803. Tel: (417) 864-4340.

I-44 Swap Meet

DATES: Saturday and Sunday, March through December, rain or shine.
TIMES: Daylight to dark.

ADMISSION: $1 per car admission and parking.
LOCATION: 2908 North Niergaard across from the Zenith TV Plant.
DESCRIPTION: "Sooner or later it's out there, if you want it." Started in 1984, this swap meet has from 200 to 300 dealers selling everything! It is on 40 acres right along I-44. Pony rides, live bands, and ten snack bars liven things up. Free camping on Friday and weekends.
DEALER RATES: For a 30' × 20' space: $5 on Saturday; $6 Sundays. Reservations are suggested.
CONTACT: Butch Koonce or Bob, 2908 North Niergaard, Springfield, MO 65803. Tel: (417) 866-7493 or 864-4340 or 864-6508.

Olde Towne Antique Mall and Flea Market

DATES: Daily except Tuesday, year round. Closed Thanksgiving, Christmas, New Years, and Easter.
TIMES: Monday through Saturday 9:30 AM–5:00 PM, Sunday 1:00 PM–5:00 PM.
ADMISSION: Free, with ample free parking.
LOCATION: 600 Booneville Avenue.
DESCRIPTION: This market, housed in a three-story 60,000 square-foot World War II clothing factory, has been operating since 1978. Over 100 dealers sell their antiques, collectibles, crafts, and new merchandise from indoor booths. They say they have "the largest collection of antique furniture in southwest Missouri." Some jewelry and primitives are on hand as well. A snack bar operates on the premises.
DEALER RATES: $60 per 6' × 10' booth per month. Reservations are not required.
CONTACT: Lana Hall, Olde Towne Antique Mall and Flea Market, 600 Booneville Avenue, Springfield, MO 65806. Tel: (417) 831-6665.

Ozark Empire Fairgrounds Flea Market

DATES: Second Friday, Saturday, and Sunday of every month.
TIMES: Friday 5:00 PM–8:30 PM, Saturday 7:00 AM–5:00 PM, Sunday 8:00 AM–4:00 PM.
ADMISSION: Free. Parking is $1.
LOCATION: Ozark Empire Fairgrounds, Main Arena, I-44 Exit 77.
DESCRIPTION: Opened in 1990, this market has 200 dealers indoors and an unlimited number outdoors (weather permitting) selling antiques, collectibles, vintage to new clothing, arts and crafts, games, toys, books, cards, new merchandise, garage sale finds, whatever.
DEALER RATES: $60 for a 10' × 10' space each weekend indoors,

$5 for an outside table space per day, or $6 each for table rentals. CONTACT: J.T. or Joyce Porter or Janet Owens, P.O. Box 3033, Springfield MO 65808. Tel: (417) 833-5119.

OTHER FLEA MARKETS

Imperial: Barnhart Flea Market, 6850 Highway 61 and 67, Imperial, MO 63052. Tel: (314) 464-5503. Open weekends 6:00 AM–5:00 PM.
Old Mines: Starlite Drive-In Market, Old Mines, MO 63630. Tel: (314) 438-4974. Open weekends 8:00 AM–4:00 PM March through November.
Villa Ridge: Ozark Trader Mall, 376 Highway 100 East, Villa Ridge, MO 63089. Tel: (314) 257-4440.

> Somewhere in northwest Missouri is a state highway that becomes a 39-mile long flea market. If you pass through it, just stop and set up. Or buy.

MONTANA

BILLINGS

Great American Bazaar

DATES: Daily except Christmas, Thanksgiving, and Easter.

TIMES: Weekdays 10:00 AM–6:00 PM, Saturday 9:00 AM–6:00 PM, and Sunday 11:00 AM–6:00 PM.

ADMISSION: Free. Parking is free.

LOCATION: 1600 Main Street.

DESCRIPTION: Opened in 1987, this market's 150 dealers sell antiques in the Lind Antique Mall, crafts in two "malls" and new merchandise, furniture, collectibles, some garage sale goodies, primitives, books, Montana sausage, buffalo, and candies among other items. There is a restaurant specializing in Chinese food on site. Generally, this market is full, but they do have spaces available for the wandering dealer coming through.

DEALER RATES: $10 per day for a 10' × 10' space for transients. Longer-term rates from $35 to $100 depending on the location within the market. Reservations are required.

CONTACT: Great American Bazaar, 1600 Main Street, Billings, MT 59105. Tel: (406) 259-6490.

GREAT FALLS

Great Falls Farmer's Market

DATES: Every Saturday and Wednesday, July 1–October 1.

TIMES: Wednesday 4:30 AM–6:00 PM; Saturday 8:00 AM–12:00 noon.

ADMISSION: Free. Ample free parking is available.

LOCATION: At the Civic Center, 21 Irish Lane.

DESCRIPTION: This outdoor market hosts about 45 dealers and has been running for six years. This traditional farmer's market has taken in the flea dealers who, as yet, don't have separate ongoing markets in the state of Montana. Handicrafts are featured alongside the traditional meat, dairy, and produce offerings of local farmers. There is food served on the premises.

DEALER RATES: Ten percent commission of items sold, with 30' × 8' space provided; or $25 per space plus two tables per day. Reservations taken for the best selling locations.

CONTACT: Mike Winters, Great Falls Farmer's Market, 21 Irish Lane, Great Falls, MT 59401.

NEBRASKA

LINCOLN
Pershing Auditorium Flea Market
DATES: Saturday and Sunday. Held monthly, dates vary.
TIMES: 10:00 AM–5:00 PM.
ADMISSION: $.75 per person, 12 and under free. Parking $1–2.
LOCATION: Pershing Auditorium, lower level. 226 Centennial Mall South, at 15th and North in downtown Lincoln. Two blocks north of the state capitol.
DESCRIPTION: This indoor show opened in 1978, and has grown from a small market of 25 booths to one of full capacity accommodating 80 dealers from a five-state area selling antiques, arts and crafts, collectibles, and new merchandise. Food is served on the premises.
DEALER RATES: 1993 rates: $40 per 8' x 13' space; $55 per 8' x 21' space; $70 per 8' x 29' space for the weekend. Reservations are required. The 1994 rates were not available at press time.
CONTACT: Mr. Derek Andersen, P.O. 81126, Lincoln, NE 68508. Tel: (402) 471-7500.

SOUTH SIOUX CITY
South Sioux City Flea Market
DATES: Held the second weekend of the month, except June, July, and August. Call for correct dates.
TIMES: Saturday 9:00 AM–5:00 PM; Sunday 11:00 AM–4:00 PM.
ADMISSION: $.50. Parking is free.
LOCATION: 5th and C Streets.
DESCRIPTION: This indoor market, initiated in 1969, has been operating in a wide open, bright, modern building since 1986. They have 225 tables where antiques, collectibles, handmade and craft items, and new merchandise are sold. At least 70 percent of the items shown are antiques. The crowds have been increasing weekly, attracted by the quality of the collections. Most of the dealers are repeats lending a good sense of quality and permanence to this market. This market is especially handicapped accessible because of its wide aisles and open spaces. Food is available on the premises.
DEALER RATES: $17 per 8' table; $60 for 6 tables. Reservations are required. Call for more information.
CONTACT: Ed & Bonnie Benson, P.O. Box 236, Sioux Falls SD 57101. Tel: (605) 361-1717.

NEVADA

LAS VEGAS
Fantastic Indoor Swap Meet
DATES: Friday, Saturday and Sunday, year round.
TIMES: 10:00 AM–6:00 PM.
ADMISSION: $1. Parking is free.
LOCATION: 1717 South Decatur at Oakey Boulevard.
DESCRIPTION: Opened in 1990, this huge market has 350 dealers selling antiques, collectibles, crafts, "the most wonderful things," from satellite dishes to more usual fare. There are four restaurants selling a variety of ethnic food, ice cream, pop corn, and hot dogs.
DEALER RATES: From $290 and up for four weeks. Advance reservations are required as there is a two-week waiting period to get a city license.
CONTACT: Alan Weir, Fantastic Indoor Swap Meet, 1717 South Decatur, Las Vegas, NV 89102. Tel: (702) 877-0087.

The Gemco Indoor Swap Meet
DATES: Friday, Saturday and Sunday, year round.
TIMES: 10:00 AM–6:00 PM.
ADMISSION: $1. Parking is free.
LOCATION: 3455 Boulder Highway and East Sahara.
DESCRIPTION: Opened in 1988 and doing very well, this market has over 450 shops run by 250 merchants selling antiques, collectibles, crafts, and "everything from A to Z" including sporting equipment, home decor, electronics, food, garden shop, tools, and more. Fast food, hot dog stand, and a barbecue restaurant are on the premises.
DEALER RATES: Booths start at $160 for four weeks. Reservations are required as they rent only by four weeks at a time. There is a two-week waiting period as dealers are required to get a city license to sell.
CONTACT: Pam Chernov, Manager, The Gemco Indoor Swap Meet, 3455 Boulder Highway, Las Vegas, NV 89121. Tel: (702) 641-7927.

NORTH LAS VEGAS
Broadacres Open Air Swap Meet
DATES: Friday, Saturday, and Sunday, year round, rain or shine.
TIMES: Friday 6:30 AM–12:30 PM, weekends 6:30 AM–2:00 PM.

ADMISSION: $.50 on Friday, otherwise $.75 per person, children under 12 free.

LOCATION: Las Vegas Boulevard North at Pecos. Four miles north of the Union Plaza Hotel on Las Vegas Boulevard North.

DESCRIPTION: Opened in 1977, this outdoor market is in its fifteenth year of business. Seven hundred dealers in the summer attract 18,000 buyers weekly, and 1,000 dealers attract 25,000 buyers during the winter months. Antiques, collectibles, handmade/craft items, vegetables, and new merchandise are available.

DEALER RATES: The charge for a booth measuring 15' x 30' is $14 on Saturday and Sunday and $7 on Friday. Advance reservations are suggested at least one week in advance. Make your reservations during business hours. They have 700 reserved spaces and only 300 daily unreserved spaces.

CONTACT: Jake Bowman, Broadacres Open Air Swap Meet, P.O. Box 3059, North Las Vegas, NV 89030-3059. Tel: (702) 642-3777.

SPARKS

El Rancho Flea Market

DATES: Saturdays and Sundays, March through November, rain or shine.

TIMES: Summer: 6:15 AM–4:00 PM: winter: 7:15 AM–4:00 PM.

ADMISSION: $.50 per person; children under 12 free. Parking is free.

LOCATION: Go north on Kietzke Lane to 555 El Rancho Drive. Two blocks north of I-80 at the "B" Street exit.

DESCRIPTION: Located in Sparks, well known for gambling casinos, near Lake Tahoe. The twin city to Reno. Opened in 1978, this outdoor flea market attracts 200 to 250 dealers selling antiques, collectibles, fresh produce, new merchandise, and garage sale items. Food is available on the premises.

DEALER RATES: $13 for booths measuring 18' × 20' or 11' × 11'. Reservations are not required; first come, first served.

CONTACT: Ruthann Smyth, El Rancho Swap, 555 El Rancho Drive, Sparks, NV 89431. Tel: (702) 331-3227.

OTHER FLEA MARKETS

Las Vegas: Discount Depot, 2655 South Maryland Parkway, Las Vegas, NV 89104. Tel: (702) 792-3983. Open Thursday through Sunday 10:00 AM–6:00 PM.

NEW HAMPSHIRE

DERRY
Grand View Flea Market

DATES: Saturday and Sunday, year round, rain or shine.

TIMES: Saturday 9:00 AM–3:00 PM, Sunday 7:00 AM–4:00 PM.

ADMISSION: Sunday only: $.50 for adults; children under 12 free.

LOCATION: At the Junction of Route 28 and Bypass 28 South.

DESCRIPTION: This show, established more than 25 years ago, is one of northern New England's first and finest. In the center of the market is a pond with a 30-foot-tall Indian totem pole. It also has a strange collection of statuary including two very large elephants, a bear, and several genies purchased from an old amusement park. Two hundred to 400 dealers work indoors and out, selling all sorts of antiques, collectibles, crystals, books, novelties, jewelry, gifts, reptiles (really, sold by a licensed humane society specialist), appliances, fabric and lace, handmades, and new items. A new addition, added in the fall of 1990 increased the indoor market by 60 spaces, then another 24,000 square feet were added in 1993. It's an interesting market always trying new things like magic shows to amuse the children. Chinese and American food is available on the premises. A golf range is next door.

DEALER RATES: $25 per 12' × 8' space indoors per day including 3 tables; $20 per "large car length" space outdoors per day. Tables are available for rental at $1.50 per day. Reservations are suggested but not required.

CONTACT: Kathi Taylor, 34 South Main Street, Derry, NH 03086. Tel: (603) 432-2326.

HOLLIS
Hollis Country Store and Flea Market

DATES: Every Sunday, first Sunday of April through the second Sunday of November; plus Memorial Day and Labor Day.

TIMES: 7:00 AM–dusk.

ADMISSION: Free. $1 parking fee.

LOCATION: On Silver Lake Road (Route 122). Take Exit 7W off Route 3 to 101A west. Go 8 miles, then turn left onto Route 122. Market is 1½ miles on the right.

DESCRIPTION: Opened in 1965, this outdoor market now attracts over 250 dealers, selling antiques and collectibles as well as new merchandise and fresh produce. This is a well-attended, busy market, attracting dealers and customers from all over New England and as far away as California. They have an excellent reputation for quality goods at reasonable prices. Food is served on the premises.

DEALER RATES: $14 per 16' × 22' space. Reservations are preferred.

CONTACT: Gil and Alice Prieto, 436 Silver Lake Road, Hollis, NH 03049. Tel: (603) 465-7813.

This'll Get 'em Department:
A woman brought in a trailer with a shed on it loaded with over $10,000 worth of power tools—and sold it all for $10. She was divorcing her husband.

LEBANON
Colonial Antiques & Flea Market

DATES: Daily indoors, Sundays outdoors, weather permitting.

TIMES: 9:00 AM–5:00 PM. However, Sundays during the dark months the whole market opens at 8:00 AM; during the light months it opens at 6:00 AM.

ADMISSION: Free. Parking is free.

LOCATION: Route 12A at Exit 20 off I-89.

DESCRIPTION: Opened in 1976, and under new management since mid-April 1993, this market's over 90 dealers sell antiques, collectibles, estate jewelry, furniture, old books, old clothes, dolls, old tools, postcards, stamps, fine glassware, paintings, bottles, crafts, and much more. Many of their dealers are recognized authorities in their field. There are "loads of fine treasures, a bargain hunters paradise," with fine smalls, genuine Tiffany lamps, and rare prints among other found prizes. This market strives for the finest quality available. They have a reputation as the "first and oldest and funnest market in New England." On Sundays, Polly Hood opens her kitchen serving simple, modestly priced food. She also brings along her prized jams and pickles which sell out quickly. When Polly isn't there and hunger attacks, there are plenty of other eateries to go to nearby.

DEALER RATES: $26 for about 7' × 10' space weekly. Reservations are mandatory as there is a waiting list. No reservations for the outside space.

CONTACT: Orin Hunt, Colonial Plaza Antiques and Flea Market, Route 12A, West Lebanon, NH 03784. Tel: (603) 298-7712 or 298-8132.

Okay, I Believe That Department:

A woman came in looking for a Christmas present for her doctor husband and "hit" on an 1820 anatomy book published in Edinburgh, Scotland. She leafed through the pages with their copper-plate pictures and found a handsome adult male skeleton. Obviously intrigued she asked, "Who is this?" The dealer, without hesitation, replied, "George Washington." That didn't faze her. Then she happened upon another skeleton picture of an infant. "Who's this?" she asked. Again, without a blink, the dealer replied, "George Washington—as an infant."

She didn't buy the book.

MEREDITH
Burlwood Antique Center

DATES: Daily, May 1–October 31.

TIMES: 10:00 AM–5:00 PM.

ADMISSION: Free. Free parking is available.

LOCATION: On Route 3. From I-93, take Exit 23, then go east on Route 104, 9 miles to Route 3, then turn right to get to Burlwood Center.

DESCRIPTION: This indoor market opened in 1983 and currently accommodates over 170 dealers. There is a variety of antiques and collectibles sold and an entire floor of furniture. Fine art is also available. Because they are open only six months a year, all the merchandise is new to the market each year.

DEALER RATES: $90 per 5' × 3' × 8' space per month. Reservations are required.

CONTACT: Thomas and Nancy Lindsey, 106 Daniel Webster Highway, Meredith, NH 03253. Tel: (603) 279-6387.

NEWINGTON
Star Center Flea Market

DATES: Every Sunday, year round.

TIMES: 9:00 AM–4:00 PM.

ADMISSION: Free. Free parking is available.

LOCATION: 25 Fox Run Road. Take Exit 2 off Route 95 to Portsmouth, then onto Spaulding Turnpike, then to Fox Run Road.

DESCRIPTION: This indoor, air-conditioned market opened in 1979. There are approximately 100 to 120 dealers, and among the items for sale are antiques, arts and crafts, and collectibles, as well as new merchandise. This is a clean and well-kept market. There is a snack bar and ice cream stand on the premises.

DEALER RATES: $17 per 8' table. Reservations are required.

CONTACT: Mr. Robert J. Hajjar, c/o Star Center, 25 Fox Run Road, Newington, NH 03801. Tel: (603) 431-9403.

NEW JERSEY

ABSECON HIGHLANDS
L'Erario's Flea Market
DATES: Every Saturday and Sunday, weather permitting.
TIMES: 7:00 AM to whenever.
ADMISSION: Free. Free parking is available.
LOCATION: At intersection of Jim Leeds Road and Pitney Road, Route 561. Only minutes from Atlantic City.
DESCRIPTION: This outdoor market began in 1968 and currently accommodates approximately 50 to 80 dealers, selling anything from antiques, arts and crafts, and collectibles to new and used merchandise. There are three snack bars and restaurants on the premises.
DEALER RATES: $12 Saturdays; $15 Sundays per 20' space. Reservations are not required.
CONTACT: L'Erario's, P.O. Box 572, Absecon, NJ 08201. Tel: (609) 652-0540.

BELVIDERE
Five Acres
DATES: Every Saturday, Sunday, and holidays, year round.
TIMES: 8:00 AM until everyone is gone.
ADMISSION: Free. Parking is also free.
LOCATION: On Route 80 take Exit 12 south to Route 46, go east 1500 feet. Market is on right.
DESCRIPTION: This indoor/outdoor flea market opened in 1965. There are 75 to 100 dealers selling anything from antiques and collectibles to arts and crafts and new merchandise. Fresh produce is also available. There are clean restrooms, a game room, and a bar on premises.
DEALER RATES: $15 per 10' × 20' space on Sunday, $10 on Saturday. Reservations are not required.
CONTACT: Totsy Phillips, P.O. Box 295, Belvidere, NJ 07823. Tel: (908) 475-2572.

BERLIN
Berlin Farmers Market
DATES: Thursday, Friday, Saturday, and Sunday, rain or shine.
TIMES: 8:00 AM–4:00 PM outside Saturday and Sunday only. Thurs-

day through Saturday 11:00 AM–9:30 PM; Sunday 10:00 AM–6:00 PM inside.

ADMISSION: Free. Free parking is available.

LOCATION: 41 Clementon Road. Just off Route 30, Route 73 or Route 42 about 40 minutes from either Atlantic City or Philadelphia.

DESCRIPTION: This market started in 1930 as a livestock auction. Today it is located on about 60 acres of land. These spacious accommodations house the outdoor flea market and parking lot. The indoor shopping market is in a building a quarter of a mile long. Between their indoor and outdoor market, on any given weekend, there are anywhere from 700 to 800 dealers. The types of merchandise to be found are unlimited: from antiques to new merchandise, from quality new and used furniture to arts and crafts and fresh produce. Seen and sold: clothing of all kinds, gold stuff, toys, tools, hardware, health & beauty aids, furniture, sports cards, video games, tapes, etc. Once a customer brought in a house on a trailer—and sold it! There are two snack bars and three other food vendors inside, and eight food vendors outside. This flea market is proudly owned and operated by the third generation of the Giberson family.

DEALER RATES: $20 per 12' × 30' booth for strictly used merchandise for 2 days; $35 per 12' × 30' booth for all new merchandise. Reservations are suggested.

CONTACT: Stan Giberson, Jr. or Ron Smith, 41 Clementon Road, Berlin, NJ 08009. Tel: (609) 767-1284.

CAPE MAY

Cape May Convention Hall "Fun Sale"

DATES: Two Monday markets a year. 1994: July 17 and August 14.

TIMES: 7:30 AM–3:00 PM.

ADMISSION: Free. Parking is metered.

LOCATION: Beach Avenue, on the Boardwalk.

DESCRIPTION: This market, started about 20 years ago, hosts 50 dealers selling antiques, collectibles, crafts, and new merchandise. There are handicapped-accessible restrooms in the market. Food is available on the Boardwalk and from surrounding restaurants.

DEALER RATES: $35 and up. Tables are provided or bring your own. Reservations are recommended.

CONTACT: Nadia Promotions, Inc., P.O. Box 156, Flourtown, PA 19031-0156. Tel: (215) 643-1396 or fax: (215) 654-0896.

CLIFTON
Boys' and Girls' Club of Clifton Flea Market

DATES: Third Sunday of every month September through March; additionally the second Sunday of November and December only.
TIMES: 10:00 AM–4:00 PM.
ADMISSION: Free admission and free parking available.
LOCATION: 802 Clifton Avenue.
DESCRIPTION: This annual indoor event has been taking place for 15 years and has about ten show dates each season, with 85 to 100 dealers selling antiques, collectibles, new merchandise, and craft items. This show is used as a fundraiser for the 1,500 children who use the Club. Food is served on the premises.
DEALER RATES: $15 per 8' × 4' table. Reservations are required. Call for current rates.
CONTACT: Kathy Tulenko, Boys' and Girls' Club of Clifton, P.O. Box 798, Clifton, NJ 07015. Tel: (201) 773-2697.

COLUMBUS
Columbus Farmer's Market

DATES: Every Thursday, Friday, Saturday, and Sunday; rain or shine.
TIMES: Inside hours: Thursday 9:00 AM–9:00 PM; Friday 10:00 AM–9:00 PM; Saturday 9:00 AM–9:00 PM; Sunday 9:00 AM–6:00 PM. Outside hours: Thursday, Saturday, and Sunday. Dawn to whenever!
ADMISSION: Free. Free parking is available.
LOCATION: On Route 206, 5 miles south of Exit 7 off the New Jersey Turnpike.
DESCRIPTION: This indoor/outdoor market began in 1929. It accommodates from 400 dealers in winter to 1,700 dealers in summer, selling antiques and collectibles as well as new merchandise and fresh produce. There are 70 permanent stores including seven restaurants, monogramming, shoe repair, sewing machine repair, a Chinese food shop, and all types of specialty shops. Food is served on the premises.
DEALER RATES: Thursday $30 per 12' × 30' space; Saturday $10; Sunday $20 per 12' × 30' booth—new items, $15 per 12' × 30' booth—used items. Reservations are not required; spaces are assigned by the management.
CONTACT: Columbus Farmers Market, 2919 Route 206 South, Columbus, NJ 08022-0322. Tel: (609) 267-0400.

DORCHESTER
Campbell's Flea Market
DATES: Saturday and Sunday, March through December, rain or shine.
TIMES: 7:00 AM–5:00 PM.
ADMISSION: Free. Parking is also free.
LOCATION: Three miles south on Route 47 from Route 55.
DESCRIPTION: This market opened in 1961 on six acres with century-old trees providing plenty of shade. Route 47 is the major highway to the beaches making this a terrific spot to attract buyers. Sixty dealers inside and 80 outside sell antiques, crafts, attic treasures, collectibles, glassware, aluminum, and flea market fare. This is a market where social time among dealers and customers is common. Rare finds are still out here. A retired baker makes the most delicious cheesecake and apple cake, said to be worth the trip. Food is available on the premises. A Texaco station, an ice cream parlor, and deli are next door.
DEALER RATES: $8 per table inside or space outside. Reservations are not required.
CONTACT: Terry Campbell, P.O. Box 131, Dorchester, NJ 08316 Tel: (609) 785-2222.

EDISON
New Dover United Methodist Church Flea Market
DATES: Every Tuesday, mid-March through December, rain or shine.
TIMES: 7:00 AM–2:00 PM.
ADMISSION: Free. Free parking is available.
LOCATION: 690 New Dover Road. Take Exit 131 on Garden State Parkway, bear right, go to first light (Wood Avenue), turn right, go to second light (New Dover Road), finally, turn left.
DESCRIPTION: This indoor/outdoor market began in 1971. Since that time it has grown to accommodate approximately 100 dealers during summer months. Many items such as collectibles, new merchandise, and fresh produce can be purchased. This market is a fundraiser for the church. There are two security guards on the premises. Restrooms are available. The church kitchen, run by volunteers, sells hot homemade food.
DEALER RATES: $20 per table, bring your own table; tables on the inside and front parking lot are rented on monthly basis only. Reservations are required for monthly.

CONTACT: New Dover United Methodist Church, 690 New Dover Road, Edison, NJ 08820. Tel: (201) 381-7904.

ENGLISHTOWN
Englishtown Auction Sales Flea Market

DATES: Saturday and Sunday, March through January; also open Labor Day, Friday after Thanksgiving, and Fridays in December until Christmas. Closed in February.

TIMES: Saturday 7:00 AM–5:00 PM; Sundays and holidays 9:00 AM–5:00 PM.

ADMISSION: Free, with free parking available.

LOCATION: 90 Wilson Avenue; New Jersey Turnpike Exit 9; access from Route 18 East and Route 527 South.

DESCRIPTION: Since 1929 this market has been known as "recreational shopping at its best." This combination indoor/outdoor show is held in five buildings and on acres of outside dealer space. There are approximately 400 dealers selling antiques and collectibles, jewelry, hubcaps, clothing, housewares, furniture, as well as new merchandise. Food items are restricted, but there is a concession stand on the premises.

DEALER RATES: Spaces start at $5 a day. Monthly reservations are suggested.

CONTACT: Manager, Englishtown Auction Sales, 90 Wilson Avenue, Englishtown, NJ 07726. Tel: (908) 446-9644. Fax: (908) 446-1220.

FLEMINGTON
The Flemington Fair Flea Market

DATES: Every Wednesday and Friday, April through November, rain or shine.

TIMES: 7:00 AM–3:00 PM.

ADMISSION: Free. Free parking is available.

LOCATION: On Highway 31, 22 miles north of Trenton; 18 miles north of New Hope, Pennsylvania; 30 miles southeast of eastern Pennsylvania; 45 miles west of New York City.

DESCRIPTION: Started in 1980, this market now accommodates anywhere from 75 to 120 dealers outdoors as well as 16 indoor shops. Although the majority of vendors sell antiques and collectibles, fine art, arts and crafts, new merchandise, and fresh produce, everything under the sun can be found. Besides the many things you can buy here, there are events for children including an Easter contest and a costume contest. There is also food available on the premises. The town of Flemington has hundreds of outlet stores. Situated in the beautiful, historic country setting of the Flemington Fairgrounds, this can be a fun day for the entire family!

DEALER RATES: $6 per 8' × 20' space outdoors; $625 per season per 10' × 12' indoor shop which includes 10' × 30' outdoors. Reservations are required for indoor space only.

CONTACT: Melissa L. Yerkes, 25 Kuhl Road, Flemington, NJ 08822. Tel: (908) 782-7326 after 5:00 PM. Day of show call main office at (908) 782-2413.

GILLETTE
Meyersville Grange Antique Mart

DATES: Every Sunday, October through April.

TIMES: 8:00 AM-3:00 PM.

ADMISSION: Free. Free parking is available.

LOCATION: On Meyersville Road, between Route 78 and Route 24, in the heart of the Great Swamp Wildlife Preserve, in southeast Morris County.

DESCRIPTION: This market started in 1970. Approximately 35 dealers specialize in antiques, collectibles, and handmade craft items. Free coffee is served to all customers, and vendors can get free doughnuts while they set up. From 10:00 AM-2:00 PM, hot dogs, homemade soup, and pastries are served.

DEALER RATES: $15-$25 per 8' table, per day. Reservations are required and can be made any evening after 6:00 PM.

CONTACT: Mr. Walter O'Neill, Jr., 149 Kline Blvd, Berkeley Heights, NJ 07922. Tel: (201) 464-1598 after 6:00 PM. Day of show call (201) 647-9727.

HOWELL
Great American Flea Market

DATES: Tuesday through Sunday, year round.

TIMES: Mini-mall open Tuesday through Thursday 10:00 AM-6:00 PM. Entire market open Friday and Saturday 10:00 AM-9:00 PM; Sunday 10:00 AM-6:00 PM.

ADMISSION: Free. Parking is free.

LOCATION: On Route 9 North in Howell Township, about one mile north of I-195, Exit 28B. Also Exit 7A off New Jersey Turnpike onto I-195 East or Exit 98 off Garden State Parkway onto I-195 West.

DESCRIPTION: Opened in July 1990, and reopened under new management, this two-level market already has over 100 dealers selling antiques, collectibles, crafts, new merchandise, mens and ladies clothing, jewelry, tools, reptiles, baby furniture and accessories, computer pictures, video games, books and magazines, and more. There are plenty of shops including a used furniture consignment shop, beauty salon, tattoo parlor, ceramic shops, and a hobby shop. There is a food court with three snack bars. They hold weekly auctions: Tailgate on Wednesdays, antiques and collectibles on Fridays, potluck on Saturdays, as well as monthly shows and auctions (call about baseball card shows!). There is a Spernell indoor carpeted RC racetrack for more thrills. They are in the process of applying for permits from the local township to sell outside.

DEALER RATES: Daily space: $15 for a 8' banquet table (they supply it). Booths are about $315 for approximately a 10' × 10' space per month. Reservations are suggested.

CONTACT: Howard Bennett, Manager, Great American, 2301 Route 9 North, Howell, NJ 07731. Tel: (908) 308-1105.

LAMBERTVILLE

Golden Nugget Antique Flea Market

DATES: Every Wednesday, Saturday, and Sunday, outdoors, year round. Indoor shops are open on weekends. Rain or shine.

TIMES: Outdoors: 6:30 AM–5:00 PM; indoors 8:30 AM–4:00 PM.

ADMISSION: Free. Free parking is available.

LOCATION: Route 29, 1 mile south of Lambertville, 5 miles north of Exit 1 on I-95.

DESCRIPTION: This indoor/outdoor market began its operation in 1960 and currently accommodates 40 indoor shops and 200 tables outdoors. The main building offers 15,000 square feet of space and is air-conditioned for use year round. Dealers offer antiques and collectibles such as furniture, glassware and porcelain, craft items, and new merchandise. Food is served on the premises. This market is located in the within a few miles of several historic sites: Washington Crossing, New Hope-Lahaska, and Lambertville.

DEALER RATES: $3 for a 8' × 3' table on Wednesday, $11 on Saturday, $18 on Sunday. Reservations are required for Sunday, recommended for Saturday. Please reserve in person.

CONTACT: Daniel Brenna, Golden Nugget Antique Flea Market, Route 29, Lambertville, NJ 08530. Tel: (609) 397-0811.

Lambertville Antique Flea Market, Inc.

DATES: Every Wednesday, Friday, Saturday, and Sunday, rain or shine.
TIMES: Outdoors: 6:00 AM–4:00 PM. Indoors: Wednesday through Friday 10:00 AM–4:00 PM.
ADMISSION: Free. Free parking is available.
LOCATION: On Route 29, 1½ miles south of Lambertville, along the Delaware River.
DESCRIPTION: Opened in 1967, this is both an indoor and outdoor market, with a pavilion covering for 56 of its spaces outside. In total, there are close to 150 dealers who attend. Although they do not specialize in one type of item, there is a wonderful assortment of antiques and collectibles on display. Friday is an "anything goes" day, but Wednesday, Saturday, and Sunday are strictly antiques and collectibles. This market was listed in *Good Housekeeping* as one of the 25 best antique markets in the United States. There is a new parking area. There are over 50 showcases of antiques indoors. The country kitchen serves homemade specials on the premises.
DEALER RATES: Wednesdays and Fridays $7 for a two-table space. Sundays $40 for a two-table space under the pavilion; Saturday $27 under the pavilion; $20 outside. Reservations for Sunday and Saturday pavilion area are required.
CONTACT: Heidi and Tom Cekoric, 1864 River Road, Lambertville, NJ 08530. Tel: (609) 397-0456.

MANAHAWKIN

Manahawkin Flea Mart

DATES: Friday, Saturday, and Sunday, year round.
TIMES: 8:00 AM–6:00 PM.
ADMISSION: Free. Parking is also free.
LOCATION: 681 East Bay Avenue, off Route 9. Take Garden State Parkway to Exit 63 Manahawkin Exit. Follow signs to Manahawkin Business District. Bay Avenue. Mart is on the right hand side.
DESCRIPTION: This show started in 1977 and hosts 90 outdoor and 45 indoor dealers, featuring antiques, collectibles, produce, meats, new merchandise, and stained glass items. Food is served on the premises.
DEALER RATES: $20 per 22' × 19' space per day outdoors; $160 monthly. Reservations are not required.

CONTACT: Warren Petrucci, P.O. Box 885, Manahawkin, NJ 08050. Tel: (609) 597-1017.

NESHANIC STATION
Neshanic Flea Market

DATES: Every Sunday, March through December, rain or shine.

TIMES: 6:00 AM–5:00 PM.

ADMISSION: Free. $.50 parking donation to the Neshanic Volunteer Fire Company.

LOCATION: Midway between Somerville and Flemington, off Highway 202.

DESCRIPTION: This outdoor market opened in 1970 and currently draws approximately 100 dealers. Some of the types of items you can find include antiques and collectibles, fine art, and arts and crafts, as well as new merchandise and fresh produce. There is also food available on the premises. This market is family owned and operated and provides a friendly atmosphere. It is located in a beautiful historic village.

DEALER RATES: $9 per 4' × 8' space. $10 per space with table. Reservations are recommended.

CONTACT: Mary and Jack Weiss, Elm Street, P.O. Box 428, Neshanic Station, NJ 08853. Tel: (908) 369-3660.

NEW BRUNSWICK
U.S. #1 Flea Market and Antiques

DATES: Every Friday, Saturday, and Sunday, year round.

TIMES: Friday 12:00 PM–9:00 PM; Saturday 10:00 AM–9:00 PM; Sunday 10:00 AM–7:30 PM.

ADMISSION: $1 per carload on Sunday only.

LOCATION: On Route 1. Take Exit 9 off the New Jersey Turnpike; or take Exit 130 off the Garden State Parkway.

DESCRIPTION: This indoor flea market began in 1975, and it currently accommodates approximately 500 dealers and 30,000 people each weekend. This is considered one of the largest flea markets on the East Coast. There is an ample supply of antiques and collectibles, as well as fine art, arts and crafts, new merchandise, and fresh produce. There is also food available on the premises. They have strolling musicians and bagpipe bands during the holidays. There is live country and western music every Sunday.

DEALER RATES: Daily, weekly, and monthly rates available upon request. Reservations are required.

CONTACT: U.S. #1 Flea Market and Antiques, Route 1, New Brunswick, NJ 08901. Tel: (908) 846-0900 or 846-0902.

NEW EGYPT

New Egypt Auction and Farmers Market

DATES: Every Wednesday and Sunday, year round.

TIMES: 7:00 AM–2:00 PM.

ADMISSION: Free. Free parking is available.

LOCATION: On Route 537 between Routes 528 and 539. Take Exit 7 or 7A off the New Jersey Turnpike. Six miles west of Great Adventure Amusement Park.

DESCRIPTION: This indoor/outdoor market has been in existence since 1959. There are approximately 100 dealers buying and selling antiques, collectibles, arts and crafts, and new merchandise, along with clothing, coins, books, furniture, scrap metals, and lots of other used items and oddities. This market is located near campsites, an amusement park and in the heart of New Jersey race horse country. Food is served on the premises. There is a terrific story at the end of this chapter written about this market by one of its longtime dealers.

DEALER RATES: $6 per 5' × 12' space on Wednesday; $7 per space on Sunday. Prices include parking space. Reservations are not required.

CONTACT: Les Heller, New Egypt Flea Market, 933 Route 537, Cream Ridge, NJ 08514. Tel: (609) 758-2082.

PALMYRA

Tacony-Palmyra Swap N' Shop Flea Market

DATES: Every Saturday, Sunday, and selected holidays, rain or shine, year round.

TIMES: 4:00 AM–3:00 PM.

ADMISSION: Free. Free parking is available.

LOCATION: On Route 73. From New Jersey follow Route 73 to Tacony-Palmyra Bridge. From Pennsylvania take I–95 exit and follow signs to Tacony-Palmyra Bridge.

DESCRIPTION: This outdoor market has been open since 1972. There are, on an average, 400 dealers selling a wide range of objects, including antiques, fine art, collectibles, and arts and crafts, along with new merchandise and fresh produce. Food is served on the premises.

DEALER RATES: $10 per 18' × 18' space Saturday and select holidays; $20 on Sunday. Reservations are not required. Dealers must have a valid NJ license.

CONTACT: Mr. Jim Ryan, P.O. Box 64, Palmyra, NJ 08065. Tel: (609) 829-3001. Day of show call the general line at (609) 829-3000.

RAHWAY

Rahway Italian-American Club Flea Market

DATES: Wednesday and Friday, year round.

TIMES: 7:00 AM–3:00 PM.

ADMISSION: Free. Parking is also free.

LOCATION: 530 New Brunswick Avenue in Rahway. Corner of Inman and New Brunswick Avenues.

DESCRIPTION: This market has been held for 18 years, featuring up to 75 dealers both indoors and out selling antiques, collectibles, handicrafts, designer clothes, baseball cards, jewelry, and new merchandise. A snack bar featuring homemade food serves the hungry.

DEALER RATES: Start at $15 per 12' booth. Reservations are suggested.

CONTACT: Bob, Rahway Italian-American Club Flea Market, 242 Front Street, Dunellen, NJ 08812. Day of show call (908) 574-3840 (the club number).

RANCOCAS WOODS

William Spencer's Antique Show

DATES: Second Sunday of the month, March through December. Rain date is the following Sunday.

TIMES: 9:00 AM–4:00 PM.

ADMISSION: Free. Free parking is available.

LOCATION: On Creek Road, 1 mile from the Rancocas Woods exit off I–295.

DESCRIPTION: This very popular market first opened in 1950. There are over 150 dealers attending this outdoor market set in a beautiful, wooded area. They specialize in antiques and collectibles, and they also have a craft show on the fourth Saturday of every month from March through November. Antique show items include jewelry, glass, vintage clothing, furniture, etc. Craft show items include handicrafts, quilted gifts, handmade toys, etc. They were written up in the *New York Times* in 1993, and people are still coming because of the recommendation. Food is served on the premises.

DEALER RATES: They request that you call for more information as there are too many variations on size and show to list here.
CONTACT: Mr. Orin Houser, c/o William Spencer, 118 Creek Road, Rancocas Woods, NJ 08054. Tel: (609) 235-1830.

WARREN

Washington Valley Fire Company Flea Market

DATES: Every Sunday, weather permitting.
TIMES: 7:30 AM–4:00 PM.
ADMISSION: Free. Free parking is available.
LOCATION: 140 Washington Valley Road. Go north from Greenbrook 1½ miles on Route 22 north.
DESCRIPTION: Formed in 1971, this outdoor market's 150 to 200 dealers sell antiques and collectibles as well as new merchandise. All this is done by and for the volunteers of the Washington Valley Fire Company so that they can provide their own fire-fighting equipment. Food is served on the premises.
DEALER RATES: $12 per 10' × 11' space, including a 3' × 10' table. Reservations are not required.
CONTACT: Jerome Boschen at (908) 469-2443 or 469-1571.

WOODSTOWN

Cowtown Bawl, Inc.

DATES: Every Tuesday and Saturday, rain or shine, year round.
TIMES: 8:00 AM–4:00 PM.
ADMISSION: Free. Free parking is available.
LOCATION: On Route 40. From South Delaware Memorial Bridge, take Atlantic City exit to Route 40 and go 5 miles to Cowtown. From North 295, take Exit 4 onto Route 48, go east 5 miles until joining Route 40. Market is 2 miles down the road on the right.
DESCRIPTION: This market opened in 1940. Nearly 700 dealers sell anything from antiques, arts, crafts, and collectibles to fresh produce, meats, cheeses, and new merchandise. This market is held both indoors and outdoors. Food is served on the premises. They draw anywhere from 15,000 to 40,000 people a day. I'm told that election day is very popular here. Maybe it has something to do with the livestock market on Tuesdays. They sell cattle, the occasional buffalo… During the summer there is a professional rodeo every Saturday night.
DEALER RATES: $15–$35 per space. Reservations are not required.

CONTACT: Robert Becker, Manager, Cowtown Bawl, Inc., US 40 Box 23A, Woodstown, NJ 08098. Tel: (609) 769-3000.

OTHER FLEA MARKETS

Atlantic City: The Sand Flea, Sovereign Avenue and Boardwalk, Atlantic City, NJ 08401. Tel: (609) 926-3006 or 823-7713. Open Thursday through Monday, May through October.

Cherry Hill: Garden State Park Flea Market, Rt 70, Cornell Avenue, Cherry Hill, NJ 08002. Tel: (609) 663-9804. Open Wednesday 8:00 AM–3:00 PM, Sundays 9:00 AM–3:00 PM.

Edgewater Park: The Route 130 Flea Market, 2176 Route 130 South, Edgewater Park, NJ 08010. Tel: (609) 877-0136. Open Friday 12:00 PM–9:00 PM, Saturday 10:00 AM–9:00 PM, Sunday 10:00 AM–6:00 PM.

East Brunswick: All New Route 18 Multi-Merchandise Market, 290 State Highway 18, East Brunswick, NJ 08816. Tel: (908) 254-5080. Open Friday and Saturday 10:00 AM–9:00 PM, Sunday 11:00 AM–6:00 PM.

East Rutherford: Meadowlands Flea Market, Giant's Stadium, Parking Lot 17, East Rutherford, NJ 07073. Tel: (201) 935-5474. Open Thursday and Saturday 9:00 AM–5:00 PM March through December. March, Saturdays only.

Estell Manor: Cedar Ridge Market, Route 50, Estell Manor, NJ 08319. Tel: (609) 628-3444. Open Thursday through Sunday from 9:00 AM until.

Lakewood: Route 70 Flea Market, 117 Route 70, Lakewood, NJ 08701. Tel: (908) 370-1837. Open Friday through Sunday, 6:00 AM until.

Somerville: Packard's Farm Market, 135 Route 206 South, Somerville, NJ 08876. Tel: (908) 369-3100. Open Thursday and Friday 6:30 AM until done.

Tom's River: Tom's River Connection, 957 Route 37 West-Box 5106, Tom's River, NJ 08754. Tel: (908) 349-4907. Open Friday 12:00 noon–9:00 PM, Saturday 10:00 AM–9:00 PM, Sunday 10:00 AM–6:00 PM.

Vauxhall: Union Market, 2445 Springfield Avenue, Vauxhall, NJ 07088. Tel: (201) 688-6161. Open Friday and Saturday 11:00 AM–9:00 PM, Sunday 11:00 AM–6:00 PM.

From the New Egypt Auction and Farmer Market
Animal Kingdom Outpost
by Fritz Davis

In the more than 35-year history of the market, animals have played as interesting a part as the management, merchants, and customers. Aside from merchants' and customers' pets, brought along for a day's outing, there have been "regulars" who came on their own.

Most memorable of these was Herman, a little three-legged mutt of a vaguely wirehair ancestry, who would show up early every market day, rain or shine, with or without his master, and stay late. In time he became the market's official closer. When Herman would finally stop, late in the day, look up and down the empty aisles and then turn reluctantly homeward, you could hear merchants calling back and forth among themselves: "Herman's going home—the market's over!"

Many merchants' pets, too, are well remembered, especially Gaby, a toy poodle of somewhat irascible dispostion who belonged to Bill H., a dealer in coins, jewelry, and small antiques. It was hard to tell just when Gaby might develop a dislike to someone, and once convinced of that person's undesirability, never forgot and never forgave. Because I was a very good friend of her master's, she tolerated me, but just barely. For years I lingered on the "pending approval list," until the matter was settled once and for all—not to my advantage. It was at the close of market day. Bill and Gaby were visiting me in my shop. I closed up, and Bill and I set off for a final cup of coffee and a rehash of the day's events. Unfortunately, by accident, I had locked Gaby in the shop.

Eventually we realized what had happened and I freed her, but it was too late. I had been put on the "no-good" list. Gaby rushed out as soon as I opened the door, grabbed my pants cuff twisting it savagely, growling ferociously. From then on, she had to be forcibly restrained—all 8½ pounds of her—whenever I came in view.

We had a merchant, a devoted cat-lover, whose family developed allergies to his pets. He begged to be allowed to rent a facility at the market for their use as he couldn't bear the thought of being parted from them. After some hesitation, the management, cat-lovers themselves, agreed and an "apartment" was set up, complete with comfortable beds, heat, food and water bowls, toilet facilities, and private entrance. The merchant came every day and visited with his feline friends and everybody was happy. Naturally, it became a running joke among the regulars that we were the only flea market in the country with a "cat house."

One day a merchant showed up peddling a variety of odds and ends, including a snapping turtle—a large and very fine specimen, completely trussed up with rope. Perspective buyers were supposed to make soup, purportedly a gourmet's delight, from this poor creature.

I felt so sorry for it, exposed as it was to the hot cruel sun, I dug into my pocket and produced the necessary ten dollars and bought its freedom. A six-year-old friend shared my feelings, and we placed the turtle in his toy wagon, took it down to the creek that runs along the western edge of the market, and after some quick and fancy maneuvering to avoid its impressive jaws, set it free.

This made a great impression on the merchant who had sold the turtle, and for years after, he pointed me out to anyone who would listen as the true eccentric, though he used another term, one who actually paid ten dollars for a turtle and then let it go! Whether he thought this strange and aberrant behaviour on my part commendable or possibly dangerous, I was never sure.

Soon we will be putting up bat houses at the market as part of a national voluntary effort to help preserve and restore this important and greatly misunderstood creature, so important for pollination and insect control. When this is done, I guess it can be truthfully said that we have finally gone batty at the New Egypt Market.

NEW MEXICO

ALBUQUERQUE
Indoor Mercado
DATES: Saturday and Sunday, year round.
TIMES: 10:00 AM–6:00 PM.
ADMISSION: $.50. Parking is free.
LOCATION: 2035 12th Street and I-40.
DESCRIPTION: This market opened in September 1991, and has 190 to 200 dealers selling mostly new merchandise, some antiques and collectibles, loads of southwestern arts and crafts and jewelry, ceramics, tools, toys, new clothes, books, art, and the "usual fare." There are two food courts, just in case.
DEALER RATES: $220 to $250 for a 10' × 10' space for four weeks depending on length of reservation. Reservations must be made at least two weeks in advance. There is some first-come, first-served space.
CONTACT: Richard Westfall, Indoor Mercado, 2035 12th Street, Albuquerque, NM 87104. Tel: (505) 243-8111.

New Mexico Open Air Flea Market
DATES: Saturday and Sunday, except for September during the State Fair.
TIMES: Sun-up to 5:00 PM.
ADMISSION: Free. $2 parking fee.
LOCATION: New Mexico State Fairgrounds at Louisiana and Central Streets, Northeast.
DESCRIPTION: This market opened in 1979 and currently has between 100 to 1,000 dealers, depending on the weather, selling everything: antiques, collectibles, arts and crafts, new merchandise—everything! Probably the largest market in New Mexico. Known for a jewelry row with exhibitors from one section of Native American arts and crafts to another section of commercial manufacturers. Race track racing next door occasionally coincides with the market. Excellent food from American to Mexican is available on the premises.
DEALER RATES: $10 per space. Reservations are not required.
CONTACT: Hugh Perry, New Mexico Open Air Flea Market, P.O. Box 8546, Albuquerque, NM 87198. Tel: (505) 265-1791.

CARLSBAD
The Bull Ring

DATES: Tuesday through Sunday, rain or shine.

TIMES: 9:00 AM–5:00 PM.

ADMISSION: Free. Parking is also free.

LOCATION: 4303 National Parks Highway. On the road to Carlsbad Caverns.

DESCRIPTION: Started in 1984, this market averages 20 vendors selling "everything from soup to peanuts," including antiques, collectibles, flea market stuff, Spanish music collections, handcrafted quilts and other crafts, rattlesnake hatbands and wallets, turquoise, T-shirts, dolls, figurines, fudge, western art painting, hand-carved miniatures, secondhand uniforms, clothes, and more. Among their collection of rather unusual items: an exploding toilet—deposit a nickel and watch it blow. Great way to save money. Food is available on the premises.

DEALER RATES: $3 per day per space. Reservations are not required.

CONTACT: Wes Reynolds, Manager, The Bull Ring, 4303 National Parks Highway, Carlsbad, NM 88220. Tel: (505) 887-9174.

FARMINGTON
Farmington Flea Market

DATES: Every Friday through Sunday, rain or shine.

TIMES: 6:00 AM–8:00 PM during summer; 7:00 AM–7:00 PM during winter.

ADMISSION: Free. Free parking is available.

LOCATION: On Highway 550, halfway between Farmington and Aztec, at 7701 East Main Street.

DESCRIPTION: This outdoor market opened in 1970 and currently accommodates up to 300 dealers during peak season. Among the articles available are antiques and collectibles, fine art, handicrafts, household items, furniture, new merchandise, and fresh produce. A notable feature of this market is that it also offers animals such as horses, goats, pigs, dogs, and cats. Food is served on the premises.

DEALER RATES: $3 per 12' × 26' space Friday and Sunday; $6.50 per space on Saturday. Reservations are required March through August only. Self-contained trailers may stay on the grounds Friday through Sunday night for no additional fee.

CONTACT: Cathey Wright, Owner, 4301 Holiday Drive, Farmington, NM 87402. Tel: (505) 325-3129.

LAS CRUCES
Big Daddy's Flea Market

DATES: Saturday and Sunday, rain or shine.
TIMES: 6:30 AM–4:00 PM.
ADMISSION: Free. Parking is also free.
LOCATION: 7320 North Main (Highway 70 East).
DESCRIPTION: Since 1981 there have been between 200 to 400 dealers selling antiques, collectibles, new and used merchandise—anything and everything. Mexican, Chinese, and other food is available as well as a convenience store and laundromat.
DEALER RATES: Available on request; one of the lowest in the nation. Reservations are not required, but they do take reservations on Fridays from 8:00 AM–5:00 PM.
CONTACT: Frank Sciortino, Big Daddy's Flea Market, 7320 N Main Street, Las Cruces, NM 88004. Tel: (505) 382-9404 or 382-1055.

ROSWELL
Dalton's Trading Village

DATES: Every Saturday and Sunday, year round.
TIMES: 7:00 AM–4:00 PM.
ADMISSION: Free. Free parking is available.
LOCATION: 2200 South Sunset at Poe.
DESCRIPTION: This show, started in 1980, has 50 to 70 dealers and has been operating indoors/outdoors for the past eight years. Antiques, collectibles, handicrafts, and new merchandise are featured, but jewelry, clothing accessories, Native American art, and traditional craft items are also to be found. A snack shack and food concessions are on the premises.
DEALER RATES: $4 per 12' × 20' space per day. Reservations for best locations are required in advance.
CONTACT: Nell Ross, Owner, Dalton's Trading Village, 2200 South Sunset, Roswell, NM 88201. Tel: (505) 622-7410.

SANTA FE
Trader Jack's Flea Market

DATES: Every Friday, Saturday, and Sunday, rain or shine.
TIMES: 7:00 AM–6:00 PM.

ADMISSION: Free. Parking is also free.

LOCATION: Seven miles north of Santa Fe on Highway 285.

DESCRIPTION: This outdoor market first opened in 1975 and outgrew its first location, moving here in the early 1980s. It accommodates approximately 400 dealers selling antiques, collectibles, Indian jewelry and pottery, Guatemalan imports, saddles, cowboy boots, Mexican imports, secondhand merchandise, household items, as well as fresh produce and livestock and "just everything." This market was written up in the *Chicago Tribune* a few years ago causing a stampede of buyers that is still continuing. Trader Jack's Cafe (Pierte Hermon, chef) is well known for superb food, homemade soups, Mexican food, and the usual kid's fare. The cafe's outdoor seating overlooks stunning views of the foothills of the nearby Sangre de Cristo Mountains.

DEALER RATES: $12 per day per 10' × 25' space. Reservations are not accepted.

CONTACT: Jack or Caggie Daniels, 500 North Guadeloupe, Suite G6, Santa Fe, NM 87501.

TAOS

Taos Rendezvous

DATES: Summer: daily; winter: Friday, Saturday, and Sunday.

TIMES: 9:00 AM–6:00 PM.

ADMISSION: Free. Parking is free.

LOCATION: 523 Paseo del Pueblo Sur.

DESCRIPTION: Opened in 1987, this market hosts approximately 100 dealers selling "everything": Indian jewelry and crafts, clothing, cowboy boots, shoes, antiques, collectibles, new merchandise, garage sale finds, whatever. There are a snack bar and restrooms on the premises. During the third weekend in October, they hold a Balloon Festival. Anywhere from 50 to 75 hot-air balloons take off in an big celebration.

DEALER RATES: $10 a day for outside space, $12 for inside space. Reservations are suggested.

CONTACT: Bob Gherardi, Taos Rendezvous, 532 Paseo del Pueblo Sur, Taos, NM 87710. Tel: (505) 758-7511.

NEW YORK

ALBANY
Country Peddler Show

DATES: October 7–9, 1994.

TIMES: Friday 4:00 PM–9:00 PM, Saturday 9:00 AM–5:00 PM, Sunday 11:00 AM–4:00 PM.

ADMISSION: Adults $5, children 2–12 $2.

LOCATION: Empire State Plaza, 52 South Pearl Street.

DESCRIPTION: This new show is one of a series of highly successful folk art shows held around the East Coast. They feature only top-quality folk artists from across the nation selling only handmade decorating and quality items such as herb arrangements, country furniture, salt-glazed pottery and more.

DEALER RATES: $375 for a 10' × 10' space, $562 for a 10' × 15' space, $750 for a 10' × 20' space. Reservations are mandatory as this is a juried show.

CONTACT: American Memories, Inc. P.O. Box 249, Decatur, MI 49045. Tel: (616) 423-8367 or fax: (616) 423-2421.

BOUCKVILLE
Bouckville Antique Pavilion

DATES: Every Sunday, from the last Sunday of April through the last Sunday of October. Special shows: Palm Sunday Two-Day Show, June Two-Day (fourth weekend in June), August Four-Day Show (third weekend in August).

TIMES: 7:00 AM–4:00 PM.

ADMISSION: Free. Parking is also free. The Palm Sunday Show only has a $2 admission fee.

LOCATION: On Route 20, in the center of Bouckville, 100 miles west of Albany, 35 miles east of Syracuse, 25 miles west of Utica. The Palm Sunday Show is held at SUNY–Morrisville Gym.

DESCRIPTION: This market started in 1984 is located "in the heart of antique country." There are 37 shops as well as seven multi-dealer shops included in this show. Close to 200 dealers specialize in antiques and collectibles including furniture, glass, toys, jewelry, paintings, baseball cards, lamps, military items, coins, dishes, dolls, and tools. During the August show, there will be around 2,000 dealers in town for this one show. Whether you are shopping outdoors or under cover, all booths are conveniently protected from the mud if it rains. When you need a break from shopping, food is available on site.

DEALER RATES: $10 for 23' × 23' space outdoors; $15 for 12' × 12' space plus 12' × 20' space for a vehicle. Reservations are advised.

CONTACT: Joe and Ann Bono, RR 1 Box 34, Bouckville, NY 13310, Tel: (315) 893-7912.

BRONXVILLE

Antiques Show

DATES: May 1 and September 25, 1994. Usually the last Sunday in April and September, weather permitting.

TIMES: 10:00 AM–4:30 PM.

ADMISSION: $4 per person; $3 with a discount card, widely available in local shops. Parking is free. Early birds $10 from 9:00 AM–10:00 AM.

LOCATION: Take Bronxville exit off Bronx River Parkway, to Boy Scout Field off Midland Avenue. Field is well marked.

DESCRIPTION: This show began in 1968, and proceeds go toward the beautification of the village of Bronxville. There are 101 quality dealers selling strictly the finest antiques, fine art, and collectibles. This show has grown in popularity since its opening. The same dealers return year after year because the show is so special. There is both a gourmet and a grill selection on the premises. Homeward Bound, a local caterer, feeds the famished.

DEALER RATES: Call for information. Reservations are required. There is very little space available each year as most of the dealers return annually.

CONTACT: Bronxville Chamber of Commerce, Bronxville, NY 10708. Tel: (914) 337-6040. Peter Phalen, 230 West Lake Drive, Valhalla, NY 10595. Tel: (914) 949-7128.

BROOKLYN

Avenue "I" Flea Market Inc.

DATES: Thursday through Sunday.

TIMES: Thursday and Friday 12:00 PM–10 PM; Saturday 10:00 AM–9:00 PM; Sunday 10:00 AM–6:00 PM.

ADMISSION: Free. Parking is also free.

LOCATION: 1080 McDonald Avenue. Take Ocean Parkway to Avenue "I," then go west to McDonald. The market is conveniently reached by public transportation.

DESCRIPTION: This indoor market began in 1978 and now attracts approximately 600 dealers who convene to sell antiques, fine art, collectibles, and new merchandise. The market accommodates an average of 10,000 people per weekend, and as many as 50,000 visitors per holiday weekend. There is a variety of foods available on the premises.

DEALER RATES: $100 and up per booth per weekend. Reservations are required.

CONTACT: Avenue "T" Flea Market, Inc., 1080 McDonald Avenue, Brooklyn, NY 11230. Call Louis Stall at (718) 338-8234.

CALLICOON
Callicoon Flea Market

DATES: Weekends June through September; also Thursdays and Fridays during July and August.

TIMES: Saturdays 9:00 AM–5:00 PM; other days 10:00 AM–3:00 PM.

ADMISSION: Free. Parking is also free.

LOCATION: Main Street, Route 17B West from Monticello.

DESCRIPTION: This market began in 1980 in the historic town of Callicoon in sight of the Delaware River. It is privately run by owners who sell a variety of interesting collectibles, antiques, crafts, lighting fixtures, depression and carnival glass, some new merchandise, furniture, and the occasional railroad and jewelry collectibles. The owners try to have a bit of something for everyone. Many of the original buildings in town are wonderful examples of 1800's architecture. There is camping and canoeing nearby, as well as local bed and breakfast inns.

DEALER RATES: Not applicable.

CONTACT: Office: Carol Kay, 29 Shetland Drive, New City, NY 10956. Tel: (914) 634-6436. Store: Callicoon Flea Market, Main Street, Callicoon, NY 12723. Tel: (914) 887-5411.

CHEEKTOWAGA
Super Flea and Farmer's Market

DATES: Every Saturday and Sunday, rain or shine.

TIMES: 9:00 AM–6:00 PM.

ADMISSION: Free. Parking is available and is also free.

LOCATION: Off New York State Thruway, Exit 52 east, at 2500 Walden Avenue.

DESCRIPTION: Begun in 1975, this is the largest indoor and outdoor flea market in western New York, with 300 dealers outside in the summer and another 200 inside year round. Offered are a wide range of antiques, collectibles, handicrafts, new merchandise, as well as fresh produce, meats, and dairy products. The Super Flea and Farmer's Market boasts four fast-food restaurants on the premises.

DEALER RATES: $20 per 7½' × 6' booth inside, $30 for a 8' × 8' booth inside per day; $10 per 11' × 22' booth outside per day. Space is available on a first-come, first-served basis.

CONTACT: Ronald A. Wagner, General Manager, 2500 Walden Avenue, Cheektowaga, NY 14225. Tel: (716) 685-2902.

CLARENCE

Antique World and Flea Market

DATES: Every Sunday, year round.

TIMES: 8:00 AM–4:00 PM.

ADMISSION: Free. Parking is available, but they may be a charge in 1994.

LOCATION: Fifteen miles east of Buffalo and 40 miles west of Rochester on Main Street (Route 5).

DESCRIPTION: There are approximately 350 dealers in winter and 650 dealers in summer displaying their merchandise. The three buildings on the premises help to separate the various sale items. One building is exclusively for antiques and collectibles, one specializes in dealers selling "flea market" merchandise, and the other building serves as an exhibition center. There is an enormous variety of items with everything from antiques and collectibles to new merchandise, meats, and cheeses for sale. Special shows are scheduled during the year including: a twice yearly EXPO featuring 600 of the finest antique and collectible dealers from 22 states and Canada; AUTO is a swap meet, flea market, and car show all in one; Arts and Crafts Faire (July), an outdoor show, featuring hundreds of the finest artisans and crafts people; and Arts and Crafts Show, (just before Easter and Christmas) an indoor show including 75 talented artisans and crafts people. There are admission charges for these special shows. There are several restaurants on the premises.

DEALER RATES: Flea market rates are $15 per 21' × 20' space outdoors; $25–$35 per 9' × 9' booth indoors. Reservations are not required outside; are required for inside space.

CONTACT: Katy Toth, Antique World, 10995 Main Street, Clarence, NY 14031. Tel: (716) 759-8483.

ELMONT
Belmont Flea Market

DATES: Saturday and Sunday, April and May and late October to Christmas, except when there is a horse race.

TIMES: 7:30 AM–4:00 PM.

ADMISSION: $1.50 per carload, $.50 per walk-in.

LOCATION: Cross Island Parkway to Exit 26A, B or C (Hempstead Turnpike East).

DESCRIPTION: This outdoor market has been operating since 1976 attracting about 1,200 dealers per show. A variety of antiques and collectibles, craft items, new merchandise, and fresh produce are available. It abounds with new and old items; from jewelry and hardware to sporting goods, automotive supplies, plants, toys, electronics, linens, leather goods, shoes, and sneakers. You name it, it's probably here. For your convenience, there are a variety of prepared foods available.

DEALER RATES: $40 up to $150 per 12' × 24' booth. Rates are daily and monthly depending on location. Reservations are suggested.

CONTACT: Harold, Belmont Flea Market, 257 Hempstead Turnpike, Elmont, NY 11003. Tel: (516) 775-8774 on Wednesdays between 10:00 AM and 2:00 PM.

GARDEN CITY
Megamarket

DATES: Friday through Sunday, year round.

TIMES: Friday 12:00 AM–9:00 PM, Saturday and Sunday 10:00 AM–6:00 PM. Daily Thanksgiving through Christmas with extended hours.

ADMISSION: Free. Parking is free.

LOCATION: 711 Stewart Avenue. Adjacent to Roosevelt Field Shopping Center. Less than 2 miles from Roosevelt Raceway. Exit Meadowbrook Parkway at M3 West to Stewart Avenue. Proceed ¾ mile on Stewart Avenue. Market is on the right.

DESCRIPTION: Opened in 1993, this huge market specializes in new merchandise and crafts. The 47th Street Fine Jewelry Exchange is housed there as well as 700 other dealers offering famous-name brand fashions and accessories and unique crafts. Seven snack bars and restaurants will satisfy any appetite.

DEALER RATES: $500 for a 10' × 7' booth monthly. Reservations are mandatory.

CONTACT: Alan Finchley, 711 Stewart Avenue, Garden City, NY 11530. Tel: (516) 745-0600.

HAMBURG
Country Peddler Show

DATES: April 22–24, 1994.

TIMES: Friday 4:00 PM–9:00 PM, Saturday 9:00 AM–5:00 PM, Sunday 11:00 AM–4:00 PM.

ADMISSION: Adults $5, children 2–12 $2.

LOCATION: Eric County Fairgrounds, International Agriculture Center. 5600 McKinley Parkway, Buffalo.

DESCRIPTION: This new show is one of a series of highly successful folk art shows held around the East Coast. They feature only top-quality folk artists from across the nation selling only handmade decorating and quality items such as herb arrangements, country furniture, salt-glazed pottery, and more.

DEALER RATES: $375 for a 10' × 10' space, $562.0 for a 10' × 15' space, and $750 for a 10' × 20' space. Reservations are mandatory as this is a juried show.

CONTACT: American Memories, Inc. P.O. Box 249, Decatur, MI 49045. Tel: (616) 423-8367 or fax: (616) 423-2421.

LEVITTOWN
Tri-County Flea Market

DATES: Thursday through Sunday.

TIMES: Thursday and Friday 12:00 PM–9:00 PM; Saturday 10:00 AM–6:00 PM; Sunday 10:00 AM–5:00 PM.

ADMISSION: Free. Parking is also free.

LOCATION: 3041 Hempstead Turnpike.

DESCRIPTION: Opened in 1981, this indoor market has 600 dealers selling literally everything—all new merchandise and collectibles including shoes, leather, furs, toys, plants, and all sorts of clothing. You could furnish your house and clothe a family from the merchandise sold here. They have 55,000 square feet of display area loaded with just furniture. One of the treats of this market is a superb train display. And no, you can't have it! Seven restaurants, including Greek, Chinese, and a bagel bakery, provide food to starving patrons. For all merchandise purchased here, there is a seven-day, money-back guarantee.

DEALER RATES: $500 to $600 for a very large space for 16 work-ing days (about one month). Reservations are required.
CONTACT: Barbara Eve, Tri-County Flea Market, 3041 Hempstead Turnpike Levittown, NY 11756. Tel: (516) 579-4500.

MAYBROOK
Maybrook Flea Market

DATES: Sundays, year round, except holidays like Easter.
TIMES: 8:00 AM–4:00 PM.
ADMISSION: Free. $.75 per vehicle.
LOCATION: Route 208, 2 miles south of I-84, Exit 5.
DESCRIPTION: For over 20 years this market has been hosting from 100 dealers in winter to 500 dealers in summer selling antiques, col-lectibles, garage sale treasures, new merchandise, or what the owner describes as "gems to junk." There is a snack bar on premises as well as clean restrooms.
DEALER RATES: Must have NY State license to sell. The 1993 rates are $23 for a liberal 18' × 18' space outdoors, $26 for 6' × 10' inside space. The rates may go up in 1994.
CONTACT: Nick Perilli, Maybrook Flea Market, Route 208, Maybrook, NY 12543. Tel: (914) 427-2715.

MONTICELLO
Alan Finchley's Famous Summer
Flea Market at Monticello Raceway

DATES: Memorial Day through Labor Day: Saturday and Sunday; and in July and August: Friday through and Sunday.
TIMES: 9:00 AM–5:00 PM.
ADMISSION: Free admission and free parking for 3,000 cars.
LOCATION: Route 17B at Quickway (Route 17), Exit 104.
DESCRIPTION: Established in 1976, this market is New York State's original summer upscale outdoor designers' and manufacturers' flea market. Their 150 dealers, from all over the country, offer recogniz-able savings on famous-maker brand-name fashions and accessories, as well as a fascinating variety of novelties, toys, and jewelry. All new and unused. Food is available on the premises.
DEALER RATES: All selling spaces accommodate vendor's vehicle. Rates range from $20 per day Fridays in July and August to $30 and up on all weekend and holiday dates. All vendors must have NY State Sales Certificate. Dealers may sign up for a month or a season and

receive a discount. Non-reserved vendors may line up at 8:00 AM the morning of the show they wish to sell. At least 20 non-reserved spaces are set aside each market day.

CONTACT: Alan Finchley, 515 Boston Post Road, Port Chester, NY 10573. Tel: (914) 796-1000. Fax: (914) 939-5046.

NEW YORK CITY
The Annex Antiques Fair and Flea Market

DATES: Every Saturday and Sunday, year round, rain or shine.

TIMES: 9:00 AM–5:00 PM.

ADMISSION: $1 for antique market. Flea market is free. Ample parking is available, but not free.

LOCATION: Avenue of the Americas, between 24th and 26th Streets in Manhattan.

DESCRIPTION: This show began over 20 years ago and is claimed to be the longest running outdoor show in the metropolitan area. The market accommodates from 400 to 500 dealers who come from all over the United States, Canada, and Europe to sell an amazing variety of merchandise, including antique jewelry, vintage clothing, bronzes, Art Deco, porcelain, and rugs. There are three outdoor selling areas and a new indoor selling area, The Garage, that holds 150 dealers. Restaurants are nearby.

DEALER RATES: Saturday: $95 per 10' × 14' booth; $60 per 5' × 14' booth. Sunday: Antique Fair $125 per 10' × 14' booth; $80 per 5' × 14'; Flea Market $100 per 9' × 12' booth; $70 per 4½ × 12' booth. The Garage is $100 for a 11' × 12' space for the weekend. Reservations are required.

CONTACT: Michael, Annex Antique Fair, P.O. Box 7010, New York, NY 10116-4627. Tel: (212) 243-5343. Day of show call 243-7922.

The 26th Street Indoor Antiques Fair

DATES: Saturday and Sunday, year round.

TIMES: 9:00 AM–5:00 PM.

ADMISSION: Free. On weekends, parking around the market is available on the streets.

LOCATION: 122 West 26th Street, between Sixth and Seventh Avenues on 26th Street.

DESCRIPTION: This hugely successful market opened January 23, 1993 and has 65 dealers on two floors of selling space specializing in antiques and collectibles only. They were featured in the *New York*

Times two months after their opening when they were the hot topic during the famous 1993 blizzard. If it's old it's probably here: furniture, lamps, jewelry, paintings, silver, toys, clothing, books, comics, whatever. They do plenty of advertising and as a result the market draws in buyers by the thousands each weekend. Lines form early every weekend before opening with people looking for the as-yet-unfound bargains. And they have been found here.

DEALER RATES: $160 for a 8' × 10' space, $210 for a 10' × 12' space for the weekend. Reservations are required.

CONTACT: Amos Balaish, Indoor Antiques Fair, 122 West 26th Street, New York, NY 10001. Tel: (212) 633-6010. Fax: (212) 633-6064.

P.S. 183 Antique Flea and Farmer's Market

DATES: Every Saturday, year round, rain or shine.

TIMES: 6:00 AM–6:00 PM.

ADMISSION: Free. Parking space is not provided. Garages are available nearby at standard city rates.

LOCATION: 419 East 66th; or 67th Street between First and York Avenues.

DESCRIPTION: This show first opened on August 12, 1979. Over 175 dealers attend this market, selling their merchandise both indoors and outdoors. One may purchase quality antiques, fine art, arts and crafts, and collectibles; of special interest are the smoked meats, cheeses, and fresh flowers that are available from farmers in the tri-state area. Proceeds are used directly for the benefit of the children, with over $100,000 given to the school each year. This market is unique as one of the first of its kind in the country whose purpose was education and support of the public school system. It is now a community event with a following of three to five thousand people attending every Saturday. Spend the day shopping and, when you are hungry, there is food available on the premises.

DEALER RATES: $55 for a 6' table inside. Reservations are required at least two weeks in advance. Ask about the special parking arrangements for vendors.

CONTACT: Bob DiTroia, 98-30 67th Avenue, Forrest Hill, NY 11374. Tel: (718) 897-5992.

NORWICH
Eighteenth Annual Antiques, Collectibles
and Toys Show and Sale

DATES: Annually on Labor Day Sunday.

TIMES: 8:30 AM–4:00 PM.

ADMISSION: $3 per person. Parking is free.

LOCATION: At the Chenango County Fairgrounds in the city, at the junction of Routes 12 and 23.

DESCRIPTION: This market started in 1977 and has grown to host approximately 300 to 350 dealers both outside and under covered spaces. This show expands each year adding a Toy Show in a new building on the grounds in 1990. It has been a real "crowd pleaser" and compliments the rest of the show with antique and collectible toys. They exhibit all types of merchandise from furniture to small collectibles and accessories, such as quilts and art glass. Specialized dealers with high standards make it a quality and growing show. This antiques and collectibles show and sale is sponsored by the Chenango County Historical Society, which also maintains a local history museum, a restored railroad guards' tower, and a canal packet replica and its "house." Special historical exhibits are a feature at the show. Food is available on the premises.

DEALER RATES: $40 for 10' × 12' covered space, includes electricity. $35 for 20' × 30' space outside. Toy space is per table. Reservations are required.

CONTACT: Arleta Miller, RD2, Manley Road, Norwich, NY 13815. Tel: (607) 336-4184.

29th Annual Antique Auto Show and Flea Market

DATES: Annually, the Saturday and Sunday of Memorial Day.

TIMES: 8:00 AM–5:00 PM.

ADMISSION: $3 daily. Shuttle buses run from city parking lots to the site. There is no on-site parking, it's already full of antique cars and dealers.

LOCATION: Chenango County Fair Grounds, East Main Street.

DESCRIPTION: This market is a car buff's dream with proud owners and dealers showing and selling antique cars, car parts, muscle cars, show cars—and then the regular antique flea market, crafts, and auctions. There were over 765 antique cars on display in 1993, over 462 car *parts* dealers, and 268 antique/flea market dealers registered three weeks before the show. By the time the show was underway, there were even more. They hold two auctions on site: the Car Auction and then the "2+2" Auction, nicknamed the Poor Man's Auction. At the 2+2 the buyer and seller each pay the auctioneer $2 as a fee. All sorts of odds and ends are sold during this auction including "cheap" cars. Naturally, the fabulous cars are sold during the Car Auction.

DEALER RATES: Reserved before May 15: 20' × 30' outdoor space or 10' × 12' inside space $35; after May 15 $40. Car parts dealers: 20' × 30' space $20 (before May 15)/$30 (after May 15); crafts space $35/$40, car sales 10' × 30' space $20 anytime.

CONTACT: Ray Hart, P.O. Box 168, Norwich, NY 13815. Tel: (607) 334-4044.

PORT CHESTER

Empire State Year Round Indoor Flea Market

DATES: Saturday, Sunday, and holidays, year round. Thanksgiving through Christmas, daily with extended hours.

TIMES: 10:00 AM–6:00 PM.

ADMISSION: Free. Parking is also free.

LOCATION: Caldor Shopping Center at 515 Boston Post Road, Port Chester, on U.S. 1 at intersection of I–95 and I–297. From NYC and south: I–95 north to Exit 21. Bear right on Exit ramp to U.S. 1, immediate right into Caldor Shopping Center.

DESCRIPTION: This market started in 1976 and is New York State's original year round, indoor, upscale flea market mall. They still use the name "flea market" even though all the merchandise is new, top-of-the-line, brand-name because flea markets are associated with a place to find great values on a tremendous variety of goods. Their success is verified by the millions of shoppers who have made this marketplace Westchester County's most attended free weekly event. A cash refund policy of seven days is strictly enforced for all 300 vendors. An Italian bakery and snack bar will keep the hungry busy.

DEALER RATES: Space is sold on a monthly basis only. A typical booth (10' × 7') rents for $388 per month ($37.50 per day). A security deposit of one month is required. All vendors must have or acquire a NY State Sales Tax Certificate licensing the collection and payment of sales tax.

CONTACT: Alan Finchley, 515 Boston Post Road, Port Chester, NY 10573. Tel: (914) 939-1800.

QUEENS
Aqueduct Flea Market

DATES: Saturday and Sunday, May through October; Tuesday, April through Christmas.

TIMES: 7:30 AM–4:00 PM.

ADMISSION: $1.50 per car load. $.50 per walk-in.

LOCATION: Take Belt Parkway to Exit 18B Lefferts Boulevard, go north to Rockaway Boulevard, then a left to 108th Street.

DESCRIPTION: This outdoor market first opened in 1974. There is a wide variety of merchandise to choose from including hardware, electronics, clothing, jewelry, household items, linens and leather, and shoes and sneakers. Everything from antiques and collectibles to new merchandise and fresh vegetables can be found. They boast of friendly merchants and customers from all over the world. There are all types of prepared foods available when you need a break from shopping.

DEALER RATES: $40 and up per 12' × 24' booth depending on location. Monthly rates available. Reservations are suggested.

CONTACT: Harold, 257 Hempstead Turnpike, Elmont, NY 11003. Tel: (516) 775-8774 Wednesday 10:00 AM to 4:00 PM.

Kennedy International Antique Toy Convention

DATES: Annually. The third Sunday in September.

TIMES: 10:00 AM–4:00 PM.

ADMISSION: $5 for adults; children free, accompanied by adult; $1 for senior citizens. Parking is free.

LOCATION: Take Van Wyck Expressway to entrance of airport, TravelLodge International Hotel on right.

DESCRIPTION: For 20 years this show has specialized in antique and collectible toys, dolls, and related items. This market is host to over 200 dealers from all over the U.S., Europe, and Japan. Food is served on the premises.

DEALER RATES: $60 per 6' × 30' table. Reservations are required. Advance shopping hours for dealers: 8:00 AM–10:00 AM.

CONTACT: Mr. Bob Bostoff, 331 Cochran Place, Valley Stream, NY 11581. Tel: (516) 791-4858.

RHINEBECK
Rhinebeck Antiques Fair

DATES: Two shows annually on the Saturday and Sunday of Memorial Day weekend and Columbus Day weekend in October.

TIMES: 11:00 AM–6:00 PM.

ADMISSION: $5. Parking is free.

LOCATION: Indoors on the Duchess County Fairgrounds, on Route 9 at northern edge of Rhinebeck. From New York Thruway, take Exit 19 to Rhinebeck Bridge, cross bridge and continue 1 mile to Route 9G, then south 1 mile to Route 9, and then south to Fairgrounds.

DESCRIPTION: 1994 marks the 19th year of this antiques fair. This indoor market attracts approximately 190 dealers exhibiting a wide variety of quality antiques and collectibles, at a wide variety of prices. Food is served on the premises.

DEALER RATES: $350 per space. Reservations are required.

CONTACT: Mr. Bill Walter, P.O. Box 310, Red Hook, NY 12571. Tel: (914) 758-6186. Show days call (914) 876-3644.

SCHENECTADY

White House Flea Market

DATES: Wednesday through Sunday, rain or shine.

TIMES: 9:00 AM–5:00 PM; Thursday 9:00 AM–9:00 PM.

ADMISSION: Free. Free parking is also available.

LOCATION: 952 State Street.

DESCRIPTION: This indoor market has been held every weekend since 1985. Approximately 40 dealers gather here to sell antiques, collectibles, handmade craft items, furniture, books, records and toys, as well as new merchandise. This is the area's largest year round indoor market and an excellent place for dealers to find great treasures.

DEALER RATES: Average $27 per week. Advance reservations are required. Permanent dealers usually fill this market.

CONTACT: Rudy or Jeanette Fecketter, 952 State Street, Schenectady, NY 12307. Tel: (518) 346-7851.

SPRING VALLEY

Spring Valley Flea Market

DATES: Friday, Saturday, and Sunday, year round. December, seven days a week.

TIMES: Friday 5:00 PM–10:00 PM; Saturday 10:00 AM–9:00 PM; Sunday 10:00 AM–7:00 PM. Call for December hours.

ADMISSION: Free. Parking is also free.

LOCATION: New York State Thruway (I-87) to Exit 14, 1 mile west on Route 59.

DESCRIPTION: This indoor market has been in operation since 1981. They feature professional vendors year-round, selling top quality merchandise at discount prices. Market is located in an excellent high volume area and is considered one of the "world's largest" indoor markets. Their 500 dealers sell a wide variety of new merchandise. Food is available on the premises.

DEALER RATES: $105 per week for an 8' × 8' booth; $200 per week for an 8' × 16' booth. Reservations are required.

CONTACT: Al Bonadonna, Spring Valley Flea Market, 122 East Central Avenue, Spring Valley, NY 10977. Tel: (914) 356-1171.

STATEN ISLAND

Antiques, Arts and Crafts Market

DATES: Three shows per year. First Sunday in June, second Sunday in September, first Sunday in October. Rain dates: the following Sundays.

TIMES: 10:00 AM–5:00 PM.

ADMISSION: $1. Parking is free.

LOCATION: At the Staten Island Historical Society, Historic Richmond Town, 441 Clarke Avenue. From Verrazano Narrows Bridge, follow New Jersey West Route to Richmond Road/Clove Road Exit; proceed to the second light and turn left onto Richmond Road, about 5 miles ahead turn left onto St. Patricks Place, and finally, turn right on Clarke Avenue. From St. George, take bus #74.

DESCRIPTION: This show has been in existence since 1974. It is an outdoor market that accommodates approximately 125 dealers from Staten Island, Manhattan, Brooklyn, Long Island, New Jersey, Pennsylvania, and Connecticut. They sell antiques, collectibles, stamps, coins, old photographs, books, baseball cards, oil and water-color paintings, plants, hand-made crafts, and much more. Hamburgers, hot dogs, soda, donuts, and coffee are available for hungry shoppers. This show attracts crowds of over 3,000 visitors. For an additional fee visitors will also have the opportunity to see the exhibit buildings and museum.

DEALER RATES: $30 per 9' × 19' space. Reservations are required.

CONTACT: Historic Richmond Town, 441 Clarke Avenue, Staten Island, NY 10306. Tel: (718) 351-1611.

Yankee Peddler Day

DATES: First Sunday in May. Rain date is third Sunday in May.
TIMES: 10:00 AM–5:00 PM.
ADMISSION: $1. Parking is free.
LOCATION: At the Staten Island Historical Society, Historic Richmond Town Restoration, 441 Clarke Avenue. From Verrazano Narrows Bridge, follow New Jersey West Route to Richmond Road/Clove Road exit; proceed to the second light and turn left onto Richmond Road, about 5 miles ahead turn left onto St. Patricks Place, and finally, turn right on Clarke Avenue. From St. George, take bus #74.
DESCRIPTION: This outdoor market began in 1968. It hosts over 130 dealers from New York, New Jersey, Connecticut, and Pennsylvania, who sell antiques, arts and crafts, silver, glass, furniture, jewelry, and collectibles. The Women's Auxiliary at the Staten Island Historical Society is responsible for this fundraising event. This is claimed to be the first large outdoor flea market on the island. This show is always well attended by dealers and buyers alike. Food is served on the premises.
DEALER RATES: $30 per 9' × 19' space. Reservations are required.
CONTACT: Historic Richmond Town, 441 Clarke Avenue, Staten Island, NY 10306. Tel: (718) 351-1611.

STORMVILLE

Stormville Airport Antique Show and Flea Market

DATES: Held annually on the last Sunday of May, first Sundays of July, August, September, and the second Sunday in October, rain or shine.
TIMES: Dawn to dusk.
ADMISSION: Free. Parking is also free.
LOCATION: At the Airport. On Route 216, Dutchess County.
DESCRIPTION: This outdoor market began in 1970. Over 600 dealers attend their shows. A variety of purchases can be made, including antiques, arts and crafts, and collectibles. Shopping for new merchandise and fresh produce can also be accomplished at this market. Food is served on the premises.
DEALER RATES: $45 prepaid per 20' × 20' space or $50 at the gate. Reservations are suggested. Advance shopping hours for dealers begin at noon on the Saturday before the show.
CONTACT: Pat Carnahan, P.O. Box 125, Stormville, NY 12582. Tel: (914) 221-6561.

WESTBURY

Roosevelt Raceway Flea Market

DATES: Every Sunday year-round; Wednesdays from fourth Wednesday in March through December, rain or shine.

TIMES: 9:00 AM–5:00 PM.

ADMISSION: Free. $1.50 fee for parking on Wednesdays. Sundays year-round and Saturdays during November and December parking is $2 per car.

LOCATION: Roosevelt Raceway. Take the Meadowbrook Parkway to Roosevelt Raceway exit.

DESCRIPTION: This flea market began as an antique show over 20 years ago. It was originally held in the horse paddock and has grown to occupy 12 acres outdoors and the entire grandstand building at Roosevelt Raceway. Almost anything can be purchased from at least 2,000 dealers. New merchandise includes anything from fur, jewelry, and sporting goods to computers, tools, and coat hangers. Even eye care and insurance can be purchased! There is also a variety of antiques and collectibles for sale. Food is available on the premises.

DEALER RATES: $45–$60 per 10' × 28' space. Reservations are required for monthly space, first come/first served for daily booths.

CONTACT: Carol De Santo, Plain and Fancy Shows of Westbury, P.O. Box 978, Westbury, NY 11590. Day of show call the Manager's office at (516) 222-1530.

YONKERS

Yonkers Raceway Market

DATES: Sundays, last Sunday in March through last Sunday in December.

TIMES: 9:00 AM–4:00 PM.

ADMISSION: $2 per car.

LOCATION: Yonkers Racetrack. Cross the George Washington Bridge, take the Major Deegan Expressway to New York Thruway Exit 2. From the other direction, from the New York Thruway take Exit 4 (Central Avenue) to the racetrack.

DESCRIPTION: This outdoor market's 400 dealers sell mostly new merchandise. Although when there are enough dealers (40 or more) in antiques and collectibles, one corner will be put aside for their wares exclusively. There are loads of different foods available: bratwurst, fish and chips, pizza, sausages, and lots more on traveling food trucks and snack bars. There are clean restrooms on site.

DEALER RATES: $40 for a 9' × 28' space with reservations; $50 without reservations.

CONTACT: Marty McGrath, Yonkers Raceway Market, Inc., Yonkers Raceway, Yonkers, NY 10704. Tel: (914) 963-3898 or 968-4200 x216. Fax: (914) 968-1121.

OTHER FLEA MARKETS

Brooklyn: Caesar's Bay Bazaar, 8973 Bay Parkway, Brooklyn, NY 11214. Tel: (718) 372-8686. Open Thursday through Sunday.

Buffalo: Super Flea and Farmers Market, 2500 Walden Avenue, Buffalo, NY at Exit 52E of NYS Thruway. Tel: (716) 685-2902. Open weekends 9:00 AM–5:00 PM.

Farmingdale: Farmingdale Flea Market, 1600 Route 110, Farmingdale, NY 11735. Tel: (516) 293-7878. Open Thursday through Sunday.

Flushing: Busy Bee Compartment Store, 37-11 Main Street, Flushing, NY 11354. Tel: (718) 961-4111. Open Wednesday through Sunday.

Kingston: Shopper's World, 1120 Ulster Avenue, Kingston, NY 12401. Tel: (914) 336-2686. Open weekends 10:00 AM–6:00 PM.

Lowman: Lowman Flea Market, Route 17, Lowman, NY 14861. Tel: (607) 734-3670. Open Sundays November through April; weekends April to November.

Massapequa Park: Busy Bee A Compartment Store, 5300 Sunrise Highway, Massapequa Park, NY 11762. Tel: (516) 799-9090. Open Thursday through Monday.

New York City: New York East Flea Market, 145 East 23rd St, New York, NY 10011. Tel: (212) 777-9609. Open daily except Sunday.

Niagara Falls: Super Flea and Farmers Market, 6000 Packard Road (at I-190 Exit 23), Niagara Falls, NY 14304. Tel: (716) 297-6443. Open weekends 9:00 AM–5:00 PM.

Ridgewood: Store World, Inc., 54-30 Myrtle Avenue, Ridgewood, NY 11385. Tel: (718) 628-5555. Open Wednesday through Sunday.

Tappan: Auto Kino Car and Flea Market, Route 303, Tappan, NY 10983. Tel: (914) 359-2008. Open weekends 9:00 AM–6:00 PM.

NORTH CAROLINA

ALBEMARLE
Albemarle Flea Market
DATES: Friday, Saturday and Sunday, year round.
TIMES: Friday and Saturday 11:00 AM–10:00 PM, Sunday 1:00 PM–9:00 PM.
ADMISSION: Free. Parking is free.
LOCATION: Stony Gap Road. Take Highway 52 South from Albemarle, at the former skating rink. Between Highways 52 and 2427.
DESCRIPTION: Located in a former dance hall and skating rink, this market houses 50 dealers, year round, selling treasured antiques to yard sale stuff including collectibles, old beer signs and advertisements, depression glass, leather, tools, new merchandise, Avon, army surplus, and crafts. It is said that Fats Domino performed on their stage during the dance hall years. Restrooms and a snack bar are on site.
DEALER RATES: $18 for space along the wall with peg boards, $12 for non-wall space. Reservations are required, as there is a waiting list.
CONTACT: Doris and Howard Dearmon or Ronald M. Ray, P.O. Box 283, New London, NC 28127-0283. Tel: (919) 982-5022. Best time to call for reservations is Sunday afternoon.

ASHEVILLE
Dreamland Flea Market
DATES: Every Wednesday, Friday, Saturday, and Sunday.
TIMES: 7:00 AM–4:30 PM.
ADMISSION: Free. Free parking is available.
LOCATION: Off I-240 at Tunnel Road Exit.
DESCRIPTION: This market began operation in 1971 and currently attracts approximately 350 dealers selling antiques, collectibles, garage sale goodies, attic treasures, craft items, fresh produce, and some new merchandise. Food is served on the premises. This market is near all major shopping in Asheville, the Blue Ridge Parkway, and Biltmore House.
DEALER RATES: $7 per day for a 20' open space; $9-$10 per day for a 12' × 8' booth. Reservations are suggested.

CONTACT: Dusty Pless, P.O. Box 5936, Asheville, NC 28813. Tel: (704) 255-7777 or (704) 254-7309.

They used to have a part-time deputy sheriff on site just to keep things in order while Dusty and his staff worked inside their office. One day an excited man burst into the office to announce that one of the dealers had brought a lion! Dusty and his partner decided to check this out. After three walks through the market, they still hadn't seen this lion. Then Dusty noticed a school bus taking up three to four spaces with something rather lion-like next to one wheel. Upon closer inspection it proved to be a young male, about 100 pounds, just growing his mane and fortunately on a very short chain. "The deputy pitched a fit!" The dealer put the lion in the school bus for the duration of the market and was never seen again.

It was here that someone bought a WW II artillery shell, took it home, fiddled around with it—and found $400 stashed in the base. You never know what you'll find.

CHARLOTTE

Metrolina Expo

DATES: First full-weekend Saturday of the month (Friday, Saturday, and Sunday); third full-weekend Saturday of the month (Saturday and Sunday).

TIMES: 8:00 AM–5:00 PM.

ADMISSION: First weekend $2.50 each day except during the Spectaculars in April and November; third weekend $1.50 each day; Spectaculars $5 each day. Free parking is available.

LOCATION: 7100 Statesville Road (Highway 21).

DESCRIPTION: This market, started in 1971, hosts between 800 and 2,000 exhibitors. The first weekend is devoted to selling antiques and antique collectibles only. The third weekend includes antiques, collectibles, handmade and craft items, new merchandise, clothing, and jewelry—just about anything and everything. The first Saturday of the month is the busier day. Food is available. In April and November they hold the Great American Antique and Collectible Spectaculars with over 5,000 dealers showing the best in antiques and antique collectibles.

DEALER RATES: Their reasonable rates vary according to location and size of space. Reservations are required for inside space, requested for outside space. Contact Metrolina Expo for the latest information. **CONTACT:** Aileen Lisk, Metrolina Expo, P.O. Box 26652, Charlotte, NC 28226-6652. Tel: (704) 596-4643 or 1-800-824-3770.

DEEP GAP
Wildcat Flea Market

DATES: Friday through Sunday, May through October.
TIMES: Friday and Sunday 10:00 AM–5:00 PM; Saturday 9:00 AM–10:00 PM.
ADMISSION: Free. Parking is free.
LOCATION: Highway 421, 8 miles east of Boone.
DESCRIPTION: High in the Blue Ridge Mountains, along the Blue Ridge Parkway, this family-run flea market has been in business since 1972. From 50 to 60 dealers sell antiques, collectibles, crafts including one dealer selling his hand-carved wood items, old and new glassware including depression, garage sale stuff, old and new gold jewelry, novelties, tools, hardware, new merchandise, coins, cards, furniture, and whatever. About 5,000 buyers show up in this market every weekend. There is an auction every Saturday night at 7:00 PM, year round. Antique auctions are held once a month on Tuesdays. There is a snack bar on premises, dubbed the "Lonesome Dove Cafe" by the market owners, serving grilled chicken and homemade hamburgers among their other culinary talents. Restrooms are on site.
DEALER RATES: Outside rates $5 a day for a shed. Inside and more permanent space available; please call for more information. Reservations are required as most space is reserved for the season. The inside spaces are rented out by February for the year.
CONTACT: Kevin Richardson, Route 7 Box 43, Boone, NC 28607. Tel: (704) 264-7757.

A piece of depression glass was purchased here for $5 and later resold for $240.

Historical note: The original market was built in 1972, and as they were putting the finishing touches on the roof, it collapsed! The builders had to rebuild the entire building again. Obviously, it stayed up this time. They've used it for 22 years.

FLETCHER

Smiley's Flea Market and Antique Mall

DATES: This market is open every Friday, Saturday, and Sunday, year round. Antique mall is open daily.

TIMES: Hours are 7:00 AM–5:00 PM. Antique mall is open 10:00 AM–5:00 PM.

ADMISSION: Free with over 10 acres of free parking.

LOCATION: Halfway between Asheville and Hendersonville on Route 25. Take Exit 13 off I-26; then travel north ½ mile on Route 25.

DESCRIPTION: This indoor/outdoor market began in 1984. The market provides over 11,000 square feet of space in the antique mall and over ½ mile of covered selling space in the flea market. It attracts an average of more than 250 dealers. A large variety of items can be found including antiques, collectibles, handicrafts, fresh produce, and some new merchandise. This place is known as the "Baseball Card Capital of Western North Carolina." Two snack bars serve the hungry. RV parking is available.

DEALER RATES: $10 per 10' × 10' space per day inside the flea market area with two tables. Outside space is $5. 10' × 25' lockable units are available at $125 per month. $105 per 10' × 12' space per month in the antique mall. Reservations are not required.

CONTACT: Wade McAbee, Smiley's Flea Market and Antique Mall, P.O. Box 458, Fletcher, NC 28732. (704) 684-3532 or at the mall 684-3515.

FOREST CITY

74 By-Pass Flea Market

DATES: Friday, Saturday, and Sundays, year round.

TIMES: 7:00 AM–5:00 PM.

ADMISSION: Free. Parking is also free.

LOCATION: 110 Frontage Road. Eight miles east of Rutherfordton and 15 miles west of Shelby, exit Alexander–Forest City off 74 by-pass.

DESCRIPTION: This indoor/outdoor market opened in 1986 and hosts up to 240 dealers in summer and 100 in winter. They sell antiques, ball cards, racing cards, collectibles, electronics, groceries, fresh produce, cheeses, baked goods, clothing, leather goods, tools, jewelry, and new merchandise. Food is available on the premises.

DEALER RATES: $7 per 10' × 10' inside booth; $6 outside under shed; $2 in the open. Reservations are suggested.

CONTACT: Gary Hardin, 110 Frontage Road, Forest City, NC 28034. Tel: (704) 245-7863 anytime.

FRANKLIN
Franklin Flea and Craft Market

DATES: Tuesday, Thursday, Friday, Saturday, and Sunday, April through November.

TIMES: Tuesday 5:00 PM–9:00 PM, Thursday all day, Saturday and Sunday 7:00 AM until you or they drop.

ADMISSION: Free. Parking is also free.

LOCATION: 199 Highlands Road, U.S. Route 64 towards Franklin.

DESCRIPTION: Opened in 1971, this market has the unusual distinction of being located in the town known as the "Gem Capital of the World." One of the local tourist attractions is "washing" gems out of purchased buckets of soil to locate raw gems. A dozen specialty shops in Franklin and about three dozen mine locations offer jewelry and gems. Their 60 to 100 dealers sell antiques, sapphires, collectibles, rubies, craft items, emeralds, fresh produce, amethyst, new merchandise, crystals, and other gems mined locally and sold in either the raw or jewelry "processed" form. They also specialize in blue-ribbon jams, jellies and preserves as well as hats, t-shirts, baskets, toys, sunglasses, tools, and more produce. "You can take a little bit of North Carolina home with you when you leave the Franklin Flea." All booths are covered and there are eight enclosed stores. Their snack bar serves "by far, the best all-beef hot dog east of the Mississippi."

DEALER RATES: $20.25 per weekend with 2 full-size tables, approximately 10' × 12' covered. $1 per booth, per vendor, per weekend for electric. Reservations are suggested.

CONTACT: Gina Torrance, Franklin Flea and Craft Market, 199 Highlands Road, Franklin, NC 28734. Tel: (704) 524-6658.

GREENSBORO
"Super Flea" Flea Market

DATES: 1994: March 19–20, April 9-10, May 14–15, June 4–5, July 9–10 for certain and generally the second weekend of each month the rest of the year. But call, just in case, on the unconfirmed months.

TIMES: Saturday 8:00 AM–5:00 PM; Sunday 10:00 AM–5:00 PM.

ADMISSION: $1.50 per person. $1 for parking.

LOCATION: Greensboro Coliseum Complex, Exhibit Hall. 1921 West Lee Street. Follow signs posted in town.

DESCRIPTION: This very successful indoor market recently attracted as many as 10,000 shoppers on a weekend, with 500 dealers selling various types of antiques and collectibles, along with arts and crafts and some new merchandise. Food is served on the premises.

DEALER RATES: $60 per 8' × 10' space. Reservations are required in advance.

CONTACT: Smith-Tomlinson Co., P.O. Box 16122, Greensboro, NC 27416. Tel: (910) 373-8515.

HICKORY

Hickory Livestock and Flea Market

DATES: Every Thursday.

TIMES: All day, starting at 5:00 AM.

ADMISSION: Free. Parking is $.50 per vehicle.

LOCATION: On Sweetwater Road, ¼ mile north of the junction of Highway 64 and Route 70.

DESCRIPTION: "There's no better Thursday market." This outdoor market, which began in 1962 and is probably the oldest in the area, has grown to include approximately 300 dealers selling a selection of antiques and collectibles, craft items, and some new merchandise. There is also a livestock auction, selling everything from cattle to birds, chickens, and rabbits, at 1:30 PM every week except during the weeks of Thanksgiving, Christmas, and July 4th. "When you mix animals and cowboys, there's never a dull moment," says Mr. Hahn of the auctions within a flea market. The Stockyard Cafe serves such special meals that people come from all over to eat here, market or not. The cafe also operates a "mobile dealer food cart" taking food to the dealers in their spaces so the dealers don't have to leave their merchandise and miss a sale. What a great idea!

DEALER RATES: $7 per 12' space on pavement. Reservations are not required.

CONTACT: George Hahn, Hickory Livestock and Flea Market, 951 Cloninger Mill Road NE, Hickory, NC 28601. Tel: (704) 256-2673 or (704) 324-7354.

Springs Road Flea Market

DATES: Saturday and Sundays, year around.

TIMES: 8:00 AM–4:00 PM.

ADMISSION: Free. Parking is free.

LOCATION: On Springs Road.

DESCRIPTION: This market opened in the Springs Road Drive-In Theater in 1981. From 200 to 300 dealers sell anything and everything imaginable including antiques, arts and crafts, collectibles, and new merchandise. There is a heated building 500' long for indoor sales which has proved so popular they added two outdoor sheds to house 80 dealers. It seems the dealers are doing so well in the sheds (and prefer them to the building!) that they are adding four more sheds over the next three years. Two concessions provide food to the hungry.

DEALER RATES: $4 per day for a 20' × 20' outdoor space (two car parking spaces), $5 under a shed with two tables, and $7 per day for a 12' × 12' space inside, if available (there is a waiting list). Monthly and yearly rates are available.

CONTACT: Al Rumley, Springs Road Flea Market, Route 2 Box 198, Hickory, NC 28601. Tel: (704) 256-7669.

LEXINGTON
Farmer's Market and Flea Market

DATES: Every Monday, Tuesday, and Wednesday of the year, rain or shine.

TIMES: Monday 3:00 PM–9:00 PM (wholesale only); Tuesday 5:30 AM–2:00 PM (wholesale and retail); Wednesday 8:00 AM–12:00 noon (retail only).

ADMISSION: Free. Free parking is available.

LOCATION: On Old Highway 64 West, ¾ mile off of the I-85 business loop.

DESCRIPTION: This outdoor market has been in business since 1973 and is run by brothers Tim and Jim Fritts. It attracts 300 to 500 dealers selling a full range of antiques and collectibles, as well as new merchandise, farm produce, and tag sale items. Tim handles the retail end of the market. There is also a wholesale market that operates on Mondays and Tuesdays at this same location. They have over 250 wholesale vendors selling all new merchandise: new clothing, novelties, toys, jewelry, crafts, and other assorted goodies. "Wholesale Alley" is not open to the general public and requires a state sales tax ID to be able to enter the area. Jim handles the wholesale market. The "wholesale alley" has been a real success story here.

DEALER RATES: $10 for a 10' × 10' sheltered booth to $8 per 12' × 16' outside space per day. Wholesale Alley rates are $200 per quarter for a sheltered space. Reservations are suggested.

CONTACT: Tim and Jim Fritts, Owners, Route 15 Box 1357, Lexington, NC 27292. Tel: (704) 246-2157 or fax: (704) 246-8693. Jim handles the Wholesale Alley and Tim handles the rest of the flea market.

> Tim bought an empty grenade shell for his young son from an army surplus dealer. Unknown to his mother, Tim's son took it to his kindergarten Show and Tell at school, wrapped in a bag. When his teacher opened the bag, she naturally freaked. "Cleaned the whole school out," says Tim. The sheriff's department was called, and of course, Tim and his wife were summoned. The janitor, fearing for his life I'm sure, carefully took the grenade out to the middle of the playing field and guarded it there. The cops arrived and did their thing. Of course, Tim's son was terribly upset that the officials were taking his favorite toy. Tim duly arrived, went to the field and pocketed the harmless casing. But not before catching a severe lecture from the deputy and the school principal.

MORGANTOWN

Jamestown Flea and Farmers Market

DATES: Saturday and Sunday, year round, rain or shine.

TIMES: 7:00 AM–5:00 PM.

ADMISSION: Free admission and free parking.

LOCATION: Jamestown Road. One-half mile off I-40 at Exit 100.

DESCRIPTION: This flea market, which attracts 300 dealers year round, has been held since 1983. Dealers sell antiques, collectibles, handmade crafts, vegetables, and new merchandise. There are clean restrooms, spacious parking, storage, showers, and security available.

DEALER RATES: $60 for a 10' × 10' booth for four weeks; advance reservations are required.

CONTACT: Clarence Clark, President, Jamestown Flea Market, P.O. Drawer 764, Morgantown, NC 28655-0764. Tel: (704) 584-4038.

RALEIGH

North Carolina State Flea Market, Inc.

DATES: Every Friday, Saturday, and Sunday, year round.

TIMES: Gates open at 7:00 AM for outside shopping; buildings open from 9:00 AM–5:00 PM.

ADMISSION: Free. Parking is also free.

LOCATION: 2200 Atlantic Avenue. From Raleigh Beltway take Exit 10, Wake Forest Highway Exit; at fourth traffic light turn left on Whittier Mill Road, go left to dead end—at the flea market.

DESCRIPTION: Forced to move two miles down the road in late 1992, due to the state's destruction of Buildings 3 through 6 at the fairgrounds, this market kept many of its original dealers. The new owner is one of the dealers who was with the original market from its inception in 1970 (see The Story.) Now housed in one 100,000 square foot building and in the process of adding two more buildings to their collection, one 80,000 square feet and the other 70,000 square feet, Harry is trying to build the market up to the 600 dealers they had before. Currently 125 dealers sell, with more coming back all the time. The market regularly donates fund-raising space for churches and non-profit organizations making the collection of goodies sold even more interesting. Among the items sought by loyal customers are quality antiques, collectibles, craft items, furniture, coins, cards, comics, garage sale and attic finds, fresh produce, and new merchandise. For your convenience, food is available on the premises.

DEALER RATES: $5 per 10' × 20' outside space with table, $5 for a 10' × 10' space with table for inside space. No charge for electricity. Overnight facilities are free to dealers.

CONTACT: Harry Johnson, NC State Fairgrounds Flea Market, Inc., 10 Westridge Drive, Durham, NC 27713. Tel: (919) 683-8438 or (919) 493-5968.

The Story

After the NC State Fair ended in October 1992, the powers-that-be decided to place their bets on horse racing instead of flea markets. The laws haven't been passed yet, but still, 4 buildings were demolished, the rates raised on the remaining dealers and eventually the news hoopla died down. Where there were 600 dealers before the state fair, now there are 150. The dealers started their own association to fight the planned demolition but failed. In the end, many of the dealers came with Harry Johnson to the Atlantic Avenue site to start over. Their aim is to build this new site to the glory of the old. They seem to have a good start.

SALISBURY
Webb Road Flea Market

DATES: Saturday and Sunday, year round, rain or shine.

TIMES: 8:00 AM–5:00 PM.

ADMISSION: Free admission and free parking.

LOCATION: Six miles south of Salisbury on I-85 at Stuckeys-Webb Road, Exit 70. Just 30 miles north of Charlotte

DESCRIPTION: Started in 1985, this market attracts 300 to 400 dealers. They sell antiques, collectibles, handmade crafts, vegetables, new merchandise, and coins, specializing in jewelry, furniture, glass, carpets and rugs, tools, auto accessories, books, and just about anything. Food is available. There are clean restrooms, spacious parking, storage, and 24-hour security.

DEALER RATES: $60 per 10' × 10' booth for four weeks inside. Advance reservations are required inside. Outside rates: $5 for open 10' × 10' space, $6 for sheltered space; first come, first served.

CONTACT: John Nash, Manager, Webb Road Flea Market, 905 Webb Road, Salisbury, NC 28146. Tel: (704) 857-6660.

SMITHFIELD
I-95 Antique and Flea Market

DATES: Daily, year round.

TIMES: Weekdays 10:00 AM–6:00 PM, Saturday 9:00 AM–6:00 PM, Sundays 12:30 PM–6:00 PM.

ADMISSION: Free. Parking is free.

LOCATION: Off I-95 at Exits 95 or 97.

DESCRIPTION: Opened in 1992 this indoor/outdoor market has about 35 permanent dealers inside and in good weather 25 or so outside. They deal mostly "in old stuff," with about 85 percent of the items sold being antiques and collectibles. Some of the listed items are glass, wood, leather, books, and crafts. On weekends, a snack bar is open. There are restrooms available. They hold special antique festivals and shows during the year.

DEALER RATES: Outside vendors: $6 open space, $10 for sheltered space. Permanent indoor vendors rent by the month. Reservations are required for indoors only.

CONTACT: Ken Vick, I-95 Antiques and Flea Market, I-95 Industrial Park Blvd, P.O. Box 2400, Smithfield, NC 27577-2400. Tel: (919) 937-1148.

WINSTON-SALEM
Country Peddler Show

DATES: May 13–15, 1994.

TIMES: Friday 4:00 PM–9:00 PM, Saturday 9:00 AM–5:00 PM, Sunday 11:00 AM–4:00 PM.

ADMISSION: Adults $5, children 2–12 $2.

LOCATION: Dixie Classic Fairgrounds, 421 West 27th Street.

DESCRIPTION: This new show is one of a series of highly successful folk art shows held around the East Coast. They feature only top-quality folk artists from across the nation selling only handmade decorating and quality items such as herb arrangements, country furniture, salt-glazed pottery and more.

DEALER RATES: $375 for a 10' × 10' space, $562.50 for 10' × 15' and $750 for 10' × 20' space. Reservations are mandatory as this is a juried show.

CONTACT: American Memories, Inc., P.O. Box 249, Decatur, MI 49045. Tel: (616) 423-8367 or fax: (616) 423-2421.

OTHER FLEA MARKETS

Fayetteville: Great American Market Place, 4909 Raeford Road, Fayetteville, NC 28304. Tel: (919) 423-4440. Open Friday through Sunday 7:00 AM–6:00 PM.

Fayetteville: US Flea Market Mall, 504 North McPherson Church Road, Fayetteville, NC 28303. Tel: (919) 868-5011. Open Friday 12:00 noon–8:00 PM, Saturday 9:00 AM–8:00 PM, Sunday 9:00 AM–6:00 PM.

Frankinville: Cedar Creek Flea Market, Highway 64, Frankinville, NC 27248. Tel: (919)625-1521. Open Friday through Sunday.

Gastonia: Great American Market Place, 761 Linwood Road, Gastonia, NC 28052. Tel: (704) 864-3130. Open Thursday and Friday 12:00 noon–7:00 PM, Saturday 8:00 AM–7:00 PM, Sunday 9:00 AM–5:00 PM.

Goldsboro: Goldsboro Flea Market, 2102 Wayne Memorial Drive, Goldsboro, NC 27530. Tel: (919) 736-4422. Open Saturday 8:00 AM–5:00 PM, Sunday 10:00 AM–5:00 PM.

Greenville: Pirate Lane Flea Market, 400 Moore Street, Greenville, NC 27834. Tel: (919) 757-1641. Open weekends 8:00 AM–5:00 PM.

Hamptonville: Vintage Village, I-77 and US 421 South, Hamptonville, NC 27020. Tel: (919) 468-8434. Open Friday 10:00 AM–4:00 PM, weekends 8:30 AM–5:30 PM.

Laurinburg: Plaza Flea Market, 1511 Atkinson Street, Laurinburg, NC 28352. Tel: (919) 277-8878. Open Wednesday through Sunday 8:00 AM–8:00 PM.

New Bern: Flea City USA, 2830 Neuse Boulevard, New Bern, NC 28560. Tel: (919) 638-5721. Open Friday 12:00 noon–8:00 PM, weekends 8:00 AM–5:00 PM.

Statesville: Statesville Flea Market, Route 18 Box 79, Statesville, NC 28677. Open weekends 8:00 AM–5:00 PM.

Winston Salem: Cooks Plaza Flea Market and Cooks Plaza 2 Flea Market, Highway 52 and Highway 8, Winston Salem, NC 27105. Tel: (919) 661-0610. The plazas are open weekends, year round; the original Cook's Flea Market is open weekends November through July.

NORTH DAKOTA

MANDAN
Dakota Midwest Flea Market and Antique Show
DATES: First weekend of every month, except January and July.
TIMES: Saturday 9:00 AM–5:00 PM; Sunday 9:00 AM–4:00 PM.
ADMISSION: $.50 per person age 13 and older.
LOCATION: At the Mandan Community Center, 901 Division Street.
Take Exit 152 off I-94, then travel south on 6th Avenue northwest to
Division Street. Signs are posted everywhere.
DESCRIPTION: This show has operated indoors since 1984, and
currently attracts an average of 80 dealers who sell a wide range of
items including antiques and collectibles, crafts and fine art works,
new merchandise, and fresh produce. Food is served on the premises.
The market is close to historic Fort Abraham Lincoln, which was
once the home of General Custer and is currently undergoing restora-
tion as a national landmark.
DEALER RATES: $10 per 8' × 4' table per day. There are special
rates for more tables and/or more dates. Reservations are required.
CONTACT: Leo and Julia Mattern, 2738 Gateway Drive, Bismarck,
ND 58501. Tel: (701) 258-5623. Day of show call the Community
Center at (701) 667-3260.

MINOT
Magic City Flea Market
DATES: Second Saturday of every month, February through Decem-
ber.
TIMES: 9:00 AM–4:00 PM.
ADMISSION: $.50 per person. Free parking is available.
LOCATION: On State Fairgrounds. Well marked in downtown Minot.
DESCRIPTION: This indoor market first opened in 1967 and cur-
rently accommodates an average of 75 dealers. There is a variety of
antiques, collectibles, and crafts available at this market. Food is served
on the premises. This is an old-fashioned flea market with plenty of
treasures dragged out of local attics and basements.
DEALER RATES: $10 per 6' × 9' space, includes table. Reserva-
tions are required.
CONTACT: Mr. Richard Timboe, Manager, P.O. Box 1672, Minot,
ND 58701. Tel: at home (701) 852-1289 or at the Antique shop (701)
838-1150.

OHIO

ALLIANCE
Alliance Flea Market

DATES: Saturday and Sunday, year round.

TIMES: 9:00 AM–5:00 PM.

ADMISSION: Free. Free parking is also available.

LOCATION: On Route 62, east of Alliance.

DESCRIPTION: This show began in 1967 and now accommodates 50 to 80 dealers. The market is held indoors for the most part, but there are some outside dealers selling antiques, collectibles, handicrafts, produce, and new merchandise. A huge draw here is over 10,000 square feet of new furniture. Food is available at this market.

DEALER RATES: $20 per 20' × 20' space and six tables per day. Single tables at $5 per day. Reservations are strongly suggested from October through April.

CONTACT: Manager, Alliance Flea Market, 1500 South Mahoning Avenue, Alliance, OH 44601. Tel: (216) 823-2302.

AURORA
Aurora Farms Flea Market

DATES: Indoor market: every Wednesday, Saturday, and Sunday, year round, rain or shine. Outdoor market: Sunday and Wednesday.

TIMES: 8:00 AM–4:00 PM.

ADMISSION: Free. Ample free parking is provided.

LOCATION: 549 South Chillicothe Road. On State Route 43, one mile south of Route 82. Take Exit 13 off the Ohio Turnpike, then go north on State Route 43.

DESCRIPTION: This indoor/outdoor market began as a livestock auction in 1929, making it among the oldest of its kind in the country. Nowadays the market attracts between 200 and 400 dealers and up to around 10,000 shoppers per market day in the summer. Items for sale can include anything from antiques and collectibles to craft items to farm-fresh foods, including Amish baked goods, smoked meats, cheeses and spices—all on 55 acres of selling space. Crowds sometimes appear as early as 7:00 AM looking for the best bargains. Auctions are also held on both days. Food is served on the premises.

DEALER RATES: $7 per 12' × 20' space. Reservations are not required.

CONTACT: Mr. Claude Hopkins, General Manager, 549 S. Chillicothe Road, Aurora, OH 44202. Tel: (216) 562-2000.

BEACH CITY
Shady Rest Flea Market

DATES: Every Sunday.
TIMES: Dawn to dusk.
ADMISSION: Free. The ample parking is free.
LOCATION: Routes 250 and 93.
DESCRIPTION: Held under the trees, this old-fashion outdoor market, started in the late 1960's, now averages about 75 to 100 dealers offering a range of miscellaneous items including produce, collectibles, new merchandise, and handmade crafts. This is the oldest flea market in Tuscarawas County. Food and toilet facilities are available. The owner of the market, Mike, is 90 years young and still helps out at the market on Sundays. Stop in and say "Hi, Mike!"
DEALER RATES: $6 per day per dealer. Advance reservations not required.
CONTACT: Mr. Mike Vukich or Mildred Dinger Miller, 1762 Johnstown Road NE, Dover, OH 44622. Tel: (216) 343-9508.

BLOOMFIELD
Bloomfield Auction and Flea Market

DATES: Every Thursday, year round, rain or shine.
TIMES: 6:00 AM–4:00 PM.
ADMISSION: Free.
LOCATION: One-half mile west of North Bloomfield on Route 87.
DESCRIPTION: Claiming to have been in business since 1943, this market is one of the oldest markets in the state of Ohio. It draws 150 to 200 dealers who sell both indoors and outdoors. Among the offerings are live poultry and other fresh farm products, as well as crafts, new goods, and antiques. Food and toilet facilities are available.
DEALER RATES: $6 per 10' × 12' stall outside; inside, when available, $8 to $10. Reservations are required for some stalls.
CONTACT: Mr. Charles Roscoe, 8183 Route 193, Farmdale, OH 44417. Tel: (216) 876-4993; day of show call (216) 685-4403.

CINCINNATI
Paris Flea Market

DATES: Sundays, April through mid-November.

TIMES: 7:00 AM–4:00 PM.

LOCATION: 2310 Ferguson Road, off 5000 Glenway or 3000 Queen City.

ADMISSION: $.75 per car.

DESCRIPTION: This market started in 1966 in Cincinnati, the home of the Bengals, the Cincinnati Reds, and the Cincinnati Zoo. It attracts up to 250 dealers selling antiques, collectibles, handmade and craft items, fresh produce, and new merchandise. Food is available on the premises.

DEALER RATES: $10 per 19' × 25' booth. Reservations are not required, first come, first served.

CONTACT: Paris Flea Market, 2310 Ferguson Road, Cincinnati, OH 45506. Tel: (513) 451-1271 or 223-0222.

CLEVELAND
Clark Avenue Flea Market

DATES: Wednesday through Saturday, year round.

TIMES: 11:00 AM–6:00 PM.

ADMISSION: Free. Free parking is available.

LOCATION: 5109 Clark Avenue.

DESCRIPTION: This small indoor market has been operating since 1986 selling antiques, collectibles, some furniture, appliances (televisions with TV repairman on premises), and new merchandise.

DEALER RATES: $16 per 8' × 10' aisle space per week, $5 a day; $18 along the wall weekly. They furnish tables. First come, first served.

CONTACT: Fred Scaife, 5109 Clark Avenue, Cleveland, OH 44102. Tel: (216) 398-5283.

COLUMBIANA
Theron's Country Flea Market

DATES: Every Sunday, year round.

TIMES: 9:00 AM–5:00 PM.

ADMISSION: Free. Ample free parking.

LOCATION: Columbiana-Lisbon Road, (County Road 440), Old State Route 1641. One mile south of downtown Columbiana, just off I-11.

DESCRIPTION: This market has been around since the mid-1960's and operates both indoors and outdoors. More than 60 dealers sell a variety of items including real antiques, furniture, collectibles, homemade pastries, jewelry, glassware, etc. An annual feast is held in October. Auctions every Saturday night at 6:00 PM. Jolinda's Restaurant features home-cooking, open daily 6:30 AM–8:00 PM; Saturday 6:30 AM–10:00 PM, closed on Mondays. Restrooms are available inside.

DEALER RATES: $4 outdoor setups for transients. Shops $40–$160. Waiting list for shops.

CONTACT: Joann or Linda, Theron's, 1641 Columbiana-Lisbon Road, Columbiana, OH 44408. Tel: (216) 482-4327.

COLUMBUS

Amos Indoor Flea Market

DATES: Fridays through Sundays, year round.

TIMES: 10:00 PM–7:00 PM.

ADMISSION: Free. Free parking nearby.

LOCATION: 3454 Cleveland Avenue at Innis Road. Take I-71 north to Webber Road; east on Webber Road to Cleveland Avenue; north about one mile on Cleveland Avenue.

DESCRIPTION: This indoor market has been open since 1980; its dealers, which number approximately 250, sell general flea market merchandise, as well as new goods and fresh produce. Food and toilet facilities are available on the premises.

DEALER RATES: $13 for a 9' × 8' space per day. Advance reservations are suggested.

CONTACT: Doug Hott and Paul Gwilym, Rainbow Enterprises, 865 King Avenue, Columbus, OH 43212. Tel: (614) 291-3133. For information call: (614) 275-4444, or call Paul at the market: (614) 262-0045.

Columbus Antique Flea Market

DATES: 1994 dates: January 16, February 27, October 2, November 13, and December 4. Call for 1995 dates, generally around the same weekend days.

TIMES: 7:00 AM–4:00 PM. (Dealers setup from 5:00 AM–7:00 AM, during which time browsing is permitted.)

ADMISSION: $1.50 per person; children under 12 free; parking available, $3 per car.

LOCATION: Ohio State Fairgrounds (Lausche Building). Take 17th Avenue exit off I–71.

DESCRIPTION: Three generations of Stockwells all chip in to run this 150-dealer market, which has been in operation since 1979 offering everything "from A to Z" in antiques and collectibles. Attendance is currently around 2,500 shoppers per show, and there is a substantial backlog of dealers waiting for a chance to peddle their wares. Food is available on the premises.

DEALER RATES: $65 per 10' × 20' space. There is currently a waiting list.

CONTACT: Stockwell Promotions, 4214 North High Street, Columbus, OH 43214. Tel: (614) 267-8163, 263-6830, or 885-2352.

Livingston Court Indoor Flea Market

DATES: Friday, Saturday, and Sunday year round.

TIMES: 10:00 AM–7:00 PM.

ADMISSION: Free. Parking is also free.

LOCATION: 3575 East Livingston Avenue. Just west of Courtright Road.

DESCRIPTION: Opened in 1988, this market has about 375 dealers selling antiques, collectibles, arts and crafts, flea market fare, and new merchandise. Food concessions are present selling mainly Amish food.

DEALER RATES: Starting at $10 per day. Reservations are preferred.

CONTACT: Doug Hott or Bill Marcum, Rainbow Enterprises, 865 King Avenue, Columbus, OH 43212. Tel: (614) 275-4444. Day of show call Doug Hott at: (614) 231-7726.

Scott Antique Market

DATES: April 23–24, June 25–26, November 26–27, December 17–18, 1994.

TIMES: Saturday 9:00 AM–6:00 PM, Sunday 10:00 AM–5:00 PM.

ADMISSION: Free. Parking is $3.

LOCATION: Ohio State Fairgrounds. Off I-71, Exit at 17th Avenue to the fairgrounds.

DESCRIPTION: This market opened in 1986 with over 1,200 dealers selling exclusively antiques and collectibles. There are four snack bars and one restaurant to perk up the weary shopper. Handicapped-accessible restrooms are also available.

DEALER RATES: $73 for a 10' × 10' space in the Multi-Purpose room; $78 in the Celeste and $54 for a 14' × 15' space outside. Reservations are required.
CONTACT: Scott Antique Markets, P.O. Box 60, Bremen, OH 43107. Tel: (614) 569-4112, fax: (614) 569-7595.

South Drive-In Theatre Flea Market

DATES: Every Wednesday, Saturday, and Sunday, April through October.
TIMES: 7:00 AM–3:00 PM.
ADMISSION: $.50 per carload includes parking.
LOCATION: 3050 High Street. Take I-71 south to Frank Road; east on Frank Road to High Street; south on High Street about 1 mile.
DESCRIPTION: In business since 1975, with an average of 350 dealers, outdoors only. Crafts, fresh produce, and new merchandise complement general flea market fare. Food and restrooms are available.
DEALER RATES: $5 for a 20' × 20' space, Saturdays and Sundays; $1 on Wednesdays. Reservations not required.
CONTACT: Doug Hott, Rainbow Enterprises, 865 King Avenue, Columbus, OH 43212. Tel: (614) 275-4444 or 491-6771.

Westland Indoor Flea Market

DATES: Friday through Sunday.
TIMES: 10:00 AM–7:00 PM.
ADMISSION: $.50 a carload.
LOCATION: 4170 West Broad Street at Georgesville Road.
DESCRIPTION: This newer market has 400 spaces for dealers selling everything from antiques and collectibles to newer merchandise. It is a sister market to three others in the Columbus area, covering north, east, and south with this one the west side.
DEALER RATES: $17 per space per day. Reservations not required.
CONTACT: Doug Hott, Rainbow Enterprises, 865 King Avenue, Columbus, OH 43212. Tel: (614) 275-4444 or 272-5678.

DAYTON

Paris Flea Market

DATES: Sunday, mid-April through mid-November.
TIMES: 7:00 AM–4:00 PM.
ADMISSION: $.75 per car.

LOCATION: 6201 North Dixie Drive. Take Needmore Exit off I-75.
DESCRIPTION: There are 60 to 250 dealers in this outdoor market, a fixture here since 1966. There are plenty of antiques for sale, as well as collectibles, arts and crafts, produce in season, and new merchandise. The Air Force Museum is three miles down the road. Dayton is the home of the Wright Brothers. Food is available on site.
DEALER RATES: $10 per 19' × 25' area. Reservations are not required, first come, first served.
CONTACT: Gary Castle, 6201 North Dixie Drive, Dayton, OH 45414. Tel: (513) 890-5513 or (513) 223-0222.

DELAWARE

Kingman Drive-In Theatre Outdoor Flea Market

DATES: Every Sunday, April through October, rain or shine.
TIMES: 7:00 AM–3:00 PM.
ADMISSION: $.50 per carload, includes parking.
LOCATION: On Route 23 North at Cheshire Road, 1 mile south of Delaware and 8 miles north of I-270.
DESCRIPTION: This outdoor market began in 1982 and currently attracts about 275 dealers selling a variety of collectibles, as well as fresh produce, handmade goods, and new merchandise. Food and restrooms are available.
DEALER RATES: $5 per 20' × 20' space. No advance reservations are required.
CONTACT: Dale Zinn, Rainbow Theatres, 865 King Avenue, Columbus, OH 43212. Tel: (614) 548-4227 or (614) 275-4444.

FREMONT

Fremont Flea Market

DATES: Year round: Second weekend of every month, rain or shine. Winter: Also fourth weekends.
TIMES: Saturday 10:00 AM–5:00 PM, Sunday 10:00 AM–4:00 PM.
ADMISSION: Free. Free parking is available.
LOCATION: 821 Rawson Avenue. At the Fremont Fairgrounds, four miles south of Exit 6 off the Ohio Turnpike.
DESCRIPTION: This began in 1976 and currently operates both indoors and outdoors. It attracts approximately 100 (winter) to 250 (summer) dealers who show up to sell antiques and collectibles, as well as handicrafts, tools, fresh produce when in season, and some new mer-

chandise. Three snack bars serve the famished. Dirt track car races are held during the market in the summer.

DEALER RATES: $13 for a 10' × 10' space indoors; $12 for a 20' × 10' space outdoors. Reservations are required for inside space; not for outside space.

CONTACT: Gary Kern, 821 Rawson Avenue, Fremont, OH 43420. Tel: (419) 332-6937.

HARTVILLE
Hartville Flea Market

DATES: Every Monday and Thursday, year round, rain or shine.

TIMES: 7:00 AM–5:00 PM.

ADMISSION: Free. Parking available, $1 per car.

LOCATION: 788 Edison Street; Take Route 77 to Exit 118 (Route 241) to Route 619 East. Go east on Route 619 six miles to market.

DESCRIPTION: This market began in 1947 as a livestock auction; it currently draws up to 750 dealers during the summertime (Mondays tend to draw the largest crowds) and 200 in the winter. Indoor and outdoor selling spaces offer a place to find all sorts of antiques and collectibles, as well as local farm goods, craft items, and new merchandise. Food is available at the Hartville Kitchen; restrooms are also available on the premises.

DEALER RATES: $6 per 12' × 30' space. Advance reservations are suggested.

CONTACT: Mr. Marion O. Coblentz, 788 Edison Street, Hartville, OH 44632. Tel: (216) 877-9860.

JOHNSTOWN
Johnstown Lions Memorial Day Flea Market

DATES: Every Memorial Day, rain or shine.

TIMES: 6:30 AM–5:00 PM.

ADMISSION: Free. Free parking is available.

LOCATION: On the public square in Johnstown, at the intersection of Routes 62 and 37.

DESCRIPTION: This annual outdoor market has been in operation since 1972 and is now the occasion for 50 or more sellers to show up to offer their collectibles, handicrafts, and sometimes new merchandise. Food is served on the square on the day of the market.

DEALER RATES: $15 per 12' × 24' space.

CONTACT: Mr. Dick Scovell, P.O. Box 428, Johnstown, OH 43031. Tel: (614) 967-1279.

LIMA

Lima Antique Show and Flea Market

DATES: First full weekend, Saturday and Sunday, every month except February, June, July, August, and September.

TIMES: 9:00 AM–5:00 PM.

ADMISSION: $.50 per person; children under 12 enter free. Free parking available.

LOCATION: At the Allen County Fairgrounds in Lima.

DESCRIPTION: This indoor market opened in 1976. Antiques and collectibles, new merchandise, and handicrafts are available from over 50 dealers. There is a food concession on the premises.

DEALER RATES: $35 per 10½' × 13' space per weekend; $55 per 20' × 10½' space per weekend. Advance reservations are required. Tables are available at $5 each per weekend.

CONTACT: Aubrey Martin, Manager, 716 South Main Street, Lima, OH 45804. Tel: (419) 228-1050, Monday through Friday, weekends and evenings (419) 339-7013.

MAUMEE

Country Peddler Show

DATES: 1994: February 25–27, September 9–11.

TIMES: Friday 4:00 PM–9:00 PM; Saturday 9:00 AM–5:00 PM; Sunday 11:00 AM–4:00 PM.

ADMISSION: Adults $5; children 2–10 years $2.

LOCATION: Lucas County Recreational Center. Exit 6 Salisbury Road. Go left until stop, turn left follow to end, straight ahead.

DESCRIPTION: This indoor market, started in 1983, features 100 folk artisans selling a variety of collectibles, arts and crafts, and fine art, the heirlooms of the future. For your convenience there is food available on the premises. This show is one of a series of Country Peddler Shows held throughout the East Coast from Florida to Michigan and Wisconsin. These are all-American made items.

DEALER RATES: $375 per 10' × 10' booth; $562.50 per 10' × 15' booth; $750 per 10' × 20' booth. Reservations are required.

CONTACT: American Memories, P.O. Box 249, Decatur, MI 49045-9093. Tel: (616) 423-8367, fax (616) 423-2421.

PROCTORVILLE

Proctorville Flea Market

DATES: Friday through Sunday.

TIMES: 8:00 AM–5:00 PM.

ADMISSION: Free. Parking is free.

LOCATION: Near the Huntington East End Bridge, 2 blocks off Route 7. Follow the signs.

DESCRIPTION: Open since February 1991, this market is readily accessible to the many travelers going through three states: West Virginia, Kentucky, and Ohio. It has 185 inside dealer spaces and 60 outdoor spaces. Dealers sell antiques, collectibles, produce, coins, stamps, books, ceramics, crafts and supplies, carpeting, tapes and records, electronics, new and used clothing, tools, lots of new merchandise, garage sale goodies, and more. There is a restaurant with clean restrooms on site.

DEALER RATES: $20 for a 10' × 14½' space for the weekend or $10 per day inside; $3 a day outside for a 16' × 26' space. Reservations are mandatory for inside space as there is usually a waiting list, outside is first come, first served.

CONTACT: Todd Riley, Proctorville Flea Market, Route 4 Box 541B, Proctorville, OH 45669. Tel: (614) 886-8207.

ROGERS

Rogers Community Auction and Open-Air Market

DATES: Every Friday, rain or shine.

TIMES: 7:30 AM on, there isn't really a closing time.

ADMISSION: Free, with plenty of free parking.

LOCATION: On State Route 154, 8 miles east of Lisbon.

DESCRIPTION: This market and auction has been operating on this site since 1955. It is mostly outdoors, with about 300 indoor traders. The 1,200 dealers sell antiques, collectibles, handmades, vegetables, fruit, meats and cheeses, as well as new merchandise. On mid-summer peak weekends as many as 30,000 shoppers and browsers show up. There is a state park campgrounds nearby, and food is served on the premises. The auction starts at 6:00 PM auctioning eggs, produce, miscellaneous items, and poultry.

DEALER RATES: $10–$12 per 15' × 30' setup space per day. Reservations are required. However, if there is a vacant space available due to a cancellation, then it's first come, first served.

CONTACT: Manager, Open-Air Market, 5640 Raley Road, New Waterford, OH 44445. Tel: (216) 227-3233.

ROSS

Stricker's Grove Flea Market

DATES: Every Thursday, year round. Except Thanksgiving and Christmas.

TIMES: 8:00 AM–1:00 PM.

ADMISSION: Free. Free parking is available on 25 acres.

LOCATION: On Route 128, 1 mile south of Ross, near Cincinnati.

DESCRIPTION: This indoor/outdoor market began July 1977 and hosts 50 to 100 dealers. There are 100 spaces under roof. Among the merchandise for sale are mostly antiques and interesting collectibles, handicrafts, and fresh produce. In the winter the market is held in a heated hall. In the summer it is held outdoors under covered pavilions, on the grounds of a privately owned amusement park. The restaurant is open from 6:00 AM to 2:00 PM.

DEALER RATES: $10 for two tables (furnished) and setup space per day. Reservations are required for indoor selling in winter; first come, first served in summer.

CONTACT: Gladys Jordan, 9468 Reading Road, Cincinnati, OH 45215. Tel: (513) 733-5885.

SOUTH AMHERST

Jamie's Flea Market

DATES: Every Wednesday and Saturday, year round, rain or shine.

TIMES: 8:00 AM–4:00 PM.

ADMISSION: Free. Free parking.

LOCATION: On Route 113, ½ mile west of Route 58. Thirty miles west of Cleveland.

DESCRIPTION: This market, opened around 1970, has 200 permanent dealers indoors and an average of 400 transient dealers outdoors. All types of goods are available here, both new and used, including books, tools, crystal, china, silver, glassware, jewelry, coins, stamps, handmade goods, baseball cards, floral displays, greenhouse plants and garden supplies, candles, Hummels and Goebels collector plates, Amish crafts, clocks, lamps, music boxes, Barbie clothes, etc. One shopper even reported seeing a kitchen sink here ($50)! Claimed to be the largest and the oldest in northeast Ohio, average daily attendance has been put at 6,000 in the summer and 2,400 in the winter. An annual Christmas special is held on the first Sunday in December from 10:00 AM–4:00 PM. Fresh farm produce featuring German, Amish, and American specialties are conveniently located for the hungry shopper. More variety of foods is available including cheese, meats, bread, health food, candy, and nuts; restrooms are also available on the premises.

DEALER RATES: $23–$25 per 10' × 12' space indoors, $8 per 10' × 15' space per day outdoors. There is a waiting list for indoors; outdoors first come, first served.

CONTACT: Jamie's Flea Market, P.O. Box 183, Amherst, OH 44001. Day of show call Ralph or Lolita Mock at: (216) 986-4402.

SPRINGFIELD
Springfield Antique Show & Flea Market

DATES: Saturday and Sunday, usually the third weekend of every month except July. May and September shows are three-day Extravaganzas—Friday through Sunday. Call for specific dates.

TIMES: Saturday 8:00 AM–5:00 PM, Sunday 9:00 AM–4:00 PM, and Extravaganza Fridays 12:00 PM–8:00 PM.

LOCATION: Clark County Fairgrounds, next to Exit 59 off I-70.

ADMISSION: $1. Extravaganzas $2. Parking is free.

DESCRIPTION: Started in 1971, this market attracts 1,500 dealers in summer and 600 indoors in winter selling quality antiques, collectibles, handmade craft items, dairy products, and new merchandise. Food available on the premises.

DEALER RATES: Reserved asphalt spaces 15' × 20' are $25 per weekend; grass spaces 14' × 30' are $40 per weekend. First come, first served spaces $15 per day or $30 per weekend. Extravaganza rates: asphalt $40, grass $50 per weekend. For other building and long-term rates call. Reservations are required.

CONTACT: R. Bruce Knight, Manager, P.O. Box 2429, Springfield, OH 45501. Tel: (513) 325-0053.

TIFFIN
Tiffin Flea Market

DATES: Two shows May and October; one weekend each month, June through September. Call for exact dates.

TIMES: 9:00 AM–5:00 PM.

ADMISSION: Free. Plenty of free parking.

LOCATION: Seneca County Fairgrounds, Hopewell Avenue. Take State Route 53 to Euclid Avenue, then turn west; or, take State Route E18 to Wendy's, then turn left; or, take State Route 224 and turn north at Wolohan's.

DESCRIPTION: Started in 1977 and sponsored by the Seneca County Junior Fair Foundation, this market operates from May through October with an average of over 200 dealers selling all types of antiques and collectibles, as well as fresh produce, handmade crafts, tools, clothing, and new merchandise. Proceeds go to promoting the welfare of the Seneca County Junior Fair and its activities. Overnight camping is available on the site for $5 per vehicle. Food is served at the fairgrounds.

DEALER RATES: $8 per day for a 10' × 10' space inside; $8 per day for a 15' × 15' space outside. Reservations are required for inside space only. Tables are available for a rental fee of $4 per table for two days; tables must be reserved in advance.

CONTACT: Mr. and Mrs. Don Ziegler, 6627 S. TR 173, Bloomville, OH 44818. Tel: (419) 983-5084.

URBANA

Urbana Antiques and Flea Market

DATES: Saturday and Sunday, first full weekend. Not in August because of the fair.

TIMES: 9:00 AM–5:00 PM. Winter hours are 9:00 AM–4:00 PM.

ADMISSION: Free. Free parking is available.

LOCATION: Park Avenue Fairgrounds.

DESCRIPTION: This very successful indoor/outdoor market, started in 1971, has a bit of everything available from over 150 indoor dealers alone. Weather permitting, from 100 to 200 dealers sell outside. There are antiques and collectibles, handicrafts and new merchandise, vegetables, meats, and cheeses. Refreshments and food are available on the premises. This is a growing market, full of very good antiques and collectibles. There are three heated buildings full of dealers year round. One of the buildings is air-conditioned for summer.

DEALER RATES: $22 and up for a three 8' table setup per weekend. Reservations are required for inside sellers. This market is more than willing to work with their dealers.

CONTACT: Elizabeth and Steve Goddard, 934 Amherst Drive, Urbana, OH 43078. Tel: (513) 653-6013 or (513) 788-2058.

WILMINGTON
Caesar Creek

DATES: Saturday and Sunday, year round, also Memorial Day and Labor Day, rain or shine.

TIMES: 9:00 AM–5:00 PM.

ADMISSION: $.35 per person. Free parking is available.

LOCATION: 7763 State Route 73 at I-71, Exit 45. Five miles east of Caesar Creek Lake State Park on Route 73. Conveniently located only 19 miles south of Kings Island Amusement Park on I-71.

DESCRIPTION: Opened in 1979 this indoor/outdoor market accommodates 600 dealers during the summer and 400 dealers during the winter. From 10,000 to 14,000 people per weekend come here to shop. Items found here include antiques, collectibles, craft items, as well as fresh produce, dairy products, and meats. They have a huge stock of famous-maker jeans list at ½ price! There are seven restaurants serving a variety of foods on the premises.

DEALER RATES: Inside: $44 to $52 for smaller 10' × 12' booths; $120 per 20' × 25' booth. Outside space: Saturdays uncovered $9, sheltered $13; Sundays uncovered $11, sheltered $15. Reservations are required for indoor space, while outside space is given out on a first come, first served basis.

CONTACT: Allen Levin, Caesar Creek Flea Market, 7763 State Route 73, Wilmington, OH 45177. Tel: (513) 382-1669 or 223-0222.

OTHER FLEA MARKETS

Cleveland: The Bazaar, 4979 West 130 Street, Cleveland, OH 44135. Tel: (216) 362-0022. Open Friday through Sunday 10:00 AM–6:00 PM.

Columbus: Livingston Court Flea Market, 3575 East Livingston Avenue, Columbus, OH 43227. Tel: (614) 231-7726. Open Friday through Sunday 10:00 AM–7:00 PM.

Dayton: Dayton Traffic Circle Flea Market, 3700 Keats, Dayton, OH 45414. Tel; (513) 275-4759. Open Friday through Sunday 10:00 AM–5:00 PM.

Dover: Dover Flea Market, 120 North Tuscarawas Avenue, Dover, OH 44633. Tel: (216) 364-3959. Open Saturday 9:00 AM–5:00 PM, Sunday 10:00 AM–5:00 PM.

Franklin: Schomy's Flea Market, 8862 Dayton-Oxford Road, Franklin, OH 45005. Tel: (513) 746-0389. Open Saturday 10:00 AM–9:00 PM.

Huber Heights: Brandt Pike Flea Market, 6123 Brandt Pike, Huber Heights, OH 45424. Tel: (513) 236-5003. Open Friday and Saturday 9:00 AM–7:00 PM, Sunday 9:00 AM–5:00 PM.

Pataskala: Red Barn Flea Market, 10501 Columbus Expressway Park, Pataskala, OH 43062. Tel: (614) 9927-1234. Open Friday through Sunday 10:00 AM–6:00 PM.

Piketon: Piketon Flea Market, US Route 23, Piketon, OH 45661. Tel: (614) 289-2593. Open Friday and Saturday 6:00 AM–5:00 PM, April through October.

Toledo: Toledo Trade Market, 1258 West Alexis Road, Toledo, OH 43611. Tel: (419) 478-1001. Open Friday through Sunday.

Troy: Troy Flea Market, 1375 South Union Street, Troy, OH 45373. Tel: (513) 339-9387. Open weekends 9:00 AM–5:00 PM.

Warren: Warren Flea Market, 428 South Main St, Warren, OH 44481. Tel: (216) 399-8298. Open Tuesday–Saturday 8:00 AM–5:00 PM.

Urbana: West Centrals Best Flea Market, Route 68, Urbana, OH 43078. Tel: (513) 653-6945. Open first weekend of the month, except August.

Youngstown: Austintown Flea Market, 5370 Clarkins Dr, Youngstown, OH 44515. Tel: (216) 799-1325. Open weekends 9:00 AM–5:00 PM.

Youngstown: Four Seasons Flea and Farm Market, Route 422 and McCartney Road, Youngstown, OH 44505. Tel: (216) 744-5050. Open Wednesday and Sunday 8:00 AM–5:00 PM.

OKLAHOMA

DEL CITY
Cherokee Flea Market

DATES: Tuesday through Sunday, year round.
TIMES: 7:00 AM–5:00 PM or whenever.
ADMISSION: Free. Parking is also free.
LOCATION: Corner of S.E. 15th and Bryant.
DESCRIPTION: Said to be one of the oldest flea markets in Oklahoma, this market has 30 to 40 dealers selling everything from antiques and collectibles to garage sale loads; attic finds; furniture; produce; and new, used, and old merchandise, VCRs, TVs, and whatever. A snack bar on premises serves breakfast, lunch, and other treats. Bragging that they are the "smallest in the area," they also invite you to drop in to watch the domino games in the Domino Room of the snack bar.
DEALER RATES: $3 per outside table setup; building space starts at $45 and up per space. Reservations are not required. No peddler's license required as they are considered their own eight-block county.
CONTACT: Lyn Frazier or Lucille Richardson, 3101 S.E. 15th Street, Del City, OK 73115. Tel: (405) 677-4056.

OKLAHOMA CITY
AMC Flea Market Mall

DATES: Saturday and Sunday, year round.
TIMES: 9:00 AM–6:00 PM.
ADMISSION: Free. Free parking is available.
LOCATION: 1001 North Pennsylvania Street.
DESCRIPTION: This indoor/outdoor market started in 1988 and has 600 booth spaces with dealers selling antiques, collectibles, baseball cards, coins, stamps, office supplies and furniture, new furniture, Indian art, garage sale treasures, 14-karat gold jewelry, and new merchandise among other things. Housed in a 135,000 square foot building, with about 50 dealers spaces outside, this is probably the largest flea market in Oklahoma. Food is available on the premises.
DEALER RATES: $40 per weekend; $144 per month. Reservations are not required. Daily rates also available: $10 per day outside.
CONTACT: Nick Adams, AMC Flea Market Mall, 1001 North Pennsylvania Street, Oklahoma City, OK 73107. Tel: (405) 232-5061.

Mary's Ole Time Swap Meet

DATES: Every Saturday and Sunday, year round, rain or shine.
TIMES: Dawn to dusk.
ADMISSION: Free admission and parking.
LOCATION: Northeast corner of 23rd Street and Midwest Boulevard.
DESCRIPTION: This market started in 1963. There are 300 dealers who sell both indoors and out. Lots of antiques, collectibles, primitives, and Western curios complement an assortment of handmade items, produce, as well as new merchandise. There is live music outdoors and food is available.
DEALER RATES: $5 and up for 12' × 20' booths, plus electric. No advance reservations are required.
CONTACT: Dennis Sizemore, 7905 Northeast 23rd Street, Oklahoma City, OK 73141. Tel: (405) 427-0051.

Old Paris Flea Market

DATES: Every Saturday and Sunday, year round, rain or shine.
TIMES: 9:00 AM–6:00 PM.
ADMISSION: Free admission and parking.
LOCATION: 1111 South Eastern Road; access from I-40 and I-35.
DESCRIPTION: This indoor/outdoor show started January 3, 1976 and hosts 400 dealers selling everything from antiques, handcrafts, and collectibles to produce, meats, cheeses, and new merchandise. Close to a KOA campground and near the Baseball Hall of Fame. Food is served on the premises.
DEALER RATES: $22.50 per 8' × 15' booth indoors per selling day. $11 for 10' × 20' outdoor space daily. Reservations are required by the Monday before the weekend requested.
CONTACT: Norma Wise, Old Paris Flea Market, 1111 South Eastern Road, Oklahoma City, OK 73129. Tel: (405) 670-2611.

OOLOGAH

Oologah Flea Market

DATES: Thursday through Monday, year round. Flea market outside in the summers.
TIMES: 9:00 AM–5:00 PM.
ADMISSION: Free. Parking is free.
LOCATION: 505 South Highway 169, 30 miles north of Tulsa.
DESCRIPTION: Although admittedly small and off the beaten path,

due to a new highway, this market sells antiques, collectibles, garage sale finds, books, jewelry, and "mostly small stuff." The owner regularly attends auctions and fills his market with treasures. There is a half-acre lot outside where dealers show up and sell in warm weather. Oologah is the birthplace of Will Rogers, whose home is five miles down the road. There are two other flea markets in this town. While there isn't any food served at the market itself, there is a pizza parlor and a donut shop nearby. Try this town's markets; they could be worth the detour.

DEALER RATES: $2 for an outside space. Reservations are not required.

CONTACT: Richard Plute, 505 South Highway 169, Oologah, OK 74053. Tel: (918) 443-2568.

TULSA

The Great American Flea Market and Antique Mall

DATES: Friday, Saturday, and Sunday, year round.

TIMES: 10:00 AM–6:00 PM.

ADMISSION: Free. Parking is also free.

LOCATION: 9212-32 East Admiral Place.

DESCRIPTION: Opened in 1989, this market holds 250 dealers inside and up to 100 outside selling antiques, collectibles, glassware, jewelry, baseball cards, garage sale stuff, and more "from A to Z." There is an electronic message board with advertising messages for dealers! A snack bar provides meals. There is a mall section adjacent to this market open from Tuesday through Sunday and a produce market on site.

DEALER RATES: Reasonable rates vary according to location, size, and length of rental. Reservations are suggested.

CONTACT: The Great American Flea Market, 9212 East Admiral Place, Tulsa, OK 74115. Tel: (918) 834-6363.

OTHER FLEA MARKETS

Tulsa: Tulsa Flea Market, P.O. Box 4511, Tulsa, OK 74159. Tel: (918) 744-1386.

OREGON

BEND
Deschutes Junction Flea Market
DATES: Friday through Sunday, and holidays.
TIMES: 9:00 AM–5:00 PM.
ADMISSION: Free. Parking is free.
LOCATION: Halfway between Bend and Redmond on U.S. Highway 97 on the site of the former Buffet Flat Flea Market.
DESCRIPTION: Opened on April 1, 1993, this market is carrying on the tradition of the famous Buffet Flat market that was closed due to a massive road building project several years ago. According to its manager, Ponch, it is growing to match its predecessor's fame and glory. As of May '93 it already had 50 dealers and is constantly adding more. You can find antiques, collectibles, crafts, produce in season, new merchandise, tools, tires, wheels, mowers, "just about anything you could name." They plan to be Oregon's largest flea market and can handle 18-wheelers on their parking lot. Take it from Ponch, they are close to all the good fishing and camping. Some fine rock climbing is just down the road at the Smith Rock State Park.
DEALER RATES: $20 for a 20' × 20' space for the weekend, $40 for a 20' × 20' for 4 weekends, or $10 a day. First come, first served.
CONTACT: Warren "Ponch" Neihart, 15820 Sparks Drive, La Pine, OR 97739. Tel: (503) 536-1467.

CORVALLIS
Heart of the Valley Flea Market and Bazaar
DATES: First Sunday of each month, except April 1994 when it is held on Saturday. No markets in June, July, or August.
TIMES: 10:00 AM–4:30 PM.
ADMISSION: $.25 per person, children under 6 free. Maximum per family $1. Free parking.
LOCATION: Benton County Fairgrounds, 110 Southwest 53rd Street, just south of 53rd and Harrison.
DESCRIPTION: This family run, indoor market has been in operation since 1971 and currently attracts between 55 and 65 dealers. A variety of antiques and collectibles including coins, brass, baseball cards, art, guns, tools, crafts, leather, and more is offered, as well as new merchandise. Snack food and restrooms are available. They hold a special two-day Christmas show.

DEALER RATES: $9 per 3' × 8' table per day. Dealer setup 7:00 AM–9:30 AM. Overnight hook-ups are available through Benton County Fairgrounds Office. Reservations are required.
CONTACT: Spike and Ileene Smith, 1010 NW 9th Street, Corvallis, OR 97330-6145. Tel: (503) 758-3019.

EUGENE
Picc-A-Dilly Flea Market
DATES: Sunday shows throughout the year, generally two per month. Call or write for 1994 dates.
TIMES: 10:00 AM–4:00 PM.
ADMISSION: $1 per adult; children under eight, enter free.
LOCATION: Lane County Fairgrounds, 796 West 13th (eight blocks west of city center).
DESCRIPTION: Claiming to be "Oregon's First Giant Flea Market," this indoor show has been going strong since February 1970 and draws 300 to 550 dealers and 1,000 to 3,000 customers depending on the season, making it one of the largest flea markets in the area. Among the items available are antiques and collectibles, handmade crafts, sports cards, coins, clocks, records, Indian artifacts, plants, gold, silver, toys, new merchandise, and fresh produce when in season. Hot and cold lunches are available.
DEALER RATES: $13 per 8' × 2½' table and cloth and 1 chair provided. Reservations are recommended. Set up time begins at 8:00 AM on day of show.
CONTACT: Rosemary Major, P.O. Box 2364, Eugene, OR 97402. Tel: (503) 683-5589. Phone open one week prior to each market.

HILLSBORO
Banner Flea Market
DATES: Fridays, Saturdays, and Sundays.
TIMES: 12:00 PM-5:30 PM.
ADMISSION: Free. Free parking.
LOCATION: 4871 S.E. Tualatin Valley Highway.
DESCRIPTION: This indoor/outdoor market is said to be the oldest in Washington County. Between 25 and 30 dealers sell all types of antiques, collectibles, jewelry, and produce in season. Food is served on the premises and toilet facilities are available nearby.
DEALER RATES: $10 per 4' × 8' space per weekend (three days). Reservations are not required.

CONTACT: Betty Henson, Banner Flea Market, 4871 SE Tualatin Valley Highway, Hillsboro, OR 97123. Tel: (503) 640-6755 or 648-8456.

KLAMATH FALLS
Linkville Flea Market

DATES: Generally one show per month, September through March. Call for dates.

TIMES: 9:00 AM–5:00 PM.

ADMISSION: $.25 per person. Free parking is available.

LOCATION: Klamath County Fairgrounds in Exhibit Building. Go east from downtown Klamath Falls on Sixth Street 2 miles.

DESCRIPTION: This show opened in 1975. It is an indoor market that accommodates approximately 100 dealers. Items sold include antiques, fine art, arts and crafts, collectibles, and new merchandise. Interesting points to visit nearby are Crater Lake, 65 miles away, and Lava Beds, also 65 miles away. Food is served on the premises.

DEALER RATES: $8 per 6' × 6' space, includes table. Reservations are suggested.

CONTACT: Elizabeth Boorman, 5420 Cottage, Klamath Falls, OR 97603. Tel: (503) 884-4352. Day of show call (503) 882-9102.

LA PINE
Wickiup Junction Flea Market

DATES: Friday, Saturday and Sunday and holiday Mondays, April through October, weather permitting.

TIMES: Friday 12:00 noon–5:00 PM, Saturday and Sunday 9:00 AM–5:00 PM.

ADMISSION: Free. Parking is also free.

LOCATION: U.S. Highway 97 about 3 miles north of La Pine.

DESCRIPTION: When the powers-that-be decided a road needed to be widened and then condemned the Buffet Flats Flea Market building, some of the regulars decided to open another market not too far away. And the dealers followed. They claim to be "Central Oregon's largest market" with 30-40 dealers per weekend. Tucked high in timber country, the Wickiup dealers trade in antiques, collectibles, crafts, handmade items, tools, and everything else. La Pine is the gateway to the brand-new Newberry National Monument and near two gorgeous lakes filled with great fishing possibilities: East and Polina Lakes.

DEALER RATES: All spaces are 22' and rent for $15 per day; or $25 per weekend. Reservations are suggested.

CONTACT: Kathleen St. Claire, Wickiup Junction Flea Market, La Pine, OR 57739. Tel: (503) 536-2211.

PORTLAND

"America's Largest" Antique and Collectible Sale

DATES: 1994 dates: March 5–6, July 16–17, October 29–30.

TIMES: Saturday 8:00 AM–7:00 PM; Sunday 9:00 AM–5:00 PM.

ADMISSION: $5 per person. Parking is available (4,000 spaces) for $4 per vehicle.

LOCATION: Multnomah County Expo Center. Exit 306B off I-5.

DESCRIPTION: This series of shows, which began operation in October 1981, is certainly one of the largest in the country, filling 1,260 dealer booths in March and October, and an additional 300 in July, in an impressive 240,000 square feet of indoor selling space devoted exclusively to antiques and collectibles. It is held three times each year in March, July, and October, and is so successful that the promoter runs similar events in Tacoma and San Francisco. Food and restrooms are available.

DEALER RATES: $80 per 10' × 10' space, with one 8' table included. Reservations are required well in advance of shows, 1991 was sold out by January.

CONTACT: Christine Skinner, Donald M. Wirfs and Associates, 4001 NE Halsey, Portland, OR 97232. Tel: (503) 282-0877, fax: (503) 282-2953.

"America's Largest" Antique & Collectible Sale

DATES: December 10–22, 1994.

TIMES: Saturday 8:00 AM–7:00 PM, Sunday 9:00 AM–5:00 PM.

ADMISSION: $5. Parking is $4.

LOCATION: Oregon Convention Center.

DESCRIPTION: This is the fifth show at this facility, which began operation in 1990. The Oregon Convention Center is one of the nicest in the country, and filling 800 plus booths you will find an excellent assortment of antiques and collectibles. Food is available on site.

DEALER RATES: $100 for a 10' × 10' booth.

CONTACT: Chuck Palmer, Palmer/Wirfs & Associates, 4001 NE Halsey, Portland, OR 97232. Tel: (503) 282-0877, or fax: (503) 282-2953.

"America's Largest" Christmas Bazaar

DATES: November 25–27, December 2–4, 1994.

TIMES: Friday and Saturday 10:00 AM–9:00 PM, Sunday 10:00 AM–6:00 PM.

ADMISSION: $5 per person, $2 under 17. Parking available (4,000 spaces) at $4 per vehicle.

LOCATION: Multnomah County Expo Center. Exit 306B off I-5.

DESCRIPTION: This annual indoor six-day show began in 1983 and currently draws around 1,000 dealers selling mostly craft items, gifts, with some new merchandise and some antiques and collectibles. The shows draws over 40,000 shoppers buying stocking stuffers and gifts for the holidays. Food and restrooms are available on the premises.

DEALER RATES: $250 per 10' × 10' space for crafters, with one 8' table and 500 watts electricity.

CONTACT: Christine Palmer, Palmer/Wirfs and Associates, 4001 NE Halsey, Portland, OR 97219. Tel: (503) 282-0967, or fax: (503) 282-2953.

Catlin Gabel Rummage Sale

DATES: Annually, first weekend in November, Thursday through Sunday.

TIMES: Thursday 5:00 PM–9:00 PM, Friday 10:00 AM–9:00 PM, Saturday 10:00 AM–6:00 PM, Sunday 10:00 AM–3:00 PM.

ADMISSION: Free. Parking is available at $3 per vehicle.

LOCATION: Multnomah County Exposition Center. Off I-5, near Jantzen Beach.

DESCRIPTION: Celebrating their 50th anniversary, this indoor "rummage sale" has been held annually since 1944 by the Catlin Gabel School, and certainly ranks among the largest markets of its type, even rating a listing once with the *Guiness Book of World Records* as the world's largest rummage sale. Imagine an average of over 8,000 shoppers rummaging through antiques, collectibles, books, hardware, furniture, standard rummage fare, cars, some new merchandise, and their spectacular Treasure Department. Once a horse was brought in for sale, another time it was a beer truck! Marilyn Cooper, the mastermind of all this, says "it's like putting on a circus." To give you some idea of the size of this haul, the loot fills 22 semi-trucks and over 60,000 square feet of space. All 650 students of the school help sort and schlep the goods to their respective "departments" come sale time. It takes a year to sort through all the stuff. The money earned from this project runs the financial aid program for this little school. Food is served on the premises.

DEALER RATES: All merchandise is donated. No independent dealers are admitted.

CONTACT: Marilyn Cooper, Catlin Gabel School, 8825 SW Barnes Road, Portland, OR 97225. Tel: (503) 297-1894.

Sandy Barr's Flea Market

DATES: Saturday and Sunday, year round.

TIMES: 8:00 AM–3:00 PM.

ADMISSION: Saturday is $.50. Sunday $1; seniors and children $.50.

LOCATION: 1225 North Marine Drive. Right next to I-5; east across the Interstate is the Expo Center.

DESCRIPTION: Opened in March 1991, there are up to 900 dealers selling everything: antiques, collectibles, office equipment, bulk food, shampoo, "world-famous sweet potato and pineapple pies from Germany (the best pies ever tasted, I'm assured!)," jewelry, dog clothes—you name it! A mini-mall sells very special antiques and collectibles including dolls, glass, and other treasures. Several restaurants serve Chinese, Mexican, American, and soul food as well as other foods.

DEALER RATES: Tables are $5 Saturday, $10 on Sunday. Reservations are required.

CONTACT: Sandy Barr's Flea Market, 1225 Marine Drive, Portland, OR 97217. Tel: (503) 283-6993 or 283-9565.

SALEM
Big Red's Shop N Swap

DATES: Saturday and Sunday, year round, rain or shine.

TIMES: 9:30 AM–5:00 PM.

ADMISSION: Free admission and free parking.

LOCATION: 3545 Portland Road NE. Five blocks south of I-5, Exit 258 (on Portland Road NE).

DESCRIPTION: Opened in the state capitol in 1983, dealers offer antiques, collectibles, handmade and craft items, and new merchandise. Ethnic products and jewelry are strong items here. About 70 percent of merchandise is new. This market is part of a six-acre business complex also housing an auto auction and furniture building all owned by the Whitneys. Food is available at a snack bar.

DEALER RATES: $7 per day for a 3' × 7' table, two or more tables.

Single tables rent for $8 per day. Advance reservations are required. Setup is Friday 2:00 PM–5:00 PM and one hour before opening on show days.

CONTACT: Duke Whitney, 3545 Portland Road NE, Salem, OR 97303. Tel: (503) 362-1252.

Salem Collectors Market

DATES: Generally two shows per month except July and August. 1994 dates: January 16, 30, February 13 (Sounds of Nostalgia), March 26–27 (Depression Glass), April 10, 24, May 8, 22 (21st Watch and Clock Show), June 12, 26, July 10, September 10–11, 25 (16th Annual Paper Caper), October 22–23 (two day "Nifty Fifties" Show), November 12-13 (Annual Toy and Doll Show), 27, December 3–4, 18 (Last Minute Christmas Shoppers Sale).

TIMES: 9:30 AM–3:30 PM.

ADMISSION: $1 per adult $.50 per senior; children under age 12 are admitted free with an adult. $8 "Early Shoppers" admission fee allows shoppers to enter between 4:00 PM–7:00 PM the evening before the show and 7:00 AM–9:00 AM day of show.

LOCATION: Oregon State Fairgrounds, 2770 17th Street, corner of Silverton Road. Take the Market Street exit off I-5, then west on Market to 17th, then north to Fairgrounds.

DESCRIPTION: This show has been in business since 1972 under the same family management (the Haley's daughter is now running these events), and currently averages 500 tables of merchandise per show. Shows generally feature antiques, collectibles, and craft items; specialty shows include "Sounds of Nostalgia," featuring old-time phonographs and records (first show in February); glassware shows in April and October; clock and watch sale, first show in May; "Paper Caper" show featuring advertising memorabilia and other Americana, first show in September; and a toy and doll show, first show in November. This is considered the largest continuous twice-monthly antique and collectibles market in the Northwest. Food is served on the premises.

DEALER RATES: $13 per 8' × 2½' table. Reservations are required.

CONTACT: Karen Haley Huston, P.O. Box 20805, Salem, OR 97307-0805. Tel: (503) 393-1261.

SUMPTER

Sumpter Valley Country Fair

DATES: 1994 dates: May 28–30, July 2–4, and September 3–5.

TIMES: 8:00 AM–5:00 PM.

ADMISSION: Free. Free parking is also available.

LOCATION: When entering town from Baker City, take first right and go three blocks to SVDA parking lot.

DESCRIPTION: Started in 1971, this flea market is one of the ways in which Sumpter is being turned into "the Liveliest Ghost Town in Oregon." Originally held in downtown Sumpter, by 1986 the event grew so large much of the market moved to the Sumpter Valley Days grounds. The event features 80–140 dealers in antiques, collectibles, handcrafts, and new merchandise. Fresh produce and food are also available. While in town, visitors can also ride the restored portion of the Sumpter Valley Railway, a steam-operated narrow-gauge railroad. In July and September, visitors enjoy an old-time fiddlers show.

DEALER RATES: $1.50 per foot with minimum space of 12 feet. Reservations are suggested.

CONTACT: Leland or Nancy Myers, SVDA, P.O. Box 513, Sumpter, OR 97877. Tel: (503) 894-2264.

OTHER FLEA MARKETS

Portland: Salvage Sally's Flea Market and Bargain Fair, 2330 SE 82nd Avenue, Portland, OR 97216. Tel: (503) 777-5058.

PENNSYLVANIA

ABINGTON
St. Anne's Annual Flea Market
DATES: Saturdays: April 23, July 16, October 1. The 1995 dates will be the same weekend each year; raindate is the following Saturday.
TIMES: 9:00 AM–3:00 PM. Dealers set up at 7:00 AM, and the public is welcome then, too.
ADMISSION: Free. Parking is also free.
LOCATION: Old Welch Road and Old York Road (Route 611).
DESCRIPTION: This 20-year-old open-air market has 75 to 100 vendors selling collectibles, crafts, and new merchandise as a fundraiser for St. Anne's Church. Food is provided by the church. Restrooms are provided indoors and are handicapped-accessible.
DEALER RATES: $13 to $18 per space per day. Reservations are required.
CONTACT: Nadia Promotions, Inc., P.O. Box 156, Flourtown, PA 19031. Tel: (215) 643-1396.

ADAMSTOWN
Renninger's #1 Antique Market
DATES: Every Sunday, year round.
TIMES: 7:30 AM–5:00 PM.
ADMISSION: Free. Free parking is available.
LOCATION: On Route 272, 1 mile north of Exit 21 on the Pennsylvania Turnpike, between Adamstown and Denver in Lancaster County.
DESCRIPTION: This indoor and outdoor market has operated since 1967 and houses up to 500 dealers in a huge, indoor building. They deal in fine antiques and all types of collectibles. No crafts or new merchandise are permitted. In fair weather, outdoor dealers number from 300 to 400. Stands are in a grove and lot behind the main market building.
DEALER RATES: $15 per day all Sundays except six special dates, when the fee is somewhat higher. Reservations for indoor stands are required. No reservations are needed for the outdoor section. Apply at the market office.
CONTACT: Renninger's Promotions, 27 Bensinger Drive, Schuylkill Haven, PA 17972. Tel: (717) 385-0104, Monday through Thursday; Friday through Sunday (215) 267-2177.

Stoudt's Black Angus Antique Mall

DATES: Every Sunday, year round, rain or shine.

TIMES: 8:00 AM–5:00 PM.

LOCATION: Route 272, 1 mile north of Pennsylvania Turnpike, Exit 21.

ADMISSION: Free. Plenty of free parking is available.

DESCRIPTION: Over 25 years old, this Sunday market is part of a huge complex including Stoudt's Black Angus Restaurant, brewery, brewery hall and tours, and the Antique Mall. They hold a Beer Fest every weekend, Friday through Sunday, with live entertainment. Polka weekend is Labor Day weekend! Only antiques and collectibles are sold at the Antiques Mall by 250 permanent indoor dealers year round and another 100 dealers setup in three outdoor pavilions in the summer. One source tells me that the Black Angus Restaurant serves the best steak dinner he has ever eaten and this man travels extensively!

DEALER RATES: Contact Carl Barto for rates. Reservations are required.

CONTACT: Carl Barto, Manager, Stoudt's Black Angus, P.O. Box 880, Route 272, Adamstown, PA 19501. Tel: (215) 484-4385, or (717) 569-3536.

BENSALEM

Farmers Market at Philadelphia Park

DATES: Friday, March through December.

TIMES: Daylight.

ADMISSION: Free. Parking is free.

LOCATION: Philadelphia Park Racetrack, located just off of I-95, Route 1 and Exit 28 of the Pennsylvania Turnpike.

DESCRIPTION: Opened in 1982, this outdoor market hosts 450 to 850 dealers selling antiques, collectibles, crafts, shoes, housewares, jewelry, carpets, clothing, kids stuff, new merchandise, and more. Ten snack bars take care of the screaming munchies.

DEALER RATES: $25 for a 12' × 30' booth for sellers of new merchandise; $10 for a 10' × 40' booth for sellers of used goods. Reservations are not required.

CONTACT: Janice Ackerman, P.O. Box 387, Voorhees, NJ 08043. Tel: (609) 795-4686.

BLOOMSBURG
Pioneer Village Sales Market

DATES: Every Saturday and Sunday, April through November.

TIMES: 9:00 AM–5:00 PM.

ADMISSION: Free. Ample free parking on premises.

LOCATION: On Route 11 North, 3 miles south of Exit 36S off I-80.

DESCRIPTION: This market, which has been in operation since 1980, was designed previously as a replica of an old western town, complete with railroad station and eight buildings copied from designs of the Old West. Currently there are between 50 and 60 dealers each week selling indoors and outdoors if weather permits. Fresh farm products and new merchandise complement antiques and collectibles to provide a variety of items to choose from. Food and toilet facilities are available.

DEALER RATES: $8 and up per 6' table outside for first two tables, $2 each additional table per day inside. Outside bulk dealer spaces $10 and up; inside booths range from $15 to $65 per week. Reservations required for indoors only.

CONTACT: Harry W. Myers, P.O. Box 32, Bloomsburg, PA 17815. Tel: (717) 784-1675. Market number: (717) 387-0734.

CHADDS FORD
Pennsbury-Chaddsford Antique Mall

DATES: Upper section open daily except Tuesday and Wednesday; lower level weekends only, year round.

TIMES: 10:00 AM–5:00 PM.

ADMISSION: Free. Free parking.

LOCATION: On Route 1, between Brandywine River Museum and Longwood Gardens.

DESCRIPTION: Located in a two-level building in historic Brandywine Valley near the Brandywine River Museum, this indoor market has 100 regular dealers selling a range of antiques and collectibles, primitives, stamps, coins, militaria, silver, jewelry, period furniture, and Oriental rugs. Food is available on the premises.

DEALER RATES: Downstairs rates start from $135 to $250 for spaces ranging from 10' × 12' to 24' × 12', per weekend. Upstairs rates are from $500 and up for prime spaces. There is a waiting list for dealers. Display cases are also available for rental for $100 a month.

CONTACT: Mr. Alfred Delduco, Owner, 31 South High Street, West Chester, PA 19382. Tel: (215) 388-6480. Or Earl Buckley, Upstairs

Manager, Pennsbury-Chaddsford Antique Mall, 640 East Baltimore Pike, Chadds Ford, PA 19317. Mall numbers are (215) 388-1620 upper level; (215) 388-6546 for lower level.

COLLEGEVILLE
Power House Antique and Flea Market

DATES: Every Sunday.

TIMES: 9:00 AM–5:00 PM.

ADMISSION: Free. Free parking available.

LOCATION: On Route 29 North. From Philadelphia: take Route 422 West to Collegeville, then north on Route 29. From Reading: take Route 422 East to Collegeville, then north on Route 29.

DESCRIPTION: This indoor market has been functioning since 1970 in an old power house, and currently holds approximately 50 dealers who sell a range of collectibles including coins, baseball cards, books, and jewelry, as well as many antique items, new merchandise, and handicrafts. Food is not served on the premises, although restrooms are available.

DEALER RATES: $15 for a 9' × 12' space. Reservations are required, and rates for larger spaces are available on request.

CONTACT: Janet McDonnell, 45 First Avenue, Collegeville, PA 19426. Tel: (215) 489-7388.

DENVER
Barr's Antique World

DATES: Every Saturday and Sunday, rain or shine.

TIMES: Saturday 10:00 AM–5:00 PM; Sunday 8:00 AM–5:00 PM.

ADMISSION: Free. Free parking.

LOCATION: Take Exit 21 off the Pennsylvania Turnpike; take Toll Booth Service Road to Route 272 North (¼ mile).

DESCRIPTION: This indoor/outdoor market has operated since 1979 and currently attracts around 150 sellers offering a range of items including antiques, Country French furniture and accessories, furniture, paintings, Oriental art, cigar labels, clocks, glassware, stamps, primitives, jewelry, quilts, tools, toy trains, postcards, and political memorabilia, as well as crafts. An auction room occupies the rear of the building with regular Monday sales. For items viewed on weekends, you can leave a 25 percent deposit as an absentee bid. There are special sale dates throughout the year. Food and clean restrooms are available.

DEALER RATES: Outdoor space is unreserved; inside space also available. Call for rates and reservations.
CONTACT: Col. Bervin L. Barr, 2152 North Reading Road, Denver, PA 17517. Tel: (215) 267-2861.

DOWNINGTOWN
Downingtown Marketplace
DATES: Friday through Sunday, year round.
TIMES: Friday and Saturday 10:00 AM–10:00 PM; Sunday 10:00 AM–6:00 PM. Front stores: Wednesday and Thursday 10:00 AM–6:00 PM.
ADMISSION: Free. Free parking on premises.
LOCATION: On Route 30. Take Exit 23 off the Pennsylvania Turnpike, head south on Route 100 to Route 30, then go west on Route 30 (market will be on right side).
DESCRIPTION: The Downingtown Marketplace is more than just a flea market—there is also an adjacent indoor shopping center which has a 116-booth under-roof outdoor flea market and a large Amish market where produce, baked goods, and crafts are readily available. The indoor market, which is devoted to collectibles, clothing, jewelry, furniture, and food is over four football fields in length and is surely one of the very largest in the state, measured either by number of dealers (minimum of a few hundred) or by the number of shoppers present (an article in *The New York Times* in 1979 suggested a July 4 weekend turnout of over 60,000, while the owners modestly limit that figure to 25,000 at most). Toilet facilities are available on the premises.
DEALER RATES: $15 per 12' × 12' space outdoors, per day. Dealer reservations are not required outside. Inside is by lease at $85 a week for a 9' × 13' space.
CONTACT: Marc Schaefer, Schaefer Management Corp., c/o Downingtown Marketplace, Route 30, Downingtown, PA 19335. Tel: (215) 269-4050.

EDINBURGH
MichaelAngelo's
DATES: Sunday, year round.
TIMES: 7:00 AM–5:00 PM.
ADMISSION: Free. Parking is free.
LOCATION: On State Route 422, 5 miles west of New Castle.

DESCRIPTION: This indoor/outdoor market, started in 1971, boasts 200 to 300 dealers offering antiques, handmades, musical greeting cards, floral arrangements, collectibles, cards, gifts, produce, meats, cheese, and new and used merchandise. Food is always available in ground's concessions, restaurant, and smorgasbord.

DEALER RATES: $7 and up for a 14' × 16' space outside; $8 and up for a 4' × 8' table plus space indoors. Reservations are not required outdoors, but are required for indoor selling.

CONTACT: Michael Carbone, MichaelAngelo's, RD 1 Box 211, Edinburg, PA 16116. Tel: (412) 654-0382 or 656-8915.

EPHRATA
Green Dragon Farmers Market and Auction

DATES: Every Friday, rain or shine.

TIMES: 9:00 AM–10:00 PM.

ADMISSION: Free. Thirty acres of free parking.

LOCATION: 955 North State Street, 1 mile north of Ephrata; also, ¼ mile off Route 272. Look for the dragon.

DESCRIPTION: Green Dragon began in 1932 and now has over 400 merchants weekly, including 250 local growers and craftsmen. Meats, fish, poultry, cheeses, and sweets are among the fresh produce available, and all types of antiques and collectibles may be found at the market. The auction offers a range of products from dry goods to livestock—a real down-home country affair for the whole family. Food is served in five restaurants and seven snack bars; restroom facilities are available.

DEALER RATES: $24 per 20' × 20' space. Advance reservations are required.

CONTACT: Larry L. Loose, Manager, The Green Dragon, 955 North State Street, Ephrata, PA 17522. Tel: (717) 738-1117.

FAYETTEVILLE
Fayetteville Antique and Flea Market

DATES: Daily.

TIMES: Monday through Saturday 9:00 AM–5:00 PM; Sunday 8:00 AM–5:00 PM.

ADMISSION: Free. Parking is also free.

LOCATION: I-81, Exit 6 on Route 30, 18 miles west of Gettysburg, or 4 miles east of Chambersburg.

DESCRIPTION: This market, located in four buildings, has 220 dealers selling mostly antiques, collectibles, cast iron, depression glass, books, toys, dolls, china, tools, postcards, primitives, furniture (in another two buildings), and more! A snack bar operates Friday through Sunday. Outside setups are available. There are six to eight smaller buildings rented by individuals selling even more items.

DEALER RATES: $45–$66 per 10' × 10' space depending on location. Reservations are required as space rents by the month.

CONTACT: L. L. Dymond, Jr., Fayetteville Antique and Flea Market, 3653 Lincoln Way East, Fayetteville, PA 17222. Tel: (717) 352-8485.

GILBERTSVILLE

Gilbertsville Firehouse Indoor Flea Market

DATES: 1994: February 6, March 13, and December 11. Try the same weekends for the following years.

TIMES: 9:00 AM–3:00 PM. Dealers setup after 7:30 AM and the public is welcome to join in.

ADMISSION: Free. Parking is also free.

LOCATION: Route 73, east of Route 100 and west of Route 663.

DESCRIPTION: Started in 1990, this indoor market's 50 to 75 dealers (from 100 tables) sell antiques, collectibles, handmade and craft items, and some new merchandise. This market started in1989. Food sold at the market helps the Gilbertsville Firehouse. There is a restaurant on premises as well. Restrooms are inside and handicapped-accessible.

DEALER RATES: $18 per 8' table and two chairs. Reservations are required.

CONTACT: Nadia Promotions, Inc., P.O. Box 156, Flourtown, PA 19031-0156. Tel: (215) 643-1396 or fax: (215) 654-0896.

Zern's Farmer's Market and Auction

DATES: Every Friday and Saturday, year round, rain or shine.

TIMES: Friday 2:00 PM–10:00 PM; Saturday 11:00 AM–10:00 PM.

ADMISSION: Free. Free parking for 5,000 cars is available.

LOCATION: On Route 73, 1 mile east of Boyertown.

DESCRIPTION: This market and auction started in 1926 with over 300 dealers currently both indoors and out. In addition to antiques, collectibles, handicrafts, clothes for the entire family, all types of produce, meats, and cheeses are for sale. You could probably furnish a house and clothe your family from the markets and auctions here;

from hearing aids to kitchens, from hats to shoes. There is a livestock auction weekly and an auto auction every Friday. Located in the heart of "Amish Country," this market is self-billed as the "World's Largest Dutch Treat." It was once voted "Best of Philly" by *Philadelphia Magazine*. There are food concessions on the premises.

DEALER RATES: $20 per 8' × 10' outside space per weekend. $150 per 10' × 10' inside space per month. Reservations are required.

CONTACT: Jake Rhoads, c/o Zern's, Route 73, Gilbertsville, PA 19525. Tel: (215) 367-2461.

GREENSBURG

Greengate Flea Market

DATES: Sundays, April through October.

TIMES: 7:00 AM–3:00 PM.

ADMISSION: Free. Parking is free.

LOCATION: Route 30 west of Greensburg, next to the Greengate Mall. From the turnpike take Exit 7, go east to market.

DESCRIPTION: Moved from Latrobe in 1993, this outdoor market has grown with their new space. They can accommodate 150 dealers and have come close in their first year. Their dealers sell antiques, collectibles, crafts, produce, household goods, garage sale finds, coins, stamps, loads of baseball cards, baked goods, furniture, new merchandise, whatever. I am assured that one of the three snack concessions serves the "best hot sausage sandwich in Pennsylvania." People drive from all over just to have a sandwich! Found among the Tupperware and stuff brought in: a hanging salt in blue spongeware (very rare item), and two beautiful handmade quilts.

DEALER RATES: $13 for a 21' × 16' space paid in advance, $8 for a 11' × 16' space, $5 for a spot in the bargain section. Reservations are suggested. They haven't had to turn anyone away from this location, yet.

CONTACT: Carol J. Craig, 214 Kenneth Street, Greensburg, PA 15601. Tel: (412) 837-6881.

HAZEN

Warsaw Township Volunteer Fire Company Flea Market

DATES: First Sunday of the month, May through October.

TIMES: Daybreak–4:00 PM, depending on weather.

ADMISSION: Free. The firehouse has five acres of free parking, but the neighbors do charge to park on their property.

LOCATION: On Route 28, ½ mile north of Hazen. Take I-80 to Exit 14, then north 6 miles on Route 28. Located in northwest Pennsylvania near Brookville, Brockway and Dubois. Only 80 miles from the Ohio stateline.

DESCRIPTION: This extremely successful outdoor market began in the early 1970s as a fundraiser for the firehouse. They average 450 dealers selling a variety of antiques and collectibles, as well as farm produce and some new items. This is truly a great place to find treasures. A violin went for $2,000 here. One customer was seen walking around with a boa constrictor around her neck. It is quite common for out-of-state dealers to fly to this area several times during the year, stock up on antiques, store them, then return later with a truck to collect their booty. Because of the success of this market, area motels and hotels have expanded to accommodate the influx of traffic. On the day of the flea market, the entire area becomes a giant yard sale. If you are a true-blue hunter of treasures and bargains, come in on Saturday when the dealers start setting up and start hunting. Food and toilet facilities are available.

DEALER RATES: $15 for 18' × 24' space outdoors. Call for reservation information. Dealers get discounts at local area hotels and motels. All dealers must have a Pennsylvania sales tax number.

CONTACT: Warsaw Township Volunteer Fire Co., RD 1 Box 76C (Brookville), Hazen, PA 15825. Call the Fire Hall at (814) 328-2528 or Clyde at (814) 328-2536.

Be specific—

An out-of-state dealer asked a seller the price of a butter churn and butter maker dish. "Two-fifty each," the seller replied. Thinking that $250 each was a bit steep, the dealer continued browsing. The next buyer admired the pair and asked the price. "Five bucks for the pair." They were sold on the spot.

Later the dealer told Clyde that he really would have paid $250 each for the items; they were more than worth it.

HULMEVILLE
Old Mill Flea Market

DATES: Thursday through Sunday, year round, rain or shine.

TIMES: Thursday and Friday 6:00 PM–9:00 PM; Saturday 12:00 noon–9:00 PM; Sunday 12:00 noon–5:00 PM.

ADMISSION: Free. Free parking is available.

LOCATION: Intersection of Hulmeville Road/Bellevue and Trenton Avenues; 2 miles from Exit 28 on the Pennsylvania Turnpike (U.S. Route 1); 2 miles from I-95 (U.S. Route 1) Exit 26.

DESCRIPTION: This small, year-round indoor market started in 1971 in a large, 1880's historic Bucks County grist mill. The market draws several hundred shoppers each weekend. A full range of antiques and collectibles is available, including dolls, books, china, textiles, jewelry, furniture, glassware, advertising, breweriana, photographica, pottery, etc. This place is a "haunt" for dealers and collectors, more so than the general public (who haven't caught on—yet), as the management buys out house contents and estates. No food is available on the premises. Restrooms are provided.

DEALER RATES: Currently there is no space available.

CONTACT: Kathy Loeffler, P.O. Box 7069, Penndel, PA 19047-7069. Tel: (215) 757-1777.

KUTZTOWN

Renninger's #2 Antique Market

DATES: Every Saturday, year round, rain or shine. Extravaganzas in April, June, and September. Pennsylvania Dutch Farmer's Market is open every Friday 12:00 noon–8:00 PM.

TIMES: 8:30 AM–5:00 PM.

ADMISSION: Free. There is an admission charge for Extravaganzas. Free parking is provided.

LOCATION: 740 Nobel Street, 1 mile south from the center of town. Midway between Allentown and Reading on Route 222.

DESCRIPTION: This indoor/outdoor market has been in operation since 1976 and now ranks among the most popular markets in the Northeast. The market attracts approximately 300 dealers during regular weekends, and up to 1,500 during the Extravaganzas. A wide range of antiques and collectibles is featured along with craft items, new merchandise, and fresh foods including smoked and fresh meats, poultry, seafood, and baked goods. For the Extravaganzas, dealers are said to arrive from as many as 42 different states, as well as from Canada and Europe. There is no flea market on Extravaganza days.

DEALER RATES: $8 per 10' × 25' outdoor pavilion space per day, $6 for special outdoor section during normal sale days. Call for rates for Extravaganzas. Reservations are required.

CONTACT: Renninger's Promotions, 27 Bensinger Drive, Schuylkill Haven, PA 17972. Tel: (717) 385-0104 Monday through Thursday; Friday through Sunday call (215) 683-6848.

LEESPORT
Leesport Farmer's Market

DATES: The flea market is every Wednesday and the first Sunday of each month from April through December; the farmer's market is held every Wednesday, year round.

TIMES: Flea market from 7:00 AM–close; first Sunday 7:00 AM–3:00 PM; farmer's market from 9:00 AM–8:00 PM.

ADMISSION: Free admission and free parking.

LOCATION: One block east off Route 61; 8 miles north of Reading.

DESCRIPTION: This family-run market has been operating since 1947, currently accommodating up to 400 dealers both indoors and out. The complete farmer's market, with a livestock auction on Wednesday, is complemented by the collectibles, jewelry, clothing, crafts and new merchandise available in the flea market. Many items are supplied by neighboring Pennsylvania Dutch merchants. Food is available on the market grounds.

DEALER RATES: $10 per 12' × 35' unsheltered space, no tables; $10 per 10' × 10' space with 8' table. Some spaces are reserved for the season. Otherwise, first come, first served.

CONTACT: Daniel "Woody" Weist, P.O. Box B, Leesport, PA 19533. Tel: (215) 926-1307.

LEOLA
Meadowbrook Market, Inc.

DATES: Fridays and Saturdays.

TIMES: Friday 9:00 AM–8:00 PM; Saturday 8:00 AM–5:00 PM.

ADMISSION: Free. Free parking is provided.

LOCATION: 345 West Main Street; 4 miles east of Lancaster on Route 23.

DESCRIPTION: This indoor market has been in operation since 1970 and currently draws approximately 196 dealers selling all types of items including antiques, collectibles, foods, furniture, spices, sheepskins, handmade goods, new merchandise, and most anything. The market is air-conditioned in summertime, and shopping carts are provided for added convenience. A new addition was added in 1991 creating more space indoors. This is a big complex that includes three restaurants "outside"; one Chinese, one Italian, and one serving Barbecue ribs, and one "inside" the market. In addition, there are six snack bars scattered throughout the complex. Tour buses regularly come from Texas making a yearly pilgrimage, as well as Canada, California and all over the East Coast. Restrooms are available.

DEALER RATES: $7 to $20 per booth for outside flea market, no tables supplied. Advance reservations are required.

CONTACT: Frank or Joe Surachi, Meadowbrook Market, 345 West Main Street, Leola, PA 17540. Tel: (717) 656-2226.

MARSHALLS CREEK

Pocono Bazaar

DATES: Every Saturday and Sunday, and major holidays.

TIMES: 9:00 AM–5:00 PM.

ADMISSION: Free. Ample free parking is available.

LOCATION: On U.S. Route 209. Take Exit 52 off I-80 (1 mile west of the Delaware Water Gap toll bridge), then drive 5 miles north on U.S. Route 209.

DESCRIPTION: Located in the Pocono Mountains and started in 1983, this rapidly expanding indoor/outdoor complex currently supports 50 indoor dealers, 140 more under outdoor pavilions, and about 400 more located in an outdoor paved lot. The indoor market is known as the Pocono Antique Bazaar, and the outdoor arrangements trade in a variety of collectibles, crafts, produce, and new merchandise. Food is available, as are restrooms.

DEALER RATES: $25 per 12' × 25' space (including car). No reservations are required.

CONTACT: Wulf and Eva Knausenberger, P.O. Box 248, Marshalls Creek, PA 18335. Tel: (717) 223-8640.

MECHANICSBURG

Silver Spring Flea Market

DATES: Every Sunday of the year, rain or shine.

TIMES: 7:00 AM–3:00 PM.

ADMISSION: Parking and admission are free.

LOCATION: 6416 Carlisle Pike, 7 miles west of Harrisburg on U.S. Route 11.

DESCRIPTION: This flea market was founded in 1969 and is the largest in the area, with 700 to 1,000 indoor and outdoor dealers attracting thousands of visitors each Sunday. Here you'll find antiques, collectibles, crafts, farm goods, and new merchandise. "You can find anything at this market." Ten restaurants and snack bars quell any screaming munchies.

DEALER RATES: $10 per 10' × 10' outside space per day; $45 per 3' × 8' table monthly rental cost. First come, first served. There are some reserved outside spaces.

CONTACT: Alan Kreitzer, Silver Spring Flea Market, 6416 Carlisle Pike, Mechanicsburg, PA 17055-2393. Tel: (717) 766-7215. Day of market call Anna Smith: (717) 766-9027.

MENGES MILLS
Colonial Valley

DATES: Every Sunday.

TIMES: 8:30 AM–4:30 PM. Special events last longer.

ADMISSION: Free. Free parking is available.

LOCATION: On Route 116, 10 minutes west of York and 10 minutes east of Hanover.

DESCRIPTION: This market grew from a little flea market into a resort. It has 140 dealers indoors and more outdoors, covering over 140 acres. Antiques, collectibles and craft items, and new merchandise are offered. In addition to regular Sunday hours, four three-day shows are held each year, and other special attractions. There are all sorts of races, rodeos and events including Civil War reenactments, an Indian pow-wow, Western shows, donkey baseball, horse shows, trail rides, rock concerts, an antique car show and a street ride show. There is even a haunted house at Halloween. At Christmas, they really light up the whole town with 100,000 lights and have a variety of carriage and sleigh rides! They now have one building devoted to Christmas year round with animated scenes and characters among other goodies. They have a real bear, llamas, 4-horn sheep, miniature horses (22" high), and a petting zoo loaded with an interesting variety of animals (unfortunately, "Clyde," their 26"-tall steer, died). Auctions are held Wednesday evenings at 6:30 PM. Bus tours frequently stop here. "Good country food" and restrooms are available.

DEALER RATES: $10 per table inside; $8 outside. Reservations are required for inside spaces.

CONTACT: Judy Phillips or Herb Sterner, Owners, or Betty Staines, Manager, Colonial Valley Resorts, P.O. Box 34, Menges Mills, PA 72346. Day of show call (717) 225-4811.

Colonial Valley has over 60 Tennessee walking horses here. Many are trained for police departments all over the country.

This is the site of one of the oldest working post offices. Former President Richard Nixon grew up around here and was at the post office when he got the call to go to China, the first sitting president to do so.

MIDDLETOWN
Saturday's Market

DATES: Every Saturday, rain or shine.

TIMES: Inside 8:00 AM–6:00 PM, outside 5:30 AM until.

ADMISSION: Free. Ample free parking is available.

LOCATION: 3751 East Harrisburg Pike, just off Route 283, on Route 230 between Middletown and Elizabethtown, Pennsylvania. Only minutes from Hershey Park and Amish country.

DESCRIPTION: This indoor/outdoor market opened in 1983 and currently attracts 200-plus dealers indoors and over 200 outdoors. Items sold include antiques, arts and crafts, and collectibles. New merchandise is also available. At the farmer's market there is always a large supply of fresh produce, along with the delicacies of 14 other eateries on the premises.

DEALER RATES: $45 per month for a 10' space inside. Outside special: two spaces for $15. Consult management, reservations are sometimes required.

CONTACT: Rod Rose, 3751 East Harrisburg Pike, Middletown, PA 17057. Tel: (717) 944-2555.

MORGANTOWN
The Market Place at Morgantown

DATES: Friday and Saturday, year round, rain or shine.

TIMES: 9:00 AM–6:00 PM.

ADMISSION: Free, with free parking available.

LOCATION: At the junction of Route 23 and Route 10 in mid-Morgantown.

DESCRIPTION: This market started in 1968. There are approximately 120 indoor and 120 outdoor dealers selling antiques, collectibles, craft items, and new merchandise. Many of the dealers specialize in antiques and collectibles. There is a new clock tower plaza that houses 10 retail stores, including a Radio Shack and travel agency. Stop in Rush's Meats and say hello. Produce, meats and cheeses are also on hand. Food is served on the premises.

DEALER RATES: $8 and $10 per 10' × 20' space outside. Reservations are suggested for outside dealing, and required indoors.

CONTACT: Guy or Patty, Market Place at Morgantown, Route 23, Morgantown, PA 19543. Tel: (215) 286-0611.

NEW HOPE
Country Host Flea Market

DATES: Every Sunday, year round, weather permitting.

TIMES: 7:00 AM–5:00 PM.

ADMISSION: Free with free parking.

LOCATION: On Route 202 in New Hope.

DESCRIPTION: This market was formed in 1970 and is run outdoors. Dealers sell primarily antiques and collectibles. There is a diner open during market hours next door. They are located in beautiful Bucks County.

DEALER RATES: $10 per one table, $15 for two; $20 for three tables setup per day. No reservations needed.

CONTACT: Manager, Country Host Flea Market, Route 202, New Hope, PA 18938. Tel: (215) 862-5575.

Rice's Sale and Country Market

DATES: Every Tuesday, rain or shine.

TIMES: 6:30 AM–2:00 PM.

ADMISSION: Free. Free parking is available. Paid parking is available for $1.

LOCATION: 144 Green Hill Road, between Aquetong and Mechansville Roads, off Route 263.

DESCRIPTION: This market is said to have started in 1857, ranking it among the very oldest existing flea markets in the state of Pennsylvania. There are currently over 1,200 spaces each week at this indoor/outdoor event, selling "everything from A to Z" including antiques, collectibles, fine art to new merchandise, and fresh produce, meats, baked goods, and zucchini. Restrooms are available.

DEALER RATES: $15 per 8' × 3' table weekly; $60 monthly.

CONTACT: Robert and Barbara Blanche, 144 Green Hill Road, New Hope, PA 18938. Tel: (215) 297-5993.

NEWRY

Leighty's 29-Acre Indoor/Outdoor Flea Market

DATES: Saturday and Sunday, year round.

TIMES: 7:00 AM–5:00 PM.

ADMISSION: Free, with ample free parking.

LOCATION: On Route 220, 2 miles south of Altoona.

DESCRIPTION: This show began 13 years ago and has grown from 60 dealers in the winter to 350 in the summer exhibiting antiques, collectibles, handmades, and new merchandise, as well as an assortment of yard sale items. Food vendors and a concession are on the property. This is a large, clean, well-managed market for the area and is located near the famous "horseshoe curve." They also have a farmer's market across the street

DEALER RATES: $8 and up per 11' × 20' outdoor sales space. Indoor spaces vary in size and price. Reservations are suggested. For walk-ins, the earlier you come the better the location for you.

CONTACT: Brent Leighty, Leighty's Flea Market, P.O. Box 310, Newry, PA 16665-0310. Tel: (814) 695-5052. Day of show call (814) 695-9120.

PHILADELPHIA

Philadelphia International Antique Toy Convention

DATES: June 5, 1994 and another in January 1995. Annually, generally the second or third Sunday in January and another in June.

TIMES: 10:00 AM–4:00 PM.

ADMISSION: $5 for adults; children free, accompanied by adult; $1 for senior citizens. Parking is free.

LOCATION: Ramada Inn Hotel and Convention Center, northeast Philadelphia (Trevose). Route 1, ½ mile south on Pennsylvania Turnpike Exit 28.

DESCRIPTION: For 20 years this show has specialized in antique and collectible toys, dolls, and related items. This market is host to over 200 dealers from all over the United States, Europe, and Japan. Food is served on the premises.

DEALER RATES: $60 per 6' × 30' table. Reservations are required. Advance shopping hours for dealers are: 8:00 AM–10:00 AM.

CONTACT: Bob Bostoff, 331 Cochran Place, Valley Stream, NY 11581. Tel: (516) 791-4858.

Quaker City Flea Market

DATES: Every Saturday and Sunday, rain or shine.

TIMES: 8:00 AM–4:00 PM.

ADMISSION: Free. Free parking nearby.

LOCATION: Tacony and Comly Streets, 2 blocks south of the Tacony-Palmyra Bridge.

DESCRIPTION: This market began operation in 1972 and currently attracts between 175 and 200 dealers on indoor and outdoor spaces, selling a variety of items including jewelry and other handmade crafts, fresh produce, antiques, and new merchandise. Food and restrooms are available.

DEALER RATES: Between $15–$20 for an outside space; $35 and up for inside space. Reservations are required in advance.

CONTACT: K. Williams, Quaker City Flea Market, Tacony and Comly Streets, Philadelphia, PA 19135. Tel: (215) 744-2022.

PITTSBURGH

Country Peddler Show

DATES: April 8–10, 1994.

TIMES: Friday 4:00 PM–9:00 PM; Saturday 9:00 AM–5:00 PM; Sunday 11:00 AM–4:00 PM.

ADMISSION: Adults $5; children 2–12 years $2.

LOCATION: Pittsburgh Expo Mart, Monroeville.

DESCRIPTION: This market is one of a series of highly successful shows specializing in folk art, collectibles, and crafts with exhibitors displaying their wares. Their specialty is the folk artisans that create the collectibles of the future. Food is available on the premises. This show is one of a series held all over the East Coast from Michigan to Florida.

DEALER RATES: $375 per 10' × 10' booth; $562.50 per 10' × 15' booth; $750 per 10' × 20' booth. Reservations are required as this is a juried show.

CONTACT: American Memories, Inc., P.O. Box 249, Decatur, MI 49045-0249. Tel: (616) 423-8367, fax: (616) 423-2421.

Wildwood Peddler's Fair

DATES: Every Sunday, year round, rain or shine.

TIMES: 6:00 AM–4:00 PM.

ADMISSION: Free. Parking on premises is available at $1 per vehicle; free parking is also available nearby.

LOCATION: 2330 Wildwood Road. From Pittsburgh: take Route 8 to Wildwood Road towards North Park (Yellow Belt).

DESCRIPTION: This indoor/outdoor market has operated year round since 1972 on the site of the Old Wildwood Coal Mine. The mine closed in the 1960s. It currently draws between 350 and 500 dealers, depending on the time of year. A wide variety of antiques, collectibles, and new merchandise is offered here. They have grown substantially having added five new rooms to the one-acre building, making a total of 300 indoor spaces, currently filled to capacity. Additional restrooms and another complete concession stand were added with the addition, making a total of two complete kitchens offering everything from homemade chili to cotton candy and candy apples. There is a festive family atmosphere at this market.

DEALER RATES: $12 per 14' × 22' space outside; starting at $18 per 8' × 12' space inside. Reservations for indoors only.

CONTACT: Mr. Vince Rutledge, President, Peddler's Fair, Inc., 2330 Wildwood Road, Wildwood, PA 15091. Tel: (412) 487-2200.

QUAKERTOWN
Quakertown Flea and Farmer's Market

DATES: Friday, Saturday, and Sunday all year round, rain or shine.

TIMES: Friday and Saturday 10:00 AM–10:00 PM; Sunday 11:00 AM–5:00 PM.

ADMISSION: Free. Ample free parking is provided.

LOCATION: 201 Station Road, ¼ mile south of Quakertown.

DESCRIPTION: Originally established as a farmer's market in 1932, this indoor/outdoor market has been in operation as a flea market since 1970. They have a 150,000 square foot building that houses permanent vendors selling hard goods, soft goods and other items. There are three more buildings for flea market goods as well as plenty of outside space attracting over 500 dealers. This market covers the gamut of antiques and collectibles, handicrafts, and new merchandise, as well as the traditional farmers' market fare. They have 12 restaurants, two grocery stores, five butchers, five delis, and five produce markets. Yes, they have food! At Christmas time they have a 99¢ photo special: "Your picture with Santa" that brings in 7,000 people. Santa Claus Day brings in another 3,000 riding or bringing their pets with them—everything from cows to cats. At Easter they gave away over $15,000 in prizes.

DEALER RATES: $10 per 16' space outdoors per day with tables;

$40 per 6' space indoors for three days. Reservations are required for indoor selling space only.
CONTACT: Joseph Kaye, Manager, 201 Station Road, Quakertown, PA 18951. Tel: (215) 536-4115.

> This market used to hold livestock auctions in the barns that now house the flea markets. One regular, Tex, attends this market with his cow. Once he stopped a president from passing, blocking the road with himself and his companion.

WAYNESBORO
23rd Annual Antiques and Collectibles Market

DATES: Annually, second Saturday in June. 1994: June 11.
TIMES: 6:30 AM–5:00 PM.
ADMISSION: Free. Free parking is available.
LOCATION: On Main Street (Route 16) in downtown Waynesboro, located in Franklin County, just 2 miles from the Mason-Dixon Line.
DESCRIPTION: This outdoor market began in 1971 and currently attracts over 100 dealers from five states, some of whom are said to have attended annually since the market's beginning. This market specializes in antiques and collectibles of varying types. Food is served on the premises.
DEALER RATES: $30 per 22' space along sidewalks. Reservations are required in advance.
CONTACT: Greater Waynesboro Chamber of Commerce, 323 East Main Street, Waynesboro, PA 17268. Tel: (717) 762-7123.

WEST MIDDLESEX
Mentzer's Antique Market

DATES: Wednesday, Saturday, and Sunday, rain or shine.
TIMES: 9:00 AM–5:00 PM.
ADMISSION: Free. There is also free parking.
LOCATION: 101 North Sharon Road. Exit 1N off I-80 and State Route 18.
DESCRIPTION: Since 1974 dealers have been displaying their goods in either an outdoor or indoor setting. They have 75 permanent booths year round and setups for another 30 dealers outside in warm weather. They specialize in antiques and collectibles, and browsers are always welcome. The market is located in a picturesque setting in the heart of Amish country. For your convenience breakfast and lunch are avail-

able on the premises. The food is wonderful!

DEALER RATES: $10 per 10' × 12' booth daily; $121 monthly. Outside space is $5. Reservations are required inside, not outside.

CONTACT: Fred Mentzer, 101 North Sharon Road, West Middlesex, PA 16159. Tel: (412) 528-2300.

WEST MIFFLIN
Woodland Flea Market

DATES: Weekends, rain or shine. Also, Memorial Day, July 4th, and Labor Day.

TIMES: 7:00 AM–3:00 PM.

ADMISSION: Free. Parking is $1 per car on Sundays and holidays.

LOCATION: 526 Thompson Run Road, West Mifflin. One mile from the Allegheny County Airport, 1½ miles from Kennywood Park and just 7 miles from downtown Pittsburgh.

DESCRIPTION: This indoor/outdoor market has been operating since 1962. It currently attracts between 250 to 500 sellers, and between 10,000 and 15,000 buyers. Antiques, collectibles, handmade and craft items, fresh produce, new merchandise, and other items are sold. Food and clean restrooms are available on the premises.

DEALER RATES: Outdoors $6 per 10' × 23' space or two spaces for $10; indoors $6 per 8' × 30' table or two tables for $10; and garage rentals 10' × 25' at $100 per month. Reservations are required for indoor and garage rentals.

CONTACT: Bob Kranack, Woodland Flea Market, 526 Thompson Run Road, West Mifflin, PA 15122. Tel: (412) 462-4370.

OTHER FLEA MARKETS

Chambersburg: Chambersburg Antique and Flea Market, 868 Lincoln Way West, Chambersburg, PA 17201. Tel: (717) 267-0886. Open daily 9:00 AM–5:00 PM.

Pittsburgh: Eastland Mall and Marketplace, 833 East Pittsburgh Boulevard, Pittsburgh, PA 15137. Tel: (412) 678-8050. Open weekends 9:00 AM–5:00 PM.

Pittsburgh: Pittsburgh Flea Market, 601 Ridge Avenue, Pittsburgh, PA 15212. Tel: (412) 323-7229. Open Sundays April through October from 8:00 AM–4:00 PM.

Washington: Al's Flea Market, Washington County Fairgrounds, 37 Woodside Drive, Washington, PA 15301. Tel: (412) 228-1119 or 225-0961. Open weekends, except August, 9:00 AM–3:00 PM.

RHODE ISLAND

ASHAWAY
Ashaway Flea Market Garage Sale

DATES: Saturday and Sunday, year round, rain or shine.
TIMES: 10:00 AM–4:00 PM.
ADMISSION: Free. Free parking is available.
LOCATION: 1 Juniper Drive. Off Route 3. Take I-95 to Exit 1; go south on Route 3 about 1½ miles to Egypt Street to Juniper.
DESCRIPTION: This indoor/outdoor market has been in operation since 1964 and currently attracts between 15 and 50 dealers, depending on the weather. Miscellaneous items are sold including antiques, collectibles, and new and used junk.
DEALER RATES: $10 per day to setup. Reservations are not required. Advance shopping hours are by appointment.
CONTACT: Mr. John Marley, 1 Juniper Drive, Ashaway, RI 02804. Tel: (401) 377-4947.

CHARLESTOWN
General Stanton Inn

DATES: Saturdays, Sundays, and Monday holidays during the summer.
TIMES: Saturdays 7:00 AM–3:00 PM, Sundays and holiday Mondays 7:00 AM–4:00 PM.
ADMISSION: Free. Parking is $1.
LOCATION: 4115A Old Post Road between Routes 1A and 1. From New York: I-95 North, Exit 92 (Route 2) 3 miles to Route 78, 4 miles to Route 1, go north 12 miles to Charlestown. From Boston: I-95 South, Exit 9 to Route 1, South Charlestown Beach exit. They are 35 miles south of Providence and 40 miles northeast of New London, Connecticut. Between Mystic and Newport.
DESCRIPTION: There is space for 200 dealers at this outdoor market, started in 1967. It is located on the property of The General Stanton Inn, one of America's oldest inns. There is everything from antiques and collectibles to handmade crafts, vegetables, and new merchandise at this market. There is one restaurant and one snack bar on the premises.
DEALER RATES: $20 for a 15' × 20' space; $35 for an end spot. Reservations are required.

CONTACT: Janice Falcone, General Stanton Inn, Route 1A Box 222, Charlestown, RI 02813. Tel: (401) 364-8888.

EAST GREENWICH
Rocky Hill Flea Market

DATES: Every Sunday, April through November.
TIMES: 5:00 AM–4:00 PM.
ADMISSION: Free. Parking is $1.
LOCATION: 1408 Division Road, corner of Division Road and Route 2. Take Exit 8A off I-95.
DESCRIPTION: This market has been around since 1960 and now attracts approximately 400 dealers and sometimes more, with virtually all types of merchandise available, including crafts, collectibles, fresh produce, and new merchandise. Food is available on the premises.
DEALER RATES: $15 per 20' × 25' space; corner spaces go for $20, smaller spaces are available for $10. Advance reservations are not required.
CONTACT: Mr. Gary Hamilton, 1408 Division Road, East Greenwich, RI 02818. Tel: (401) 884-4114.

TIVERTON
Route 177 Flea Market

DATES: Saturday, Sunday, and holidays, year round.
TIMES: Saturday 9:00 AM–4:00 PM; Sunday and holidays 8:00 AM–5:00 PM.
ADMISSION: Free admission and free parking.
LOCATION: 1560 Bulgar Marsh Road.
DESCRIPTION: Opened in 1964, this indoor/outdoor flea market has been in business for over 26 years and has been called one of the finest fleas markets on the East Coast.
DEALER RATES: $15 for outside space measuring 15' × 10'; $10 for inside space measuring 10' × 5'. Advance reservations are not required; first come, first served.
CONTACT: Thomas G. Ouellette, 8 Campion Avenue, Tiverton, RI 02878. Tel: (401) 624-9354 or 625-5954.

WARWICK
Rocky Point Flea Market

DATES: Every Saturday and Sunday, November through April.

TIMES: 9:00 AM–4:30 PM.

ADMISSION: Saturday free, Sunday $.50. Children under 10 free. Free parking is available.

LOCATION: At Rocky Point Park, 1 Rocky Point Avenue in Warwick. From north: take I-95 South to Exit 14; follow signs to park. From south: take I-95 to Exit 10 East; follow signs to park.

DESCRIPTION: This indoor market, housed in the Shore Dinner Hall, has run since 1981 and offers approximately 150 booth spaces to sellers of collectibles including toys, jewelry, clothing, new merchandise, crafts, electronics, and more. On Sunday afternoons, shoppers are treated to live country and western music.

DEALER RATES: $28 for weekend; $17 per day for 8' × 10' spaces. Reservations are required. Dealers must have Rhode Island license.

CONTACT: Al, Rocky Point Park, 1 Rocky Point Avenue, Warwick, RI 02889. Tel: (401) 737-8000 × 214.

WOONSOCKET

Blackstone Valley Flea Market

DATES: Friday through Sunday, year round.

TIMES: Friday 1:00 PM–8:00 PM, Saturday and Sunday 9:00 AM–5:00 PM.

ADMISSION: Friday and Saturday free; Sunday $.50, children under 12 free with parent. Parking is free.

LOCATION: 401 Clinton Street.

DESCRIPTION: Opened December 19, 1992, this market has room for over 200 dealers. The owners describe it as a "truly unique shopping experience." Their dealers peddle antiques, collectibles, loads of crafts and new merchandise. The Eldorado Snack Bar is part of the market and serves the famished. There are also homemade pastries sold.

DEALER RATES: $25 and up for a 8' × 10' space for the weekend. Reservations are not required.

CONTACT: Edward Perkins, Cap Promotions, Inc., P.O. Box 1361, Westport, MA 02790. Tel: (508) 677-2244. Day of show call market at (401) 762-9101.

Woonsocket Flea Market

DATES: Saturday and Sunday, year round, rain or shine.

TIMES: 9:00 AM–5:00 PM.

ADMISSION: $.50 adults, children under 12 free. Parking is free.

LOCATION: 6 Davidson Avenue. Corner of Route 122 (Hamlet Avenue) and Davidson Avenue.

DESCRIPTION: Since 1989, this indoor market of 250 spaces has offered a wide variety of new and used merchandise, antiques, collectibles, sport cards, coins, stamps, dolls, and anything else that wanders in. Freshly made homecooked food is served in a large snack bar.

DEALER RATES: $18 and up depending on area and amount of space. Reservations are not required.

CONTACT: Edward Perkins, Cap Promotions, Inc., P.O. Box 1361, Westport, MA 02790. Tel: (508) 677-2244. Day of show call the market at (401) 762-9101.

SOUTH CAROLINA

ANDERSON/BELTON

Anderson Jockey Lot and Farmer's Market

DATES: Saturday and Sunday, rain or shine.

TIMES: Saturday 7:00 AM–6:00 PM; Sunday 9:00 AM–6:00 PM.

ADMISSION: Free. Parking is free.

LOCATION: Highway 29 between Greenville and Anderson, 10 miles from Anderson.

DESCRIPTION: Opened in 1974, this huge market hosts between 1,500 and 2,000-plus dealers selling everything, quite literally. To prove their point, their crowds average 30–40,000 in summer to 50–60,000 in winter! "If we don't have it, you don't need it." Just some of the items sold are: antiques, collectibles, tons of produce, clothing, comics, cleaning supplies, pantyhose (see?), pharmaceuticals, office supplies, cologne, stamps, coins, garage sale goodies, and other new merchandise. There are "lots of restaurants and snack bars" and clean restrooms on site.

Just as an aside, they have an Anderson exchange telephone at the front of the market, a Williamston exchange telephone at the back of the market, and a Belton address. That's what you get for operating at the junction of three separate entities.

DEALER RATES: Inside: $10 for one day with a wooden table. Outside, pick a vacant, non-reserved space and one of the owners will tap you for $6 for the space and one concrete table for each day. Reservations are required for inside space only. Those spaces can be hard to get. You must reserve in person.

CONTACT: Anderson Jockey Lot and Farmer's Market, 4530 Highway 29 North, Belton, SC 29627. Tel: (803) 224-2027.

CHARLESTON

Lowcountry Flea Market and Collectibles Show

DATES: Third Saturday and Sunday of each month, year round, except November and December, the second weekend. Call for specific dates.

TIMES: 9:00 AM–6:00 PM.

ADMISSION: $1.50 per person; kids free.

LOCATION: At Gaillard Auditorium, 77 Calhoun Street, in Charleston, between Meeting Street and Calhoun Street.

DESCRIPTION: This show has been operating since 1973 in the historic downtown area. Over 100 dealers offer antiques, collectibles, estate merchandise, and handcrafts from indoor stalls. This is strictly an antiques and collectibles show. For your convenience food is available on the premises.

DEALER RATES: $55 per 10' × 10' booth per weekend. Reservations are required in advance.

CONTACT: Mr. and Mrs. Nelson Garrett, 513 Pelzer Drive, Mount Pleasant, SC 29464. Tel: (803) 884-7204.

COLUMBIA
Barnyard Flea Market

DATES: Friday, Saturday, and Sunday, rain or shine.

TIMES: 8:00 AM–6:00 PM and later in summer.

ADMISSION: Free. Paved parking is also free.

LOCATION: Between Lexington and Columbia on Highway 1. Just 2.3 miles from Exit 58 off I-20. Three miles from Exit 111A of I-26.

DESCRIPTION: Built as a new market in April 1988, this collection of ten red-tin-roofed buildings houses 552 spaces for dealers. The number of dealers varies by how many spaces each dealer will rent. They are usually full. The buildings are lit inside and out allowing late evening shopping in summertime. There are 75 to 100 dealer tables outside without cover. Four restaurants, including a brand new barbecue restaurant, take care of hungry shoppers. Among the fares sold are antiques, collectibles, boiled peanuts, car stereos, t-shirts, sunglasses, hardware, fishing supplies, used appliances, fashion jewelry, handbags, new and used clothes, "and the usual generic flea market stuff." Also notable are air-conditioned restrooms and the Barnyard RV park next door.

DEALER RATES: $10 per day for 4' × 8' tables undercover in a 10' × 10' space; $5 for 4' × 8' tables outside. Reservations are suggested as they do fill up fast.

CONTACT: Manager, Barnyard Flea Market, 4414 Augusta Road, Augusta, SC 29211. Tel: 1-800-628-7496 or (803) 957-6570.

GREENVILLE
Fairgrounds Flea Market

DATES: Saturday and Sunday, rain or shine.

TIMES: Saturday 5:00 AM–5:00 PM, Sunday 6:00 AM–5:00 PM.

ADMISSION: Free. Parking is also free.

LOCATION: 2600 White Horse Road. From I-85 South, take the White Horse Road exit, turn right, go 1 mile to market.

DESCRIPTION: This market, opened in March 1990, hosts 600 to 800 dealers selling everything: some antiques and collectibles, lots of crafts and produce, garage sale goodies, some new merchandise, racing material, tools, pantyhose (is there a run on these in SC?), windows and siding, and lots of cards. Pets are sold here, from the occasional goat to chickens, rabbits, dogs, and cats. Home-cooking and the usual snack bar fare feed the famished. There are plenty of restrooms, inside and out, just in case.

DEALER RATES: $7 under the shed, $5 for a 10' × 10' space and table outdoors, $8 inside. Reservations are recommended.

CONTACT: Monika Baker, Fairgrounds Flea Market, 1300 White Horse Road, Greenville, SC 29605. Tel: (803) 295-1183.

Country Peddler Show

DATES: May 20–22.

TIMES: Friday 4:00 PM–9:00 PM; Saturday 9:00 AM–5:00 PM; Sunday 11:00 AM–4:00 PM.

ADMISSION: $5; children 2–12 $2 each day.

LOCATION: Palmetto Expo Center, Exposition Avenue.

DESCRIPTION: This show is one of a series of highly successful shows specializing in folk art, collectibles, and crafts with 75 exhibitors displaying their wares. Their specialty is the folk artisans that hold the collectibles of the future. Food is available on the premises. This show is one of a series held all over the East Coast from Michigan to Florida.

DEALER RATES: $375 per 10' × 10' booth; $562.50 per 10' × 15' booth; $750 per 10' × 20' booth. Reservations are required as this is a juried show.

CONTACT: American Memories, Inc., P.O. Box 249, Decatur, MI 49045. Tel: (616) 423-8367 or fax: (616) 423-2421.

LADSON

Coastal Carolina Flea Market

DATES: Every Saturday and Sunday, rain or shine.

TIMES: 8:00 AM–6:00 PM.

ADMISSION: Free. Free parking is available on six acres.

LOCATION: At the junction of College Park Road and Highway 78.

Take I-26 to Exit 203 (College Park Road); or take Highway 78. Flea market is next door to the local fairgrounds.

DESCRIPTION: This indoor/outdoor market started in June 1981, and now has 600 indoor booths available. It usually draws 400 to 450 dealers selling a full range of antiques and collectibles such as tools, jewelry, furniture, old and new clothing, baby items, pets and pet supplies, birds, as well as fresh produce, garage sale items, and new merchandise. There is often a local airbrush artist on hand for portraits. Computer portraits are also a draw. Food is available on the premises.

DEALER RATES: $10 per 10' × 10' space per day inside, $6 per table outside. Reservations required for inside space; first come, first served outside.

CONTACT: Michael W. Masterson, Coastal Carolina Flea Market, Inc., P.O. Box 510, Ladson, SC 29456. Tel: (803) 797-0540.

NORTH CHARLESTON
Palmetto Flea Market

DATES: Saturday and Sunday, year round, rain or shine.
TIMES: 9:00 AM–6:00 PM.
ADMISSION: Free. Parking is also free.
LOCATION: Just off Ashley-Phosphate Road on Rivers Avenue.
DESCRIPTION: Imagine 22 spaces, an entire wing, filled with some of the finest antiques! From dishes to furniture, crystal, depression glass—whatever antiques you can think of in one spot. However this market, opened in 1988, has another 99 dealers selling everything else that you can ever think of: junk, collectibles, a carpet outlet, new furniture, and typical flea market fare. They have added about 60 outside covered spaces. There is a full concession on premises.
DEALER RATES: $10 per day for 10' × 10' space with 8' table. Outside spaces will go for $6 a space on a first-come, first-served basis. Reservations are strongly advised.
CONTACT: Kenneth Childress, Palmetto Flea Market, 7225 Rivers Avenue, North Charleston, SC 29407. Tel: (803) 764-3532.

The Flea Market

DATES: Saturday and Sunday, year round, rain or shine.
TIMES: 8:30 AM–6:00 PM.
ADMISSION: Free. Parking is also free.
LOCATION: 2935 Ashley-Phosphate Road.

DESCRIPTION: Opened in 1990, this new market has room for up to 250 inside dealers and 700 outside. Dealers trade in oil paintings (local artist), Avon products, clothing—from fancy to motorcycle—glass, jewelry, attic treasures and junk, candy goodies, and more. Lunch here is a treat. Restaurant daily specials include homemade fried chicken, flounder and shrimp specialties, and other scrumptious treats.

DEALER RATES: $10 per 8' × 10' space and $15 per 10' × 10' space. Reservations are not required.

CONTACT: The Flea Market, 2935 Ashley-Phosphate Road, North Charleston, SC 29418. Tel: (803) 552-4824.

SPRINGFIELD

Springfield Flea Market

DATES: Saturday through Monday, rain or shine.

TIMES: Saturday and Monday 5:00 AM until afternoon, generally around 2:00 PM. Sundays during the afternoon only. There is no set opening or closing times; however, most people work during these times.

ADMISSION: Free. Free parking is available nearby.

LOCATION: At the intersection of Routes 3 and 4, approximately 1 mile east of Springfield.

DESCRIPTION: This market evolved from an auction held at a livestock market, and has been running as a flea market since 1966. The farmers would often bring along farming tools and "whatever" to auction off as well. Soon, the auctioneer, Oscar Cooper, decided it was time the farmers sold their own stuff and sent them off to the "yard" adjacent to the Stockyard. At first, it was slow going with only ten "dealers," but in the mid-70s this market blossomed turning sleepy Springfield into a lively town one day a week. The market moved to its current 35-acre location in 1983. It now accommodates between 750 and 1,000 dealers inside and outside, selling a varied selection of antiques and collectibles, fresh farm goods, and some new merchandise. According to its current owner, Oscar's son Henry, while there are many regular dealers, the "first-timers" cleaning out their houses generally bring in a wonderful variety of merchandise. Food is served by a concession stand and a convenience store is on the premises. Clean restrooms are available, and law enforcement officers patrol the grounds. It is said that many people come so early they must use flashlights to find their way to the bargains and treasures.

DEALER RATES: For a 12' × 12' booth outdoors, $4 without a table, $5 with a table; $6 per 10' × 10' shed space with table. Advance reservations are not required.

CONTACT: Mr. Henry Cooper, Owner and Manager, P.O. Box 74, Springfield, SC 29146. Tel: (803) 258-3192.

WEST COLUMBIA
U.S. #1 Metro Flea Market

DATES: Friday, Saturday, and Sunday, rain or shine.

TIMES: Friday 8:00 AM–6:00 PM; Saturday 7:00 AM–6:00 PM; Sunday 9:00 PM–6:00 PM.

ADMISSION: Free. Free parking is available.

LOCATION: On U.S. Highway 1. From I-26, take U.S. Highway 1 south to Lexington (Exit 111A South), approximately 1½ miles; from I-20, take U.S. Highway 1 (Exit 58) to West Columbia, 3½ miles.

DESCRIPTION: This show began in March 1980, and currently draws 600 dealers inside (in permanent stalls) and outside, peddling antiques, collectibles, crafts, fresh farm produce, and some new merchandise. They are the oldest and "most popular" market in the Columbia area drawing between 5,000–15,000 per weekend depending on weather. There is even a vendor selling medical supplies—one wheelchair went for $2.95! This place is garage sale heaven! Full of surprises. Food is available on the premises. Wednesday is open for a special wholesalers market only. (Vendors need a business license to get into the wholesalers market. Open from 7:00 AM–1:00 PM.) Only five miles from the state capitol.

DEALER RATES: $5 for first table, $2 each additional table on Friday—no reservations required; $10 per day for covered stalls and $7 per open outdoor stalls Saturday and Sunday. Advance reservations are recommended for Saturday and Sunday only—at least a week to two weeks in advance.

CONTACT: Manager, U.S. #1 Metro Flea Market, 3500 Augusta Road, West Columbia, SC 29169. Tel: (803) 796-9294.

OTHER FLEA MARKETS

Florence: Florence Flea Market, 4001 East Palmetto Street, Florence, SC 29501. Tel: (803) 667-9585. Open Friday through Sunday.

Garden City: Garden City Flea Market, Highway 175, Garden City, SC 29576. Tel: (803) 651-4533. Open daily summer months, Friday through Sunday the rest of the year, from 7:00 AM on.

North Myrtle Beach: North Myrtle Beach Flea Market, Highway 17 North, North Myrtle Beach, SC 29582. Tel: (803) 249-4701. Open Friday through Sunday 8:00 AM–5:00 PM.

SOUTH DAKOTA

RAPID CITY
Antique, Craft Show and Flea Market

DATES: September through January, usually the first and third weekends; February through April, usually the first weekend. But call, just to make sure.
TIMES: Saturday 9:00 AM–5:00 PM; Sunday 10:00 AM–4:00 PM.
ADMISSION: Free. Parking is also free.
LOCATION: Rushmore Plaza Civic Center, 444 Mt. Rushmore Road.
DESCRIPTION: Started by the daughter of a local antique shop owner in 1974, this market has between 50 and 100 vendors concentrating on selling antiques, collectibles, rummage goods, baked goods, coins, and baseball cards to name a few. It is considered more of a antiques and collectibles show in the original concept of a flea market (without the fleas, of course). Crafts are quite popular and plentiful around the Christmas holidays. There is a concession open on the premises.
DEALER RATES: $25 per space per weekend. Tables and chairs are furnished. Reservations are advised.
CONTACT: Verlyn Orelup Brents, HC 73 Box 1741, Deadwood, SD 57732. Tel: (605) 342-2524.

Black Hills Flea Market

DATES: Friday, Saturday, Sundays, and national holiday Mondays, May through September. Rain checks given for days completely rained out outdoors.
TIMES: 7:00 AM–dusk, both days.
ADMISSION: Free. Plenty of easy parking is available.
LOCATION: 5500 Mount Rushmore Road. Take Exit 57 off I-90 on U.S. 16W south of Rapid City limits.
DESCRIPTION: This indoor/outdoor market, which began operation in 1973, is located on the main highway to Mount Rushmore and therefore has high exposure to the many thousands of tourists who visit this national memorial annually. A lovely panoramic view of the Black Hills is among the many attractions of this market. There are currently an average of 150 dealers on hand selling antiques and collectibles, and a special arts and crafts section featuring locally made handicrafts. Some new merchandise is available, and fresh produce when in season. This market operates on the concept that "Flea Mar-

kets are Fun!" and has invited the public to "Come out, enjoy the outdoors, and fly your kites" with them.

DEALER RATES: $8 per inside table (arts and crafts) per day; $7 per outside tailgate; $8–$13 for an indoor booth. Tables are furnished. Eight-foot tables are available outside for $2 rental per day. Reservations are recommended for indoor booths.

CONTACT: Paul or Maybelle Ashland, 909 Francis, Rapid City, SD 57701. Tel: (605) 348-1981 or (605) 343-6477.

Sioux Falls Flea Market

DATES: Saturday and Sunday, first weekend of every month. No shows in June, July, or August.

TIMES: Saturday 9:00 AM–5:00 PM; Sunday 11:00 AM–4:00 PM.

ADMISSION: $.50 per person. Ample free parking.

LOCATION: Expo Building at 12th and Fairgrounds.

DESCRIPTION: This indoor market first opened in 1970. There are 250 dealers selling antiques, collectibles, arts and crafts items as well as new merchandise. At least 70 percent of the items shown are antiques. The crowds keep growing every weekend and have more than doubled in size in this good, clean, smoke-free atmosphere. Handicapped access throughout the market is very easy as this is a large well-lit building with wide aisles. Food is available on the premises.

DEALER RATES: $19 per 8' table and space per weekend; $70 for four tables. Advance reservations are required as there is a waiting list.

CONTACT: Ed and Bonnie Benson, P.O. Box 236, Sioux Falls, SD 57101. Tel: (605) 361-1717.

OTHER FLEA MARKETS

Sioux Falls: Koenig's Antiques and Flea Market, 1103 North Main Street, Sioux Falls, SD 57101. Tel: (605) 338-0297.

Yankton: Yankton Flea Market, 601 Burleigh, Yankton, SD 57078. Tel: (605) 665-8130. Open daily.

TENNESSEE

CLARKSVILLE

Clarksville Fairgrounds Flea Market

DATES: Wednesdays, starting the first Wednesday in April through Wednesday before Thanksgiving.

TIMES: 5:00 AM–5:00 PM.

ADMISSION: Free. Parking is also free.

LOCATION: Highway 48 and 13, 1 block south of the by-pass. Turn off the by-pass beside auto dealership, go 1 block south on Highway 48 and 13 to fairgrounds on right.

DESCRIPTION: This indoor/outdoor market started in April 1984, and has 60 to 90 vendors selling antiques, collectibles, crafts, new and used merchandise, produce and "whatever the dealers bring, including rabbits and pigs." Many dealers return to the same spaces year after year building up a faithful clientele. A snack bar and restrooms are on site.

DEALER RATES: $8 for a 10' × 18' outside space and $10 for a 10' × 18' booth inside the pavilion. Reservations and prepayment are recommended for inside space only.

CONTACT: Ray Reed, 863 Lennox Drive, Clarksville, TN 37042-3709. Tel: (615) 647-2273 or 647-9558 on Wednesdays at the Pavilion.

CLEVELAND

Flea Hollow

DATES: Every Saturday and Sunday, rain or shine. Yard sales daily.

TIMES: 8:00 AM until happy exhaustion.

ADMISSION: Free. Free parking is available.

LOCATION: Exit off I-75, from south Exit 20, or from north Exit 25; follow by-pass around Cleveland; exit State Highway 60 toward Cleveland.

DESCRIPTION: This mostly outdoor market has been in business since 1978 and attracts 50 to 100 dealers selling a full range of antiques and collectibles, as well as new merchandise and farm goods. All of the covered booths are taken by area residents who are cleaning house. This market is small, clean, and friendly with a down-home atmosphere. Food is served on the premises.

DEALER RATES: $6 per booth per day single; $10 double. Advance reservations suggested.

CONTACT: Luke and Ann Johnson, 2240 Dalton Pike, Cleveland, TN 37311. Tel: (615) 476-4133 or (615) 476-8894.

CROSSVILLE
Crossville Flea Market

DATES: Saturday, Sunday, and Monday holidays.

TIMES: 7:00 AM–4:00 PM.

ADMISSION: Free. Parking is free.

LOCATION: Highway 70 North, midway between Knoxville and Nashville. Take I-40, Exit 317 towards Crossville, turn right at second traffic light. Right at the next traffic light. Market is about 1½ miles down the road on the right.

DESCRIPTION: A flea market in the original sense, operating under covered sheds, this market has been running since 1970. Depending on the season, there are 200 to 400 dealers selling antiques, collectibles, furniture, dogs, coins, cats, cards, chickens, garage sale goodies, livestock, new merchandise, crafts, produce, nursery stock, stamps, and whatever else shows up. Because of the nature of this market, much of the merchandise is old and/or used. Think "unfound treasures." There are four snack bars and a restaurant as well as handicapped-accessible parking and restrooms. Member of the Tennessee Flea Market Association.

DEALER RATES: $4.25 for a 10' × 12' open space; $7.25 for a 10' × 12' covered space. Reservations are suggested.

CONTACT: Mary Gunter or Lois Wilbanks, P.O. Box 30264, Knoxville, TN 37930. Tel: (615) 484-9970 or tel/fax: (615) 691-4126.

HUMBOLDT
Antique City

DATES: Thursday through Saturday.

TIMES: 8:00 AM–5:00 PM.

ADMISSION: Free. Parking is free.

LOCATION: Between Jackson and Humboldt, 4 miles from Humboldt on Route 2.

DESCRIPTION: Since 1976, this market's 20 to 40 dealers have been specializing in antiques and collectibles. There are some reproductions, a coin dealer, some garage sale goodies, but no novelties or new merchandise. Food and restrooms are available on site.

DEALER RATES: $30 for a 10' × 12' space for the three-day weekend. Reservations are required.

CONTACT: George Henley, Route 2 Box 130, Humboldt, TN 38343. Tel: (901) 784-1544.

JACKSON
Friendly Frank's Flea Market
DATES: First weekend of every month, except January and September, from Friday night through Sunday.
TIMES: Saturday and Sunday 9:00 AM–6:00 PM and Friday evenings.
ADMISSION: Free. Parking is free.
LOCATION: Highway 45 South. One mile south of Jackson.
DESCRIPTION: Opened in 1983, this indoor/outdoor market's 200 dealers sell antiques, collectibles, coins, stamps, cards, furniture, garage sale clean-outs, new merchandise, and crafts. Two snack bars serve to quell the munchies. There are clean handicapped-accessible restrooms on site.
DEALER RATES: $50 for the weekend for a 9' × 10' space. Reservations are required.
CONTACT: Frank Mullikin, P.O. Box 328, Cordova, TN 38088. Tel: (901) 755-6561.

KNOXVILLE
Esau's Antique and Collectible Market
DATES: Saturday and Sunday, third weekend of each month, except September when it is held the fourth weekend. October and April dates are huge three-day extravaganzas.
TIMES: 9:00 AM–5:00 PM.
ADMISSION: $3 per person. Thirty acres of free parking is provided.
LOCATION: Take the Rutledge Pike Exit 392 off I-40 East.
DESCRIPTION: This indoor market has run since 1975 and now includes 300 dealers selling a range of antiques and collectibles, craft items, and new articles. Antiques and collectibles account for about 70 percent of the merchandise. Food is available on the premises. Members of the Tennessee Flea Market Association.
DEALER RATES: $60 per 10' × 10' space per weekend.
CONTACT: Ruby Hughes, Esau, Inc., P.O. Box 50096, Knoxville, TN 37950-0096. Tel: (615) 588-1233.

KODAK

Great Smokies Craft Fair/Flea Market

DATES: Friday, Saturday, and Sunday, year round, and the week before Christmas.

TIMES: Weekdays 10:00 AM–6:00 PM, Saturday and Sunday 9:00 AM–6:00 PM.

ADMISSION: Free. Parking is also free.

LOCATION: 220 Dumplin Valley Road West. Off I-40, Exit 407, turn onto Dumplin Valley Road, about ¼ mile down the road. Sixteen miles from Gatlinburg. Only 12 miles from Dollywood.

DESCRIPTION: Ideally situated on 25 acres next to the Interstate, this very successful market opened on August 3, 1990. The dealers are housed in a 230-space air-conditioned building, with unlimited outdoor space. They have a special section of wonderful antiques and collectibles, including player pianos! The dealers are noted for their friendliness, courtesy and helpfulness. They are more than willing to help each other and their customers out. There is a tremendous variety of superb handmade crafts as well as manufacturer-direct booths. There is a food court selling homemade pizzas and corn bread, soup beans, gourmet burgers and regular burgers, hot dogs, and daily specials. A video arcade keeps the kids busy. The market is kept spotlessly clean. They welcome RVs, tour buses, and tractor-trailers. Ninety percent of their dealers are permanent, 80 percent have been here since they opened. Definitely a family market including vendors with kid's stuff. They choose their vendors to meet the wants and desires of all of their customers. The management strives to be the best market in the business and was chosen as one of the top ten markets in the state by the Tennessee Flea Market Association. Nearby are 15,000 motel and hotel rooms, and there are plenty of restaurants around the area. Over 71,000 cars go by this market each day! Member of the Tennessee Flea Market Association.

DEALER RATES: Winter: $10 Friday; $20 Saturday and Sunday each day. Outside open spaces $8 a day, covered sheds $10 a day. Tables $2 a day. Summer rates can vary, but within this scale. Reservations are required because of a long waiting list.

CONTACT: Great Smokies Craft Fair and Flea market, 220 Dumplin Valley Road West, Kodak, TN 37764. Tel: (615) 932-FLEA (3532).

LEBANON

Parkland Flea Market

DATES: Every Saturday and Sunday, March 1 through December 15.

TIMES: 7:00 AM–dark.

ADMISSION: Free. Ample free parking is provided.

LOCATION: Across the street from the entrance to Cedars of Lebanon State Park. From I-40 take Exit 238, go 6 miles south. Between Lebanon and Murfreesboro on Highway 231.

DESCRIPTION: This indoor/outdoor market has operated since 1977 near the center of the state of Tennessee. It has enjoyed steady growth with a "great group of family-type dealers where 90 percent of the 300 are regulars." They are housed in a complex of seven buildings on ten acres of land, with another 40 acres available for further expansion. Large and small items, both new and used, can be found including boats, trailers, vans, and trucks, as well as the traditional flea market fare. Free weekend camping is available for dealers, and food is available at the site. Another attraction nearby is the Grand Olde Opry and Opryland only 30 miles away. Member of the Tennessee Flea Market Association.

DEALER RATES: $10 for 12' × 12' space under shed; $7 per 15' × 15' outside space. Reservations are strongly suggested.

CONTACT: Gwynn or Nancy Lanius, 403 Cambridge, Lebanon, TN 37087-4207. Tel: (615) 444-1279. Day of show call (615) 449-6050.

LOUISVILLE

Green Acre Flea Market

DATES: Saturday and Sunday, rain or shine.

TIMES: 6:00 AM–5:00 PM.

ADMISSION: Free. Plenty of free parking is available. Space is also available for vehicles such as motor homes and trailers.

LOCATION: On Alcoa Highway 129 between Knoxville and the Knoxville Airport.

DESCRIPTION: This indoor/outdoor show has been in operation since 1976, and draws an average of 772 dealers in 400 available spaces outdoors and over 300 indoors; miscellaneous antiques and collectibles, gold, and furniture old and new can be found, as well as new items and farm goods. There is a large restaurant and large breakfast bar on the premises selling yogurt, cotton candy, pork skins, and corn dogs. Member of the Tennessee Flea Market Association.

DEALER RATES: $7 per space, approximately 20' × 20'. Reservations are suggested. Dealers can come on Friday and stay overnight.
CONTACT: Tom Smith, Route 5 Box 344, Louisville, TN 37777. Tel: (615) 681-4433 or fax: (615) 681-1091.

MEMPHIS
Memphis Flea Market

DATES: Third weekend of each month, Friday through Sunday, rain or shine.
TIMES: 9:00 AM–6:00 PM.
ADMISSION: Free. Parking is $1.
LOCATION: Memphis Fairgrounds at Central and East Parkway.
DESCRIPTION: Opened in 1969, this indoor/outdoor market of 900 to 1,200 dealers sells anything from antiques, collectibles, crafts, produce, housewares, and clothing, to new merchandise. Nearby attractions, all within walking distance, include Libertyland, Children's Museum, Mid-South Coliseum, and the Tim McCarver Stadium. A snack bar is on the premises.
DEALER RATES: $50 for a 10' × 8' inside space per weekend, $40 for a 10' × 12' outside space for the weekend. Reservations are suggested.
CONTACT: Mike Hardage, 955 Early Maxwell Boulevard, Memphis, TN 38104. Tel: (901) 276-3532.

Mid-South Flea Market

DATES: First and fourth weekends of each month (fifth weekend if applicable), rain or shine.
TIMES: 9:00 AM–6:00 PM.
ADMISSION: $.50. Free parking is available.
LOCATION: Mid-South Fairgrounds, mid-town Memphis. Follow signs throughout the city.
DESCRIPTION: This indoor/outdoor market has operated since 1971 and has grown from the original 19 dealers to its present size, encompassing an average of 200 dealers indoors. Antiques, collectibles, and arts and crafts are offered. This market is known to local people and the trade as the Coleman-Simmons Market, after the names of its operators. Food is served on the premises.
DEALER RATES: $50 per 8' × 10' booth per weekend. 8' folding tables are available at $5 each per weekend. Reservations and booth rent are required in advance.

CONTACT: Coleman-Simmons Promotions, P.O. Box 40776, Memphis, TN 38174. Call Sam or Mary Simmons or Kathryn Coleman at (901) 725-0633.

NASHVILLE

The Flea Market at the Nashville Fairgrounds

DATES: Fourth weekend of every month, rain or shine.
TIMES: Summer hours: Saturday 6:00 AM–6:00 PM, Sunday 7:00 AM–6:00 PM. Winter hours: Saturday 7:00 AM–6:00 PM, Sunday 7:00 AM–5:00 PM.
ADMISSION: Free. Free parking is available for 6,000 cars.
LOCATION: Tennessee State Fairgrounds, at Wedgewood and Nolensville Road. Easy access from Nashville and middle Tennessee via I-65, I-440, and I-24.
DESCRIPTION: The Flea Market at the Nashville Fairgrounds was established in 1971 and has been operating under new management since 1985. The popular indoor/outdoor market has, on average, about 950 dealers per month, with the April, May, and October markets being the largest shows of the year, having an estimated attendance of 50,000 to 70,000 per market. The market consists mainly of antiques and collectible items. Also sold are handmade craft items and some new merchandise. Nearby hotel accommodations are available with a special rate for their flea market dealers. There are a variety of delicious foods available on the premises for your dining enjoyment. Member of the Tennessee Flea Market Association.
DEALER RATES: $55 for 10' × 10' outside or shed space; $70 for a 10' × 10' inside booth. Reservations and prepayment are required. Advance shopping hours begin at 3:00 PM on the Friday before the show.
CONTACT: Gerri Luther, Manager, Nashville Fairgrounds Flea Market, P.O. Box 40603, Nashville, TN 37204. Tel: (615) 383-7636. Or contact the office at: P.O. Box 40208, Nashville, TN 37204. Tel: (615) 862-5016. Office is open Monday through Friday 8:30 AM–5:00 PM and during show hours.

Trinity Flea Market

DATES: Friday through Sunday, year round.
TIMES: Daylight to sunset.
ADMISSION: Free. Parking is free.

LOCATION: 120 Trinity Lane. Take I-65 North, Exit 87A at Trinity Lane, about ¼ mile from the I-65.

DESCRIPTION: Described as "truly an old-fashioned-open air flea market," this outdoor market's 30 to 50 dealers sell antiques, collectibles, crafts, produce, new merchandise, garage sale goodies, furniture, cards, and "all types of junk and merchandise."

DEALER RATES: $12 for a 20' × 20' space. Reservations are recommended.

CONTACT: Juanita Ellis, Trinity Flea Market, 150 West Trinity Lane, Nashville, TN 37207. Tel: (615) 228-9131 or 226-1600.

SWEETWATER

Fleas Unlimited

DATES: Saturday and Sunday, rain or shine.

TIMES: 8:00 AM–5:00 PM.

ADMISSION: Free. Parking is also free.

LOCATION: Directly off I-75 at Exit 60. Between Knoxville and Chattanooga.

DESCRIPTION: Opened in December of 1989, this indoor/outdoor market is housed in a new 160,000 square foot building and on 95 acres of land. It attracts 500 dealers inside and there are another 100 spaces outdoors. A new "log cabin" building is devoted to antiques and crafts, while the other buildings house everything from collectibles to car tires and mechanic tools; from jewelry and crafts to furniture. There is a bit of everything here including plenty of cards, coins, stamps, garage sale finds, and some new merchandise. They have an in-house deli, camping facilities with bath house, and a restaurant/candy factory! Member of the Tennessee Flea Market Association.

DEALER RATES: Inside $15 per day per space or $11 on a monthly basis. Outside $10 per day. Reservations are recommended.

CONTACT: Sheila Moore, Fleas Unlimited, 121 County Road 308, Sweetwater, TN 37874. Tel: (615) 337-3532.

OTHER FLEA MARKETS

Athens: Athens Flea Market Mall, Congress Parkway, Athens, TN 37331. Tel: (615) 263-7414. Open Friday and Saturday 8:00 AM–7:00 PM, Sunday 10:00 AM–5:00 PM.

Baxter: Baxter Flea Market, Route 3, Baxter, TN 38544. Tel: (800) 868-5152. Open weekends 8:00 AM–5:00 PM.

Chattanooga: 23nd Street Flea Market, off I-24W or I-2E at 4th Avenue exit. Open weekends sun-up to sundown.

Jonesborough: Jonesborough Flea Market, 11-E Highway. Alan Shelton, 702 East Main Street, Jonesborough, TN 37659. Open Sundays.

Kingsport: Traders Village Mall, 2745 East Stone Drive, Kingsport, TN 37660. Tel: (615) 288-8204. Open weekends 8:30 AM–5:30 PM.

Knoxville: I-75 Flea Market, I-75 and Emory Road, Exit 112, Knoxville, TN 37849. Tel: (615) 938-7880. Open weekends, 8:00 AM–dusk.

Knoxville: River Breese Flea Market, 6110 Ashville Highway, Knoxville, TN 37924. Open weekends during daylight.

Madison: Pricetown USA, 1210 Gallatin Road South, Madison, TN 37115. Tel: (615) 865-5001.

Nashville: American International Flea Market and Mini Mall, 3030 Dickerson Pike, Nashville, TN 37207. Tel: (615) 262-4500. Open Friday 12:00 noon–6:00 PM, Saturday 9:00 AM–8:00 PM, Sunday 10:00 AM–6:00 PM.

Nashville: Metro Farmers Market, 618 Jackson Street, Nashville, TN 37219. Tel: (615) 862-6765. Open daily 5:00 AM–10:00 PM.

Nashville: Nashville Flea Mart and Antique Center, 1364 Murfreesboro Road, Nashville, TN 37217. Tel: (615) 360-7613. Open Friday 3:30 PM–8:30 PM, Saturday 9:00 AM–7:30 PM, Sunday 12:00 noon–6:00 PM.

TEXAS

ALAMO
All Valley Flea Market

DATES: Saturday and Sunday, rain or shine.
TIMES: Daylight to dark.
ADMISSION: Free. Parking is also free.
LOCATION: Intersection of Morningside Road and Expressway 83.
DESCRIPTION: Started in 1969 after a visit to another successful market elsewhere gave Mr. Bruns the idea, he opened his first of four markets in Pharr. Also the first in Valley area. When a highway was built through the market, they moved to Alamo. Now, there are around 1,000 dealers presenting "everything!" And 20,000 to 30,000 buyers coming through every weekend buying everything including antiques, collectibles, used items, and some new merchandise. Food is served on the premises. There are 40 trailer hook-ups available.
DEALER RATES: Saturdays $3.50 outdoors includes tables and all the space you need; Sundays $6 in sun and $6.50 in shade, $.50 per table and, if you need it, $1 for electricity. Reservations are strongly suggested.
CONTACT: Harvey Bruns, All Valley Flea Markets, P.O. Drawer 1099, Alamo, TX 78516. Tel: (210) 781-1911.

AMARILLO
T-Anchor Flea Market

DATES: Every Saturday and Sunday, year round, rain or shine.
TIMES: 9:00 AM–5:00 PM.
ADMISSION: Free. Free parking is available.
LOCATION: 1401 Ross Street, off I-40.
DESCRIPTION: This market began in 1978 and is run indoors. One hundred seventy-five vendors in 365 spaces from all over the country sell antiques, collectibles, handmade/craft items, produce, and new merchandise. During summer months vendors rent space outdoors. Produce vendors are furnished with a permit. There is food on the premises.
DEALER RATES: $7.50 per day outside and $10–$12 inside. Reasonable daily rates for 10' × 10' and 10' × 30' spaces. Reservations are not required, except during the Christmas season.
CONTACT: H.D. and Claudia Blyth, P.O. Box 31182, Amarillo, TX 79120. Tel: (806) 373-0430.

AUSTIN

Austin Country Flea Market

DATES: Saturday and Sunday, year round, rain or shine.

TIMES: 10:00 AM–6:00 PM.

ADMISSION: Free admission.

LOCATION: 9500 Highway 290 East.

DESCRIPTION: This is central Texas' largest flea market, with over 550 selling spaces. It averages over 500 dealers in summer and winter, selling antiques, collectibles, handmade crafts, vegetables, and new merchandise. Open every weekend, it offers good food, family fun, and big bargains. The entire market is covered.

DEALER RATES: $35 per 10' × 8' booth (20' dealer parking directly behind each space if desired, or dealer's vehicle may be moved to an authorized area and parking space can be used as additional selling area). One display table is provided. RV electricity is available in limited areas. Gates are open to dealers at 7:00 AM; gates close 10:00 PM. Advance reservations required.

CONTACT: Buz Cook, Austin Country, 9500 Highway 290 East, Austin, TX 78724. Tel: (512) 928-2795. Office is open 8:00 AM–7:00 PM on Saturday and Sunday, and 9:00 AM–5:00 PM weekdays, except Wednesday when the office is closed.

Pirate's Den

DATES: Every day, rain or shine.

TIMES: 10:00 AM–6:00 PM.

ADMISSION: Free. Free parking is available behind market.

LOCATION: 11704 N. Lamar. From I-35 take Braker Lane exit to Lamar, go north ¾ mile.

DESCRIPTION: One of the oldest flea markets in the Austin area, started in 1969, the Pirate's Den's dealers sell antiques and collectibles including fifties memorabilia, dolls, furniture, toys, used household items, vintage clothing, glassware, and costume jewelry. Nothing new here. There are tables of old records, salt and pepper shakers, and other goodies. This market has quite a history! It was once an old restaurant, then transformed into a bar, a dance hall, fruit stand, a furniture store and finally a flea market. Food is not available; there are toilet facilities.

DEALER RATES: Not applicable, but sometimes there is room.

CONTACT: Lillie Mae Williams, 11704 N. Lamar, Austin, TX 78753. Tel: (512) 836-4966.

BEAUMONT
Larry's Antique Mall and Flea Market

DATES: Saturday and Sunday, year round.
TIMES: Saturday 9:00 AM–5:00 PM; Sunday 1:00 PM-6:00 PM.
ADMISSION: Free, with free parking.
LOCATION: 7150 Eastex Freeway, Exit 105 in Beaumont.
DESCRIPTION: The mall has 50 permanent dealers indoors, year round, selling antiques, collectibles, and handmades. There is some flea market space available outside. The major part of the flea market has moved to Winnie and grown to 500 to 1,000 dealers.
DEALER RATES: $125 per month. Call for the flea market space.
CONTACT: Larry and Justine Tinkle, Owners, Larry's Antique Mall and Flea Market, 7150 Eastex Freeway, Beaumont, TX 77708. Tel: (409) 892-4000.

BUFFALO GAP
Buffalo Gap Flea Market

DATES: Friday, Saturday, and Sunday, third Saturday of each month from February through December (weather permitting in December).
TIMES: 7:00 AM–10:00 PM.
ADMISSION: Free. Parking is available nearby.
LOCATION: In Buffalo Gap, 6 miles south of Abilene on Highway 89.
DESCRIPTION: This outdoor market began in 1974, and currently draws around 250 dealers selling a wide range of antiques, collectibles, fresh produce, handicrafts, and new merchandise. They have well-lit night shopping on Saturday night, "under the stars and trees." This market is described by its owner as the "prettiest market in the west." Food and toilet facilities are available.
DEALER RATES: $14 per 12' x 18' space for a three-day weekend; plus electricity–$3 per day, if needed. All electric wiring has been updated. Reservations are required *at least one week in advance*, as they have had to turn away dealers before. A $2 city permit is required to sell.
CONTACT: John Brolls, P.O. Box 575, Buffalo Gap, TX 79508. Tel: (915) 572-3327.

CANTON

First Monday Trade Days

DATES: Begins on Friday before the first Monday of each month, and runs Friday through Monday, rain or shine.

TIMES: 7:00 AM–dark.

ADMISSION: Free. Parking is available for $2 per vehicle. RV spaces are available with advance reservations.

LOCATION: Two blocks north of downtown square. Easy access on Highway 19, Highway 64 and FM Road 859. I-20, Exit 526, 2 miles south on left.

DESCRIPTION: This is surely one of the most popular and well-known flea markets in the country, if not the world. Originating in 1876 as the town's court day, people at that time began to take care of their trading and purchasing of animals, produce, etc., while waiting for the judge. In 1965, the city of Canton acquired a three-acre plot of land two blocks north of the Court House, which now holds all antique and collectible dealers. (The dealers selling animals can be found four blocks east of the Court House on the property known as Curry's Trade Grounds or Dog Grounds.) Since 1965, the number of available lots has grown from 150 to well over 4,000. First Monday Trade Days began advertising its unique market in 1974, and since then has appeared on NBC's "Today Show," the front page of *The Wall Street Journal*, in *National Geographic* and in several other local and national media. All kinds of antiques, collectibles, new merchandise, handmade crafts, and food are available. Six restrooms with showers are provided.

DEALER RATES: $40 for each lot. Dealer spaces are approximately 12' × 20'. Dealers who reserve in advance may renew for following sale. Unreserved lots are also available.

CONTACT: City of Canton, P.O. Box 245, Canton, TX 75103. Tel: (903) 567-6556.

CHANNELVIEW

White Elephant, Inc.

DATES: Every Saturday and Sunday, rain or shine.

TIMES: 7:30 AM–5:30 PM.

ADMISSION: Free. $1 a car for parking.

LOCATION: 15662 I-10 east. Take the Sheldon-Channelview exit; the market is on the Service Road of I-10.

DESCRIPTION: Between 350 and 375 dealers show up each week for this indoor/outdoor market, which has been in operation since 1971. Articles for sale include antiques, collectibles, garage sale items such as tools, furniture, and jewelry, as well as some new items and fresh produce. Food and toilet facilities are available on the premises.

DEALER RATES: $12 per space on Saturday, $14 on Sunday. Reservations not required. $14 for shed space for vehicles on Saturday and $16 on Sunday.

CONTACT: Ruth McDaniel, P.O. Box 209, Channelview, TX 77530. Tel: (713) 452-9022.

DALLAS
Big "T" Bazaar

DATES: Thursday through Monday, year round.

TIMES: 10:00 AM–9:00 PM.

ADMISSION: Free. Acres of free parking.

LOCATION: 4515 Village Fair Drive. At I-35 and Loop 12 in Oak Cliff section of Dallas, behind Bud's Wholesale.

DESCRIPTION: This 160,000 square foot air-conditioned indoor market opened in July 1989. It keeps its community in mind by donating thousands of dollars worth of food and turkeys at Thanksgiving to the local needy and homeless of Dallas. The 140 dealers sell everything from collectibles and craft items to electronics, clothing, shoes, furniture, toys, jewelry, auto repair, comic books, music, wheel rims, shoe repair, cleaning service—you name it. Plenty of food in three restaurants is available on the premises.

DEALER RATES: $.70 to $1.65 per square foot per month depending on location and booth size.

CONTACT: Kenneth Lee, Manager, Big "T" Bazaar, 4515 Village Fair Drive, Dallas, TX 75224. Tel: (214) 372-9173.

GARLAND
Vikon Village Flea Market

DATES: Saturdays and Sundays, year round.

TIMES: 10:00 AM–7:00 PM.

ADMISSION: Free. Free parking for up to 750 cars is available nearby.

LOCATION: 2918 South Jupiter. On the corner of Kingsley and Jupiter, 2 blocks north of Route 635.

DESCRIPTION: This indoor market began in 1975, and averages around 350 booths with 175 dealers selling such items as books, baseball cards, coins, jewelry, furniture, clothing, and plants, as well as new merchandise. Snacks are available from snack bars. Toilet facilities are provided.

DEALER RATES: Lease available at $140 and up per month (minimum one month). Reservations and a refundable $50 security deposit required. Call for information Thursdays from 10:00 AM–5:00 PM or Fridays 10:00 AM–6:00 PM.

CONTACT: Vikon Village Flea Market, 2918 South Jupiter, Garland, TX 75041. Tel: (214) 271-0565.

GRAND PRAIRIE
Traders Village

DATES: Every Saturday and Sunday, year round, rain or shine.

TIMES: 8:00 AM–dusk.

ADMISSION: Free. Parking for over 7,000 cars is available at $2 per vehicle. Handicapped parking is available.

LOCATION: 2602 Mayfield Road in Grand Prairie. In the heart of the Dallas/Fort Worth area, 5 miles south of Six Flags Over Texas Theme Park off Highway 360. Or, take Highway 360 north 1 mile off I-20.

DESCRIPTION: Traders Village is a 106-acre complex, which opened in November 1973. Since that date, over 55 million people have visited this market, roughly 2.5 million a year. The market currently attracts between 1,500 and 1,600 dealers who set up on open, covered, and enclosed spaces. Crowds average 35,000–75,000 per weekend. Special events include a chili cook-off (April), a Cinco de Mayo Fiesta (May), an antique auto swap meet (June), an authentic Indian pow-wow (September), a barbecue cook-off (October), an Oktoberfest celebration, and more throughout the year. Most of the special events are open to the public for free. Traders Village runs its own food and beverage department, with over 30 stands selling everything from German specialties to pizza by the slice, from chicken-fried steak to funnel cakes. Produce vendors and bulk-food dealers are also on hand. Other features include kiddie rides, an arcade, stroller and wheelchair rentals, shaded rest areas, an ATM machine, and a first-aid room. There is also a sister market in Houston.

DEALER RATES: $20 per 14' × 25' open lot per day. $25 per covered space per day. Reservations are required for two-day rentals only.

CONTACT: Mr. Irving L. "Tag" Taggart, President and General Manager, c/o Traders Village, 2601 Mayfield Road, Grand Prairie, TX 75051. Tel: (214) 647-2331. Day of show call Tag or Mr. Jeff Jones, Director of Operations, at the above number.

> Traders Village is a continuing extension of the trading that went on between various Indian tribes over the centuries. An historical marker, dedicated in 1980, marks the site of the million acre "Cross Timbers" area where Shoshoni, rooted out by Apaches, in turn chased out by Comanches, traded until white men showed up in the 17th and 18th centuries. In the 1840s, white settlers stayed, leading to the Battle of Village Creek on May 24, 1841, marking the end of the Indian domination of the area.

HOUSTON
Traders Village

DATES: Every Saturday and Sunday year round, rain or shine.
TIMES: 8:00 AM–dusk.
ADMISSION: Free. Parking for over 4,000 cars is available at $2 per vehicle. Handicapped parking is available.
LOCATION: 7979 Eldridge Road. Off Northwest Freeway (Highway 290), Eldridge Exit, .3 mile south.
DESCRIPTION: Traders Village is a 100-acre complex, which opened in May 1989. Roughly 7 to 9 million people visit a year. The market currently attracts over 600 dealers who set up on open, covered, and enclosed spaces selling imports, antiques, collectibles, crafts, produce, garage sale merchandise, pets, clothes, furniture, auto parts, flowers and plants, electronics, and lots more. Crowds average 10,000-15,000 a weekend. Special events include chili and barbecue cook-offs in January—chili on Saturday and barbecue on Sunday—an antique auto swap meet (March), an authentic Indian pow-wow (May), an Oktoberfest celebration, and more throughout the year. Most of the special events are open to the public. Traders Village runs its own food and beverage department, with over 30 stands selling everything from German specialties to pizza by the slice, from chicken-fried steak to funnel cakes. Produce vendors and bulk-food dealers are also on hand. Other features include kiddie rides, an arcade, stroller and wheelchair rentals, shaded rest areas, an ATM machine, and a first-aid room. There is also a sister market in Grand Prairie.

DEALER RATES: $20 per 14' × 25' open lot per day. $25 per covered space per day. Reservations are required for two-day rentals only.
CONTACT: Ron Simmons, President and General Manager, Traders Village–Houston, 7979 Eldridge Road, Houston, TX 77041. Tel: (713) 890-5500.

Trading Fair

DATES: Every Friday, Saturday, and Sunday, rain or shine.
TIMES: 10:00 AM–6:00 PM.
ADMISSION: Free. Parking $1.
LOCATION: 5515 South Loop East. Midway between the Astrodome and the Galveston Freeway on Loop 610. Use the Crestmont exit either way.
DESCRIPTION: This indoor market started in 1974 and currently draws approximately 400 dealers selling a wide range of antiques and collectibles, as well as craft items. They are possibly the largest indoor market in the Houston area. Their two floors of 60,000 square feet each and an additional 30,000 square foot annex in the back houses 300 dealers downstairs on a weekly basis. The owner says, "I can drive my Cadillac in an easy circle on the second floor, and the wheelie skaters love the tile floor." They fill that second floor with cat shows, antique-collectible shows, Indian pow-wows, and whatever. Their selection of sale items is described as "some of everything, a lot of some things." Two restaurants and one snack bar take care of hunger problems. They do plenty of advertising and as well as everything they can to gain the notice, goodwill, and support of the buying public.
DEALER RATES: $200 to $1,000 per month for a 10' × 10' space. Dealer reservations are suggested.
CONTACT: Warren S. Henkle, 5515 South Loop East, Houston, TX 77033. Tel: (713) 731-1111.

LOCKHART
Lockhart Flea Market

DATES: Saturday and Sunday, year round.
TIMES: 8:00 AM–sundown, more or less.
ADMISSION: Free and parking is free.
LOCATION: From Austin: take the third traffic light in Lockhart, go left at the Super S Market, take an immediate right onto Brownsboro

Road (aka Commerce Street within city limits). Flea market is 1 mile on the right. You can't miss it; it has a huge sign sticking up in the air.
DESCRIPTION: Since 1988, this outdoor market, held under cover, attracts anywhere from the 25 to 50 regulars up to 150 dealers selling antiques, collectibles, used clothing, jewelry, t-shirts, wall-hangings, and loads of other goodies. The market is part of a complex including a dance hall and bar and grill with all the associated goodies. They use the dance hall stage to bring in live shows featuring well-known singers, folkfests and even a wedding. "Just your basic down-home folk," says Mrs. Kaufman. She also adds that this property was once a chicken farm, and warns people to "watch your head! Eggs may fall on you." The walls of the dance hall are covered with antiques and the bar has old newspapers under cover—still readable.
DEALER RATES: $7.50 per day for a 10' × 11' space.
CONTACT: Henrietta Kaufman, 1621 South Commerce Street, Lockhart, TX 78644. Tel: (512) 398-4901.

LUBBOCK
National Flea Market
DATES: Every Wednesday through Sunday, except Thanksgiving and Christmas week.
TIMES: Wednesday and Friday 9:00 AM–5:00 PM, Saturday and Sunday 9:00 AM–6:00 PM.
ADMISSION: Free. Parking is also free.
LOCATION: 1808 Clovis Road, ½ block west of Avenue Q. Look for their flags.
DESCRIPTION: This market first opened in 1982. It is both an indoor and outdoor market attracting from 100 to 150 dealers selling everything from antiques and collectibles to handmade crafts and vegetables. New merchandise including clothing, tools, and electronics are also available. For your convenience, a snack bar and concession stand are on the premises.
DEALER RATES: There are two buildings available and outdoor space available: weekly rates in the main building range from $37.63 and up for 10' × 10' booth depending on location; rates in the other building, which usually houses the weekend dealer, vary from $15–$30, while space varies from 10' × 10' to 10' × 20'.
CONTACT: Debie Grant, National Flea Market, 1808 Clovis Road, Lubbock, TX 79415. Tel: (806) 744-4979.

MCALLEN
All Valley Garage Sale

DATES: Third weekend in February.

TIMES: Daylight to dusk.

ADMISSION: $.50. Parking is free.

LOCATION: McAllen Civic Center.

DESCRIPTION: Started in 1976, this market is really a one-shot-a-year garage sale! As its owner describes it "you are liable to find anything here." Rather than have separate garage sales, everyone who entertained the idea of holding a sale saves it for this weekend. It is possible to find the usual antiques, collectibles, and fresh produce. Food is available on the premises.

DEALER RATES: $17 per space for the weekend. Reservations are suggested.

CONTACT: Harvey Bruns, All Valley Flea Markets, P.O. Drawer 1099, Alamo, TX 78516. Tel: (210) 781-1911.

MCALLEN-MISSION
All Valley First Sunday Flea Market

DATES: First Sunday of every month.

TIMES: Daylight to dusk.

ADMISSION: $.50. Parking is free.

LOCATION: Villa Real Convention Building. Bentsen Road, between McAllen and Mission on Expressway 83.

DESCRIPTION: This market first opened in 1976 as one of four markets in the Valley area. The other markets are in McAllen, Mercedes and Alamo. This one attracts quantities of tourists to the 285 dealers and their wares. Mostly antiques and collectibles are shown here Food is available on the premises.

DEALER RATES: $8.50 per table per day. Reservations are a must!

CONTACT: Harvey Bruns, All Valley Flea Markets, P.O. Drawer 1099, Alamo, TX 78516. Tel: (210) 781-1911.

MERCEDES
Mercedes Flea Market

DATES: Saturday and Sunday, year round.

TIMES: Daylight to dusk.

ADMISSION: $.25. Parking is free.

LOCATION: Mile 2 West and Expressway 83.

DESCRIPTION: Opened in 1973 as the second of the All Valley Flea Markets and now owned by Mr. Kim, this market attracts over 600 vendors selling predominately antiques and collectibles, as well as fresh produce, used and some new merchandise. From 10,000 to 12,000 local people come here each weekend. Thirteen concession stands provide a cure for the munchies.

DEALER RATES: Saturdays $3.50 outdoors in sun; $5 under shelter per space; Sundays $5 in sun and $6 in shade. Reservations are strongly suggested.

CONTACT: Tack Kim, Mercedes Flea Market, Mile 2 West and Expressway 83, Mercedes, TX 78570. Tel: (210) 843-2644. Market number is (210) 565-2751.

PEARLAND

Cole's Antique Village and Flea Market

DATES: Every Saturday and Sunday, rain or shine.
TIMES: 7:30 AM–6:00 PM.
ADMISSION: Free. $1 for parking.
LOCATION: 1014-1022 North Main Street, 4 miles south of the Hobby Airport on Telephone Road (Highway 35).
DESCRIPTION: This indoor/outdoor market started in 1969 and currently draws approximately 700 dealers selling a range of antiques and collectibles such as furniture, tools, and glassware; fresh produce and plants, handicrafts, and new items are also available. Food is available on the premises. They added 140 new covered tables outside in 1993.

DEALER RATES: $40 per 10' × 11' space indoors per weekend; $34 per outdoor covered space per weekend. Reservations are not required.

CONTACT: Cole's Antique Village and Flea Market, 1014 North Main Street, Pearland, TX 77581. Tel: (713) 485-2277.

SAN ANTONIO

Austin Highway Flea Market and Trade Center

DATES: Friday, Saturday and Sunday, year round, rain or shine.
TIMES: 7:30 AM–dusk.
ADMISSION: Free admission and free parking for 1,000 cars.
LOCATION: Located between Broadway and Harry Wurzbach on Austin Highway (U.S. Highway 81). Take I-Loop 410 to either Broadway or Harry Wurzbach and follow south to Austin Highway.
DESCRIPTION: This flea market is conveniently located four miles

from downtown and the historic Alamo, two miles from San Antonio International Airport, one mile from Fort Sam Houston, and five miles from Randolph Air Force Base. Starting in 1976, it attracts 266 dealers selling antiques, collectibles, crafts, vegetables, and new merchandise, including Mexican imports, music instruments, books, new and estate jewelry, bicycles, lawn equipment, new and vintage clothing, and plants. A snack bar provides food.

DEALER RATES: Inside spaces vary depending on size; the charge for outside space is $19 for a 10' × 20' covered booth for three days. Reservations are preferred.

CONTACT: Ed Barley, Austin Highway Flea Market, 1428 Austin Highway, San Antonio, TX 78209. Tel: (512) 828-1488; (512) 828-9188.

Eisenhauer Road Flea Market

DATES: Everyday, rain or shine.

TIMES: Weekends 9:00 AM–7:00 PM; weekdays 12:00 noon–7:00 PM.

ADMISSION: Free. Ample free parking is available.

LOCATION: 3903 Eisenhauer Road.

DESCRIPTION: This market, started in 1979, operates 90 percent indoors in an air-conditioned space with over 200 steady dealers plus transients. A variety of antiques and collectibles is sold, along with fresh produce, crafts, and some new merchandise. Food is served at five snack bars on the premises. There is a free country jam session every Sunday from 1:00 PM to 6:00 PM.

DEALER RATES: $5 per 8' table per day. Reservations are suggested.

CONTACT: Mr. Harry Weiss or Mrs. Pat Walker, 3903 Eisenhauer Road, San Antonio, TX 78218. Tel: (210) 653-7592/3.

SCHERTZ

Bussey's Flea Market

DATES: Saturday and Sunday, year round, weather permitting.

TIMES: 7:00 AM–dusk.

ADMISSION: Free. $1 per car.

LOCATION: 18738 I-35 North.

DESCRIPTION: This outdoor show began in 1979. There are 513 dealer spaces, with most of them filled on the weekends. Anything from antiques and collectibles to produce, new merchandise, and handmade craft items are available—"anything that's legal." Generally 90 percent used, ten percent new merchandise. Plenty of garage sale items. There are many Mexican imports and a variety of curios as well. Food is available on the premises with five fantastic snack bars and plenty of homemade cinnamon rolls, pizzas, hamburgers, hot dogs (among other delights, like a sausage on a stick), breakfast tacos and special hand-me-down recipes. This is a family operated market.

DEALER RATES: Very reasonable rates. No reservations needed.

CONTACT: Harold Smith, General Manager, Bussey's Flea Market, 18738 I-35 North, San Antonio, TX 78154. Tel: (210) 651-6830.

Tear Your Hair Out

A woman, cleaning out her attic, brought in a crystal punch bowl and cup set and put them out for $25. She was offered $15 by a professional dealer and refused it. Another dealer offered her $20 which started a screaming match between the two dealers. Eventually one won and 20 minutes later the victor sold the set for a 900% profit.

WICHITA FALLS
Holliday Street Flea Market

DATES: Every Saturday and Sunday, year round.

TIMES: 7:00 AM–dark.

ADMISSION: Free, with free parking available.

LOCATION: 2820 Holliday Street. Near Highways 281 and 287 on Holliday Road near Holliday Creek.

DESCRIPTION: This market, formerly "Wichita Falls Flea Market and Trade Center" runs both indoors and out. Under the same ownership as before, it began in 1966 and currently hosts 200 to 250 dealers. The property was originally an amusement park, swimming pool and trailer park before becoming a flea market. There are antiques, collectibles, and crafts for sale, alongside produce and new merchandise. In addition, there are Mexican imports, musical instruments, saddles, boots, clothes—new and used, t-shirts, furniture, appliances and tack offered. There are 19 acres of selling space, including individual buildings with inside lock-ups. There are food concessions on the premises.

DEALER RATES: $6 per 12' × 12' space uncovered; $8 per 12' × 12' covered shed per day; $65 to $100 per lock-up stall indoors per month. Reservations are required for indoor spaces.

CONTACT: Jim and Vivian Parish, Owners, 2820 Holliday Street, Wichita Falls, TX 76301. Tel: (817) 767-1712 or 767-9038.

WINNIE

Old Time Trade Days Flea Market

DATES: The weekend following the first Monday, year round.
TIMES: Daylight to dusk.
ADMISSION: Free. Parking is $2 a carload. Tour buses are free.
LOCATION: I-10, Exit 829 at Winnie. When you get off the Interstate, you are there. Between Beaumont and Houston.
DESCRIPTION: Formerly a part of Larry's Antique Mall and Flea Market in Beaumont, this market opened in 1992, taking the major part of the flea market with it. Housed in permanent shops, big top tent, covered pavilions, or outdoors, it hosts 500 to 1,000 dealers specializing in antiques, collectibles, and crafts. The crafters have their own space showing their wares from the Ozarks to the South Texas coast. Decorators come from all over the country to find those "special somethings" to furnish their jobs. There is a special designated place for garage sales and everyone is invited to use it. With the publicity from the move from Beaumont, this market put the town of Winnie on the Texas map, so much so that all the major fast-food companies have space there including McDonald's, Burger King, Taco Bell, and plenty more. There are clean restrooms available. Very quickly, this market has become "family" to some and a capsule history of Texas in that there have already been at least one wedding, a two-foot flood, tornados, and hurricanes—"some real hair-raisers," says Mrs. Tinkle, one of the owners. "But our customers are loyal, our vendors are loyal, and somehow the market just keeps growing."
DEALER RATES: $25 and up depending on location and size: outdoors, covered pavilion, big top tent, indoors, shop; 20' × 20' to 20' × 50'. Reservations are recommended.
CONTACT: Larry and Justine Tinkle, 7135 Concord Road, Beaumont, TX 77708. Tel: (409) 892-4000. Day of show call: (409) 296-3300.

OTHER FLEA MARKETS

Cleveland: Frontier Flea Market, Route 2, Cleveland, TX 77327. Tel: (214) 793-7700. Open weekends, daylight to dark.
Denton: 380 Flea Market, 4200 East University, Denton, TX 76201. Tel: (817) 566-5060. Open Friday through Sunday 6:00 AM–10:00 PM.
El Paso: Ascarte Drive-In Flea Market, 6701 Delta Drive, El Paso, TX 79905. Tel: (915) 779-2303. Open weekends 6:00 AM–4:00 PM.

El Paso: Bronco Swap Meet, 8408 Alameda Avenue, El Paso, TX 79907. Tel: (915) 858-5555. Open weekends 7:00 AM–6:00 PM.

Houston: Town and Country Bazaar, 919 West Sam Houston Parkway South, Houston, TX 77024. Tel: (713) 973-8080. Open weekends 10:00 AM–7:00 PM.

Lubbock: The Flea Market of Lubbock, 2323 Avenue K, Lubbock, TX 79408. Tel: (806) 747-8281. Open weekends 7:00 AM–6:00 PM.

McAllen: The Flea Market, 2400 South 23 Street, McAllen, TX 78502. Tel: (512) 687-4513. Open weekends from 7:00 AM.

McKinney: Third Monday Trade Day, Highway 380 West, McKinney, TX 75069. Tel: (214) 542-7174. Open the weekend before the third Monday.

North of Dallas: Southfork Ranch 3rd Monday Trade Days, Parker Road and FM 2551, North of Dallas, TX 75215. Tel: (214) 442-4868. Open Friday through Sunday, the weekend before the third Monday of each month from 8:00 AM–dark.

Pasadena: Capitan Flea Market, 1001 East Shaw Street, Pasadena, TX 77506. Tel: (713) 477-9137. Open weekends 10:00 AM–6:00 PM.

Royse City: I-30 Country Village USA, Route 1 Box 74C, Royse City, TX 75189. Tel: (214) 635-9501. Open weekends 8:00 AM on.

San Antonio: Marbach Flea Market, 7014 Marbach Road, San Antonio, TX 78227. Tel: (210) 674-7540. Open Thursday through Sunday 10:00 AM–6:00 PM.

San Antonio: Mission Open Air Market, 207 West Chavaneaux, San Antonio, TX 78221. Tel: (210) 921-1569. Open Wednesday through Sunday 7:00 AM–6:00 PM.

San Antonio: Northwest Center Flea Market, 3600 Fredricksburg Road, Suite 126, San Antonio, TX 78201. Tel: (210) 736-6655. Open weekends 8:30 AM–6:00 PM.

Waco: Unlimited Flea Market, 2728 and 2729 Lasalle, Waco, TX 76706. Tel: (817) 662-6616. Open weekends, dawn to dusk.

UTAH

PARK CITY

Park City Resort Center Antique Show and Sale

DATES: Fridays, Saturdays, and Sundays in August.

TIMES: 9:00 AM–7:00 PM.

ADMISSION: Free. Parking is free.

LOCATION: On the ice rink at the base of the alpine slide.

DESCRIPTION: Started in 1991, this antique and collectible market is located in one of the finest summer resorts in the nation. Their 75 dealers specialize in antiques and collectibles, good pine furniture (Mormon and otherwise), Indian artifacts, Western memorabilia, jewelry, toys and dolls, Oriental carpets, and other treasures. Five restaurants are on the premises. "Park City has more art galleries per capita than any other city." As this is an international resort, people from all over the world shop here.

DEALER RATES: $135 for a 10' × 12' booth. Reservations are required.

CONTACT: Jan or Jeffrey Perkins, 2902 Breneman Street, Boise, ID 83703. Tel: (208) 345-0755 or 368-9759.

SALT LAKE CITY

Antiques Fair and Collectibles Flea Market

DATES: 1994: February 25–27; April 30–May 1; June 25–27; August 20–21; October 22–23. Generally the third or fourth weekend during even months starting with February (except December).

TIMES: Saturday 10:00 AM–6:00 PM; Sunday 10:00 AM–5:00 PM.

ADMISSION: $3, $2 with ad from local newspaper (in the classified section). Early bird admission for Saturday 9:00 AM–10:00 AM: $5.

LOCATION: Salt Palace Convention Center, in the heart of downtown Salt Lake City.

DESCRIPTION: Limited to antiques and collectibles only, this market opened in 1986 and hosts 60 to 75 dealers during its six shows per year. Savvy shoppers and other dealers come from all over the country to restock their own inventory buying jewelry, vintage clothing, glassware, a huge variety of oak furniture, primitives, kitchenware, Mormon pine, prints, dolls, postcards, books, old tools, and more. Plenty of hotels, motels, and restaurants surround the Center. This is the only market of its type between Denver and the West Coast. Food is available on the premises.

DEALER RATES: $85 for a 11' × 13' booth; 20% additional for a wall or aisle end position. Dealers may drive into the room to set up from Friday 10:00 AM–7:00 PM. Security is provided by the Salt Palace. RV parking within 3 miles of site.

CONTACT: James Reece Antique Promotion, P.O. Box 510432, Salt Lake City, UT 84151. Tel: (801) 532-3401.

Redwood Swap Meet

DATES: Every Saturday and Sunday.

TIMES: Winters 9:00 AM–3:00 PM; summers 8:00 AM–4:00 PM.

LOCATION: 3600 South Redwood Road. Take I-15 to 3300 South. Go west to 1700 West, south to Redwood Swap Meet.

ADMISSION: $.50 per person. Parking is free.

DESCRIPTION: This indoor/outdoor market started in 1972 and currently draws approximately 170 dealers in winter, and up to 700 dealers in summer. The merchandise available includes antiques, collectibles, tools, electronics, hundreds of garage sales, and new merchandise. Fresh farm goods and craft items are also available. Food is served on the premises. Showers and overnight parking are available on premises.

DEALER RATES: $12 per dealer (as much space as needed) on Saturday; $15 and up on Sunday. Reservations are suggested.

CONTACT: Redwood Swap Meet, 3688 South Redwood Road, West Valley, UT 84119. Tel: (801) 973-6060.

VERMONT

BROWNINGTON

Antique Gas and Steam Engine Show and Flea Market

DATES: 1994: June 18–19. Next to last full weekend in June.

TIMES: 9:00 AM–4:00 PM.

ADMISSION: Free. Parking is free.

LOCATION: Old Stone House Museum. Ten miles south of Newport. Three miles from Orleans, Exit 26 off I-91. Follow the signs to Old Stone House Museum.

DESCRIPTION: Located in Vermont's spectacular Northeast Kingdom, this flea market attracts 15 to 20 dealers selling crafts, junk, collectibles, food, garage sale goodies, and several dealers specializing in particular treasures—one in antique camera equipment. This is held in conjunction with the Vermont Gas and Steam Engine Association's Antique Gas and Steam Engine Show. Lunch is served as part of the flea market and engine show.

DEALER RATES: $10 a day for officially a 20' x 20' space. Reservations are strongly suggested.

CONTACT: Old Stone House Museum, RFD 1 Box 500, Orleans, VT 05860. Tel: (802) 754-2022.

The Rev. Alexander Twilight, who built the Stone House in 1836, is believed to be the first black to graduate from an American college.

Legend has it that Rev. Twilight built the Old Stone House, a massive four-story structure of native granite blocks, single-handedly. Okay, he did have the help of an ox whose scaffolding grew higher and higher as the walls rose. When the building was finished, there wasn't any way to get the ox down. The ox was slaughtered and roasted. It made for one very large celebration. Since there are no records to prove or disprove any of this, the legend stands.

The museum is well worth the visit. It was originally built as a dormitory for a school, later abandoned, but subsequently reincarnated as a museum. Many artifacts from early Vermont history are located in rooms dedicated to specific people, times or events. One huge room on the top floor is an historian's dream of old school textbooks and the bestsellers of yesteryear.

CHARLOTTE
Charlotte Flea Market

DATES: Saturday and Sunday, April through October, weather permitting.

TIMES: 8:00 AM–5:00 PM or later.

ADMISSION: Free. Parking is free.

LOCATION: Route 7, just south of the Wildflower Farm. Ten miles south of Burlington. About 5 miles south of the Shelburne Museum.

DESCRIPTION: Located next door to the Wildflower Farm and just south of the Shelburne Museum (the second largest tourist attraction in Vermont) this market enjoys the crowds driving scenic Route 7. One of the oldest and biggest in Vermont, this market attracts an average of 100 dealers selling literally everything: old tools, books, clothing, garage sale items, paper, jewelry, crafts, glass and bottles, used and antique furniture, "stuff," new merchandise, whatever. A snack bar serves the hungry.

DEALER RATES: For a three-table setup, tables included: $5 on Saturday and $10 on Sunday. Reservations are not required.

CONTACT: Larry Lavalette, P.O. Box 415, Shelburne, VT 05482. Tel: (802) 425-2844.

CHELSEA
Chelsea Flea Market

DATES: Second Saturday of July.

TIMES: 10:00 AM–4:00 PM.

ADMISSION: Free. Parking is free.

LOCATION: On the North and South Common of Chelsea, on Route 110, south of Barre.

DESCRIPTION: Started in 1971 by the Ladies Service Guild, as a fundraiser to repair the United Church of Chelsea, this show has grown to include 125 vendors from all over New England. Over 3,000 visitors choose from antiques, collectibles, and whatever. The Fish and Game Department runs the famous chicken barbecue (a special Vermont treat); hot dogs and sodas are sold by the Ladies Service Guild. Chelsea is another of Vermont's beautiful towns stretched along the back roads. Definitely worth the trip.

DEALER RATES: $15 per space. Reservations are required as there is a long waiting list.

CONTACT: Charlene R. Edmondson, Box 281, Chelsea, VT 05038. Tel: (802) 685-2207.

CRAFTSBURY COMMON
Craftsbury Antique and Unique Festival

DATES: Second Saturday in July, come heck or high water!
TIMES: 10:00 AM–4:00 PM.
ADMISSION: Free. Parking is free.
LOCATION: On Craftsbury Common itself. From the south: take Route 100 heading north through Morrisville to Route 15 East to Route 14 North, follow the signs to Craftsbury, then Craftsbury Common. From the north: Route 14 South from Newport and follow the signs.
DESCRIPTION: Set in the picturesque village of Craftsbury Common, this special market, started in 1970, helps raise funds for the Vermont Children's Aid Society. The dealers specialize in antiques, collectibles and unique crafts including stuffed animals, jewelry, handmade wooden clocks and other treasures. Sterling College is next door and the local sports center is home to some wild mountain-bike races. Food is provided by local bakers. The Anderson sisters bring in 15 to 20 homebaked pies and there are lines backed up to buy their mouth-watering specialties before they ever get there! This is considered a "four-plunger day" by the two directors of the Festival. You'd better ask either Judy or Alice about this one.
DEALER RATES: $50 for a 16' frontage and ample space behind. Reservations are a must and should be in by sometime in January as the invitations to sell are sent in February.
CONTACT: Judith Reiss, VCAS, P.O. Box 127, Winooski, VT 05404-0127. Tel: (802) 655-0006.

ELY
Conval Antique Mall

DATES: Daily.
TIMES: 10:00 AM–5:00 PM.
ADMISSION: Free. Parking is free.
LOCATION: I-91, Exit 15 to Route 5 South, 2 miles on left.
DESCRIPTION: Located along what the owners call the "Chicken to Chippendale Corridor" of Vermont's Route 5 with 20 miles of auctions, flea markets, and antique shops almost end to end from Thetford to Bradford. This indoor market started in 1990 with the concept of the old-time flea market in mind. Nothing new. With three floors and room to grow, they host between 80 to 120 dealers selling good quality antiques, collectibles, cards, coins, toys, household ware, aged flea market items, and crafts. Auctions are held bi-weekly, usually

the first and third Thursdays of the month. Think of this as the Filene's of the antique and collectible world: their basement houses the less-expensive treasures and their main floors house the extraordinary treasures. Outside space is proposed for the future.

DEALER RATES: Indoor $1.75 per square foot in the basement, as much as you need; main floors $2.90 per square foot. Proposed outdoor rate $10 per 5' x 10' space. Reservations are suggested.

CONTACT: Marty and Kitty Diggins, P.O. Box 37, Ely, VT 05044. Tel: (802) 333-9971.

FAIRLEE
Railroad Station Flea Market

DATES: Saturday, Sunday, and holidays, May through October.

TIMES: Daylight.

ADMISSION: Free. Parking is free.

LOCATION: On Route 5, in the center of Fairlee. Exit 15 off I-91; follow the signs to the town of Fairlee.

DESCRIPTION: Located outside an old train station, near the famous Lake Morey Inn resort, this little market draws its share of the Route 5 "Chicken to Chippendale corridor" crowd. The shop inside the station is loaded with the most wonderful treasures! Furniture, magazines (old only), books by the ton, household items (brass, pewter, silver, etc.), clothes, signs, cards, whatever. If you're hungry, try the Fairlee Diner down the road a piece. As to the outside, about 25 dealers set up under the trees along the road. It's a lovely spot along a picturesque wandering road. The town of Fairlee also boasts several other antique shops including Attic Collectables. This is a great place to ferret out treasures.

DEALER RATES: $15 for a 15' x 20' space. Reservations not necessary—first-come, first-served—but they are nice to have.

CONTACT: Barry LeBarron, LeBarron's Antiques and Auction Service, P.O. Box 57, Fairlee, VT 05045. Tel: (802) 333-4574 or (603) 787-6758.

LYNDONVILLE
Route 5 Antiques Flea Market

DATES: The last Saturday of the month, May through September.

TIMES: 8:00 AM–4:00 PM.

ADMISSION: Free. Parking is free.

LOCATION: On Route 5, just before Lyndonville. Exit 23 off I-91, head towards Lyndonville; it's on the left before you get to the railroad tracks.

DESCRIPTION: Started in 1993 as an aside to the Antiques and Collectibles shop, this market hosts 20 to 30 dealers selling antiques, collectibles, garage sale goodies, whatever comes in. There is a superb bakery next door, Holly Berry's, serving all homemade pasteries, breads, soup and sandwiches. Lyndonville in is the extraordinary Northeast Kingdom of Vermont near beautiful Lake Willoughby, Burke Mountain (skiing, hiking and biking), St. Johnsbury (with its unusual Fairbanks Museum and Planetarium, with plenty of kid things to do—Vermont schools regularly send their students here by the bus load), and the quiet, but historic town of East Burke.

Most of the houses and farms in East Burke are painted yellow instead of the usual Vermont farmhouse white. This is to honor the memory of one man's contribution to the town—the library, the school and many other amenities larger towns take for granted.

Elmer Darling, spurned by his true love as being too poor, went to New York City and joined the family business of hotelry. He became very rich and returned to East Burke where he built the most astonishing yellow mansion and complete farm with creamery, dairy barns and more (all in yellow), on a hilltop overlooking East Burke.

His former love married another wealthy man, who went broke.

Just down the road from Elmer's mansion is the Wildflower Inn with a view of Willoughby Lake. They specialize in families if you happen to be passing through on an antique scouting mission.

MANCHESTER CENTER
Manchester Flea Market

DATES: Every Saturday, May through October, rain or shine.
TIMES: 9:00 AM–5:00 PM.
LOCATION: Junction of Routes 11 and 30. Take Bromley Mountain Road 3 miles from the center of Manchester.
ADMISSION: Free. Free parking is available.
DESCRIPTION: This indoor/outdoor show has operated since 1970

in the heart of the Green Mountains and ski country. Stratton, Magic and Bromley ski areas surround Manchester. It currently attracts 35 to 40 dealers of primarily antiques, with collectibles, crafts, some farm goods also available. There is an exhibit of antique farm machinery here, and this is also the location of a locally well-known Thursday auction. Robert Todd Lincoln's historic home Hildene is nearby and open to the public. Food is served on the premises.

DEALER RATES: $15 per 20' x 15' space. Advance reservations are suggested.

CONTACT: Albert H. Wessner, RR1 Box 1960, Manchester Center, VT 05255. Tel: (802) 362-1631.

NEWFANE

The Original Newfane Flea Market

DATES: Every Sunday, May through October, rain or shine.

TIMES: 7:00 AM–5:00 PM.

ADMISSION: Free. Ample free parking is available.

LOCATION: On Route 30, 1 mile north of downtown Newfane.

DESCRIPTION: This outdoor market has been around since 1963 and is claimed to be the oldest and largest in Vermont. It is well known throughout the state, attracting between 150 and 200 dealers who come from near and far to exhibit such diverse items as antiques, collectibles, craft items, new merchandise, and fresh produce—in a word: "Everything." There is a cider mill on site, along with other foods served on the premises.

DEALER RATES: $20 per space. No reservations period! Dealers may camp free Saturday nights.

CONTACT: Mr. Earl Morse, Proprietor, P.O. Box 5, Newfane, VT 05345. Tel: (802) 365-7775.

SALISBURY

Flea Mart Center

DATES: Daily, year round.

TIMES: 10:00 AM–5:00 PM.

LOCATION: On Route 7 just south of Middlebury.

ADMISSION: Free. Free parking is available.

DESCRIPTION: This market, which began operation in 1983, has an indoor section that is open seven days a week all year round. Antiques and collectibles including furniture and primitives, glassware, pottery, jewelry, and ephemera are sold here. Now a five-year tradition, tailgate auctions are held every Friday night with an auctioneer going around the parking lot from one "sellers" car to another auctioning off the contents.

DEALER RATES: Not applicable as all inside spaces are permanently filled. Friday nights, just bring your car.

CONTACT: Joyce McGettrick, P.O. Box 186, Salisbury, VT 05769. Tel: (802) 352-4424.

WATERBURY
3rd Annual American Red Cross Flea Market

DATES: Sunday, April 24, 1994.

TIMES: 9:00 AM–3:00 PM.

ADMISSION: $1. Parking is free.

LOCATION: Waterbury Armory. Off Route 2. Use Exit 10 West off I-89. At the intersection, turn a hard left onto Union Street, *not* under the railroad tracks on Route 2. Take a left again onto Armory Street and continue to the Armory. It's the "big gray building."

DESCRIPTION: This popular annual indoor flea market is the fundraiser for the local Central Vermont/NH Valley Chapter of the American Red Cross. At least 30 dealers come from New York, Vermont, and New Hampshire to sell their collectibles, attic finds, garage sale clean-outs, trinkets, and what-have-yous to eager patrons. The management gives away door prizes; one of which is free entry to all the other winter markets at the Armory. Believe it or not, that is the most prized door prize of all! The Armory kitchen serves up homemade soup, hot dogs and hamburgers to starving visitors. However, the management is trying hard to con their patrons into eating healthier fare. Restrooms are available on the premises.

The same management of this show also puts on seven other shows at this location throughout the winter. These shows have been local events since 1981. All are fundraisers for one excellent charity or another. Call for more information.

DEALER RATES: $25 a table. Reservations are required.

CONTACT: Dorothy Willis, Willis & Willis, P.O. Box 182, Waterbury Center, VT 05677. Tel: (802) 244-5519.

Waterbury Flea Market

DATES: Saturday, Sunday, and holidays, weather permitting, May through October.

TIMES: Daybreak to exhaustion.

ADMISSION: Free. Parking is free.

LOCATION: Route 2, just north of the Waterbury. Exit 10 West off I-89.

DESCRIPTION: Opened in 1979, this outdoor market attracts anyone and everyone with up to 100 vendors selling everything from classic antiques, attic treasures, ancient books and old magazines, new merchandise, jewelry, tools—new and very old, furniture, yardsale and house clean-outs, collectibles and "stuff." I remember one dealer buying a huge box of ladies intimate apparel and trying to flog it off to his various lady acquaintances in another town—"Such a deal, such a deal." The sizes were so huge, however, no one could fit into them. A snack concession with delicious hot dogs sates hungry appetites. Then again, there is Ben & Jerry's Ice Cream around the corner and down Route 100.

DEALER RATES: $7 Saturday, $9 Sunday for a 20' x 25' space. Dealers may camp over the weekend for free and set up on Friday. No dogs, please.

CONTACT: Hartley McHone, P.O. Box 178, Waterbury, VT 05676. Tel: (802) 244-5132.

WATERBURY CENTER
Stowe Road Flea Market

DATES: Saturday and Sundays, June through October's fall foliage season. Weather permitting.

TIMES: 9:00 AM–5:00 PM.

ADMISSION: Free. Parking is free.

LOCATION: Route 100. Only 4 miles from I-89, Exit 11 East, Waterbury/Stowe on the road to Stowe. Just 3 miles north of Ben & Jerry's Ice Cream Factory.

DESCRIPTION: This market, opened in 1992, has the unique distinction of being surrounded by some of Vermont's biggest attractions: Ben & Jerry's Ice Cream Factory (the largest tourist attraction in the state), the Cold Hollow Cider Mill across the street, and the resort town of Stowe just north down scenic Route 100. They host anywhere from 20 to 50 dealers selling antiques, collectibles, Vermont crafts, glass, furniture, garage sale goodies and whatever turns up. New merchandise is rare and discouraged. If you are hungry, try B&J's or the cider mill. Enjoy!

DEALER RATES: $8 for a 25' x 20' space per day, or $15 for the weekend. Reservations are not required. Tents are available by advance reservation.
CONTACT: Sir Richard's Antiques, P.O. Box 10, Waterbury Center, VT 05677. Tel: (802) 244-8879.

WILMINGTON
Wilmington Outdoor Antique and Flea Market
DATES: Saturday, Sunday, and holiday Mondays, from the weekend before Memorial Day through the weekend after Labor Day.
TIMES: No specific times, really. Say dawn on...
ADMISSION: Free. Parking is free.
LOCATION: Junction of Routes 9 and 100.
DESCRIPTION: Since 1982 this market has been located on a choice 10-acre lot at the junction of two heavily traveled scenic roads through Vermont. They do a lot of advertising and draw crowds. Their dealers sell antiques, collectibles, garage sale items, all manner of stuff.
DEALER RATES: $15 per space. Reservations are not required.
CONTACT: Sally Gore, P.O. Box 22, Wilmington, VT 05363-0022. Tel: (802) 464-3345 evenings.

Sign on the Millbrook Store at Lake Willoughby, Vermont:

FLEE MARKET
INSIDE

OTHER FLEA MARKETS
Poultney: Green Mountain College Flea Market and Craft Fair, Poultney, VT 05764. Tel: (802) 287-9313 ×224. Open second Saturday in October.

VIRGINIA

ALTAVISTA
First Saturday Trade Lot

DATES: First Saturday of each month, year round.
TIMES: Friday 12:00 noon until 4:00 PM on Saturday.
ADMISSION: Free. Parking is also free.
LOCATION: On Seventh Street, 1 block off Business Highway 29, between Lynchburg and Danville.
DESCRIPTION: This outdoor market first opened in 1911. There are more than 200 dealers selling mostly antiques, collectibles, crafts, new and secondhand merchandise, as well as some produce. There is also food available on the premises. Don't miss the hot dogs. I'm assured they are terrific! The Altavista Band Boosters now run this show and man the concession stand to help pay their expenses. Uncle Billy's Day (the first Saturday weekend in June, including the preceding Friday) is a town-wide celebration that lasts three days centered around the Trade Lot. Uncle Billy started the Trade Lot by trading animals at the turn of the century. Fireworks, old-timers ballgame, children's entertainment, and more are featured on this weekend.
DEALER RATES: $7.50 per 9' × 20' space for the weekend. Six-month reservations are $6 per weekend. Reservations are strongly suggested, or else.
CONTACT: Carl Davis, Altavista Band Boosters, P.O. Box 333, Altavista, VA 24517.

CHESAPEAKE
Oak Grove Flea Market

DATES: Every Saturday and Sunday, year round, rain or shine.
TIMES: 10:00 AM–6:00 PM.
ADMISSION: Free. Parking is also free.
LOCATION: From I-64, go 2 miles south on Battlefield Boulevard.
DESCRIPTION: This indoor/outdoor market first opened in 1972. There are 20 permanent dealers inside and 12 permanent dealers outside, with room for more. Available are antiques and collectibles, arts and crafts, guns, coins, and stamps to name a few. There is no food available on the premises, unless you like peanuts.
DEALER RATES: Indoor space $125 to $135 monthly. Outdoor space $5 per day. Reservations are not required.

CONTACT: John Corbman, Oak Grove Flea Market, 910 Oak Grove Road, Chesapeake, VA 23320. Tel: Monday through Friday (804) 482-1919, Saturday and Sunday (804) 547-1500.

CHRISTIANBURG
A-1 Flea Market and Antique Emporium

DATES: Daily.
TIMES: 8:00 AM–7:00 PM.
ADMISSION: Free. Parking is also free.
LOCATION: 940 Radford Street. Route 11.
DESCRIPTION: Open since 1982, this market houses 20 permanent dealers selling everything including guns, knives, antiques, dolls, tools, vintage glassware (Fenton, Cambridge, Heisey, Fostoria—loads of these treasures), custom-made clothing, sports (race and ball) cards, comics, and much more. A snack bar serves the hungry. Every weekend and Thursday nights they hold remote-control car races both on paved and off-road track!
DEALER RATES: $115 per month for a 12' × 24' space. Reservations are required.
CONTACT: Kathryn Minnick, 940 Radford Street, Christianburg, VA 24073. Tel: (703) 382-9811.

FREDERICKSBURG
Manor Mart Flea Market

DATES: Saturday and Sunday, year round.
TIMES: 7:00 AM–dusk.
ADMISSION: Free. Parking is also free.
LOCATION: U.S. Highway 1, just south of Fredericksburg.
DESCRIPTION: An indoor/outdoor flea market established in 1983, the Manor Mart offers antiques, collectibles, handicrafts, and new merchandise, as well as fresh produce. It is located near historic Fredericksburg, scene of much Civil War fighting and near other historic battlefields. For your convenience there is food available on the premises.
DEALER RATES: $10 per 16' × 10' booth (indoors and out). Reservations are not required.
CONTACT: Nick or Jeannie Dommisse, Route 18, Box 173, Fredericksburg, VA 22408. Tel: (703) 898-4685.

HAMPTON

The Big Flea Market

DATES: One show a month; call for specific dates.

TIMES: 12:00 noon–6:00 PM.

ADMISSION: $1.50; children under 12 free. There is a parking fee.

LOCATION: Hampton Coliseum. Off I-64 just before Hampton Roads Tunnel.

DESCRIPTION: Established 19 years ago, this show is one of a series held in Virginia. There are over 300 spaces available for dealers selling antiques, collectibles, crafts, and some new merchandise. The other shows are held in Virginia Beach, Richmond, and Roanoke. Food is available on the premises.

DEALER RATES: $45 per space for a one-day show; $70 per space for a two-day show. Reservations are required.

CONTACT: Joan Sides, 504 Central Drive, Suite 106, Virginia Beach, VA 23454. Tel: (804) 431-9500.

HILLSVILLE

V.F.W. Labor Day Gun Show and Flea Market

DATES: Friday through Monday Labor Day weekend, rain or shine.

TIMES: 8:00 AM–8:00 PM.

LOCATION: At the V.F.W. Complex. On U.S. Route 58-221 West (Galax Road), 1 mile east of I-77.

ADMISSION: $1 per person; children under 12 admitted free. Parking is free on V.F.W. property; private property owners do charge.

DESCRIPTION: The population of the town of Hillsville expands five-fold during this annual event sponsored by the Grover King Post 1115 Veterans of Foreign Wars. The show has been held each year since 1967, and in 1986 it brought over 250,000 shoppers despite rain and cold weather, according to local police records. Well over 1,500 dealers are expected in 1994, selling a variety of items that goes beyond fire arms and militaria to encompass all types of antiques and collectibles including coins, jewelry, glassware, tools, toys, and other Americana. For the 1986 show, visitors registered from 40 different states plus four foreign countries, and attendance is growing each year. Food is served on the premises.

DEALER RATES: $35 per 9' × 20' space for four days, plus $10 for town license. Dealer reservations are required. Advance shopping hours for dealers are held Thursday afternoon before the show.

CONTACT: Ernest Martin, Route 2 Box 107, Hillsville, VA 24343. Tel: (703) 728-7188.

MONTROSS

Montross Day

DATES: First Saturday each May through September, weather permitting. The first Saturday in May is the special Crafts Fair; the first Saturday in October is the huge Fall Festival celebration.

TIMES: 9:00 AM–4:00 PM.

ADMISSION: Free. Parking is also free.

LOCATION: Route 3 on the middle of Montross, literally.

DESCRIPTION: Anywhere from 20 to 100 dealers, depending on who is sponsoring the market day, selling "just about everything" gather here each first Saturday. Antiques, baked goods, ceramics, and produce, and fruit in season are sold. Dealers set up on the road around the Court House and across the street from the Court House and anywhere else there is room. Food is available on the premises.

DEALER RATES: $10 per table for the regular Montross Day; higher on the two festivals. Reservations are suggested.

CONTACT: Thelma Belfield, Route 1 Box 3330, Montross, VA 22520. Tel: (804) 493-0241.

OAK GROVE

Red Barn Flea Market

DATES: Friday through Sunday. Auctions held periodically.

TIMES: Winter: Friday and Saturday 9:00 AM–4:00 PM, Sundays 12:00 noon-4:00 PM; Summer: Friday and Saturdays 9:00 AM–5:00 PM, Sundays 12:00 noon–5:00 PM.

ADMISSION: Free. Parking is also free.

LOCATION: Westmoreland County, 36 miles east of Fredericksburg on State Route 3. On left of road, look for the big red barn.

DESCRIPTION: This market started in August 1989 as an addition to an auction house, which started originally as a huge horse barn "the size of a football field." Crammed with 38-plus dealers inside and growing, they sell antiques, collectibles, glassware, toys, books, TVs, appliances—"everything." The local Baptist Church handles the snack stand.

DEALER RATES: $35 per month inside, $7.50 a day for outside table space. Reservations are not required.

CONTACT: Curtis Bartmess, 330 Circle Lane, Colonial Beach, VA 22443. Tel: (804) 224-1119.

RICHMOND
Bellwood Flea Market

DATES: Saturday and Sunday, year round, weather permitting.
TIMES: 8:00 AM–4:30 PM.
ADMISSION: $1 per person. Free parking.
LOCATION: 9201 Jefferson Davis Highway. Exit 61 off I-95 and Willis Road, south of Richmond.
DESCRIPTION: This market has been run since 1969 outdoors. Between 150 and 300 dealers offer antiques, collectibles, handmades, produce, meats, musical instruments, auto parts, appliances, real estate, furniture, clothing, and new merchandise, as well as tools and curios. A large air-conditioned food concession opens early and remains open all day. There are still reminders of the fierce Civil War battle fought on the Bellwood property as people are occasionally finding mini-balls and some trench-works are still visible.
DEALER RATES: $8 per 20' × 20' space. First come, first served.
CONTACT: Alvin Kline, c/o Bellwood Flea Market, 9201 Jefferson Davis Highway, Richmond, VA 23237. Tel: (804) 275-1187.

The Big Flea Market at the Richmond State Fairgrounds

DATES: Ten two-day shows a year in January, February, March, April, May, June, August, September, October, and November; call for specific dates.
TIMES: Saturday 12:00 noon–7:00 PM; Sunday 12:00 noon–5:00 PM.
ADMISSION: $1.50; children under 12 free. Parking is free.
LOCATION: Richmond State Fairgrounds.
DESCRIPTION: Part of a series of shows started in 1974, this show has between 300 to 600 spaces filled with dealers from 13 states. They sell primarily antiques and collectibles and some new merchandise. This market is considered the largest flea market in Virginia. Food is available on the premises.
DEALER RATES: $60 per space per show. $110 for two spaces per show. Reservations are required.
CONTACT: Joan Sides, 544 Central Drive, Suite 106, Virginia Beach, VA 23454. Tel: (804) 431-9500.

ROANOKE
The Big Flea Market
DATES: Five two-day shows a year in January, February, April, August, and November; call for specific dates.
TIMES: Saturday 10:00 AM–6:00 PM; Sunday 12:00 noon–5:00 PM.
ADMISSION: $1; children under 12 free.
LOCATION: Roanoke Civic Center.
DESCRIPTION: Though this show started in 1986, it is part of a series of shows held in Virginia. The other shows are in Richmond, Virginia Beach, and Hampton. Here 80 dealers primarily vend antiques, collectibles, and crafts. Rarely is new merchandise allowed in the market, by City Ordinance. Food is available on the premises.
DEALER RATES: $60 for a single space; $110 for a double space. Reservations are required.
CONTACT: Joan Sides, 554 Central Drive, Suite 106, Virginia Beach, VA 23454. Tel: (804) 431-9500.

Happy's Flea Market
DATES: Tuesday through Sunday, year round.
TIMES: Tuesday through Friday 8:00 AM–5:00 PM; Saturday and Sunday 6:30 AM–5:30 PM.
ADMISSION: Free. Parking is free.
LOCATION: 5411 Williamson Road N.W. Off Route 581, exit for Airport Road.
DESCRIPTION: Obviously successful, this market has been open since 1978. There are 400 inside dealers, another 500 outside with 200 of those spaces permanently reserved. The dealers sell an endless variety of everything: antiques, batteries, collectibles, used and new merchandise, and much more. A restaurant is on the premises.
DEALER RATES: $7 Saturday and Sunday; $2 Tuesday; $4 Wednesday through Friday. First come, first served.
CONTACT: Happy's Flea Market, 5411 Williamson Road, Roanoke, VA 24012. Tel: (703) 563-4473/4.

VIRGINIA BEACH
The Big Flea Market
DATES: One two-day show in May and another in September; call for specific dates.
TIMES: Friday 5:00 PM–10:00 PM; Saturday 11:00 AM–7:00 PM.
ADMISSION: $1.50; children under 12 free.

LOCATION: Virginia Beach Pavilion. Follow the signs.

DESCRIPTION: For 19 years this show has been attracting up to 300 dealers, from 13 states, selling predominantly antiques, collectibles, jewelry and crafts. This show is considered one of Virginia's largest antiques and collectibles shows and is part of a series of shows held in Richmond, Hampton, and Roanoke. Food is available on the premises.

DEALER RATES: $60 per 10' × 10' space per show; $110 per 20' × 10' space per show. Reservations are required. Dealer space sells out fast.

CONTACT: Joan Sides, 544 Central Drive, Suite 106, Virginia Beach, VA 23454. Tel: (804) 431-9500.

OTHER FLEA MARKETS

Alexandria: The Circuit Flea Market, 8750 Richmond Highway, Alexandria, VA 22309. Tel: (703) 644-2611. Open Wednesday through Sunday 10:00 AM–8:00 PM.

Gloucester: Holland's Stagecoach Markets, Route 17 and Route 1420, Gloucester, VA 23061. Tel: (804) 693-3951. Open weekends.

Manassas: The Many Market, 9808 Grant Avenue, Manassas, VA 22309. Tel: (703) 644-2611. Open Friday through Sunday 10:00 AM–8:00 PM.

Petersburg: Southside Station Flea and Farmer's Market, 5 River Street, Petersburg, VA 23803. Tel: (804) 733-5050. Open weekends and holidays.

Richmond: American International Flea Market and Mini Mall, 4000 Mechanicsville Turnpike, Richmond, VA 23223. Tel: (804) 321-0067. Open Friday 12:00 noon–9:00 PM, Saturday 9:00 AM–9:00 PM, Sunday 10:00 AM–6:00 PM.

Richmond: Richmond Super Flea, 5501 Midlothian Turnpike, Richmond, VA 23225. Tel: (804) 231-6687. Open weekends 9:00 AM–5:00 PM.

Temperanceville: Shore Flea Market, Route 13, Temperanceville, VA 23442. Tel: (804) 824-3300 or 824-5020. Open weekends.

WASHINGTON

EVERETT
Puget Park Swap-O-Rama

DATES: Saturday and Sunday, April through October, rain or shine.
TIMES: 9:00 AM–4:00 PM.
ADMISSION: $.75 per person. Free parking is provided.
LOCATION: 13020 Meridian Avenue South. The 128th Street exit off I-5.
DESCRIPTION: Started in 1975, this market currently attracts between 200 and 300 dealers who set up to sell a wide range of objects including antiques, collectibles, fine art, handicrafts, fresh produce, and some new merchandise. Food is served on the premises.
DEALER RATES: $11 for a 20' × 20' space per day; $15 for a 20' × 25' space with electricity. Advance reservations are advised and can be made in person Fridays from 12:00 noon–5:00 PM or during market hours.
CONTACT: Jamie Chatham, Puget Park Swap-O-Rama, 13020 Meridian Avenue South, Everett, WA 98204. Tel: (206) 743-7711 or 337-1435.

PROSSER
Prosser Harvest Festival

DATES: Friday and Saturday, last weekend of September.
TIMES: 9:00 AM–6:00 PM or later.
LOCATION: At the corner of 6th and Meade in downtown Prosser.
ADMISSION: Free. Free parking is available nearby.
DESCRIPTION: This outdoor market started in 1972 and is held in conjunction with the annual Great Prosser Balloon Rally. This is the annual Harvest Festival (formerly known as the Prosser Flea Market) that includes the entire town of Prosser. There are sidewalk sales, farmers' market stands and vendors everywhere. It currently attracts 100 outside dealers selling a large variety of antiques and collectibles, unbelievable arts and crafts "to die for," fresh herbs, new merchandise, and loads of freshly harvested produce. Food is available on the premises. There is entertainment for the children. The balloons go up early Sunday morning and the night before they light the balloons up in a spectacular display.

DEALER RATES: $50 per dealer for two days. Reservations are required.
CONTACT: Chamber of Commerce, 1230 Bennett Avenue, Prosser, WA 99350. Tel: (509) 786-3177.

TACOMA

"America's Largest" Antique and Collectible Sale

DATES: June 4–5 1994.
TIMES: Saturday 8:00 AM–7:00 PM; Sunday 9:00 AM–5:00 PM.
LOCATION: Tacoma Dome, Tacoma Dome exit off I-5.
ADMISSION: $5. Parking is handled by the Tacoma Dome and costs $4–$5.
DESCRIPTION: The first Tacoma Dome market was held June 1988. This market and its more than 400 dealers deal only in high quality antiques and collectibles. Food is available on the premises.
DEALER RATES: $100 per 10' × 10' booth.
CONTACT: Christine Palmer, Palmer/Wirfs & Associates, 4001 NE Halsey, Portland, OR 97232. Tel: (503) 282-0877.

OTHER FLEA MARKETS

Kent: Midway Swap and Shop, 24050 Pacific Highway South, Kent, WA 98032. Tel: (206) 878-1802. Open weekends 6:30 AM–4:00 PM.
Tacoma: Star Lite Swap and Shop, 8327 South Tacoma Way, Tacoma, WA 98409. Tel: (206) 588-8090. Open weekends 9:00 AM–4:00 PM indoor and outdoor; Tuesday through Friday 10:00 AM–6:00 PM, indoor only.

WEST VIRGINIA

BLUEFIELD
City of Bluefield Parking Facilities Flea Market

DATES: Every Saturday, March through November.

TIMES: 6:00 AM–2:00 PM.

ADMISSION: Free. Metered parking is available.

LOCATION: On Princeton Avenue, at the junction of Routes 19 and 460, in the heart of Bluefield.

DESCRIPTION: This indoor market began in 1981 and now draws approximately 175 dealers selling a wide range of items including antiques and collectibles, crafts, fresh produce, and new merchandise. Shopping can begin as early as 5:30 AM as people hurry to catch the best bargains. Two snack bars serve the hungry.

DEALER RATES: $5 per 14' × 20' space. First come, first served.

CONTACT: Sharon Leffel, City of Bluefield, Parking Commission, 514 Scott Street, Bluefield, WV 24701. Tel: (304) 327-8031.

FAIRMONT
Mom and Pop's Indoor Flea World

DATES: Friday through Sunday. Summer has outside flea market, weather permitting.

TIMES: 9:00 AM–5:00 PM.

ADMISSION: $.50. Senior citizens over 60 free. Children under 18 must be accompanied by an adult. Parking is free.

LOCATION: 500 Quincy Street. Go down Adams Avenue (one-way street) to Quincy, turn left, second building on right.

DESCRIPTION: This indoor market opened in April 1990 and has six permanent dealers and swells with the warm weather. During the summer, local charities and vendors set up outside in the parking area and sell more items. The permanent dealers sell fans, marble items, glassware, flower arrangements, furniture and refurbished appliances, loads of books and records, guns, pots and pans, some clothing, and whatever else comes by. They have complete, clean restrooms, and one snack bar. The Bunner's Ridge Volunteer Fire Department holds bingo games every Monday and Friday nights from 5:00 PM until they finish. The money raised is used to run the fire department.

DEALER RATES: $8 and up, depending on size and location. Call for inside reservations.

CONTACT: Isadore Moshien, Owner, or Douglas Keener, Manager, 500 Quincy Street, Fairmont, WV 26544. Tel: (304) 366-3265.

FAYETTEVILLE
Bridge Day

DATES: Third Saturday in October (by state law!).
TIMES: 9:00 AM–3:00 PM.
ADMISSION: Free. Parking isn't anywhere near here; try in town.
LOCATION: New River Gorge Bridge, U.S. 19 between Fayetteville and Lansing, on the bridge (really).
DESCRIPTION: Remember the TV ad where a "Jimmy" car was shoved over the side of a bridge attached to a bungee cord? This is the bridge; the longest single arch bridge in the world, the second highest in the United States at 176 feet. Bridge Day is the celebration of the building of this bridge. One day a year the police close off the northbound lanes of this four-lane bridge and all traffic is narrowed down to the two remaining lanes causing a six-mile traffic backup on each side of the bridge. Tourists come from all over to watch the goings on. Last year 174 vendors set up along the north side of the 3,030-foot-long bridge selling or performing West Virginia crafts, food, produce, tourism, gospel singing—whatever! Over 210,000 people invade the bridge on foot to participate. Parachutists fling themselves off the bridge trying to land on the "landing pad." Some don't make it onto the dry parts and have to be fished out of the water. The dealers must meet and get organized starting at 6:30 AM and then line up in their assigned order of booth number. At the appointed moment, they charge the bridge to their space, set up and sell like mad until 3:00 PM when the state police comes by to tell them it's time to pack up. They must be off the bridge by 4:00 PM, otherwise they *will* be run over.
DEALER RATES: $100 if you reserve before August 1, $200 for a 10' space after August 1, 1994. Reservations are mandatory.
CONTACT: Cindy Whitlock, Executive Director, Bridge Day, 310 Oyler Avenue, Oak Hill, WV 25901. Tel: 1-800-927-0263.

A couple married on the bridge during one Bridge Day, then "took the plunge" parachuting down the gorge.

Ace Whitewater runs rafting trips with a special on Bridge Day. They stop under the bridge, serve a gourmet meal and watch, from safe river banks, the shenanigans of parachutists and bungee jumpers—plunging into space.

HARPERS FERRY

Harpers Ferry Flea Market

DATES: Saturday, Sunday, and Monday holidays, weather permitting.

TIMES: Dawn to dusk.

ADMISSION: Free. Parking is also free.

LOCATION: On Highway 340, about 1 mile from Harpers Ferry Historical Park.

DESCRIPTION: Started in 1983, this market hosts an average of 200-plus dealers selling antiques, collectibles, yard sale treasures, crafts, and homemade treasures—a veritable variety of goodies. This is definitely a family market! Funnel cakes, fries, and hot dogs, as well as breakfast are sold at the snack bar. Visitors come from all over the East Coast including Florida.

DEALER RATES: $10 per day per space. Reservations are not required. First come, first served.

CONTACT: Harpers Ferry Flea Market, Box 1038 Conestoga, Harpers Ferry, WV 25425. Tel: (304) 725-4141.

HUNTINGTON

Country Peddler Show

DATES: September 1 through October 2.

TIMES: Friday 4:00 PM–9:00 PM, Saturday 9:00 AM–5:00 PM, Sunday 11:00 AM–4:00 PM.

ADMISSION: Adults $5, children 2–12 $2 each day.

LOCATION: Huntington Civic Center, One Civic Center Plaza.

DESCRIPTION: One of a series of highly successful folk art shows held around the East Coast from Michigan to Florida. Their artisans make and sell such items as baskets, salt-glazed pottery, country furniture, herb arrangements, tin, jewelry, and much more.

DEALER RATES: $375 for a 10' × 10' space, $562.50 for a 10' × 15" space and $750 for a 10' × 20' space. Reservations are mandatory as this is a juried show.

CONTACT: American Memories, Inc., P.O. Box 249, Decatur, MI 49045. Tel: (616) 243-8367 or fax: (616) 423-2421.

MARTINSBURG

I-81 Flea Market

DATES: Friday, Saturday, and Sunday, year round.

TIMES: 8:00 AM–5:00 PM.

ADMISSION: Free. Parking is free.

LOCATION: Off Exit 20, off I-81, Spring Mills area.

DESCRIPTION: Opened in 1989, this indoor/outdoor market has 75 inside dealers and up to 140 outside dealers selling antiques, collectibles, crafts, new merchandise, and many Pennsylvania Dutch farmers selling meats, cheeses, sandwiches, meals, bread, soups, and other delicious foods. They hold special shows during the year including an antique car show, a country cruise, and in the past an antique tractor show. In addition to the Pennsylvania Dutch foods, other concessions include: ice cream, fries, and standard snack bar fare.

DEALER RATES: Vary by location and length of stay.

CONTACT: Betty Kline, I-81 Flea Market, Route 2 Box 230, Martinsburg, WV 25401. Tel: (304) 274-1313.

MILTON

Milton Flea Market

DATES: Friday, Saturday, and Sunday.

TIMES: Friday 8:00 AM–4:00 PM, weekends 8:00 AM–5:00 PM.

ADMISSION: Free. Parking is free.

LOCATION: Take Exit 28 (Milton WV) off I-64, turn north to junction U.S. 60, turn east ¼ mile. You can't miss it.

DESCRIPTION: Open since 1989, this indoor/outdoor market has 500 dealers inside and spaces for 100 outside (number of dealers depends on the weather!) selling "really old antiques," collectibles, crafts, tools, new and used clothing, musical instruments, baseball cards, books (you can trade in the ones you've read), trains, toys, comic books, *fudge*, woodwork, and a variety of other goods. One restaurant and two snack bars deal with the hunger not quelled by the fudge. There are restrooms (handicapped-accessible) on the premises. In 1993 they added roofs to the outside spaces as well as 60 new vendor spaces. The local Chamber of Commerce recommended this market and said it was one of the biggest around.

DEALER RATES: $25 and up for the weekend indoors (there is a waiting list) for a 10' × 14' space; $6 and up for 10' wide and whatever deep outside space (depends on the location of the space).

CONTACT: Boyd and Betty Meadows, P.O. Box 549, Milton, WV 25541-0549. Tel: (304) 743-9862 or 743-1123.

WHEELING

Wheeling Civic Center Antique Flea Market

DATES: Once a month.

TIMES: 8:00 AM–4:00 PM

ADMISSION: $1 per person. $1 parking in municipal garages.

LOCATION: Four blocks from I-70 on the banks of the Ohio River, in the heart of downtown Wheeling.

DESCRIPTION: Begun 1986 this indoor market has between 140 and 200 dealers of antiques, art, collectibles, crafts, and new merchandise. The glassware and china available are of special interest as many items were made in the local factories and are just now being brought in to the market. They include both hand-blown and factory-made articles from this historic glass-manufacturing area. Collectors will also find loads of sports cards, rings, and brass items. Buffet-style breakfast and lunch are served on the premises.

DEALER RATES: $15 per 10' × 10' space plus a table and two chairs. Parking is free to exhibitors. Reservations are suggested.

CONTACT: Lela Karges, c/o Wheeling Civic Center, 2 East 14th Street, Wheeling, WV 26003. Tel: (304) 233-7000.

OTHER FLEA MARKETS

Martinsburg: Route 9 Community Auction, Route 9, Martinsburg, WV 25401. Tel: (304) 263-3313. Open daily, 9:00 AM–5:00 PM.

Rockview: Pineville Drive-In Theater, Route 10, Rockview, WV 24880. Tel: (304) 732-7492. Open Thursdays from 6:00 AM on, January through November.

WISCONSIN

ADAMS
Adams Flea Market

DATES: Every Saturday and Sunday, May through October; also open Memorial Day, July 4th, and Labor Day.

TIMES: Dawn to dusk.

ADMISSION: Free. Free parking available.

LOCATION: 2151 Highway 13 South, by the railroad tracks in Adams.

DESCRIPTION: This market has been operating since 1980 and growing each year. There are 43 permanent indoor dealers and 70 outdoors, with 15 acres of grounds on which to expand. This is a country market with plenty of trees, grass, wildflowers, birds, and small animals around to awe the newcomers. There's a bit of everything here, from antiques, collectibles, and handcrafted items, to farm produce, meats and cheeses, and a good mix of old and new merchandise. For your convenience, there is a lunch wagon on the premises. A dog racing track opened in the nearby Lake Delton-Wi Dells area.

DEALER RATES: $7 per day with one table provided free; $14 for two tables and there's space for a three-table "U" setup if you have extra tables. No advance reservations are taken.

CONTACT: Ms. Irene Steffen, 2151 Highway 13, Adams, WI 53910. Tel: (608) 339-3192. Day of show call (608) 339-9223. 1-800-232-3192 in Wisconsin only.

CALEDONIA
7 Mile Fair Flea Market

DATES: Saturday and Sunday, year round.

TIMES: April through October 7:00 AM–5:00 PM; November through March 9:00 AM–5:00 PM.

ADMISSION: $1.25 for adults, senior citizens $1. Children under 12 free with parents. Free parking is provided.

LOCATION: 2720 West 7 Mile Road. At the intersection of I-94 and 7 Mile Road, exit at 7 Mile Road. It is 15 miles south of Milwaukee in Caledonia; 25 miles north of the Illinois-Wisconsin state line.

DESCRIPTION: This indoor/outdoor market began in 1961. With the addition of a new 45,000 square foot building in 1989 there are now approximately 1,000 dealers in summer and 250 in winter marketing a wide variety of antiques, crafts and handmades, collectibles, and new merchandise. A large farmer's market sells fresh vegetables, meats, and cheeses. Outside concessions are restricted because this market has eight permanent food concessions on the premises!

DEALER RATES: $15 per 12' × 24' space per weekend outside, first come, first served; $40 per 8' × 10' booth inside per weekend, reservations required. Office hours are Monday through Friday 8:00 AM–4:00 PM, weekends 9:00 AM–5:00 PM.

CONTACT: Scott T. Niles, 7 Mile Fair, Inc., P.O. Box 7, Caledonia, WI 53108. Tel: (414) 835-2177.

CEDARBURG

Maxwell Street Days

DATES: Four shows a year: May 29, July 31, September 5, October 2. Always the last Sunday in May and July, Labor Day Monday, first Sunday in October, rain or shine.

TIMES: 4:30 AM to between 3:00 PM–5:00 PM.

ADMISSION: Free. Parking $2 on the Park grounds.

LOCATION: Firemen's Park. 796 North Washington Avenue. Follow the cars (or pedestrians), and if you find an empty parking space grab it!

DESCRIPTION: This is an all-volunteer firemen-run market and the main fund-raiser for the Cedarburg Fire Department. Opened in the 1960s, it is one of the largest markets in the Midwest. There are over 1,000 spaces for dealers. Representative of what is available include: lots of antiques and collectibles, junk, flea market goodies, fresh produce, garage sale items, a sign-maker, a construction company selling gazebos, and a siding company plying their trade. (No animals, firearms, or fireworks.) Some spaces have been property settlements in divorce cases! The firemen handle all the food concessions, including specialties like bratwurst, sauerkraut, pizza, health food, ice cream, and the usual fare.

DEALER RATES: $25 and up per space per event. Reservations are absolutely necessary. Their waiting list reached 500! Keep trying, as it is worth the wait. They do have a postcard drawing for vacant spaces. Send your name, address, and phone to the address below. Or call the number and follow instructions on the tape message.

CONTACT: Cedarburg Firemen's Park, P.O. Box 344, Cedarburg, WI 53012-0344. Tel: (414) 377-8412.

EAGLE RIVER
ERRA Flea Market

DATES: Sunday of Labor Day weekend.

TIMES: 9:00 AM–5:00 PM.

ADMISSION: $1. Parking is free.

LOCATION: Eagle River Recreation Arena. One mile east of Eagle River on Route 70.

DESCRIPTION: Started in 1989 to celebrate the last weekend of the summer season, this market of 100-plus vendors sells antiques, collectibles, new merchandise, junk, tools, crafts, and whatever. This area is a summer resort attracting thousands of visitors from all over the country. They close out the season having a field day checking out and buying new "finds." Food is available on the premises.

DEALER RATES: $19.50 per space. Reservations are suggested.

CONTACT: Zurko's Midwest Promotions, 211 West Green Bay Street, Shawano, WI 54166. Call Eileen Potasnik or Bob Zurko at (715) 526-9769.

HAYWARD
Hayward Fame Flea Market

DATES: Every Tuesday and Wednesday during summer months. Also open the weekend of the Log Rolling Contest. Call for dates.

TIMES: 7:30 AM–4:00 PM.

ADMISSION: Free admission and free parking.

LOCATION: Junction of Highway 27 South and Highway "B."

DESCRIPTION: This outdoor flea market, started in 1978, is located across from the National Fishing Hall of Fame. It attracts between 70 and 80 dealers in the summer who sell antiques, collectibles, crafts, vegetables, and new and used merchandise. They hold their own special events with a Musky Festival on Memorial Day weekend, and World Log Rolling. An annual log rolling contest is held two blocks down the street from this market. Food is available.

DEALER RATES: $7 per 12' × 25' booth. Reservations are required.

CONTACT: Jan Thiry, Route 10 Box 195, Hayward, WI 54843. Tel: (715) 634-4794.

KENOSHA
Kenosha Flea Market

DATES: Friday, Saturday, and Sunday, year round.

TIMES: Friday 10:00 AM–5:00 PM; Saturday and Sunday 9:00 AM–5:00 PM; Christmas season hours are longer.

ADMISSION: Free. Parking is also free.

LOCATION: 5535 22nd Avenue.

DESCRIPTION: Started in 1985 this small but solid market has 40 vendors selling some antiques, collectibles, handmade decorated dolls and clothing, fresh produce, surgical supplies, new appliances, more new merchandise, jewelry, household goods, electronics, and more. The variety of items changes as dealers leave and are replaced with different dealers and merchandise.

DEALER RATES: $15 and up depending on booth, location, and size. Reservations are required, as they are currently full.

CONTACT: Beth or Don Goll, 5535 22nd Avenue, Kenosha, WI 53140. Tel: (414) 658-3532.

LADYSMITH

Van Wey's Community Auction and Flea Market

DATES: Generally the 5th and 20th of each month between April and October, plus added dates.

TIMES: 6:30 AM–sundown.

ADMISSION: Free. $.50 per vehicle parking.

LOCATION: On Highway 8, 4½ miles west of Ladysmith.

DESCRIPTION: Now run by the third generation of the same family, this outdoor market began as a small community consignment auction on April 20, 1926, and has operated since on the 5th and 20th of summer months, as these are the farmers' pay days. The flea market originally developed beside the auction and now has grown to attract nearly 200 dealers at peak season, along with thousands of shoppers from all over the country. As far as the range of items available, the managers have commented boldly that, "If you don't find it here you don't need it." Aside from the standard flea market fare, antiques, collectibles, auto parts, farm machinery, used clothing, and fresh farm products are available, along with miscellaneous and new merchandise. An auction starts at 10:00 AM on market days. Food and toilet facilities are available.

DEALER RATES: $7 per 14' × 20' space. Reservations are not required.

CONTACT: Mark and Judy Van Wey, W10139 Van Wey Lane, Ladysmith, WI 54848. Tel: (715) 532-6044.

MILWAUKEE

Rummage-O-Rama

DATES: 1994: January 8–9, February 5–6, 19–20, March 19–20, April 16–17, May 21–22, August 27–28, September 17–18, October 1–2, 15–16, November 5–6, 19–20, December 3–4, and 17–18. For future years, the market dates follow about the same weekend schedule depending on holidays.

TIMES: 10:00 AM–5:00 PM.

ADMISSION: $1.50–$1.75; seniors $1–$1.25; children 12–16 $.50; under 12 is free. Parking is free.

LOCATION: State Fair Park Grounds in Milwaukee. Off I-94, Exit 306.

DESCRIPTION: Classified as the "largest indoor show in the Midwest" and rated "one of the top ten in the USA," this market started in 1973 and has 450 to 750 dealers selling antiques, collectibles, flea market treasures, new clothes, rummage goods, crafts, oak furniture, reproduction furniture, and a bit of everything. The dealers must stand behind products, with refund or replacement for new goods sold. This is such a family market/local affair that events are planned around these market dates, including weddings! Early birds come and line up their purses and bags to hold their places in line while they go chat and catch up on local gossip. An excellent biergarten restaurant serves luscious meals including sauerkraut and sausages, and there are booths selling homemade sausages and cheeses and low-cholesterol cookies. "Candid Camera" made an appearance here in September 1992 for one of their shows.

DEALER RATES: $63–$75 for a 10' × 10' space per weekend. Reservations are required.

CONTACT: Rummage-O-Rama, P.O. Box 51619, New Berlin, WI 53151-061969. Tel: (414) 521-2111.

SHAWANO

Shawano County Fairgrounds Flea Market

DATES: Every Sunday, April through October, except Labor Day weekend.

TIMES: Dawn–5:00 PM.

ADMISSION: $1 per person Sunday. Free parking (2,000 spaces).

LOCATION: Shawano County Fairgrounds. On Highway 29, just a 30-minute drive west of Green Bay.

DESCRIPTION: This indoor/outdoor market has been around since

1972 and attracts over 200-plus dealers, as well as thousands of tourists seeking bargains on such items as folk art, advertising items, antiques, tools, produce, gift items, fresh produce, etc. Special events include a "Super-Special" Memorial Day sale and Collector Car Show, a "Special Chicken Picnic" in mid-July, a July 4th "Big Bang" annual sale, stock car races every Saturday evening, and many other attractions. Campgrounds and hotels are available nearby, and there are lots of food sellers, including popcorn and barbecue. Toilets are available.

DEALER RATES: $19.50 for a 21' × 15' space. Reservations are not required.

CONTACT: Zurko's Midwest Promotions, 211 West Green Bay Street, Shawano, WI 54166. Call Eileen Potasnik or Bob Zurko at (715) 526-9769.

ST. CROIX FALLS
Pea Pickin' Flea Mart

DATES: Saturday and Sunday and holidays, starting the third weekend in April through third weekend in October.

TIMES: 6:00 AM–5:00 PM.

ADMISSION: Free. Free parking is provided.

LOCATION: On Highway 8, 5 miles east of St. Croix Falls near the junction of Route 35N.

DESCRIPTION: This indoor/outdoor market has been in business since 1968, selling a "good variety of things" including new and used merchandise, fresh produce, and "sophisticated junque." Dealers and shoppers come from all over, and camping space is provided for those who want to come on Friday afternoon and spend the night. There is plenty of food available, including a taco stand and snack bar with mini doughnuts and popcorn. Toilet facilities are available.

DEALER RATES: $7 per day. Reservations are suggested.

CONTACT: Steve and Judy Hansen, 1938 Little Blake Lane, Luck, WI 54853. Tel: (715) 857-5479 or 483-9460.

WAUTOMA
Wautoma Flea Market

DATES: Saturday and Sunday, mid-April through October; Sundays, October through early November; weather permitting.

TIMES: Saturday 7:00 AM–dusk; Sunday 6:00 AM–dusk.

ADMISSION: Free admission and free parking.

LOCATION: Junction of Highways 21 and 73, 1 mile east of Wautoma.

DESCRIPTION: Since 1978, this outdoor flea market has been located in "the Christmas Tree Capital of the World." Enjoying a reputation as a friendly market, it attracts approximately 20 dealers on Saturday and 50 on Sunday, offering antiques, collectibles, handmade crafts, vegetables, new merchandise, furniture, and rummage items. Food is available. Historic Waushara County boasts an abundance of outdoor recreation facilities, including 96 lakes, 151 miles of trout streams, fine restaurants, a challenging 18-hole golf course open to the public, and a historical museum.

DEALER RATES: $8 for a booth measuring 22 feet. Space is allocated on a first come, first served basis.

CONTACT: Milton F. Sommer, Route 4 Box 42, Wautoma, WI 54982. Tel: (414) 787-2300. Or Ron Hayman, W2498 Cumberland Drive, Berlin, WI 54923. Tel: (414) 361-2264.

OTHER FLEA MARKETS

Kenosha: Bargain Showcase Indoor Outdoor Market, 8501 75th Street, Kenosha, WI 53142. Tel: (414) 697-9770. Open Friday through Sunday 9:00 AM–5:00 PM.

WYOMING

CASPER
Antique Show and Sale
DATES: The first full weekend in June and October.
TIMES: Saturday 10:00 AM–5:00 PM; Sunday 10:00 AM–4:00 PM.
ADMISSION: $1.25 per person. Free parking is provided.
LOCATION: Central Wyoming Fairgrounds. Take C.Y. Avenue (Highway 220) from downtown Casper.
DESCRIPTION: This indoor show began in 1971 and currently draws a select 40 dealers selling only antiques and collectibles. Run by a non-profit organization, The Casper Antique and Collectors Club, which donates to Wyoming museums and other charities, this show is said to be among the largest in the state. Food is served on the grounds.
DEALER RATES: $25 per 8' table, four-table minimum. Reservations are required. There is a long waiting list.
CONTACT: Casper Antique and Collectors Club, Inc., c/o Mr. Bruce Smith, 1625 South Kenwood, Casper, WY 82601. Tel: (307) 234-6663.

Casper Flea Market
DATES: January, March, July, and November, the first weekend after the third Friday of the month.
TIMES: Saturday 10:00 AM–5:00 PM; Sunday 10:00 AM–4:00 PM.
ADMISSION: Free. Parking is also free.
LOCATION: Eagles Club, 306 North Durbin, 2 blocks east of the post office in downtown Casper.
DESCRIPTION: Started in 1974, this indoor flea market is sponsored by the Casper Antique and Collectors Club, a non-profit organization. Fifteen dealers gather to trade in quality antiques and collectibles.
DEALER RATES: $15 per 8' table. Reservations are required.
CONTACT: Casper Antique and Collectors Club, Inc., c/o Mr. Bruce Smith, 1625 South Kenwood, Casper, WY 82601. Tel: (307) 234-6663.

CHEYENNE
The Bargain Barn

DATES: Daily, year round.

TIMES: Monday through Saturday 10:00 AM–6:00 PM; Sunday 12:00 noon–5:00 PM.

ADMISSION: Free. Free parking is also available.

LOCATION: 2112 Snyder Avenue.

DESCRIPTION: This small indoor shop of 25 dealers started in 1987 offering antiques, collectibles, new merchandise, as well as tools, costume jewelry, books, records, used furniture, and consignment items. "Frontier Days, the World's Largest Rodeo" is held in Cheyenne the last full week in July.

DEALER RATES: $110 per 9' × 10' booth per month, $100 per 9' × 9' space. Advance reservations are required as there is a waiting list.

CONTACT: Bill M. Lucas, 3556 Concord Road, Cheyenne, WY 82001. Tel: (307) 635-2844.

JACKSON HOLE
Mangy Moose Antique Show and Sale

DATES: Annually, in July, rain or shine. Call for specific dates.

TIMES: 9:00 AM–7:00 PM.

ADMISSION: Free. Free parking is available.

LOCATION: In Teton Village.

DESCRIPTION: This outdoor show opened in 1985 and is considered Wyoming's biggest and best antique show. It currently accommodates approximately 65 dealers and is growing fast. This show specializes in fine antiques; dealers display furniture, carpets, jewelry, dolls, accessories, china, silver, Indian items, vintage clothes, books, and much more. All of this is sponsored by the Mangy Moose Restaurant. Food is served on the premises.

DEALER RATES: $135 per 10' × 12' space, for all three days. Reservations are required.

CONTACT: Jan Perkins or Jeffrey, 2902 Breneman Street, Boise, ID 83703. Tel: (208) 345-0755 or 368-9759. Day of show call (307) 733-4913.

CANADA

ONTARIO
BOWMANVILLE

21st Bowmanville April Antiques and Folk Art Show

DATES: April 1–2, 1994.

TIMES: Saturday 7:00 AM–10:00 PM, Sunday 10:00 AM–5:00 PM.

ADMISSION: Free. Parking is free.

LOCATION: The new Sports Complex. Highway 2. Take Exit 431 from Highway 401.

DESCRIPTION: Considered a prestige event for 21 years, this market sells exclusively pre-1870 country furniture and accessories plus old folk art.

DEALER RATES: Call for information.

CONTACT: Bill Dobson, RR1, Smiths Falls, Ontario, Canada K7A 5B8. Tel: (613) 283-1168.

QUÉBEC
BROMONT

Marché aux Puces de Bromont

DATES: First Sunday of May through second Sunday of November.

TIMES: 9:00 AM–5:00 PM.

ADMISSION: Free. Parking is free.

LOCATION: Motorway 10 at Bromont.

DESCRIPTION: This indoor market's 350 dealers sell crafts, produce, garage sale finds, furniture, coins, stamps, cards, and new merchandise. It is *the* market in the township and, for a visitor, it has a lot to offer: factory outlets, a chocolate museum, and vineyards. This is home to one of the World Championship Mountain Bike races.

MONTREAL

Super Mercado

DATES: Thursday through Sunday, year round.

TIMES: 9:00 AM–5:00 PM.

ADMISSION: Free.

LOCATION: Brossard, just south of Montreal.

DESCRIPTION: This is the "hot" place to shop around Montreal—which means it is very crowded. While they don't sell antiques, per se, they do sell just about anything else.

SAINT EUSTACHE

Marché aux Puces de Saint Eustache

DATES: Thursday through Sunday.
TIMES: 9:00 AM–5:00 PM.
ADMISSION: Free. Parking is free.
LOCATION: Road 640 West. Just north of Montreal, 3 miles before Saint Eustache.
DESCRIPTION: This year round, indoor/outdoor market's dealers sell antiques, collectibles, crafts, produce, garage sale finds, furniture, new merchandise, stamps, coins, and cards among others. This is one of the biggest markets around and apparently crammed full of customers on Sundays. So beat the crowd and go another day.

OTHER FLEA MARKETS–BRITISH COLUMBIA

Clearbrooke: Abbottsford Flea Market, Exhibition Park, Clearbrooke, BC. Tel: (604) 859-7540. Open Sunday 6:00 AM–4:00 PM.
Cloverdale: Cloverdale Fairgrounds, Cloverdale, BC. Tel: (604) 530-0612. Open Sunday 6:00 AM–4:00 PM.

OTHER FLEA MARKETS–ONTARIO

Barrie: The 400 Market, Inc., Exit 85 Innisfil Beach Road, Highway 400, Barrie, Ontario. Tel: (705) 436-1010.
Hamilton: Steel City Flea Market, 29 Linden Street, Hamilton, Ontario L8L 3H6. Tel: (416) 545-4747. Open Sunday 10:00 AM–5:00 PM.
Mississauga: Fantastic Flea Markets, Ltd., Dixie Mall, QEW and Dixie Road, Mississauga, Ontario. Tel: (416) 274-9403. Open weekends 10:00 AM–5:00 PM.
North York: Fantastic Flea Market, 2375 Steels Avenue West, North York, Ontario M3J 3A8. Tel: (416) 650-1090. Open weekends 10:00 AM–6:00 PM, Thursday and Friday 10:00 AM–8:00 PM.
Oshawa: Oshawa Flea Market, 727 Wilson Road, Oshawa, Ontario. Tel: (416) 683-5290. Open Sunday 9:00 AM–4:30 PM.
Snelgrove: Snelgrove Flea Market, 12231 Hurontario Street, Snelgrove, Ontario L0P 1M0. Tel: (416) 846-0960. Open Sunday 8:30 AM–4:30 PM.
Stouffville: Stouffville Country Flea Market, Highway 47 North, Stouffville, Ontario L4A 7Z6. Tel: (416) 640-3813. Open Saturday 8:00 AM–4:00 PM, Sunday 9:00 AM–4:00 PM.

INTERNATIONAL

A note about European markets in the big cities: generally everyone just walks about the market—no admission fees—and in the cities, take the subway and save yourself a lot of aggravation.

In Paris, the markets seems to run all daylight hours depending on whether you are visiting shops or wandering among the street vendors.

In England, all the markets I have personally visited or my friends have checked and visited lasted through the mornings only. Most of the fun and excitement was gone after lunch, although there may be a few stragglers.

In the provincal markets, Saturdays are the day—usually a farmer's market in season, like in the small town of Jonquières in Provence and the woman selling homemade goat's cheese out of the back end of a small pickup truck, or the occasional roving market like the one we happened upon in northern Germany.

I haven't put any times and admission information in with the listing, therefore, unless it was pertinent.

PARIS

Marché aux Puces

DATES: Saturday through Monday, year round.

TIMES: Daylight and then some; just get there.

LOCATION: Outside the Porte de Clignancourt Metro station (Line 4—Porte D'Orleans to Porte de Clignancourt). Just about due north at the edge of Paris.

DESCRIPTION: This market, started last century when people gathered to sell old clothes, is an institution. Visitors used to eat french fries and dance the polka. In the twenties, masterpiece paintings were found by chance here and made the market famous. Nowadays, it's practically its own village. You can find "anything you want, or don't want, or could ever dream about." You can find the most fabulous antiques and collectibles to the standard flea market t-shirts, bracelets, and what-nots. From food to junque. Vendors are all over the place—on the sidewalks, in shops, filling the streets, wherever. It's a treat. The atmosphere is electric, pulsing, bright, lively, and loud. Hold onto the kids and be prepared to use your elbows.

LONDON

Bermondsey Market (aka New Caledonia Market)
DATES: Sundays.
TIMES: 5:00 AM–6:00 AM for the serious dealings, but open all day.
LOCATION: Walk over Tower Bridge (heading south) to the crossroad (past the vinegar factory), turn right and you are there.
DESCRIPTION: This is *the* market in London. The serious antique deals are made here. Just be there very early. If you happen to watch *Lovejoy* on A&E, you'll understand. He mentions this market. It is also the one market where "unauthorized" goods get "legally" traded, according to my source.

Brick Lane Market
DATES: Sundays, year round, 9:00 AM–2:00 PM.
LOCATION: Shoreditch tube station, in the East End.
DESCRIPTION: Described as "straight out of Dickens," "with the best curry in town" by a London friend of mine, although he also describes the area as "Jack-the-Ripper-type." Everything here is second- to fourth-hand, at least.

Camden Lock Market
DATES: Sundays, year round.
LOCATION: Camden Town tube station (Northern Line).
DESCRIPTION: This is the current trendy market selling antiques, clothes and jewelry.

Camden Passage (or Walk) Market
DATES: Sundays, year round.
LOCATION: Outside the Angel tube station, turn right, then turn right again.
DESCRIPTION: This outdoor market is mostly shops selling antiques. But they are excellent antiques.

Petticoat Lane
DATES: Sundays, year round.
TIMES: Early to noon, after that the excitement is gone.
LOCATION: Middlesex Street in East End of London. Take the tube to Liverpool Street (take the road facing the station and the road will take you directly to the market), Aldgate or Aldgate East and follow the noise and crowd.

DESCRIPTION: All around the area, vendors are in a garage, on the streets, in shops, wherever. Hold on to anything of yours that you value. Better yet, don't take anything of value with you. This is a granddaddy of markets. Full of new merchandise, used stuff, clothing of all sorts, dishes (you have to see the way the vendors display and demonstrate their wares to believe it— spinning, tossing, balancing—it's a performance!), electronics, the usual flea stuff, literally whatever. Called Petticoat Lane because petticoats were made here a very long time ago.

In the '70s when I was in London, there was a brass band made up of older gents (doing this to raise money for charity) who would play and entertain here. On Wednesdays they entertained us as we boarded the tube for work from the Earl's Court Station. Their band leader would recognize me from Wednesdays and always dance a little jig and wave to say "hi." I have him immortalized on film.

Portobello Road

DATES: Saturdays, year round for the big market, daily for the shops.
TIMES: Morning is best.
LOCATION: West End of London. Take the tube to Notting Hill Gate.
DESCRIPTION: This was the classic antique and collectible market of London. If you ever saw the movie *Bedknobs and Broomsticks*, this is where the "market" part was filmed. Saturdays is the open air market, otherwise the shops are open normal hours. Now it's rather "old hat."

AN ADDITIONAL NOTE

Just about every major city in Europe has its own flea market, usually on the weekend. I know there are markets in Frankfurt, Rome, and Morocco, for starters. Maybe next edition we can stuff them in here. If you are interested, let me know! Use the address on the next page.

HOW TO BE INCLUDED
IN THIS DIRECTORY

If you own or operate a flea market and would like to have your market considered for inclusion in the next edition of *The Official Directory to U.S. Flea Markets*, either write us a letter requesting a questionnaire form or send complete information corresponding to the format currently employed in this directory. Market listings must be complete in order to be considered for publication. For a full explanation of the acceptable format for market listings, refer to the section entitled "How to Use This Book."

Address all mail to:

> *House of Collectibles*
> *Editorial Department*
> *201 East 50th Street*
> *New York, NY 10022*